CW00550171

Muhammad Ibn Sa'd's

Kitab at-Tabaqat al-Kabir

Volume VI:

The Scholars of Kufa

Muhammad Ibn Sa'd's

Kitab at-Tabaqat al-Kabir

Volume VI:

The Scholars of Kufa

translated by

Aisha Bewley

Ta-Ha Publishers Ltd

First published in March 2012/1433 AH

This edition published by

Ta-Ha Publishers Ltd.
Unit 4, The Windsor Centre
Windsor Grove, West Norwood
London, SE27 9NT, UK

www.tahapublishers.com

Translated by Aisha Bewley
Typeset by Bookwork, Norwich

A catalogue record of this book is available from the British Library

ISBN 978-1-84200-124-0

Printed and bound by IMAK Ofset, Turkey

Contents

Introduction

The *Kitab at-Tabaqat* by Abu 'Abdullah Muhammad ibn Sa'd is one of the earliest collections of biographical details of the early Muslims, extending from the Prophet 🕮 to Ibn Sa'd's own time (148 AH/764 CE to 230 AH/844 CE or 236 AH/850 CE). This is Volume VI, which deals firstly with the scholars of Makka, Ta'if, Yemen, Yamama and Bahrayn and then the bulk of the book is devoted to the scholars of Kufa.

The Companions are mentioned first in each locality, and then the next generation, the Tabi'un, and then the following generations. The scope of Ibn Sa'd covers the time of the Rashidun khalifs, the Umayyads and the 'Abbasids, and so some brief comments about Islamic history are necessary in order to put the events and individuals mentioned into perspective, and to make the events and comments described more comprehensible.

The Founding of Kufa

Kufa was founded in 17/638 by the famous Companion of the Prophet 🕮, Sa'd ibn Abi Waqqas, after the capture of Mada'in-Ctesiphon from the Persian Sasanids. The Arabs did not like the climate in Mada'in nor its urban environment. They were also badly affected by the mosquitoes there. 'Umar noticed that messengers from Mada'in were becoming flabby and their complexions sallow. When he asked the reason for that, he was told that it was due to the climate and the mosquitoes. 'Umar wrote to Sa'd telling him that only land that was suitable for camels was suitable for the Arabs. He ordered that Salman al-Farisi and Hudhayfa ibn al-Yaman (the two main scouts of the army) be tasked with locating a new site. It was to be suitable for their camels: located on the edge of the desert, with easy access to water and not cut off from Arabia by a bridge or major body of water.

The two men set off in different directions but both ended up at the same place. The site chosen was located on the edge of the desert, but on the bank of the middle course of the Euphrates River on a tongue of grey sand mixed with gravel, higher than the water level - which eliminated the mosquito problem. It did not experience flooding, had ample water and a healthy climate.

The origin of the name "Kufa" is unclear and there are various theories about its source. According to at-Tabari, *"kufa"* is the name for coarse land where sand and gravel are mixed. Others say that it derives from 'Aqola or Aqula, an existing monastic site between Hira and the Euphrates. Whatever the origin of the name, the site guarded the access to Babil and Mada'in and was near Qadisiyya, the site of the major Muslim victory over the Sasanids. It basically replaced Hira, the former capital of the Lakhmids, but was closer to the fertile crop region of the Sawad. Kufa also guarded the bridge of boats which crossed the river and which was a major link in the commercial route between Yemen and Asia.

An additional reason for the founding of Kufa is that 'Umar wanted the Muslims to have their own place apart from the conquered Persians to maintain the cohesion and strength of the Muslim forces. Fundamentally, Kufa started as a military camp for the thirty thousand veterans of the Battle of Qadisiyya. This would be the first city designed and built by the Muslims to plan and 'Umar sent detailed instructions about it.

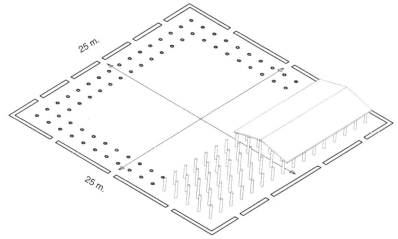

Plan of Early Kufa Mosque
showing the columns and covered area

Sa'd picked the site for the mosque and governor's residence and had a man shoot an arrow in four directions and then marked out the resulting square (*maydan*) which was then surrounded by a ditch. The central focus of the square was the mosque which was the first building to be constructed. Adjoining it was the governor's palace which contained the treasury. The mosque could be entered from any side and it had no walls, but arcades of marble columns. There was a roof built over the front part which was supported by marble columns. The governor's house was separated from the mosque by a narrow alley.

Initially the dwellings consisted of tents laid out in rows. Then they asked 'Umar for permission to use reeds as the people in Basra did. 'Umar said, "Living in an army camp is easier for you to mount your military operations from and more convenient, but I do not like to disagree with you." (at-Tabari) So huts were constructed from the local reeds. Then there were fires both in Kufa and Basra, the worst of which occurred in Kufa. Eighty structures were destroyed in a single fire and Sa'd sent some of the victims to 'Umar to obtain permission to use bricks. 'Umar said, "Go ahead and do it. But no one should build more than three rooms for himself and no one should build a house higher than another. If you hold to what is recognised as *sunna*, then you will thrive."

Abu al-Hayyaj ibn Malik was given the task of laying out the roads and residential lots. following detailed instructions from 'Umar. The main thoroughfares (*manahij*) were to be forty cubits wide, between which were other roads (*sikak*) of thirty cubits wide and between them others which were twenty cubits wide, and no alley should be narrower than seven cubits. The plots (*khitat*) of land were sixty cubits square, except for that of the Banu Dabba. There were fifteen main thoroughfares from the centre which separated the tribal communal areas. Those who were proficient in that area were appointed with the task of surveying and marking out the plots.

There were also markets where the sites were on a first-come-first-serve basis. The first one was next to the mosque in the square and then the local tribal areas had their own markets. There were reception camps for new arrivals where they stayed until Abu al-Hayyaj ibn Malik allotted them sites.

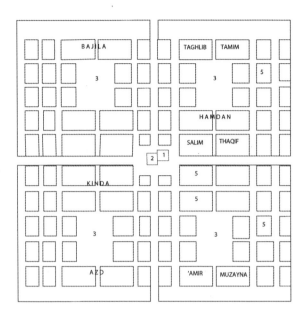

Layout of Kufa showing the location of main tribes

1. Mosque
2. Dar al-Imara
3. Square
4. Governor's companions
5. Residential quarters

The residence of the governor (*dar al-imara*) was next to the mosque and the treasury was kept inside it. Then a problem arose with the treasury when some robbers dug a tunnel to the treasury and stole from it. Sa'd informed 'Umar who told him to move the spot closer to where the prayer was performed and to place it in the direction of the prayer so that people would keep an eye on it.

Sa'd hired a *dihqan* called Ruzbih ibn Buzurgumihir to build the residence. Ruzbih told him that he would construct a citadel and make a connection between the two buildings. It was to be built from baked bricks taken from Hira, three miles west of Kufa. Sa'd set up a wooden gate on the citadel with a lock, as the market was right in front of Sa'd's quarters. People started to gossip and called it "Sa'd's citadel". 'Umar heard about this and sent Muhammad ibn Maslama, his troubleshooter, to the citadel to burn down the gate. He gave Sa'd a letter which said that he had built a citadel as his personal fortress and had a gate separating him from the people. He said, "It is not your property. Have you taken leave of your senses? Go and find a place to live near the treasury and lock that, but do not have a gate in the citadel preventing people from entering and depriving them of their right to sit freely with you in counsel."

Sa'd informed Maslama that he had not taken it as his private quarters. Muhammad ibn Maslama, not even staying to eat, turned around and returned to Madina to report to 'Umar what Sa'd had said.

Initially, Sa'd divided the area into two: one for the northern 'Adnani or Nizari Arabs, and one of the southern Yemeni areas. They drew lots and the Nizaris were on the western side and the Yemenis on the eastern. The term *khitta* is used for a settlement lot.

This division proved unworkable as it became imbalanced in numbers and was not conducive to having military groups ready for action. Distribution of stipends was also difficult. It was decided to re-balance the tribes into seven groups on the basis of genealogy and alliances. They were divided into seven groups (*asba'*). Sa'd wrote to and received permission from 'Umar to do this. The seven groups were:

1. The *Ahl al-'Aliya* (people of prestige): Kinana and their allies. Kinana was Makkan and Quraysh was one of its branches. Jadila was a branch of Qays 'Aylan from the Hijaz and had connections with Kinana. There was also a prior alliance called Khindif between Kinana, Quraysh and others.

2. Quda'a, Ghassan, Bajila, Khath'am, Kinda, Hadramawt and Azd: a powerful Yemeni grouping. Bajila was lead by Jarir ibn 'Abdullah and Kinda included al-Ash'ath ibn Qays.

3. Madhhij, Himyar, Hamdan and their allies, another powerful Yemeni grouping.

4. Tamim, Rihab and Hawazin, all of Mudar.

5. Asad, Ghatafan, Muharib, Nimr, Dubay'a and Taghlib, mostly Nizari from the larger groups of Rabi'a and Bakr.

6. Iyad, 'Akk, 'Abd al-Qays, Ahl al-Hajar and Hamra', a roughly Nizari grouping of disparate more or less local groups.

7. Tayy', a Yemeni tribe.[1]

The people were then divided into units or *'irafa*s, each of which was in charge of one hundred thousand dirhams. An *'arif* was in

---

1. Probable although not mentioned by at-Tabari.

charge of each *'irafa*. Stipends were handed to the commanders of the seven groups and then they passed them on the *'arif*s who distributed them.

These groupings lasted for nineteen years until 36/656 when 'Ali came to Kufa after the Battle of the Camel and made some changes:

1. Hamdan and Himyar, which was Yemeni.
2. Madhhij, Ash'ar and Tayy', also Yemeni.
3. Kinda, Hadramawt, Quda'a and Mahra, also Yemeni.
4. Azd, Bajila, Khath'am and Ansar, Yemeni.
5. All Nizari banches of Qays, 'Abs, Dhubya, and 'Abd al-Qays of Bahrayn.
6. Bakr, Tahglib and all branches of Rabi'a, all Nizari.
7. Quraysh, Kinana, Asad, Tamim, Dabba, and Ribab, Nizari.

Then there developed the small mosques of clans or tribes, about a dozen *jabbanat* or tribal cemeteries (which were also used for meetings and mobilisation). Various events occurred there. Each tribal area eventually had its own mosque, cemetery and gates. Then came the vaulted covered markets for the tribal areas and each trade had its own quarter in the market (*suq*).

There was also the Kunasa, which was initially the dump and then developed other functions: the unloading of caravans, an animal market, an execution site, and a fair for poets.

More complaints were received about Sa'd and 'Umar again sent Muhammad ibn Maslama to ask people about Sa'd. Everyone spoke well of him except for someone from the Banu 'Abs who said that he did not divide fairly. Sa'd said that the man was lying and at one point, according to al-'Abbas an-Narsi, exclaimed in exasperation, "O Allah, let no ruler be satisfied with them, and let them never be satisfied with a ruler!"

'Umar asked Sa'd who his deputy was and he told him it was 'Abdullah ibn 'Abdullah ibn 'Itban. 'Umar appointed him governor. Then he was removed and sent elsewhere and Ziyad ibn Hanzala appointed. Ziyad also immediately asked to be removed and 'Ammar ibn Yasir was sent as governor.

Then 'Ammar ibn Yasir was dismissed at the request of the Kufans after twenty-one months. 'Ammar himself requested it.

'Umar said, "What am I to do with the people of Kufa? If I appoint a strong man over them, they attribute transgression to him. If a weak man, they despise him!" He asked them who they wanted and they said, "Abu Musa al-Ash'ari." He was governor for a year and then the Kufans complained that his servant sold animal fodder. So he dismissed him and sent him to Basra.

'Umar had his governors come to him before *hajj* every year so that he could manage them and give their people a chance to register complaints against them. 'Umar complained about the situation with the Kufans and al-Mughira ibn Shu'ba said that it needed a strong, tough man. So 'Umar sent him as governor. Two years later, he was going to send Sa'd again, but was murdered before he could do so.

'Uthman acted on 'Umar's instructions and sent Sa'd as governor again. But in 26/647, at-Tabari reports "the first *shaytan*ically inspired event among the inhabitants of Kufa." Sa'd had borrowed a sum from the treasury from 'Abdullah ibn Mas'ud. Ibn Mas'ud then demanded immediate repayment for it and Sa'd asked for a deferral as he was unable to pay. A violent and very public quarrel broke out between the two of them. 'Uthman was furious and sacked Sa'd and sent al-Walid ibn 'Uqba as governor. Al-Walid had previously been 'Umar's agent over the Banu Rabi'a in Jazira. Once in Kufa, al-Walid was well-liked by the people and remained governor for five years.

Things went well with al-Walid until a group of Kufan youths were involved in a murder and their relatives resented the fact that they had been executed and spread rumours about al-Walid drinking wine. They burst in on him and found nothing. Another time they accused him of harbouring a sorcerer. They eventually plotted to get him deposed by testifying that he had been drinking wine. The same individuals were later involved in the plots against 'Uthman.

After al-Walid was dismissed, Sa'id ibn al-'As arrived in Kufa as the new governor and said, "Civil unrest (*fitna*) has raised its snout and eyes. I will strike it in the face until I suppress it or it defeats me. I am truly troubled today."

After examining the situation, according to at-Tabari, he wrote back to 'Uthman: "The affairs of the Kufans are in turmoil. The nobles among them, the men of distinguished families and the veterans of the early campaigns have been overwhelmed, and the dominant elements in these lands are recent immigrants and bedouin who have attached themselves to the regular forces. It has gotten to the point that one does not see a man of noble lineage or experience among the settlers or youth." (pp. 57-58, vol. xv) He tried to reorganise things but at-Tabari says, "It was as if Kufa were dry tinder engulfed by a fire."

'Uthman decided that the answer was to send more Madinans there by doing a property exchange: selling lands conquered in Iraq in exchange for holdings in the Hijaz. Those in Iraq who had not been involved in the initial conquest and hence were receiving lower stipends were further put out by this.

In 33 AH there was an incident in the governor's presence, a fight started in the presence of the governor, led by some of those who had worked against al-Walid - and typically, it was about land and wealth. Two of the Banu Asad were beaten unconscious and Sa'id was unable to stop the troublemakers from inflicting the beating.

Stirrings continued and the chiefs wrote to 'Uthman asking him to expel the dissidents. They were sent to Mu'awiya ibn Abi Sufyan in Syria who was to question them. He spoke to them and decided that they were troublemakers who desired only wealth and land. As he wrote to 'Uthman, "Their only aim is unrest (*fitna*) and the wealth of the non-Muslim subjects." They demanded that Mu'awiya resign and attacked him.

Mu'awiya sent them back to Kufa where they caused even more trouble. Then 'Uthman exiled them to Hims to 'Abd ar-Rahman ibn Khalid ibn al-Walid, the governor of Jazira, and they started to defame 'Uthman. When Sa'id was on *hajj* in 34 AH, and most of his deputies were away from Kufa on military duty, there was an opportunity for the dissidents to act. Yazid ibn Qays entered the mosque and the dissidents gathered around him. When one of Sa'id's deputies threw him out, Yazid sent word to the exiles to summon them back.

Al-Ashtar, one of the exiles, arrived and claimed to have come from 'Uthman and further claimed that Sa'id was trying to get their stipends cut and taking their land as a private garden of Quraysh. Yazid ibn Qays went out and called on people to join him in seeking the expulsion of 'Uthman. He and al-Ashtar established a camp at al-

Jara'a, near al-Qadisiyya. When Sa'id returned to Kufa, he was turned back by what amounted to a mob and so went back to Madina. He told 'Uthman that they wanted Abu Musa al-Ash'ari to be their governor and he agreed.

Negotiations between the malcontents, who had spread out in other areas as well, continued and in 35 AH, they plotted to take advantage of the *hajj*. They went to 'Uthman and presented their demands. They made an agreement with him containing five or six stipulations: that the exiles be returned, that the governor give to the one who was deprived, that the booty be given in full, that he be fair in the division and that he appoint those who had trustworthiness and strength. They wrote down all of that in a document. He enjoined them not to cause divisions in the community nor leave the community. Then they went back seemingly content. When the groups were returning, a rider appeared who ostensibly had a letter ordering their execution. There were also letters purporting to be from 'Ali and 'A'isha, both of whom denied writing them. The groups from Egypt and Kufa all arrived back in Madina simultaneously where al-Ashtar and Hukaym were waiting and they laid siege to 'Uthman which, as is well known, ended in his murder and 'Ali becoming caliph.

Kufa and the *Fitna*

After 'Uthman's murder and the allegiance had been given to 'Ali in Madina, 'Ali sent 'Umara ibn Shihab to Kufa as governor, but he was turned back. When a summons was made to call people in Kufa to take part in the Battle of the Camel, Abu Musa, who was still the governor there, advised people not to become involved, saying, "Staying here leads to the Next World and joining up leads to this world. Make your choice." When pressed, he said that the killers of 'Uthman needed to be dealt with. 'Ali told al-Ashtar to sort things out, and then al-Hasan ibn 'Ali and 'Ammar ibn Yasir were sent. At the same time a public letter arrived from 'A'isha telling the people to stay in their houses except to take action against the murderers of 'Uthman. After a heated discussion, several thousand men set out from Kufa with al-Hasan. Al-Ashtar then deposed Abu Musa and threw all his belongings out of the governor's residence. 'Ali sent al-

Hasan and 'Ammar to mobilise the men, and appointed Qaraza ibn Ka'b governor. Kufa became the de facto capital when 'Ali went there after the Battle of the Camel.

The forces of Mu'awiya, demanding justice for 'Uthman, met 'Ali in the Battle of Siffin which lasted for three days after which the parties agreed to arbitration. This is the point at which the group who were to become the Kharijites left 'Ali, objecting to the very arbitration which they had previously demanded. When 'Ali went to Kufa, they went to Harura', where twelve thousand of them encamped. They accused 'Ali of being an unbeliever and set about killing those who did not follow them. Their forces met at the canal of Nahrawan and 'Ali with a force of Kufans comprehensively defeated them. He wanted to resume the fight with the Syrians immediately. The Kufans complained that they needed time to recover. 'Ali camped at Nukhayha and told them to remain in camp and prepare to fight. After a couple of days all except a few of the leaders had slipped away and the camp was empty.

'Ali returned to Kufa. He tried to get the people there to confront the Syrians again but got no response. He addressed them, "Whoever trusts in you is duped and whoever draws you draws a useless lot!" When he was murdered in Kufa by the Kharijite 'Abd ar-Rahman ibn Muljam in 40/661 in revenge for the Kharijites killed in the Battle of Nahrawan, the Kufans gave their allegiance to his son, al-Hasan.

In dealing with the Kufans, al-Hasan had similar problems to those his father had experienced. He was attacked twice by them: once when his tent was looted, which led to him moving to Mada'in, and again on the way to Mada'in where he was stabbed in the leg. Defections continued rapidly. According to Ibn A'tham, after he was informed of the desertions, al-Hasan addressed them and said:

"People of Iraq, what should I do with your people who are with me? Here is the letter of Qays ibn Sa'd informing me that even the nobles from among you have gone over to Mu'awiya. By Allah, what abominable behaviour on your part! You were the people who forced my father to accept arbitration at Siffin; and when the arbitration to which he yielded took place, you turned against him. When he called upon you to fight Mu'awiya once again, then you showed your slackness and lassitude. After the death of my father, you came to me and gave me allegiance on your own initiative. I accepted your allegiance and came out against Mu'awiya ... Now you are behaving in the same manner as before. People of Iraq, it would be enough for me from you if you would not defame me in my religion, because now I am going to hand over this affair to Mu'awiya."

Al-Hasan surrendered Kufa and Mu'awiya entered it in 41 AH. Reports about the exact day or even month vary. Al-Hasan and al-Husayn went back to Madina. The Kharijites attacked soon after and Mu'awiya insisted that the Kufans join the fight against them and the Kharijites were defeated at Shahrazur. Mu'awiya then put 'Abdullah ibn 'Amr ibn al-'As in charge of Kufa, but al-Mughira pointed out that having him in charge of Kufa while his father, 'Amr, was in charge of Egypt, was not a good idea. So Mu'awiya made al-Mughira ibn Shu'ba governor of Kufa.

Kufa under the Umayyads

In 45/665, al-Mughira asked to be dismissed, but Mu'awiya refused. In 49/669, the plague struck Kufa. Al-Mughira left the city and then returned when he thought it had passed, but caught it and died. At this point Mu'awiya added Kufa to the governorship of Ziyad ibn Abi Sufyan who was already governor of Basra and much of Iraq. From this point on, most of the time, Iraq was governed as a single entity. Ziyad then alternated, residing six months in Basra and six in Kufa.

Ziyad ascended the minbar in Kufa but when he spoke he was pelted with pebbles. He sat down and ordered some of his guards to stand at the gates of the mosque. He then made people swear that they had not thrown pebbles and cut off the hands of those who did not.

It was only shortly before that pebbles had begun to be used to cover the mosque floor because people's hands had become covered in dust and they would clap to remove the dust. One of the unexpected consequences was the tendency of people to throw pebbles at speakers. Matting was later used to remove this problem.

Ziyad also expanded the mosque and rebuilt it using kiln-fired bricks and mortar. Stone from Ahwas was used for the columns and

Persian masons were employed. It was also covered with a flat roof of teak resting on the stone columns drilled and filled with lead and iron. It meant that the mosque could hold sixty thousand rather than forty thousand people. He also added halls (*suffa*) on three of the walls. He also moved the minbar to the side of the *qibla* rather than the middle and made a door for the imam to enter rather than passing through the people. He installed a *maqsura* (protected enclosure) inside of the mosque. The governor's house was rebuilt with brick and clay against the south (*qibla*) wall of the mosque. Fortifications were put around the mosque, governor's palace, treasury and prison, making an inner citadel of the whole complex.

Kufa was also a place where the silver coins of the Sasanids met the gold coins of Byzantium. There was a special area between the Suhayl mosque and the Central Mosque for the money-changers (*sayarifa*) who were originally Christians and soon after some Jews. Muslims took over the positions and it developed under the 'Abbasids into the *Diwan al-Jahbadhah*. A lot of the funding for the various Shi'ite movements came from this group. The main market was to the north of the mosque. There were also markets and mosques in the tribal areas which gradually sprang up. Khalid al-Qasri later oversaw the actual construction of the markets in their vaulted form and in different groupings according to function. The dump to the west, al-Kunasa, also developed into a market.

The population was diverse and large and crucial for the campaigns to the east. In the first phase al-Baladhuri says that there were between twenty thousand and thirty-thousand inhabitants. Yaqut says forty thousand. Abu Mikhnaf mentions that 'Ali mobilised all the fighters: fifty-seven thousand (forty thousand adults and seventeen thousand adolescents). So the population had jumped in number. Ziyad ibn Abu Sufyan later enlarged the mosque in order to be able to accommodate sixty thousand men. To this number, add the women and children and the number of Arabs is one hundred and forty thousand. To this add the unregistered inhabitants, slaves and *mawali*. It was a huge jump in numbers in a short period of time. Hence Arab men were sent on expeditions to the east and the gap was then filled by non-Arabs who were attracted to the city. This made the situation

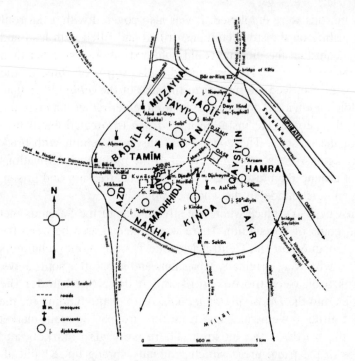

Map of the location of the tribes in Kufa

more volatile.

There was a final administrative change in Kufa. In 50/670, Ziyad abolished the seven groups and made them into four blocks, applying the system used in Basra, hoping to eliminate some of the inter-tribal rivalries:

1. Ahl al-'Aliya, the Makkans and Quraysh.
2. Tamim and Hamdan.
4. Rabi'a and Kinda.
4. Madhhij and Asad.

Each of the last three had one lot of Yemenis and one of Nizaris.

Ziyad died of the plague in 53/673. He appointed 'Abdullah ibn Khalid as his successor who lasted for two years and was replaced by ad-Dahhak ibn Qays.

After the death of Yazid, closely followed by the death of his successor a few months later, there was a civil war between the

Umayyads, who chose Marwan ibn al-Hakam as their leader, followed by his son, 'Abd al-Malik, and the forces of 'Abdullah ibn az-Zubayr who had proclaimed himself caliph in Makka.

The Shi'a

There always remained partisanship for 'Ali in some quarters and an incident which resulted in the execution of Hujr ibn 'Adi in 51/ 671 showed the potential for trouble in the city. Al-Mughira ibn Shu'ba had always forgiven his outbursts, but Ziyad was not so tolerant. When he heard that partisans of 'Ali had gathered to Hujr and openly cursed Mu'awiya and thrown stones at his deputy, 'Amr ibn al-Hurayth, he went to Kufa. There was an incident in the mosque with Hujr which Ziyad exaggerated to Mu'awiya and he was sent to Mu'awiya and beheaded.

When Mu'awiya died in 60/680 and Yazid I became caliph, the Kufans wrote to al-Husayn ibn 'Ali, inviting him to revolt. He sent his cousin Muslim ibn 'Aqil to Kufa to see what the situation was. When Muslim arrived, twelve thousand Kufans gave their allegiance to him and through him to al-Husayn. The governor, an-Nu'man, did nothing. Because of his inaction, it was suggested that Kufa be added to the governorship of 'Ubaydullah ibn Ziyad, the governor of Basra, and Yazid did that. 'Ubaydullah arrived in Kufa veiled and sent a *mawla* pretending to be a supporter of al-Husayn, who was taken to Muslim to whom he gave money and offered allegiance. He then reported back to 'Ubaydullah.

After an initial positive assessment of the situation, Muslim had written to al-Husayn telling him to come to Kufa. Muslim then heard that his host, Hani', had been arrested and went with four thousand Kufans to the governor's palace. 'Ubaydullah already had his men there. By late afternoon, only five hundred men remained with Muslim. When night fell, even those five hundred had disappeared. Muslim was caught and executed as was Hani'. Husayn ibn 'Ali was heading to Kufa when he was stopped and killed at Karbala by the Umayyad governor, 'Ubaydullah ibn Ziyad.

After the death of Yazid I in 64 AH, the Basrans gave their allegiance to 'Ubaydullah until the time a new caliph was chosen.

'Ubaydullah sent a messenger to Kufa asking them to do the same and they threw pebbles at him. That unrest spread to Basra and 'Ubaydullah fled to Syria. This was the time of the civil war between Marwan, and then his son 'Abd al-Malik, and 'Abdullah ibn az-Zubayr. At the same time, the Kharijites were active and then the Shi'a partisans entered the fray in the form of the *Tawwabun*.

The *Tawwabun*, or Penitents, were a group of Kufans led by Sulayman ibn Surad who regretted their desertion of al-Husayn and wanted to redeem themselves. They gained the support of a large number of Kufans. Al-Mukhtar ibn Abi 'Ubayd ath-Thaqafi arrived around the same time, claiming to come from Muhammad ibn al-Hanafiyya, another son of 'Ali (but not Fatima) whom he called the *mahdi*, as his *wazir*. The situation in Kufa was chaotic with three groups (not to mention the Kharijites) contending for authority. Given the fierce struggle for leadership in Syria, the Umayyads were unable to enforce their authority and 'Ubaydullah was forced to flee to Syria and control over the region was given to Ibn az-Zubayr.

Sulayman informed the Zubayrid authorities that they intended to fight 'Ubaydullah and the killers of al-Husayn, so he let them agitate. The *Tawwabun* set out in Rabi' al-Akhir 65 AH. When they stopped at their camp at an-Nukhayla, Sulayman discovered that only four thousand of sixteen thousand pledged supporters had turned up. They then decided that they were atoning rather than defeating the enemy. They spent three days at their camp and another thousand slipped away. Then they visited the grave of al-Husayn and set out. They met the Umayyad army at 'Ayn al-Warda. The battle lasted for three days and they were slaughtered.

Some of their number had gone over to al-Mukhtar and his movement. Al-Mukhtar had first approached 'Ali ibn Husayn Zayn al-'Abidin who refused to be involved in any public activity. He did not get any public support from Ibn al-Hanafiyya either.

The revolt of al-Mukhtar took place in 66/685. After the slaughter which took place at the battle of 'Ayn al-Warda, the supporters of the Shi'a who had high rank among the Arabs were dead, so al-Mukhtar brought in the Persian *mawali* and promised them booty and stipends. He promised to free any slaves who joined him. Given their background and situation, they latched onto the idea of a messianic

Mahdi who would deliver them from tyranny and injustice. Al-Mukhtar had a chair which was supposed to have belonged to 'Ali covered in silk and brocade. It was set on a grey mule and used as a quasi-Ark of the Covenant. He concentrated on the role of *mahdi* rather than that of *imam*. He quickly gained control of the town and the citadel.

Al-Mukhtar succeeded in beheading most of those responsible for the death of al-Husayn. He sent the head of the man most responsible, 'Ubaydullah ibn Ziyad, to 'Ali Zayn al-'Abidin.

But now he had aroused the opposition of the *ashraf* who were complaining about their *mawali* having riding animals and their slaves disobeying them. They attempted to overthrow al-Mukhtar when he had gone out to fight the Umayyads. It is said that ten thousand Kufans joined the Zubayrid general, Mus'ab ibn az-Zubayr, in Basra, and they urged him to attack. Al-Mukhtar's army was defeated by Mus'ab ibn az-Zubayr at Madhar. Mus'ab then marched against al-Mukhtar who was killed on a sortie from the citadel in Kufa by his forces. Al-Mus'ab then proceeded to kill seven thousand of al-Mukhtar's supporters, mostly *mawali*.

In 71 AH 'Abd al-Malik ibn Marwan defeated Mus'ab and entered Kufa. After putting Qatan ibn 'Abdullah in charge for forty days, he replaced him with Bishr ibn Marwan. In 73 AH Bishr was put in charge of both Basra and Kufa. His deputy in Kufa was 'Amr ibn Hurayth. When Bishr died in 75 AH, 'Abd al-Malik appointed al-Hajjaj ibn Yusuf as governor. He arrived in Kufa with his face covered by a red turban. When the men assembled in the mosque, he rose and gave his famous address in which he said, "By Allah! I take full reckoning of wickedness, match it and pay it back in kind. I see heads ripe and ready for plucking while the blow is ready to fall between turbans and beards!" Any able-bodied man who did not join the army which was about to set out against the Kharijites was deemed a traitor and beheaded.

This was the time when the Kharijites were being successful in their attacks on the establishment. Although the Kharijite groups mostly operated in the area around Basra, they also attacked in the region around Kufa. Shabib, the famous Kharijite leader, actually entered Kufa on a couple of occasions and the authorities were unable to do anything about it. Shabib died in 78 AH.

Another major event in Kufa's history was the revolt of Ibn al-Ash'ath, one of the Kinda tribe. In 80 AH al-Hajjaj dispatched a force of Kufans and Basrans, known as the Peacock Army, to put down a rebellion in Kabulistan. Ibn al-Ash'ath, the commanding general, decided to wait until spring before continuing his campaign. Al-Hajjaj pressed for immediate action and the dispute led to a revolt by Ibn al-Ash'ath and his troops. Ibn al-Ash'ath picked up a lot of malcontents among the *ashraf*. 'Abd al-Malik had offered to dismiss al-Hajjaj but they rejected the offer. Al-Hajjaj defeated them at Dayr al-Jamajim outside of Kufa even though he was vastly outnumbered. Supporters began to disappear and Ibn al-Ash'ath and his supporters finally defeated at Maskin.

Al-Hajjaj ruled Iraq for twenty years and died in 95/713. He left Yazid ibn Abi Kabsha in charge of Kufa and Basra and he was confirmed in the post. Once Hisham ibn 'Abd al-Malik came to power, the governor of Iraq for fifteen years was Khalid ibn 'Abdullah al-Qasri. Hisham's rule also saw a Shi'ite revolt in Kufa: that of Zayd ibn 'Ali, the brother of Muhammad al-Baqir. He went to Kufa and rebelled against the government in 122/740 and was killed in a street battle in Kufa. His son, Yahya, fled to Khurasan and fell in a battle in 125/743.

After Hisham's death in 125/743, things started to unravel for the Umayyads. In 127/744, there was another rebellion in Kufa, led by 'Abdullah ibn Mu'awiya, a Hashimite who was not a descendant of 'Ali but of his brother, Ja'far ibn Abi Talib. It lasted for two years simply because Marwan II was too busy elsewhere to spare the time to put down the rising. When he did turn his attention to 'Abdullah ibn Mu'awiya, 'Abdullah fled to Persia, and then to Herat, where he was eliminated in 129/746 at the instigation of the Shi'ite agent, Abu Muslim, who was the mover behind the 'Abbasids. The first 'Abbasid, Abu al-'Abbas as-Saffah, began his caliphate with the Friday prayer in the Kufa Mosque.

Al-Hashimiya, just outside of Kufa on the east bank of the Euphrates, was the first capital of the 'Abbasids. Al-Mansur also began his caliphate by leading the Friday prayers in the Kufa Mosque.

Then in 141 AH, the caliph al-Mansur was besieged in his residence by extreme Shi'ite elements of his guard known as the Rawandiyya. They saw al-Mansur as a divine incarnation and marched around his residence. Things progressed and developed into an insurrection and al-Mansur could easily have been killed. There was another Shi'ite of rising in 145/762 of Muhammad an-Nafs az-Zakiyya in Madina and his brother Ibrahim in Basra, which was put down. Reports say that "a hundred thousand of the Kufa rabble were ready to rise against al-Mansur." Al-Mansur decided that he needed a new capital since he had no confidence in the people of Kufa and wanted to distance himself from them. He finally decided to build a new city and chose the site of Madinat as-Salam (Baghdad) in 145-6/762-3 and he moved the treasury and diwans from Kufa to the new city.

Later, at the end of the third/ninth century, Kufa was the crucible of the Isma'ili Qarmatian movement and it never completely recovered from the damage that they inflicted on it.

Mosque of Kufa in 1912

Sects in Kufa

In general Kufa was a turbulent unruly city which easily suc-
cumbed to the lure of insurrection. As well as the various tribes inter-
acting and the conflict over wealth there also was some
Persianisation – even in language. For instance crossroads were
called *chaharsuj* and a market *wazar* (rather than *suq*). There were
the northern Arabs who had no tradition of hereditary kingship and
the southern Arabs who did. And there were many southern Arabs in
Kufa.

Umayyad Shi'ism is a veritable chaos of ideas. The early 'Alid
movement was a political movement, partly consisting of those who
followed 'Ali for religious reasons, and partly of the *rawadif*, the
later arrivals or those who had participated in the Ridda, or the still
later *lawahiq*, who wanted a larger slice of the pie: which was the
fertile agricultural land of the Sawad.

There was no widespread recognition that the imamate went
through al-Husayn. It could go through al-Husayn, al-Hasan, children
of 'Ali not by Fatima, or the wider Hashimite family, i.e. al-'Abbas.
Al-Mukhtar claimed to act for Muhammad ibn al-Hanafiyya, the son
of 'Ali by a Hanafi woman. When he died, some claimed that the
imam was his son Abu Hashim. Some took Muhammad an-Nafs az-
Zakiyya, a great grandson of al-Hasan. There was the movement of
'Abdullah ibn Mu'awiya, a descendant of the brother of 'Ali. The
'Abbasids first claimed their right from Abu Hashim, but later from
al-'Abbas.

The first Shi'ites, or 'Alawites, were distinguished by their accep-
tance of 'Ali rather than 'Uthman without having any position about
Abu Bakr and 'Umar. Then when Mu'awiya designated Yazid as his
successor, opposition to him took various forms. The Kharijites
rejected the idea that the imamate was only for Quraysh. Others said
that it was for Quraysh alone, which allowed for Ibn az-Zubayr to
claim the caliphate. The Shi'ite position was that it was only for the
house of Hashim (and hence not the Banu Umayya).

There also a stronger position called *rafd* (rejection) which led to
the use of the term 'Rafidites' which developed in in the 680s. Those

who espoused this position held that 'Ali should have been the caliph and that all of the Community (with the exception of six people) fell into error when they accepted Abu Bakr and 'Umar as caliphs. And we see this beginning in the movement of al-Mukhtar although the term Rafidite came into use somewhat later. They condemned the first three caliphs as usurpers, said that the community had gone astray by accepting them, and that 'Ali and his three sons, al-Hasan, al-Husayn and Muhammad ibn al-Hanafiyya, were the divinely appointed successors to the Prophet and possessed supernatural powers. This led to cursing the first three caliphs and those who supported them.

Initially there was a general feeling that the world would come to an end in the year 100 AH and then, when it did not happen, everyone but the Shi'a largely ignored the idea of the Mahdi until many years later. The idea of a reviver of the *deen* every hundred years took greater prominence. As we said, al-Mukhtar was also the first to use the term "*mahdi*" in a real messianic sense. He called himself the *wazir* of the Mahdi. He called for vengeance for the family of the Prophet and protection of the weak (i.e. the *mawali*). The personal followers of al-Mukhtar, who were known as "the Khashabiyya" because they were armed with wooden staffs (*khashab*), or "the Kaysaniyya" after Kaysan, the former *mawla* of al-Mukhtar and the head of his bodyguard.

The *mawali* who supported this position incorporated various ideas into their beliefs. One was that Muhammad ibn al-Hanafiyya was the Mahdi and had secret knowledge about souls and the celestial spheres which he had received from al-Hasan and al-Husayn. After his death in 81/700, various Kaysani groups emerged. The Kuraybiyya believed that he was alive, but concealed (*ghayba*) at Mount Radwa north of Madina, guarded by lions and tigers and fed by mountain goats and that he would return and emerge from his hiding place, gather his followers and establish the authority of true Islam. (This concealment was meant to be as penance for giving allegiance to 'Abd al-Malik.) Various ideas seeped in to this line of thought, including reincarnation and transmigration of souls which resulted in numerous extreme Shi'ite sects, known as *ghulat*.

The other branch became the Hashimiyya who said that the imamate passed to his son, Abu Hashim, and the line went on to the 'Abbasids. An illustration of the oscillations of the time is found in the poet as-Sayyid al-Himyari (d. 171/787-8). He started as a Khariji, became a Kaysani and then became a follower of Ja'far as-Sadiq when the 'Abbasids came to power. He said that he had "Ja'farised himself."

There were a series of people who were called *mahdis* by their followers. The second prominent *mahdi* was Muhammad an-Nafs az-Zakiyya (100-145/718-762). When he died, his followers said that he was in concealment in 'Ilmiyya, a hill on the route between Makka and Najd and would return. A group called the Nawusiyya said that Ja'far as-Sadiq (d. 765) was the Mahdi and would return. After his son, Musa al-Kazim, died in 183/799-800 in an 'Abbasid prison, another group claimed that he was the Mahdi. Isma'il, another son of as-Sadiq, was also believed to be the Mahdi. Others said that it was his son, Muhammad ibn Isma'il, who would not die until he had conquered the world. This was the start of Isma'ilism.

Al-Mukhtar's group were also accused of being "Saba'ites", after 'Abdullah ibn Saba', a Jew from San'a who converted to Islam in the time of 'Uthman and travelled about espousing the idea that Muhammad would return and that 'Ali was his executor and hence no one else had the right to the imamate. He was exiled by 'Ali and his followers joined up with al-Mukhtar.

Irja' and the Murj'ites

This is a term which began to be used after the revolt of al-Mukhtar. It was first used by al-Hasan, the son of Muhammad ibn al-Hanafiyya, stating approval of Abu Bakr and 'Umar and "postponing" judgement about 'Uthman, 'Ali and Ibn az-Zubayr and leaving judgement to Allah. So it was, as many things are, originally a political position. Then it was later applied to doctrine.

Some said that the term means that a grave sinner is a believer and his judgement is up to Allah and that it means "giving hope." This moved to the definition of faith and the statement that a believer is the one who recognises Allah and the Messenger, believes this to be true and professes it with the tongue, whether or not he acts by it. Opponents to this called them Murji'a or Murji'ites.

The Murji'ites arose in opposition to the Kharijites who believed that if someone committed a major wrong action he was no longer a believer. The more extreme Murji'ites went so far as to say that no Muslim would enter the Fire and for them faith does not increase or decrease.

The term also had different meanings for different people. The Shi'a used the term 'Murji'ites' for those who did not put 'Ali above 'Uthman (unless they were Kharijites). The Kharijites said that anyone who did not assert that 'Ali was a grave sinner was a Murji'ite. The Hanbalis applied it to someone who believed that faith did not increase or decrease according to one's actions.

There is also the issue of saying, "I am a believer if Allah wills" or "I am truly a believer." The Murji'ites objected to saying this and claimed that it expresses doubt. The Ash'arites agreed with including the conditional phrase and point out that it is a manifestation of being a humble servant and subject to Allah's will and what He decrees the ultimate seal will be.

Ahl as-Sunna wa al-Jama'a

The concept of *Ahl as-Sunna wa al-Jama'a* as a title developed slowly. We find it around the time of Sulayman at-Taymi, Ayyub as-Sakhtiyani, Ibn 'Awn and Yunus ibn 'Ubayd. Various terms were used before this one gained popularity: *Ahl as-Sunna, Ahl as-Sunna wa al-Athar, Ashab al-Hadith, Ahl al-Kitab wa as-Sunna, Ahl al-Haqq* and others. Al-Ash'ari used *Ahl as-Sunna wa al-Jama'a* once and *Ahl as-Sunna wa al-Istiqama* several times.

The impetus for this originated in Basra. The concept of *Sunna wa Jama'a*, the people of the *Sunna* and the Community, developed in opposition to the numerous sects which abounded in Iraq, but inclusion of rivals into the term took some time. It really solidified as a definitive term after al-Mutawakkil and then of the *Mihna* or Inquisition and represented communal solidarity (*jama'a*), not passing becoming embroiled in events of the civil wars, and accepting all the Companions.

Chapter One: Makka
The Names of the Companions of the
Messenger of Allah ﷺ who settled in Makka

Abu Sabra ibn Abi Ruhm

Abu Sabra ibn Abi Ruhm ibn Abi Qays ibn 'Abd Wudd ibn Nasr ibn Malik ibn Hisl ibn 'Amir ibn Lu'ayy. His mother was Barra bint 'Abd al-Muttalib ibn Hashim ibn 'Abd Manaf ibn Qusayy.

Muhammad ibn 'Umar said, "We do not know of any of the Muhajirun among those who were present at Badr who returned to Makka after the death of the Prophet ﷺ and took up residence there other than Abu Sabra. He returned to Makka after the death of the Prophet ﷺ and settled there. His son and the Muslims disliked him doing that. They objected to it and tried to dissuade him from returning to Makka and settling there after he had emigrated from it and they were angry about that. Abu Sabra ibn Abi Ruhm died while 'Uthman ibn 'Affan was caliph.

'Ayyash ibn Abi Rabi'a

'Ayyash ibn Abi Rabi'a ibn al-Mughira ibn 'Abdullah ibn 'Umar ibn Makhzum. His mother was Asma' bint Makhrama ibn Jandal ibn Ubayr ibn Nahshal ibn Darim of the Banu Tamim. He was the brother of Abu Jahl ibn Hisham by the same mother. 'Ayyash was one of those who emigrated to Abyssinia and then returned and stayed in Madina until the Prophet ﷺ died. Then he went to Syria and performed *jihad* in the Cause of Allah. Then he returned to Makka and stayed there until he died. His son, 'Abdullah ibn 'Ayyash, remained in Madina until he died.

'Abdullah ibn Abi Rabi'a

'Abdullah ibn Abi Rabi'a ibn al-Mughira ibn 'Abdullah ibn 'Umar ibn Makhzum. His mother was Asma' bint Makhrama ibn Jandal ibn Ubayr ibn Nahshal ibn Darim. In the *Jahiliyya*,

'Abdullah's name had been Buhayr. When he became Muslim, the Messenger of Allah ﷺ re-named him 'Abdullah. 'Umar appointed him governor of Yemen.

Al-Harith ibn Hisham

Al-Harith ibn Hisham ibn 'Abdullah ibn 'Umar ibn Makhzum. His mother was Asma' bint Makhrama ibn Jandal ibn Ubayr ibn Nahshal ibn Darim. Al-Harith ibn Hisham became Muslim on the day of the Conquest of Makka and continued to live in Makka until the Messenger of Allah ﷺ died. He went to Syria while Abu Bakr as-Siddiq was caliph and was present at the battles of Fihl and Ajnadayn. He died in the 'Amwas plague in 18 AH while 'Umar ibn al-Khattab was caliph.

'Ikrima ibn Abi Jahl

Abu Jahl's name was 'Amr ibn Hisham ibn al-Mughira ibn 'Abdullah ibn 'Umar ibn Makhzum. His mother was Umm Mujalid bint Yarbu' of the Banu Hilal ibn 'Amir. 'Ikrima became Muslim on the day of the Conquest of Makka and lived in Makka. In the Farewell *Hajj*, the Messenger of Allah ﷺ appointed him over the tribe of Hawazin to collect their *zakat*. The Messenger of Allah ﷺ died while 'Ikrima was at Tabala. Then he went on *jihad* to Syria and was killed as a martyr in the Battle of Ajnadayn while Abu Bakr as-Siddiq was caliph.

'Abdullah ibn as-Sa'ib

'Abdullah ibn as-Sa'ib ibn Abi as-Sa'ib ibn 'Abid ibn 'Abdullah ibn 'Umar ibn Makhzum. His *kunya* was Abu 'Abd ar-Rahman. His mother was Ramla bint 'Urwa Dhi al-Burdayn of the Banu Hilal ibn 'Amr ibn Sa'sa'a. He became Muslim on the day of the Conquest of Makka and continued to live in Makka until he died there in the time of 'Abdullah ibn az-Zubayr's rule.

'Abdullah ibn Numayr reported from 'Abd al-Malik ibn Jurayj that 'Abdullah ibn Abi Mulayka said, "I saw 'Abdullah ibn 'Ayyash when he finished the grave of 'Abdullah ibn as-Sa'ib. The people rose from it and Ibn 'Abbas stood at it and made supplication for him and then left.

Al-Fudayl ibn Dukayn reported from Ibn 'Uyayna that Dawud ibn Shabur said that he heard Mujahid say, "We used to boast about ourselves in respect of other people for four reasons: our *faqih*, our qadi, our *mu'adhdhin* and our reciter. Our *faqih* was Ibn 'Abbas. Our *mu'adhdhin* was Abu Mahdhura. Our reciter was 'Abdullah ibn as-Sa'ib. Our qadi was 'Ubayd ibn 'Umayr."

Khalid ibn al-'As

Khalid ibn al-'As ibn Hisham ibn al-Mughira ibn 'Abdullah ibn 'Umar ibn Makhzum. His mother was 'Atika bint al-Walid ibn al-Mughira ibn 'Umar ibn Makhzum. He was the father of 'Ikrima ibn Khalid and the poet, al-Harith ibn Khalid. Khalid ibn al-'As became Muslim on the day when Makka was conquered and lived there and had descendants.

Al-Fudayl ibn Dukayn reported from Ibn 'Uyayna from Ibn Jurayj that 'Ata' said, "I saw that Abu Mahdhura did not give the *adhan* until he saw Khalid ibn al-'As enter the door of the mosque."

Qays ibn as-Sa'ib, the *mawla* of Mujahid

Muhammad ibn 'Umar said that 'Abd al-Hamid ibn 'Imran reported from Musa ibn Abi Kathir that Mujahid said, "This *ayat* was revealed about my *mawla*, Qays ibn as-Sa'ib: '*For those who are able to fast [but with difficulty], their* fidya *is to feed the poor.*' (2:184) He broke the fast and fed a poor person for each day."

'Attab ibn Usayd

'Attab ibn Usayd ibn Abi al-'Is ibn Umayya ibn 'Abd Shams ibn 'Abd Manaf ibn Qusayy. His mother was Arwa bint Abi 'Amr ibn Umayya ibn 'Abd Shams. He became Muslim on the day of the Conquest of Makka. When the Messenger of Allah ﷺ left Makka for Hunayn, he put 'Attab ibn Usayd in charge of the people in Makka and the prayer. He asked him, "Do you know whom I have put you in charge of?" He answered, "Allah and His Messenger know best." He said, "I have appointed you over the people of Allah." 'Attab established the *hajj* for people that year, 8 AH. The Messenger of Allah ﷺ died while 'Attab ibn Usayd was in charge of Makka.

Khalid ibn Usayd

'Attab's brother, Khalid ibn Usayd ibn Abi al-'Is ibn Umayya ibn 'Abd Shams. He became Muslim on the day of the Conquest of Makka and remained in Makka.

Al-Hakam ibn Abi al-'Is

Al-Hakam ibn Abi al-'Is ibn Umayya ibn 'Abd Shams. His mother was Ruqayya bint al-Harith ibn 'Ubayd ibn 'Umar ibn Makhzum. He became Muslim on the day of the Conquest of Makka and remained there until the caliphate of 'Uthman ibn 'Affan. He gave him permission to enter Madina and he died there while 'Uthman ibn 'Affan was caliph. He was the father of Marwan ibn al-Hakam and the uncle of 'Uthman ibn 'Affan.

'Uqba ibn al-Harith

'Uqba ibn al-Harith ibn 'Amir ibn Nawfal ibn 'Abd Manaf ibn Qusayy. His mother was Khadija or Umama bint 'Iyad ibn Rafi' ibn Khuza'a. 'Uqba became Muslim on the day of the Conquest of Makka.

'Arim ibn al-Fadl reported from Hammad ibn Zayd from Ayyub that 'Abdullah ibn Abi Mulayka said that he heard 'Uqba ibn al-Harith say, "Ibn Abi Mulayka said, and a companion of mine also related to me when I remembered more of the *hadith* than my companion: 'I married Umm Yahya bint Abi Ihab. A black woman came to us and claimed that she had suckled both of us. I mentioned that to the Prophet ﷺ and he turned away from me. I stated, "She is lying." He said, "How do you know she is lying when she said what she said? Divorce her."'"

'Uthman ibn Talha ibn Abi Talha

Abu Talha's name was 'Abdullah ibn 'Abd al-'Uzza ibn 'Uthman ibn 'Abd ad-Dar ibn Qusayy. His mother was as-Sulama the younger bint Sa'd ibn ash-Shuhayd of the Ansar.

Muhammad ibn Sa'd said that Muhammad ibn 'Umar said, "'Uthman returned to Makka and stayed here until he died there while Mu'awiya ibn Abi Sufyan was caliph."

Shayba al-Hajib

Shayba al-Hajib ibn 'Uthman ibn Abi Talha ibn 'Abd Manaf ibn 'Abd ad-Dar ibn Qusayy. His mother was Umm Jamil bint 'Umayr ibn Hashim ibn 'Abd Manaf ibn 'Abd ad-Dar ibn Qusayy. Shayba went with Quraysh to face Hawazin at Hunayn and became Muslim there. Shayba was the father of Safiyya bint Shayba. He lived until the time of Yazid ibn Mu'awiya.

An-Nudayr ibn al-Harith

An-Nudayr ibn al-Harith ibn 'Alqama ibn Kalada ibn 'Abd Manaf ibn 'Abd ad-Dar ibn Qusayy. His *kunya* was Abu al-Harith. His mother was the daughter of al-Harith ibn 'Uthman ibn 'Abd ad-Dar ibn Qusayy. He became Muslim at Hunayn and the Messenger of Allah ﷺ gave him a hundred camels from the booty of Hunayn. He was the brother of an-Nadr ibn al-Harith who was slain by 'Ali ibn Abi Talib in the Battle of Badr at as-Safra' following the command of the Messenger of Allah ﷺ. The descendants of an-Nudayr included Muhammad ibn al-Murtafi' ibn an-Nadir from whom Sufyan ibn 'Uyayna and others related.

Abu as-Sanabil ibn Ba'kak

Abu as-Sanabil ibn Ba'kak ibn al-Harith ibn as-Sabbaq ibn 'Abd ad-Dar ibn Qusayy. His mother was 'Amra bint Aws ibn Abi 'Amr of the Banu 'Udhra. He was the one who spoke to Subay'a bint al-Harith al-Aslamiyya [regarding the end of her *idda*.]

Safwan ibn Umayya

Safwan ibn Umayya ibn Khalaf ibn Wahb ibn Jumh ibn 'Amr ibn Husays ibn Ka'b ibn Lu'ayy. His *kunya* was Abu Wahb. His mother was Safiyya bint Ma'mar ibn Habib ibn Wahb ibn Hudhafa ibn Jumah. Safwan became Muslim at Hunayn and the Messenger of Allah ﷺ gave him fifty camels from the booty of Hunayn.

'Ali ibn 'Abdullah ibn Ja'far reported from Yahya ibn Adam from Ibn al-Mubarak from Yunus from az-Zuhri from Sa'id ibn al-Musayyab that Safwan ibn Umayya said, "On the Day of Hunayn, the Messenger of Allah ﷺ gave to me although he was one of the people whom I most hated. He continued to give to me until he was the person I most loved."

Muhammad ibn 'Umar said, "It was said to Safwan ibn Umayya, 'There is no Islam for someone who does not emigrate.' He went to Madina and told that to the Prophet ﷺ who said to him, 'I adjure you, Abu Hazim, to return to the flats of Makka.' So he returned to Makka and remained there until he died in the time when the people left Makka for the Battle of the Camel in Shawwal 36 AH. He encouraged people to go to the Battle of the Camel.'"

Abu Mahdhura

His name was Aws ibn Mi'yar ibn Lawdhan ibn Rabi'a ibn 'Uwayj ibn Sa'd ibn Jumah. His mother was from Khuza'a. I heard someone give the ascription of Abu Mahdhura and said that his name was Samura ibn 'Umayr ibn Lawdhan ibn Wahb ibn Sa'd ibn Jumh. He had a full brother whose name was Aws who was killed at the Battle of Badr as an unbeliever. Abu Mahdhura became Muslim on the day of the Conquest of Makka and remained in Makka and did not emigrate.

Muhammad ibn 'Umar reported from Yahya ibn Khalid ibn 'Abdullah ibn Abi Dujana from az-Zubayr ibn al-Mundhir ibn Abi Usayd as-Sa'idi from his father that his grandfather said, "When the Messenger of Allah ﷺ came on the day of Makka's conquest, Abu Mahdhura went to speak to him and asked, 'Messenger of Allah, shall I give the *adhan* for you?' The Messenger of Allah ﷺ told him 'Give the *adhan*.' He used to give the *adhan* with Bilal. When the Messenger of Allah ﷺ returned to Madina, Abu Mahdhura remained behind giving the *adhan* and did not emigrate."

Muhammad ibn 'Umar said, "The task of giving the *adhan* was inherited afterwards from his son to his son and so on until today in the Masjid al-Haram. Abu Mahdhura died in Makka in 59 AH."

Muti' ibn al-Aswad

Muti' ibn al-Aswad ibn Haritha ibn Nadla ibn 'Awf ibn 'Abid ibn 'Awij ibn 'Adi ibn Ka'b. His mother was al-'Ajma'. She is Unaysa bint 'Amir ibn al-Fadl of Khuza'a. Muti' became Muslim on the day of the Conquest of Makka.

Muhammad ibn 'Ubayd at-Tanafisi reported from Zakariyya ibn Abi Za'ida that 'Amir said, "He did not meet any of the 'rebels' of Quraysh except for Muti'. His name had been al-'As (disobedient) and the Messenger of Allah ﷺ renamed him Muti' (obedient)."

Muhammad ibn 'Umar said that Muti' died in the caliphate of 'Uthman.

Abu Jahm ibn Hudhayfa

Abu Jahm ibn Hudhayfa ibn Ghanim ibn Ghanim ibn 'Amir ibn 'Abdullah ibn 'Uwayj ibn 'Adi ibn Ka'b. His mother was Bashira bint 'Abdullah of the Banu 'Adi ibn Ka'b. He became Muslim on the day of the Conquest of Makka and died after 'Umar ibn al-Khattab was murdered.

Abu Quhafa

His name was 'Uthman ibn 'Amir ibn 'Amr ibn Ka'b ibn Sa'd ibn Taym ibn Murra ibn Ka'b ibn Lu'ayy. His mother was Qutayka bint Ada ibn Rabah ibn 'Abdullah ibn Qurt ibn Razzah ibn 'Adi ibn Ka'b.

'Abd ar-Rahman ibn Muhammad al-Muharibi reported from Muhammad ibn Ishaq from Yahya ibn 'Abbad ibn 'Abdullah ibn az-Zubayr from his father that Asma' bint Abi Bakr said, "When the Messenger of Allah ﷺ entered Makka, was relaxed and sat in the mosque, Abu Bakr brought [his father] Abu Quhafa to him. When the Messenger of Allah ﷺ saw him, he said, 'Abu Bakr, would you not leave the old man until I could walk to him?' He said, 'Messenger of Allah, it is more proper for him to walk to you than for you to walk to him.' So the Messenger of Allah ﷺ had him sit in front of him and put his hand over his heart. Then he said, 'Abu Quhafa, become Muslim and you will be safe.' He became Muslim and gave a true testimony. When he came to him his head and beard were white like worm-wood. The Messenger of Allah ﷺ said, 'Change this white hair, but avoid black dye.'"

Isma'il ibn Ibrahim ibn 'Ulayya reported from Layth from Abu az-Zubayr that Jabir said, "Abu Quhafa was brought on the day of the conquest of Makka and it was as if his hair was [white as] wormwood. The Messenger of Allah ﷺ said, "Take him to one of his wives and change its colour, but avoid black dye."

Ma'n ibn 'Isa reported from 'Abdullah ibn Mu'ammil that 'Ikrima ibn Khalid said, "Abu Quhafa was brought to the Prophet ﷺ and it was as if his head was wormwood and the Messenger of Allah ﷺ accepted his allegiance and then said, 'Change the colour hair of the old man with henna.'"

'Amr ibn al-Haytham Abu Qatan reported from Abu Hanifa from Yazid ibn 'Abd ar-Rahman that Anas ibn Malik said, "It is as if I could see the beard of Abu Quhafa red like flame of firewood."

Muhammad ibn 'Umar said, "Abu Quhafa remained in Makka and did not emigrate. When [his son] Abu Bakr as-Siddiq died, Abu Quhafa inherited a sixth from him and he gave it back to the children of Abu Bakr. Then Abu Quhafa died in Makka in Muharram 14 AH at the age of ninety-seven."

Al-Muhajir ibn Qunfudh

Al-Muhajir ibn Qunfudh ibn 'Umayr ibn Jud'an ibn 'Amr ibn Ka'b ibn Sa'd ibn Taym ibn Murra. His mother was Hind bint al-Harith ibn Masruq of the Banu Ghanm ibn Malik ibn Kinana. Al-Muhajir's name was 'Amr. He became Muslim on the day Makka was conquered. Qunfudh's name was Khalaf. Al-Muhajir related from the Prophet ﷺ.

Al-Muttalib ibn Abi Wada'a

His name was al-Harith ibn Dubayra ibn Su'ayd ibn Sa'd ibn Sahm ibn 'Amr ibn Husays ibn Ka'b ibn Lu'ayy. His mother was Arwa bint al-Harith ibn 'Abd al-Muttalib ibn Hashim ibn 'Abd Manaf.

Suhayl ibn 'Amr

Suhayl ibn 'Amr ibn 'Abd Shams ibn 'Abd Wudd ibn Nasr ibn Malik ibn Hisl ibn 'Amir ibn Lu'ayy. His mother was Hubayy bint Qays ibn Dubays of Khuza'a. Suhayl ibn 'Amr left Makka for Hunayn with the Prophet ﷺ while he was still an idolater and became Muslim at al-Ji'irana. On that day the Messenger of Allah ﷺ gave him a hundred camels from the booty of Hunayn. Suhayl related from the Prophet ﷺ.

Muhammad ibn 'Umar reported from 'Abd al-Hamid ibn Ja'far from his father from Ziyad ibn Mina that Abu Sa'd ibn Abi Fadla al-Ansari, who was a Companion, said, "I accompanied Suhayl ibn 'Amr to Syria in the nights when Abu Bakr as-Siddiq attacked us. I heard Suhayl say that he heard the Messenger of Allah ﷺ say, 'Standing in the Cause of Allah for an hour is better than what one does for family for one's entire life.' Suhayl said, 'I will fight on the frontiers until I die and will never return to Makka!" He died in the 'Amwas plague in Syria in 18 AH. Suhayl's *kunya* was Abu Yazid.

'Abdullah ibn as-Sa'di

His name was 'Amr ibn Waqdan ibn 'Abd Shams ibn 'Abd Wudd ibn Nasr ibn Malik ibn Hisl ibn 'Amir ibn Lu'ayy. His mother was the daughter of al-Hajjaj ibn 'Amir ibn Hudhayfa ibn Su'ayd ibn Sahm. 'Abdullah ibn as-Sa'di became Muslim on the day when Makka was conquered.

Huwaytib ibn 'Abd al-'Uzza

Huwaytib ibn 'Abd al-'Uzza ibn Abi Qays ibn 'Abd Wudd ibn Nasr ibn Malik ibn Hisl ibn 'Amir ibn Lu'ayy. His *kunya* was Abu Muhammad. His mother was Zaynab bint 'Alqama ibn Ghazwan ibn Yarbu' ibn al-Harith ibn Munqidh. Huwaytib ibn 'Abd al-'Uzza became Muslim on the day when Makka was conquered.

Muhammad ibn 'Umar reported from Abu Bakr ibn 'Abdullah ibn Abi Sabra from Musa ibn 'Uqba from al-Mundhir ibn al-Jahm that Huwaytib ibn 'Abd al-'Uzza al-'Amiri reached the age of one hundred and twenty: he lived sixty years in the *Jahiliyya* and sixty years in Islam. He became Muslim on the day when Makka was conquered and was present with the Messenger of Allah ﷺ at Hunayn and Ta'if. The Messenger of Allah ﷺ gave him a hundred camels from the booty of Hunayn. Huwaytib died in 54 AH in the caliphate of Mu'awiya ibn Abi Sufyan.

Dirar ibn al-Khattab

Dirar ibn al-Khattab ibn Mirdas ibn Kabir ibn 'Amr ibn Habib ibn 'Amr ibn Shayban ibn Muharib ibn Fihr.

He said that he was the horseman and poet of Quraysh. He became Muslim on the day when Makka was conquered. He remained in Makka until he went to Yamama and was killed as a martyr in the battle there.

Abu 'Abd ar-Rahman al-Fihri

I heard someone say that his name was Kurz ibn Jabir.

'Affan ibn Muslim reported from Hammad ibn Salama from Ya'la ibn 'Ata' from Abu Hammam that Abu 'Abd ar-Rahman al-Fihri was present at the Hunayn expedition with the Prophet 鸞, and he related a long *hadith* about that.

'Utba ibn Abi Lahab

Abu Lahab is 'Abd al-'Uzza ibn 'Abd al-Muttalib ibn Hashim ibn 'Abd Manaf ibn Qusayy. His mother was Umm Jamil bint Harb ibn Umayya ibn 'Abd Shams ibn 'Abd Manaf ibn Qusayy. He became Muslim on the day when Makka was conquered. He remained in Makka and did not emigrate. He went with the Prophet 鸞 in the expedition of Hunayn. He remained firm with the Messenger of Allah 鸞 on that day among those of the people of his house and his Companions who remained steadfast. None of the men of the Banu Hashim remained in Makka after it was conquered except for 'Utba and Mu'attab, the sons of Abu Lahab.

Mu'attab ibn Abi Lahab

His mother was Umm Jamil bint Harb ibn Umayya. He became Muslim on the day when Makka was conquered and went out to Hunayn with the Messenger of Allah 鸞. He remained firm with him among those of the people of his house and his Companions who remained steadfast. He lost his eye on that day.

Ya'la ibn Umayya

Ya'la ibn Umayya ibn Ubayy ibn 'Ubayda ibn Hammam ibn al-Harith ibn Bakr ibn Zayd ibn Malik ibn Hanzala ibn Malik ibn Zayd Mana ibn Tamim. His mother was Munya bint Jabir ibn Wuhayb ibn Nusayb ibn Zayd ibn Malik ibn al-Harith ibn 'Awf ibn Mazin ibn Mansur. Ya'la ibn Umayya was an ally of the Banu Nawfal ibn 'Abd

Manaf. He, his father Umayya and his brother, Salama ibn Umayya, became Muslim. Ya'la and Umayya were present at Tabuk with the Messenger of Allah ﷺ. Ya'la related from 'Umar.

Isma'il ibn 'Ulya reported from Ibn Jurayj from 'Ata' from Safwan ibn Ya'la that Ya'la ibn Umayya said, "I went on an expedition with the Messenger of Allah ﷺ in the Army of Hardship [to Tabuk in 9 AH]. It was one my actions about which I have the most confidence."

Hujayr ibn Abi Ihab

Hujayr ibn Abi Ihab ibn 'Aziz ibn Qays ibn Suwayd ibn Zayd ibn 'Abdullah ibn Darim of the Banu Tamim. He was an ally of the Banu Nawfal ibn 'Abd Manaf.

'Umayr ibn Qatada

'Umayr ibn Qatada ibn Sa'd ibn 'Amir ibn Jundu' ibn Layth ibn Bakr ibn 'Abd Manat ibn Kinana. He was Abu 'Ubayd ibn 'Umayr al-Laythi.

Musa ibn Isma'il reported from Suwayd Abu Hatim, the quartermaster, from 'Abdullah ibn 'Ubayd ibn 'Umayr from his father that his grandfather said, "While I was sitting with the Messenger of Allah ﷺ, a man came and asked, 'Messenger of Allah, what is Islam?' So he told him its laws." It is a long *hadith*.

Abu 'Aqrab

His name was Khuwaylid ibn Khalid ibn Bujayr ibn 'Amr ibn Hamas ibn 'Uwayj ibn Bakr ibn 'Abd Manat ibn Kinana. He became Muslim and was a Companion of the Prophet ﷺ.

'Amr ibn Abi 'Aqrab

The son of Abu 'Aqrab. He met the Prophet ﷺ, saw him and related from him. He was the grandfather of Abu Nawfal ibn Abi 'Aqrab. The name of Abu Nawfal was Mu'awiya ibn Muslim ibn 'Amr ibn Abi 'Aqrab. Abu Nawfal later settled in Basra and the Basrans related from him.

Abu at-Tufayl

His name was 'Amir ibn Wathila ibn 'Abdullah ibn 'Umayr ibn Jabir ibn Humays ibn Jaz' ibn Sa'd ibn Layth.

Kalada ibn Hanbal

He was the half-brother of Safwan ibn Umayya by the same mother.

Ad-Dahhak ibn Makhlad and Rawh ibn 'Ubada reported from 'Umar ibn Abi Safwan from 'Amr ibn 'Abdullah ibn Safwan that Kalada ibn al-Hanbal said, "Safwan ibn Umayya sent me to the Prophet ﷺ on the day of the Conquest of Makka with some milk, a gazelle, and some small cucumbers when the Prophet ﷺ was at the highest part of the valley. I entered when he had not given permission for me to enter and I had not become Muslim. The Prophet ﷺ said, 'Go out and then say, '*As-salamu 'alaykum*. May I enter?' That was after Safwan had become Muslim." 'Amr reported it from Umayya ibn Safwan from Kalafa. Umayya did not say that he heard it from Kalada.

Busr ibn Sufyan

Busr ibn Sufyan ibn 'Amr ibn 'Umaymir ibn Sirma ibn 'Abdullah of Khuza'a. He is the one to whom the Prophet ﷺ wrote to call him to Islam.

Kurz ibn 'Alqama

Kurz ibn 'Alqama ibn Hilal ibn Jurayba ibn 'Abd Nuhm ibn Hulayl ibn Hubshiyya ibn Salul of Khuza'a. He is the one who followed the tracks of the Prophet ﷺ and Abu Bakr when they went to Madina. The tracks led to the opening of the cave where they were and he said, "The tracks end here." He is the one who looked at the foot of the Prophet ﷺ and said, "This foot is part of that foot in the Maqam," meaning the footprint of Ibrahim ﷺ in the Maqam. Kurz lived a long life and he became Muslim on the day Makka was conquered. Mu'awiya ibn Abi Sufyan wrote to his governor over Makka, "If Kurz ibn 'Alqama is alive, command him to acquaint you with the demarcations of the Haram." He did that and they will be its demarcations until the Final Hour.

Tamim ibn Asad

Tamim ibn Asad ibn Suwayd ibn As'ad ibn Manshu' ibn Habtar of Khuza'a. He was a poet. On the day when Makka was conquered, the Prophet ☀ commanded him to renew the supporting stones of the Haram.

Al-Aswad ibn Khalaf

Al-Aswad ibn Khalaf ibn As'ad ibn 'Amir ibn Bayada ibn Subay' ibn Ju'thuma ibn Sa'd ibn Mulayh ibn 'Amr ibn Rabi'a of Khuza'a. He related a *hadith* from the Prophet ☀. He was present with him on the day of the Conquest of Makka.

'Abd ar-Razzaq reported from Ibn Jurayj from 'Abdullah ibn 'Uthman ibn Khuthaym from Muhammad ibn al-Aswad ibn Khalaf that his father, al-Aswad ibn Khalaf, told him that he saw the Prophet ☀ accepting the allegiance of the people on the day of the Conquest at Qarn. Al-Aswad said, "I saw him when people, women, children and old people, were coming to him to give allegiance to him in Islam and the testimony that there is no god but Allah and Muhammad is His slave and Messenger.

Budayl ibn Warqa'

Budayl ibn Warqa' ibn 'Abd al-'Uzza ibn Rabi'a ibn Jurayy ibn 'Amir ibn Mazin ibn 'Adi ibn 'Amr ibn Rabi'a of Khuza'a. He is the one to whom the Messenger of Allah ☀ wrote to invite him to Islam.

Abu Shurayh al-Ka'bi

His name was Khuwaylid ibn Sakhr ibn 'Abd al-'Uzza ibn Mu'awiya ibn al-Mukhtarash ibn 'Amr ibn Zimman ibn 'Adi ibn 'Amr ibn Rabi'a of Khuza'a. Zimman and Mazin were brothers.

Nafi' ibn al-Harith

Nafi' ibn al-Harith ibn Hubala ibn 'Umayr ibn al-Harith who is Ghubshan ibn 'Abd 'Amr ibn 'Amr ibn Buwayy ibn Milkan ibn

Qusayy of Khuza'a. Nafi' ibn al-Harith was the governor of Makka for 'Umar ibn al-Khattab.

'Alqama ibn al-Faghwa'

'Alqama ibn al-Faghwa' ibn 'Ubayd ibn 'Ammar ibn Zimman ibn 'Adi ibn 'Amr ibn Rabi'a of Khuza'a.

Muharrish al-Ka'bi

Some of them said that his name is Muharrash.

'Abd ar-Rahman ibn Safwan

Hisham Abu al-Walid at-Tayalisi reported from Jarir ibn 'Abd al-Hamid from Yazid ibn Abi Ziyad from Mujahid that 'Abd ar-Rahman ibn Safwan said, "I donned my clothes on the day when Makka was conquered and then went and came upon the Prophet 🐝 when he left the House. I asked 'Umar, 'What did the Prophet 🐝 do when he entered the House?' He answered, 'He prayed two *ra'kats*.'"

Laqit ibn Sabra al-'Uqayli

He lived in the area of Rukba and Jildan close to Makka. He often went to Makka and stayed there.

Kaysan

'Uthman ibn al-Yaman said from 'Amr ibn Kathir al-Makki from 'Abd ar-Rahman ibn Kaysan that his father said, "I saw the Prophet 🐝 praying one of the two afternoon prayers, *Zuhr* or *'Asr* at Thaniyya al-'Ulya in a single garment, wrapped in it with alternate ends."

Muslim

Mu'adh ibn Hani' al-Bahrani al-Basri reported from 'Abdullah ibn al-Harith ibn Abza al-Makki from his mother Ra'ita bint Muslim that his father was present at Hunayn with the Messenger of Allah 🐝. He asked him, "What is your name?" He said, "Ghurab (crow)." He said, "Rather your name is Muslim."

'Abd ar-Rahman ibn Abza, a *mawla* of Khuza'a

Ad-Dahhak ibn Makhlad reported from Shu'ba from al-Hasan ibn 'Imran from 'Abdullah ibn 'Abd ar-Rahman ibn Abza that his father prayed with the Messenger of Allah ﷺ. When he made it light, he did not say the *takbir* (meaning when he prostrated).

Muhammad ibn 'Umar said, "'Abd ar-Rahman ibn Abza was in charge of Makka. He was the deputy of Nafi' ibn 'Abd al-Harith when he went to 'Umar ibn al-Khattab."

'Abdullah ibn Hubsha al-Khath'ami and **Iyas ibn 'Abd al-Muzani** were also part of this generation.

First Generation
of the people of Makka who related from 'Umar ibn al-Khattab and others

'Ali ibn Majida as-Shami

He is Abu Majida. He related from Abu Bakr and 'Umar ibn al-Khattab.

'Ubayd ibn 'Umayr

'Ubayd ibn 'Umayr ibn Qatada al-Laythi. His *kunya* was Abu 'Asim. He was trustworthy, and had many *hadiths*.

'Affan ibn Muslim reported from Sakhr ibn Juwayriya from Isma'il al-Makki that Abu Khalaf, the *mawla* of the Banu Jumah, related a *hadith* from 'A'isha in which he mentioned that the *kunya* of 'Ubayd ibn 'Umayr was Abu 'Asim.

'Affan ibn Muslim reported that Hammad ibn Salama reported that Thabit said, "The first of those to recount stories was 'Ubayd ibn 'Umayr in the time of 'Umar ibn al-Khattab."

'Abd al-Wahhab ibn 'Ata' reported from Habib ibn ash-Shuhayd that a man asked 'Ata', "Who was the first to recount stories?" He answered, "'Ubayd ibn 'Umayr."

Al-Fadl ibn Dukayn reported from Abu Bakr ibn 'Ayyash from 'Abd al-Malik that 'Ata' said, "'Ubayd ibn 'Umayr and I visited 'A'isha and she asked, 'Who is it?' He stated, 'I am 'Ubayd ibn 'Umayr.' She said, 'The one who is the storyteller of the people of Makka?' 'Yes,' he replied. She said, 'Lighten it. The reminder is weighty.'"

Al-Fadl ibn Dukayn reported that 'Abd al-Wahid ibn Ayman said, "I saw 'Ubayd ibn 'Umayr who had locks that reached the back of his neck or thereabouts."

Al-Fadl ibn Dukayn reported that 'Abd al-Wahid ibn Ayman said, "I saw 'Ubayd ibn 'Umayr and his beard was yellow."

16

Abu Salama ibn Sufyan

Abu Salama ibn Sufyan ibn 'Abd al-Asad al-Makhzumi. His mother was Umm Jamil bint al-Mughira ibn Abi al-'As ibn Umayya. He related from 'Umar ibn al-Khattab.

Al-Harith ibn 'Abdullah

Al-Harith ibn 'Abdullah ibn Abi Rabi'a ibn al-Mughira al-Makhzumi. His mother was an *umm walad*, and he had few *hadith*s.

'Abdullah ibn Abi 'Ammar

He was a man of Quraysh. He said, "I saw 'Umar ibn al-Khattab pray on a rug." He had few *hadith*s.

Siba' ibn Thabit

He was an ally of the Banu Zuhra. He related from 'Umar and had few *hadith*s.

Hisham ibn Khalid al-Ka'bi

He was from Khuza'a. He had few *hadith*s and listened to 'Umar. He lived at Qudayd at the base of Thaniyya Laft. His father, Khalid al-Ash'ar, and Kurz ibn Jabir al-Fihri were killed on the day Makka was conquered. They mistook the route and the cavalry of the idolators found them and killed them. He is Abu Hizam ibn Hisham from whom 'Abdullah ibn Maslama ibn Qan'ab, Abu an-Nasr Hashim ibn al-Qasim, Muhammad ibn 'Umar and others related.

'Abdullah ibn Safwan

'Abdullah ibn Safwan ibn Umayya ibn Khalaf. He related from 'Umar ibn al-Khattab.

Sa'id ibn al-Huwayrith

He had few *hadith*s.

Khuthaym

He was a man of al-Qara. He was the grandfather of 'Abdullah ibn 'Uthman ibn Khuthaym. He related from 'Umar.

Al-Fadl ibn Dukayn reported from Sa'id ibn Hassan from 'Iyad ibn Wahb that 'Ubaydullah ibn Abi Habiba said, "Khuthaym, a man from al-Qara, informed me that Sa'id, who is Jadd ibn Khuthaym, went to 'Umar ibn al-Khattab when he was giving land grants to the people at Marwa and said, 'Amir al-Mu'minin, give me and my descendants a land grant.' 'Umar turned from him and said, 'It is the Haram of Allah in which both the resident and desert dweller are equal.'"

Second Generation

Mujahid ibn Jabr

His *kunya* was Abu al-Hajjaj. He was the *mawla* of Qays ibn as-Sa'ib al-Makhzumi.

Waki' ibn al-Jarrah reported from al-Awza'i from Wasil from Mujahid ibn Jabr Abu al-Hajjaj, a *mawla* of as-Sa'ib, from al-Fadl ibn Dukayn from Isma'il ibn 'Abd al-Malik ibn Abi as-Sufayra' from Yunus ibn Khabbab that Mujahid said, "I used to lead my master as-Sa'ib who was blind. He said, 'Mujahid, has the sun declined?' If I answered, 'Yes,' he stopped and prayed *Zuhr*."

Humayd ibn 'Abd ar-Rahman ar-Rawasi reported from al-Hasan ibn Salih from Ibrahim ibn 'Abd al-A'la that Mujahid's *kunya* was Abu al-Hajjaj.

Muhammad ibn 'Abdullah al-Ansari reported from al-Fadl ibn Maymum that he heard Mujahid say, "I read the Qur'an to Ibn 'Abbas thirty times."

Al-Fudayl ibn Dukayn reported that Fitr said, "I saw Mujahid with white hair and beard."

Muslim ibn Ibrahim reported that Qurra ibn Khalid said, "I saw Mujahid had a white head and beard."

Sa'id ibn 'Amir reported from Hammam that Layth said, "'Ata', Tawus and Mujahid did not wear rings."

'Abdullah ibn Numayr reported that al-A'mash said, "When I saw Mujahid, I thought that he was donkey-driver. His donkey was missing and he was concerned."

Muhammad ibn 'Abdullah al-Asadi reported from Sufyan from Qays ibn Muslim that Mujahid disliked using black hair dye.

Abu Bakr ibn 'Ayyash reported, "I said to al-A'mash, 'Why are they careful about the *tafsir* of Mujahid?' He said, 'They used to relate that he used to question the People of the Book.'"

Someone other than Abu Bakr said, "They used to think that Mujahid related from the pages of Jabir."

Waki' ibn al-Jarrah reported from one of his Companions that Mujahid died while in prostration.

Muhammad ibn 'Umar said, "Sayf ibn Sulayman related to me that Mujahid died in Makka in 103."

Muhammad ibn 'Umar reported from Ibn Jurayj that Mujahid had reached the age of eighty-three when he died.

Al-Fadl ibn Dukayn reported that Mujahid died in 102 AH while in prostration.

Yahya ibn Sa'id al-Qattan reported that Mujahid died in 104 AH. He was a *faqih*.

'Ata' ibn Abi Rabah

Abu Rabah's name was Aslam. 'Ata' was one of the *muwallad*s of the army from the different parts of Yemen. He grew up in Makka. He was the *mawla* of the family of Abu Maysara ibn Abi Khuthaym al-Fihri.

Ya'la ibn 'Ubayd and Asbat ibn Muhammad reported from 'Abd al-Malik that the *kunya* of 'Ata' was Abu Muhammad.

Ma'n ibn 'Isa reported from 'Abdullah ibn al-Mu'ammil that 'Ata' used to teach the Book. They said that he was trustworthy, a knowledgeable *faqih* with many *hadith*s.

Muhammad ibn al-Fudayl ibn Ghazwan reported that Aslam al-Minqari said, "I was sitting with Abu Ja'far when 'Ata' ibn Abi Rabah passed by and he said, 'No one remains on the surface of the earth who has better knowledge of the *hajj* practices than 'Ata' ibn Abi Rabah.'"

Muslim ibn Ibrahim reported that Sallam ibn Miskin reported that he heard Qatada say, "'Ata' was the most knowledgeable of people about the *hajj* practices."

Qabisa ibn 'Uqba related from Sufyan that Aslam al-Manqari said, "A bedouin came and began to say, 'Where is Abu Muhammad?' They pointed about Sa'id ibn Jubayr. He said, 'Where is Abu Muhammad?' Sa'id said, 'Here we have nothing with 'Ata.'"

Al-Fadl ibn Dukayn reported from Sufyan that Salama said, "I have not seen anyone desiring this knowledge for the Face of Allah other than these three: 'Ata', Tawus and Mujahid."

'Ali ibn 'Abdullah ibn Ja'far reported from Sufyan that Isma'il ibn Umayya said, "'Ata' used to speak and when he was asked about a question, it was as if he was supported."

Ahmad ibn Muhammad ibn al-Walid al-Azraqi reported from Muslim ibn Khalid that Ya'qub ibn 'Ata' said, "I have not seen my father retain anything the way he retained sales transactions."

Isma'il ibn 'Abdullah ibn Khalid as-Sakkari reported from Yahya ibn Sulaym that Muhammad ibn 'Abdullah ibn 'Amr ibn 'Uthman ibn 'Affan said, "I have not seen a *mufti* better than 'Ata' ibn Abi Rabah. Allah was remembered in his gathering and he did not cease while they were delving. If he spoke or was asked about something, he gave the best answer."

'Amr ibn 'Asim al-Kilabi reported from Mahdi ibn Maymun that Mu'adh ibn Sa'id al-A'war said, "We were with 'Ata' when a man related a *hadith* and another man confronted him. 'Ata' became angry and said, 'What are these manners? What is this temper? By Allah, a man may recount a *hadith* when we know it better than he does. Perhaps he even heard it from me. I remain silent for it and appear to him as if I had not heard it before that.'"

'Amr ibn 'Asim said, "I related this *hadith* to 'Abdullah ibn al-Mubarak and he said, 'I will not remove my sandals until I have gone to someone guided and heard it from him."

'Abdullah ibn Ja'far reported from Abu al-Malik who said, "I and another man went on *hajj* and I went to 'Ata' ibn Abi Rabah to ask him about a matter. I sat with him and there was a black man using henna dye. The messenger of the master of Makka came and he had him sit and I did not go to him.'"

Qabisa ibn 'Uqba reported from Sufyan that Abu Jurayj said, "When 'Ata' related something, I said, 'Knowledge or opinion?' If it was a tradition, he said, 'Knowledge.' If it was opinion, he said, 'Opinion.'"

Ahmad ibn 'Abdullah ibn Yunus reported from Abu Shihab from Layth that 'Abd ar-Rahman said, "By Allah, I do not think that the faith of the people of the earth is equal to the faith of Abu Bakr, and I do not think that the faith of the people of Makka was equal to the faith of 'Ata'."

Al-Fudyal ibn Dukayn reported from Sufyan from Ibn Jurayj that 'Ata' used to feed people for his parents who were dead. He did that until his death.

Abu Nu'aym said, "He meant the *zakat al-fitr*."

Ma'n ibn 'Isa reported that Abu Mu'awiya al-Maghribi said, "I saw 'Ata' ibn Abi Rabah with the mark of prostration between his eyes."

Al-Fudayl ibn Dukayn reported from Fitr who said, "I saw 'Ata' using yellow dye on his beard."

Muhammad ibn 'Umar said, "I heard one of the people of knowledge saying that 'Ata' was black, blind in one eye, flat-nosed, semi-paralysed and lame and then he went blind after that. The *fatwa* of the people of Madina went to him and Mujahid in their time. It mostly went to 'Ata'.""

Sufyan ibn 'Uyayna, al-Fadl ibn Dukayn and Muhammad ibn 'Umar said that 'Ata' died in Makka in 115 AH.

Muhammad ibn 'Umar said, "He was eighty-eight on the day he died."

'Abdullah ibn Ja'far ar-Raqqi reported that Abu al-Malih said, "'Ata' died in 114. When news of his death reached Maymun, he said, 'None like him will replace him.'"

Yusuf ibn Mahak

He related from his mother. Her name was Musayka.

Hajjaj ibn Muhammad reported that Ibn Jurayj said, "I said to 'Ata', 'This Yusuf ibn Mahak desires death.' He criticised that and said, 'What will inform him about what it is from?'"

Musa ibn Isma'il reported from 'Umar ibn Abi Khalifa that the mother of Yusuf ibn Mahak said, "When Yusuf was dying, he instructed that he be shrouded in his clothes and he used to be gathered in them and that *hanut* not be put on his face or garment which was spread on his bier. He said, 'Bind my feet with a turban.'"

Muhammad ibn 'Umar said, "Yusuf ibn Mahak died in 113."

He said, "I heard someone else say that he died in 114." He was trustworthy, with few *hadith*s.

Miqsam

The companion of 'Abdullah ibn 'Abbas, the *mawla* of 'Abdullah ibn al-Harith ibn Nawfal ibn 'Abd al-Muttalib, His *kunya* was Abu al-Qasim. He clung to Ibn 'Abbas and related from him. Some people call him the *mawla* of Ibn 'Abbas because of how close he kept to him and served him, but he was actually the *mawla* of 'Abdullah ibn al-Harith. They all agree that he died in 101 AH. He had a lot of weak *hadith*s.

'Abdullah ibn Khalid

'Abdullah ibn Khalid ibn Usayd ibn Abi al-'Is ibn Umayya ibn 'Abd Shams ibn 'Abd Manaf. His mother was Rayta bint 'Abdullah ibn Khuza'i ibn Usayd of Thaqif. 'Abdullah ibn Khalid's children were Khalid, Umayya and 'Abd ar-Rahman, whose mother was Umm Hujayr bint Shayba ibn 'Uthman ibn Abi Talha ibn 'Abd al-'Uzza ibn 'Uthman ibn 'Abd ad-Dar ibn Qusayy; 'Uthman, whose mother was Umm Sa'id bint 'Uthman ibn 'Affan; 'Abd al-'Aziz and 'Abd al-Malik, whose mother was Umm Habib bint Jubayr ibn Mut'im ibn 'Adi ibn Nawfal ibn 'Abd al-Manaf; 'Imran, 'Umar, al-Qasim, Umm 'Amr, and Zaynab, whose mother was as-Sariyya bint 'Abd 'Amr ibn Hisn ibn Hudhayfa ibn Badr al-Fazari; Muhammad, al-Husayn, al-Mukhariq, Umm 'Abd al-'Aziz, Umm 'Abd al-Malik, Umm Muhammad and Maryam, whose mother was Mulayka bint al-Husayn ibn 'Abd Yaghuth ibn al-Azraq of Murad; Abu 'Uthman by an *umm walad*, and al-Harith by an *umm walad*. He had few *hadith*s.

'Abdullah ibn 'Ubaydullah

'Abdullah ibn 'Ubaydullah ibn 'Abdullah ibn Abi Mulayka ibn 'Abdullah ibn Jud'an ibn 'Amr ibn Ka'b ibn Sa'd ibn Taym ibn Murra. His mother was Maymuna bint al-Walid ibn Abi Husayn ibn al-Harith ibn 'Amir ibn Nawfal ibn 'Abd Manaf. Abu Mulayka's name was Zuhayr. 'Abdullah ibn 'Ubaydullah did not have descendants.

'Affan ibn Muslim reported that Sulaym ibn Hayyan said that he heard Ibn Abi Mulayka say, "I was qadi for Ibn az-Zubayr."

'Arim ibn al-Fadl reported from Hammad ibn Zayd from Ayyub that Ibn Abi Mulayka said, "Ibn az-Zubayr sent me to be qadi of Ta'if and I said to Ibn 'Abbas, 'This one sent me as qadi of Ta'if but I must pose questions to you.' He said to me, 'Yes, write to ask to me in what appears to you.'"

Al-Fudayl ibn Dukayn reported from Isma'il ibn 'Abd al-Malik ibn Abi as-Sufayra' that Ibn Abi Mulayka said, "I was qadi at Ta'if."

Abu Bakr ibn Muhammad ibn Abi Murra al-Makki reported from Nafi' ibn 'Umar, "Ibn Abi Mulayka said to me when he heard some people making the recitation of their reciters heavy, 'I used to recite *Surat al-Mala'ika* in one *rak'at* and no one complained.'"

Muhammad ibn 'Umar said, "Ibn Abi Mulayka used to lead the people in prayer in Ramadan in Makka after 'Abdullah ibn as-Sa'ib." 'Abdullah ibn Abi Mulayka died in Makka in 117 AH. He related from Ibn 'Abbas, 'A'isha, Ibn az-Zubayr and 'Uqba ibn al-Harith. He was trustworthy and had many *hadith*s.

Abu Bakr ibn 'Ubaydullah

'Abdullah's brother, Abu Bakr ibn 'Ubaydullah ibn 'Abdullah ibn Abi Mulayka ibn 'Abdullah ibn Jud'an. His mother was Maymuna bint al-Walid ibn Abi Husayn ibn al-Harith ibn 'Amir ibn Nawfal ibn 'Abd Manaf. Abu Bakr ibn 'Ubaydullah had 'Abd ar-Rahman whose name was 'Awna bint Mus'ab ibn 'Abd ar-Rahman ibn 'Awf ibn 'Abd 'Awf ibn 'Abd al-Harith ibn Zuhra. He is related from and had few *hadith*s.

Abu Zayd

He is Abu 'Ubaydullah ibn Abi Zayd. His son related from him.

Abu Najih

A *mawla* of Thaqif. He is Abu 'Abdullah ibn Abi Najih. Abu Najih's name was Yasar. He had few *hadith*s.

Al-Waqidi said that he died in 109 AH.

'Abdullah ibn 'Ubayd

The son of ibn 'Umayr ibn Qatada al-Laythi.

Shihab ibn 'Abbad al-'Abdi reported that Dawud al-'Attar said, "'Abdullah ibn 'Ubayd ibn 'Umayr was one of the most eloquent among the people of Makka."

'Arim ibn al-Fadl reported from Hammad ibn Zayd that Ayyub said, "A man who used to be with 'Abdullah ibn 'Ubayd ibn 'Umar when he was ill related something to me. He was asked, 'What do you want?' He said, 'I only want a man with trustworthy recitation to recite in my presence.'"

Muhammad ibn 'Umar said, "'Abdullah ibn 'Ubayd ibn 'Umayr died in Makka in 113." He was trustworthy and righteous, and had *hadith*s.

'Amr ibn 'Abdullah

'Amr ibn 'Abdullah ibn Safwan ibn Umayya ibn Khalaf ibn Wahb ibn Hudhafa ibn Jumah al-Jumahi. His mother was the daughter of Muti' ibn Shurayh ibn 'Amir ibn 'Awf ibn Abi Bakr ibn Kilab. 'Amr ibn Dinar and az-Zuhri related from him. He had few *hadith*s.

Safwan ibn 'Abdullah

Safwan ibn 'Abdullah ibn Safwan ibn Umayya ibn Khalaf ibn Wahb ibn Hudhafa ibn Jumah. His mother was Hiqqa bint Wahb ibn Umayya ibn Abi as-Salt ath-Thaqafi. Safwan had 'Abdullah and Amina whose mother was Umm al-Hakam bint Umayya ibn Safwan. Az-Zuhri related from him. He had few *hadith*s.

Yahya ibn Hakim

Yahya ibn Hakim ibn Safwan ibn Umayya ibn Khalaf. His mother was the daughter of Ubayy ibn Khalaf. He had a son Shurahbil whose mother was Husayna bint Kalada ibn al-Hanbal. Yahya ibn Hakim was the governor of Makka for Yazid ibn Mu'awiya. He is related from.

'Ikrima ibn Khalid

The son of Khalid ibn al-'As ibn Hisham ibn al-Mughira ibn 'Abdullah ibn 'Umar ibn Makhzum. His mother was the daughter of Kulayb ibn Hazn ibn Mu'awiya ibn Khafaja ibn 'Amr ibn 'Uqayl. His children were 'Abdullah whose mother was 'Atika bint 'Abdullah ibn Kulayb ibn Hazm of the Banu 'Uqayl ibn Ka'b, Khalid, whose mother was Hafsa bint 'Abdullah ibn Ka'b ibn Hazm, Sulayman and Umm Sa'id by an *umm walad*, and Umm 'Abd al-'Aziz whose mother was Julala bint 'Abdullah ibn Kulayb ibn Hazm. He was trustworthy and had *hadith*s.

Muhammad ibn 'Abbad

Muhammad ibn 'Abbad ibn Ja'far ibn Rifa'a ibn Umayya ibn 'Abid ibn 'Abdullah ibn 'Umar ibn Makhzum. His mother was Zaynab bint 'Abdullah ibn as-Sa'ib al-Makhzumi. He was trustworthy and had few *hadith*s.

Hisham ibn Yahya

The son of Yahya ibn Hisham ibn al-'As ibn Hisham ibn al-Mughira ibn 'Abdullah ibn 'Amr ibn Makhzum. His mother was Umm Hakim bint Abi Habib ibn Umayya ibn Abi Hudhayfa ibn al-Mughira ibn 'Abdullah ibn 'Amr ibn Makhzum. His children were Yahya, 'Abd ar-Rahman and Isma'il whose mother was Umm Hakim bint Khalid ibn Hisam ibn al-'As ibn Hisham ibn al-Mughira. He had *hadith*s.

Musafi' ibn 'Abdullah

Musafi' ibn 'Abdullah the elder ibn Shayba ibn 'Uthman ibn Abi Talha whose name was 'Abdullah ibn 'Abd al-'Uzza ibn 'Uthman ibn 'Abd ad-Dar ibn Qusayy. His mother was an *umm walad*. His children were 'Abdullah, Mus'ab and 'Abd ar-Rahman whose mother was Sa'da bint 'Abdullah ibn Wahb ibn 'Uthman ibn Abi Talha ibn 'Abd al-'Uzza ibn 'Uthman ibn 'Abd ad-Dar ibn Qusayy. He had few *hadith*s.

'Abd al-Hamid ibn Jubayr

'Abd al-Hamid ibn Jubayr ibn Shayba ibn 'Uthman ibn Abi Talha. His mother was the daughter of Abu 'Amr ibn al-Hajn ibn al-Muraqqa' from Azd and then from Ghamid.

Muhammad ibn 'Umar said that Hisham ibn Muhammad ibn as-Sa'ib al-Kalbi mentioned that al-Hajn ibn al-Muraqqa' came to visit the Prophet ﷺ. 'Abd al-Hamid was trustworthy and had few *hadith*s. Ibn Jurayj and Sufyan related from him.

'Abd ar-Rahman ibn Tariq

'Abd ar-Rahman ibn Tariq ibn 'Alqama ibn Ghanm ibn Khalid ibn 'Urayj ibn Jadhima ibn Sa'd ibn 'Awf ibn al-Harith ibn 'Abd

Manat ibn Kinana. 'Abd ar-Rahman had few *hadith*s.

Nafi' ibn Sarjis

He was trustworthy and had few *hadith*s.

Muslim ibn Yanaq

He had few *hadith*s.

Iyas ibn Khalifa al-Bakri

He had few *hadith*s.

Abu al-Minhal

His name was 'Abd ar-Rahman ibn Mut'im. He had few *hadith*s.

Abu Yahya al-A'raj

His name was Misda'. He was the *mawla* of Mu'adh ibn 'Afra' of the Ansar. He had *hadith*s.

Abu al-'Abbas the poet

His name was as-Sa'ib ibn Farrukh, a *mawla* of the Banu Jadhima ibn 'Adi ibn ad-Dil ibn Bakr ibn 'Abd Manat ibn Kinana. He had few *hadith*s. He was a poet. He was in Makka in the time of Ibn az-Zubayr and he sided with the Umayyads.

'Ata ibn Mina

He had few *hadith*s.

Third Generation

Umayya ibn 'Abdullah

Umayya ibn 'Abdullah ibn Khalid ibn Usayd ibn Abi al-'Is ibn Umayya ibn 'Abd Shams. His mother was Umm Hujayr bint Shayba ibn 'Uthman ibn Abi Talha ibn 'Abd al-'Uzza ibn 'Uthman in 'Abd ad-Dar ibn Qusayy. He had few *hadith*s.

Ibrahim ibn Abi Khidash

Ibrahim ibn Abi Khidash ibn 'Utba ibn Abi Lahab ibn 'Abd al-Muttalib ibn Hashim ibn 'Abd Manaf ibn Qusayy. His mother was Safiyya bint Araka of the Ban ad-Dil. He had a son 'Utba whose mother was Hind bint Qays ibn Tariq of the Sakasik, the allies of Himyar.

Muhammad ibn al-Muraqqa'

Muhammad ibn al-Muraqqa' ibn an-Nadir ibn al-Harith ibn 'Alqama ibn Kalada ibn 'Abd Manaf ibn 'Abd ad-Dar ibn Qusayy. His mother was an *umm walad*. He had a son called Ja'far by an *umm walad*. He had few *hadith*s.

Ibn ar-Rahin

One of the children of an-Nadr ibn al-Harith ibn Kalada who was killed as an unbeliever in the Battle of Badr.

Al-Qasim ibn Abi Bazza

A *mawla* of one of the people of Makka.

Muhammad ibn 'Umar said that he died in Makka in 124 AH. He was trustworthy and had few *hadith*s. Abu Bazza's name was Nafi' according to what Muhammad ibn 'Umar transmitted.

Al-Hasan ibn Muslim ibn Yanaq

He died before Tawus and Tawus died in 106 AH. Hirz, the brother of Hasan ibn Muslim, said to a man, "When you go to Kufa, forbid

Layth ibn Sulaym and tell him that unless he returns the book of Hasan ibn Muslim, it will be taken from him." He was trustworthy and had *hadith*s.

'Amr ibn Dinar

A *mawla* of Badhan among the *abna'*.

'Affan ibn Muslim reported from Hammad ibn Zayd that a man related to him that Tawus said, "This ibn Dinar retained what every scholar said."

Muhammad ibn Sa'd said that he reported from Sufyan ibn 'Uyayna from Zam'a ibn Salih that Ibn Tawus said, "My father said, 'When you go to Makka, you must have 'Amr ibn Dinar. His ears retain what scholars say.'"

Sufyan said, "'Amr did not stop coming to the mosque. He was carried on a donkey and I only found him when he was seated. I could not carry him due to my youth. Then I became strong enough to carry him. His house was far away and we were not sure of his age. Ayyub used to say, 'What did 'Amr relate from so-and-so?' I would tell him and then say, 'Do you want for me to write for you?' He answered, 'Yes.'"

Sufyan said, "'Amr ibn Dinar was told that Sufyan used to write. Then he lay down and wept. He said, 'Get someone who can write from me.'"

Sufyan said, "I did not write anything from him. We used to memorise."

'Abd ar-Razzaq said that Ma'mar said, "I heard 'Amr ibn Dinar say, 'They ask us about our opinion. We tell them and they write it as if it was engraved in stone. Perhaps we might retract it tomorrow.' A man asked 'Amr ibn Dinar about something and he did not answer. A man said to him, 'There is something about it in me, so answer me.' 'Amr said, 'By Allah, I prefer that you have something in yourself the size of the mountain of Abu Qubays to having something of it in myself as fine as a hair.'"

'Abd ar-Rahman ibn Yunus reported that Sufyan said that 'Amr ibn Dinar said, "Ibn Hisham asked me, 'Will you sit to give *fatwa* to people for pay?' I replied, 'I do not want to.'"

'Abd ar-Rahman ibn Yunus reported that Sufyan said, "''Amr used to relate meanings [rather than exact words]. He was a *faqih*."

'Abd ar-Rahman ibn Yunus reported that Sufyan said, "''Amr did not use hair dye."

Al-Fadl ibn Dukayn said that 'Amr ibn Dinar died in 126 AH. He gave *fatwa* in the town. When he died, Ibn Abi Jurayj gave *fatwa* after him. 'Amr was trustworthy and firm and had a lot of *hadith*s.

Abu az-Zubayr

His name was Muhammad ibn Muslim ibn Tadrus.

Yazid ibn Harun reported from Yahya ibn Sa'id from Abu az-Zubayr, the *mawla* of Hakim ibn Hizam ibn Khuwaylid. Muhammad said that he was told by Hushaym ibn Hajjaj and Ibn Abi Layla that 'Ata' said, "We were with Jabir ibn 'Abdullah and he related to us. When we left him, we discussed his *hadith*." He said, "It was as if Abu az-Zubayr had better memory of the *hadith*."

'Abd ar-Rahman ibn Yunus reported that Sufyan said, "Abu az-Zubayr did not use hair dye."

Harun ibn Ma'ruf said from Ibn 'Uyayna that Abu az-Zubayr said, "''Ata' used to go before me with Jabir to ask for *hadith* for them. He was trustworthy and had a lot of *hadith*s although Shu'ba left him because of something that he claimed that he saw in his behaviour. People related from him."

'Ubaydullah ibn Abi Yazid

A *mawla* of the family of Qa'iz. They are from the Banu Kinana, the allies of the Banu Zuhra. Ibn Jurayj and Sufyan ibn 'Uyayna related from him.

Sufyan said, "I asked 'Ubaydullah ibn Abi Yazid, 'With whom did you visit Ibn 'Abbas?' He answered, 'With 'Ata' and the common people. Tawus used to enter with the elite.'" Sufyan said, "I used to say to him, 'What did you see Ibn 'Abbas do? How did you see him produce it and bring him what he wanted?' He replied, 'Before Ibn Jurayh met him, he used to relate from him and we asked him about that and he said, "This is an old man who made me think that he had died. While I was at the door of a house in Makka on an errand, I heard a man say, 'Take us to 'Ubaydullah ibn Abi Yazid.' I asked, 'Who is 'Ubaydullah ibn Abi Yazid?' He replied, 'An old man in this house who met Ibn 'Abbas. However he has become weak so that he cannot go outside.' I asked, 'Can I visit him with you?' They said, 'Yes.' We visited him and they began to ask him and he related to them. I said, 'Give him what Ibn Jurayj related from him.' He began to relate what I heard of *hadith*s from him on that day. Then I went to Ibn Jurayj and sat with him and he began to relate to me until he said, "Ubaydullah ibn Abi Yazid related such-and-such.' I said, "Ubaydullah (i.e. Ibn Abi Yazid) related it?' He said, 'I came upon him.' He said, 'I continued to frequent him until he died.'"'

Muhammad ibn 'Umar said, "I asked Sufyan ibn 'Uyana, 'When did 'Ubaydullah ibn Abi Yazid die?' He said, 'In 126.'" He was trustworthy and had a lot of *hadith*s.

Al-Walid ibn 'Abdullah ibn Abi Mughith

He had few *hadith*s.

'Abdullah ibn 'Amr al-Qari

He had few *hadith*s.

Qays ibn Sa'd

His *kunya* was Abu 'Ubaydullah. He frequented 'Ata' ibn Abi Rabah in his gathering. He used to give *fatwa* based on his position. He thought little of that, but he did not live long. He died in 119 AH in the caliphate of Hisham ibn 'Abd al-Malik. He was trustworthy and had few *hadith*s.

'Abdullah ibn Abi Najih

His *kunya* was Abu Yasar, the *mawla* of Thaqif.

'Abd ar-Rahman ibn Yunus reported that Sufyan said, "Ibn Abi Najih did not use hair dye. He died before the plague which broke out in 131."

Muhammad ibn 'Umar said, "'Abdullah ibn Abi Najih died in Makka in 132. He was trustworthy and had a lot of *hadith*s. They used to say that he espoused *qadar* (free will)."

Sulayman al-Ahwal

He was the maternal uncle of Ibn Abi Najih. He was trustworthy and had sound *hadith*s.

'Abd al-Hamid ibn Rafi'

He related from Sufyan ath-Thawri. He had few *hadith*s.

Hisham ibn Hujayr

Sufyan ibn 'Uyayna said, "Ibn Shubruma said to me, 'His like does not exist in Makka.'" He meant Hisham ibn Hujayr. He was trustworthy and had *hadith*s.

Ibrahim ibn Maysara

A *mawla* of one of the people of Makka.

'Abd ar-Rahman ibn Yunus reported that Sufyan said, "Ibrahim ibn Maysara used to relate as he heard."

'Abd ar-Rahman ibn Yunus reported that Ibrahim ibn Maysara died in the caliphate of Marwan ibn Muhammad. He was trustworthy and had a lot of *hadith*s.

'Abd ar-Rahman ibn 'Abdullah

'Abd ar-Rahman ibn 'Abdullah ibn Abi 'Ammar, a man of Quraysh whose father related that he saw 'Umar praying on a rug. He was trustworthy and had *hadith*s.

'Abdullah ibn Kathir ad-Dari

He was trustworthy and had *hadith*s.

Isma'il ibn Kathir

Abu Nu'aym al-Fadl ibn Dukayn said, "Isma'il's *kunya* was Abu Hashim." He was trustworthy and had many *hadith*s.

Kathir ibn Kathir

Kathir ibn Kathir ibn al-Muttalib ibn Abi Wada'a ibn Dubayra ibn Su'ayd ibn Sa'd ibn Sahm. His mother was 'A'isha bint 'Amr ibn

Abi 'Aqrab, who is Khuwaylid ibn 'Abdullah ibn Khalid ibn Bujayr ibn Himas ibn 'Urayj ibn Bakr ibn 'Abd Manat ibn Kinana. Sufyan ibn 'Uyayna saw him and related from him. He died without any descendants. He was a poet and had few *hadith*s.

Sudayq ibn Musa

Sudayq ibn Musa ibn 'Abdullah ibn az-Zubayr ibn al-'Awwam His *kunya* was Abu Bakr and his mother was Umm Ishaq bint Mujamma' ibn Zayd ibn Jariya ibn 'Attaf of the Banu 'Amr ibn 'Awf. Ibn Jurayj related from Sudayq.

Sadaqa ibn Yasar

He was one of the *abna'*, and a *mawla* of one of the people of Makka. He died at the beginning of the 'Abbasid caliphate.

Sufyan ibn 'Uyayna said, "I said to Sadaqa ibn Yasar, 'They claim that you are Kharijites.' He replied, 'I was one of them and then Allah cured me.'" His family were from the people of Jazira. He was trustworthy, with few *hadith*s.

'Abdullah ibn 'Abd ar-Rahman

'Abdullah ibn 'Abd ar-Rahman ibn Abi Husayn. He was trustworthy, with few *hadith*s.

'Uthman ibn Abi Sulayman

The son of Abu Sulayman ibn Jubayr ibn Mut'im ibn 'Adi ibn Nawfal ibn 'Abd Manaf ibn Qusayy. He was trustworthy and had *hadith*s.

Humayd ibn Qays al-A'raj

He was a *mawla* of the family of az-Zubayr ibn al-'Awwam. He was the reciter of the people of Makka. He was trustworthy, and had a lot of *hadith*s.

Muhammad ibn Yazid ibn Khunays reported that he heard Wuhayb ibn al-Ward say, "Al-A'raj used to recite in the mosque and people would gather around him when he finished the Qur'an. 'Ata' went to him on the night when he finished the Qur'an."

Sufyan ibn 'Uyayna said, "Humayd al-A'raj was the best of people in his knowledge of reckoning and shares of inheritance, i.e. among the people of Makka. They only gathered to him for his recitation. He used to recite to Mujahid and there was no one in Makka who recited more than than me and 'Abdullah ibn Kathir."

'Umar ibn Qays

Humayd's brother. His title was Sandal. There was some coarseness in him. People first hastened to him and then held back from his *hadith*s and discarded them. He was weak in *hadith* and is nothing.

Muhammad ibn Sa'd said, "'Umar ibn Qays is the one who wasted Malik. He said, 'Sometimes he would err and sometimes he was not correct.' That was when the governor of Makka said to him, 'Malik!' and he remarked, 'That is just how people are. They neglect the shaykh.' Malik heard that and said, 'I will never speak to him.'"

Mansur ibn 'Abd ar-Rahman

Mansur ibn 'Abd ar-Rahman ibn Talha ibn al-Harith ibn Talha ibn Abi Talha ibn 'Abd al-'Uzza ibn 'Uthman ibn 'Abd ad-Dar. His mother was Safiyya bint Shayba al-Hajib ibn 'Uthman ibn Abi Talha. His children were Umm al-Karim and Safiyya whose mother was an *umm walad*.

Hisham ibn Muhammad related that his father said, "I saw Mansur ibn 'Abd ar-Rahman at the time of Khalid ibn 'Abdullah who was the door-keeper of the House when he was an old man. He was trustworthy and had few *hadith*s.

Sa'id ibn Abi Salih

He died in 129 AH. He had few *hadith*s.

'Abdullah ibn 'Uthman

'Abdullah ibn 'Uthman ibn Khuthaym from al-Qara, an ally of the Banu Zuhra. He died at the end of the caliphate of Abu al-'Abbas as-Saffah and the beginning of the caliphate of Abu Ja'far Mansur. He was trustworthy and had good *hadith*s.

Dawud ibn Abi 'Asim

He was trustworthy and had few *hadith*s.

Muzahim ibn Abi Muzahim

He had few *hadith*s.

Mus'ab ibn Shayba

Mus'ab ibn Shayba ibn Jubayr ibn Shayba ibn 'Uthman ibn Abi Talha ibn 'Abd al-'Uzza ibn 'Uthman ibn 'Abd ad-Dar. His mother was Umm 'Umayr bint 'Abdullah al-Akbar ibn Shayba ibn 'Uthman ibn Abi Talha. He had few *hadith*s.

Yahya ibn 'Abdullah

Yahya ibn 'Abdullah ibn Sayfi al-Makhzumi. He was trustworthy and had *hadith*s.

Wuhayb ibn al-Ward ibn Abi al-Ward

A *mawla* of the Banu Makhzum. He lived in Makka and was one of the worshippers. He had *hadith*s about admonitions and asceticism. His name was 'Abd al-Wahhab. The dimunitive was made from his name: Wuhayb. 'Abdullah ibn al-Mubarak and others related from him.

'Abd al-Jabbar ibn al-Ward

Wuhayb's brother. He related from Ibn Abi Mulayka and others.

Sulayman

A *mawla* of the Banu al-Barsa'. He had few *hadith*s.

'Amr ibn Yahya ibn Qabta

He had few *hadith*s.

Ya'qub ibn 'Ata' ibn Abi Rabah

He had *hadith*s.

'Abdullah

A *mawla* of Asma'. He had few *hadith*s.

Manbudh ibn Abi Sulayman

Ibn 'Uyayna related from him. He had few *hadith*s.

Wardan

A goldsmith in Makka. Sufyan ibn 'Uyayna related from him. He said, "I asked Ibn 'Umar about exchanging gold for gold."

Zurzur

Sufyan ibn 'Uyayna said that he was a *mawla* of Jubayr ibn Mut'im. He had few *hadith*s.

'Abd al-Wahid ibn Ayman

Al-Fadl ibn Dukayn reported from 'Abd al-Wahid ibn Ayman: "My father related to me. He had belonged to 'Utba ibn Abi Lahab. 'Utba died and his sons inherited from him. Ibn Abi 'Amr bought him and set him free. The sons of 'Utba stipulated that they would have the *wala'* and he went to 'A'isha and related to him the *hadith* of Barira from the Prophet ﷺ."

Muhammad ibn Sharik

Waki' al-Jarrah and Abu Nu'aym al-Fadl ibn Dukayn related from him.

Also of this generation are: **'Abd ar-Rahman ibn Ayman, 'Abd ar-Rahman ibn Ma'bad, Khalla' ibn ash-Shaykh, 'Umar ibn Sa'id ibn Abi Husayn, Khalid ibn Mudarris** and **'Abd ar-Rahman ibn Farrukh.**

Fourth Generation

'Uthman ibn al-Aswad al-Jumahi

He died in Makka in 150 AH. He was trustworthy and had a lot of *hadith*s.

Al-Muthanna ibn as-Sabbah

He was one of the *abna'*. Muhammad ibn 'Umar said that he died in 149 AH. Someone else said that it was 147 AH.

Ibn Muhammad ibn al-Walid al-Azraqi said, "Dawud ibn 'Abd ar-Rahman al-'Utaridi said to me, 'I did not meet anyone in the mosque with more worship than al-Muthanna ibn as-Sabbah and az-Zanji ibn Khalid.'" He had *hadith*s and he is weak.

'Ubaydullah ibn Abi Ziyad

A *mawla* of one of the people of Makka. He died in 150 AH.

'Abd al-Malik ibn 'Abd al-'Aziz ibn Jurayj

His *kunya* was 'Abdullah ibn Khalid ibn Usayd ibn Abi al-'Is ibn Umayya. His ascription was derived from his *wala'*. He was born in 80 AH, the Year of the Torrent, a flood in Makka.

Muhammad ibn "Abdullah al-Anari reported: "Ibn Jurayj came to us in Basra while Sufyan ibn Mu'awiya was governor, a year before Ibrahim ibn 'Abdullah rebelled."

Muhammad ibn 'Umar said, "I asked Ibn Jurayj about reading *hadith*s to a relater and he said, 'Someone like you asks about this? People disagree about taking a written page and saying, "I relate what is in it" without reading it out. If he actually reads it, then it is the same.'"

Muhammad ibn 'Umar said, "Abu Bakr ibn 'Abdullah ibn Abi Sabra related to me that Ibn Jurayj said, 'Write for me the *hadith*s of the *sunan*.' He said, 'I wrote a thousand *hadith*s and then I sent them to him. He did not read them to me nor did I read them to him.'"

Muhammad ibn 'Umar said, "I heard Ibn Jurayj after that relate. He said, 'Abu Bakr ibn Abi Sabra related to us about many *hadith*s.'"

Muhammad ibn 'Umar reported that 'Abd ar-Rahman ibn Abi az-Zinad said, "I was present when Ibn Jurayj went to Hisham ibn 'Urwa. He said, 'Abu al-Mundhir, the page which you gave to so-and-so is your *hadith*s?' 'Yes,' he answered."

Muhammad ibn 'Umar said, "I listened to Ibn Jurayj after that say, 'Hisham ibn 'Urwa related to us what I cannot count.'"

Ibn Jurayj said, "I went around the town and spread for them a bag of knowledge," i.e. Yemen.

Muhammad ibn 'Umar said that Ibn Jurayj died at the beginning of 10 Dhu al-Hijja 150 AH at the age of seventy-six. He was trustworthy and had a very large amount of *hadith*s.

Hanzala ibn Abi Sufyan

Hanzala ibn Abi Sufyan ibn 'Abd ar-Rahman ibn Safwan ibn Umayya ibn Khalaf ibn Wahb ibn Hudhafa ibn Jumah. His mother was Hafsa bint 'Amr ibn Abi 'Aqrab of the Banu 'Urayj ibn Bakr ibn 'Abd Manat ibn Kinana. He died in 151 in the caliphate of Abu Ja'far Mansur. He was trustworthy and had *hadith*s.

Zakariyya ibn Ishaq

'Abd ar-Razzaq said, "Abu Alzam Zakariyya ibn Ishaq said to me when I saw him with Ibn Abi Najih in a place, 'He came to me when he was forgotten and he stayed in the desert. It reached me that Ibn al-Mubarak went to him and he brought out his book to him.'" He was trustworthy and had a lot of *hadith*s.

'Abd al-'Aziz ibn Abi Rawwad

A *mawla* of al-Mughira ibn al-Muhallab ibn Abi Sufra al-'Utaki.

Ahmad ibn Muhammad al-Azraqi reported that 'Abd al-'Aziz ibn Abi Rawwad died in Makka in 159 AH. He had *hadith*s. He was a Murji'ite. He was known for righteousness, scrupulousness and worship.

Sayf ibn Sulayman

One of them said that Ibn Abi Sulayman was the *mawla* of the Banu Makhzum. He died in Makka in 156 AH. He was trustworthy and had a lot of *hadith*s.

Talha ibn 'Amr al-Hadrami

He died in Makka in 152 AH. He had a lot of *hadith*s and was very weak. They related from him.

Nafi' ibn 'Umar al-Jumahi

Shihab ibn 'Abbad al-'Abdi reported to us that Nafi' ibn 'Umar al-Jumahi died in Makka in 169 AH. He was trustworthy and had few *hadith*s. There is something questionable about him.

'Abdullah ibn al-Mu'ammil al-Makhzumi

Shihab ibn 'Abbad al-'Abdi reported to us that 'Abdullah ibn al-Mu'ammil died in Makka in the year of al-Husayn at Fakhkh or a year after that. He was trustworthy and had few *hadith*s.

Sa'id ibn Hassan al-Makhzumi

He had few *hadith*s.

'Abdullah ibn 'Uthman ibn Abi Sulayman.

He had few *hadith*s.

Muhammad ibn 'Abd ar-Rahman

Muhammad ibn 'Abd ar-Rahman ibn 'Abdullah ibn Abi Rabi'a. He had few *hadith*s.

Ibrahim ibn Yazid al-Jawzi

A *mawla* of 'Umar ibn 'Abd al-'Aziz. He was called al-Jawzi because he lived at Shi'ab al-Jawz in Makka. He died in Makka in 151 AH. He had *hadith*s and is weak.

Rabah ibn Abi Ma'ruf

He had few *hadith*s.

'Abd ar-Rahman ibn Abi Bakr ibn Abi Mulayka

He is the one who is called "husband of Jabra". He has weak *hadith*s.

Sa'id ibn Muslim ibn Qamadhin

He had few *hadith*s.

Hizam ibn Hisham

Hizam ibn Hisham ibn Khalid al-Ash'ari al-Ka'bi. He lived at Qudayd. Abu an-Nadr Hashim ibn al-Qasim, Muhammad ibn 'Umar, 'Abdullah ibn Maslama ibn Qa'nab and others related from him. He was trustworthy and had few *hadith*s.

'Abd al-Wahhab ibn Mujahid ibn Jabr

He related from his father. He was weak in *hadith*.

Also from this generation are: **'Abdullah ibn Lahiq, Ibrahim ibn Nafi'** and **Ibn Abi Sara.**

Fifth Generation

Sufyan ibn 'Uyayna ibn Abi 'Imran

His *kunya* was Abu Muhammad. He was a *mawla* of the Banu 'Abdullah ibn Ruwayba of the Banu Hilal ibn 'Amir ibn Sa'sa'a.

Muhammad ibn 'Umar reported from Sufyan ibn 'Uyayna that he was born in 109 AH. His family came from Kufa. His brother was one of the deputies of Khalid ibn 'Abdullah al-Qasri. When Khalid was dismissed from the governorship of Iraq and Yusuf ibn 'Umar ath-Thaqafi appointed, he sought out Khalid's agents who fled from him. 'Uyayna ibn Abi 'Imran went to Makka and stayed there.

'Abd ar-Rahman ibn Yunus reported that he heard Sufyan ibn 'Uyayna say, "The first person I sat with was Abu Umayya 'Abd al-Karim. I sat with him when I was fifteen and he died in 126."

Sufyan said, "I went on *hajj* in 116 and then in 120. We went to az-Zuhri with Ibn Hisham, the caliph in 123. He left in 124. I questioned him when Sa'd ibn Ibrahim was with him, and he did not answer me about *hadith*. Sa'd said to him, 'Answer the boy about what he asks you.' He said, 'I will give him his due.'"

Sufyan said, "I was sixteen on that day."

Sufyan said, "I went to Yemen in 152 while Ma'mar was alive. Ath-Thawri went a year before me."

Al-Hasan ibn 'Imran ibn 'Uyayna ibn Abi 'Imran reported that the nephew of Sufyan said, "I went on *hajj* with my uncle Sufyan in the last *hajj* he performed in 197. When we were at Jam', he prayed and laid down on his bed. Then he said, 'I have come to this place for seventy years. I said in each year, 'O Allah, do not make the end of the contract at this place.' I am ashamed before Allah of the great number of times I asked that.' He returned and died in the following year on Saturday, the first day of Rajab 198. He was buried at al-Hajun. He was trustworthy and firm. He had many *hadith*s and was an authority. He died at the age of ninety-one."

Dawud ibn 'Abd ar-Rahman al-'Attar

Ahmad ibn Muhammad ibn al-Walid al-Azraqi al-Makki said, "Dawud's father, 'Abd ar-Rahman al-'Attar, was a Christian. He was one of the people of Syria. He used to make perfume. He went to Makka and stayed there. He had children there who became Muslims. He taught them the Book, the Qur'an and *fiqh* and had a *wala'* with the family of Jubayr ibn Mut'im ibn Adi ibn Nawfal ibn 'Abd Manaf. Dawud ibn 'Abd ar-Rahman was born in 100. His father 'Abd ar-Rahman used to sit at the bottom of the minaret of the Masjid al-Haram facing Safa. He was used as an example and it was said, "More of an unbeliever than 'Abd ar-Rahman" because of his proximity to the *adhan* and the mosque and the state of his children and their being Muslim. He used to consent to their actions and encourage them to have proper manners and keep to the people of good among the Muslims." Dawud ibn 'Abd ar-Rahman died in Makka in 174 AH. He had a lot of *hadiths*.

Az-Zanji

His name was Muslim ibn Khalid ibn Sa'id ibn Jurja. His family was from Syria. He was a *mawla* of the family of Sufyan ibn 'Abd al-Asad al-Makhzumi. It is said that it was based on alliance, and there was no emancipation involved.

Abu Bakr ibn Muhammad ibn Abi Murra al-Makki reported that the complexion of Muslim ibn Khalid was white mixed with red. Az-Zanji was a title that he was given when he was young.

Ahmad ibn Muhammad ibn al-Walid al-Azraqi reported: "Az-Zanji ibn Khalid was a *faqih* and man of worship who fasted all the time." His *kunya* was Abu Khalid. He died in Makka in 180 while Harun was caliph. He had a lot of *hadiths*, but there were many mistakes and errors in his *hadith*. He was an excellent man in his body, but he used to err. Dawud al-'Attar was superior to him in *hadith*.

Muhammad ibn 'Imran al-Hajibi

He had few *hadiths*.

Muhammad ibn 'Uthman al-Makhzumi

He had few *hadiths*.

Yahya ibn Sulaym at-Ta'ifi

He settled in Makka and lived there until he died. He used to cure leather. He related from Isma'il ibn Kathir and 'Abdullah ibn Khuthaym. He was trustworthy and had a lot of *hadith*s.

Al-Fudayl ibn 'Iyad

One of Tamim, and then one of the Banu Yarbu'. His *kunya* was Abu 'Ali. He was born in Khurasan in the district of Abiward. He went to Kufa when he was old and listened to *hadith*s from Mansur ibn al-Mu'tamir and others. Then he devoted himself to worship and moved to Makka and lived there until he died in 187 AH in the caliphate of Harun. He was trustworthy and firm, excellent, worshipping, scrupulous with a lot of *hadith*s.

'Abdullah ibn Raja'

His *kunya* was Abu 'Imran. He was trustworthy and had a lot of *hadith*s. He was lame. He was one of the people of Basra. He moved and settled in Makka where he died.

'Abd al-Majid ibn 'Abd al-'Aziz ibn Abi Rawwad

His *kunya* was Abu 'Abd al-Hamid. He had a lot of *hadith*s and was weak and a Murji'ite.

Hamza ibn al-Harith ibn 'Umayr.

He was trustworthy and had few *hadith*s.

Abu 'Abd ar-Rahman al-Muqri'

His name was 'Abdullah ibn Yazid. He died in Makka in Rajab 213 AH. His family came from Basra. He was trustworthy and had a lot of *hadith*s.

'Uthman ibn al-Yaman ibn Harun

His *kunya* was Abu 'Amr. He died in Makka at the beginning of the day of 10 Dhu al-Hijja 212 AH. He had *hadith*s.

Mu'ammil ibn Isma'il

He was trustworthy, but had many errors.

Al-'Ala' ibn 'Abd al-Jabbar al-'Attar

His family came from Basra and he settled in Makka. He had a lot of *hadith*s.

Sa'id ibn Mansur

His *kunya* was Abu 'Uthman. He died in Makka in 227 AH.

Ahmad ibn Muhammad ibn al-Walid al-Arzaqi

He was trustworthy and had many *hadith*s.

'Abdullah ibn az-Zubayr al-Humaydi al-Makki

He was one of the Banu Asad ibn 'Abd al-'Uzza ibn Qusayy. He was the companion of Sufyan ibn 'Uyayna and his transmitter. He died in Makka in Rabi' al-Awwal 219 AH. He was trustworthy and had many *hadith*s.

❀❀❀

Also in this generation were: **Bishr ibn as-Sari** and **'Abdullah ibn al-Harith al-Makhzumi**.

Chapter Two: Ta'if
The Names of the Companions of the Messenger of Allah ﷺ who lived in Ta'if

'Urwa ibn Mas'ud

'Urwa ibn Mas'ud ibn Mu'attib ibn Malik ibn Ka'b ibn 'Amr ibn Sa'd ibn 'Awf ibn Thaqif, who is Qusayy ibn Munabbih ibn Bakr ibn Hawazin ibn Mansur ibn 'Ikrima ibn Khasafa ibn Qays ibn 'Aylan ibn Mudar. His *kunya* was Abu Ya'fur. His mother was Subay'a bint 'Abd Shams ibn 'Abd Manaf ibn Qusayy.

Muhammad ibn 'Umar reported from 'Abdullah ibn Yahya that more than one of the people of knowledge said, "'Urwa ibn Mas'ud was absent from Ta'if when the Prophet ﷺ besieged it. He was in Jurash learning how to use the testudo and catapult. When he came to Ta'if after the Messenger of Allah ﷺ had left, Allah cast Islam into his heart and so he went to the Messenger of Allah ﷺ in Madina in the month of Rabi' al-Awwal 9 and became Muslim. The Messenger of Allah ﷺ explained Islam to him. He stayed with Abu Bakr as-Siddiq. Al-Mughira ibn Shu'ba kept at him until he moved and stayed with him."

Then 'Urwa asked permission from the Messenger of Allah ﷺ to go out to his people to call them to Islam. He told him, "Then they will fight you." He said, "If they find me asleep, they will not wake me up." So 'Urwa went out and travelled for five days and then entered Ta'if in the evening and went into his house. Thaqif came to him and greeted him with the greeting of the *Jahiliyya*. He disliked them using it and said, "You must have the greeting of the people of the Garden: 'Peace.'" They insulted and harmed him but he endured it. They left his house and began to plot against him.

At dawn he went to an upper home in his house and gave the *adhan* for the prayer and Thaqif came against him from every side. A man of the Banu Malik called Aws ibn 'Awf shot him and hit the vein in his arm, but the blood did not rise. Ghaylan ibn Salama, Kinana ibn 'Abd Yalil, al-Hakam ibn 'Amr and the nobles of allies stood, put on their weapons, gathered and said, "We will die to the last of us or take revenge on ten of the leaders of the Banu Malik." When 'Urwa ibn Mas'ud saw what they were doing, he said, "Do not fight over me. I have given my blood as *sadaqa* to my companion so that by that I would make peace between them. It is a mark of honour with which Allah honoured me and martyrdom which Allah gave me. I testify that Muhammad is the Messenger of Allah ﷺ. He told me that you would kill me." Then he called for a group and said, "When I die, bury me with the martyrs who were killed with the Messenger of Allah ﷺ before he left you." He died and they buried him with them. The Prophet ﷺ heard about his killing and said, "'Urwa is like the companion of Yasin. He called his people to Allah and they killed him."

Abu Malih ibn 'Urwa ibn Mas'ud ibn Mu'attib ibn Malik

When 'Urwa ibn Mas'ud was killed, his son Abu Malih ibn 'Urwa and his nephew, Qarib ibn al-Aswad ibn Mas'ud, said to the people of Ta'if, "We will never join with you on anything. You have slain 'Urwa." Then they joined the Messenger of Allah ﷺ and became Muslim. The Messenger of Allah ﷺ said to them, "Take as friends whomever you wish." They said, "We take Allah and his Messenger." The Prophet ﷺ said, "Ally with your uncle, Abu Sufyan ibn Harb." They did that and stayed with al-Mughira ibn Shu'ba. They stayed in Madina until the delegation of Thaqif came in Ramadan 9 AH. They called on the Prophet ﷺ to judge and became Muslim. They returned with the delegation. Abu Malih said, "Messenger of Allah, my father was killed while owing a debt of two hundred *mithqal*s of gold. I think that you should settle it from the jewellery of the Lady (i.e. the idol al-Lat). The Messenger of Allah ﷺ said, "Yes."

Qarib ibn al-Aswad ibn Mas'ud ibn Mu'attib ibn Malik

He was the nephew of 'Urwa ibn Mas'ud. When Abu Malih ibn 'Urwa spoke to the Messenger of Allah ﷺ about the judgement of the debt of his father, Qarib ibn al-Aswad, said, "Messenger of Allah, and for al-Aswad ibn Mas'ud, my father. He left a debt like that of 'Urwa. Settle it for him from the property of the idols." The Messenger of Allah ﷺ said, "Al-Aswad died an unbeliever." Qarib answered,

"You will maintain ties of kinship by it. The debt falls on me and I am the one who is answerable for it." The Messenger of Allah 鬱 said, "Then do it." So he settled the debts of both 'Urwa and al-Aswad from the money of the idols.

Al-Hakam ibn 'Amr ibn Wahb ibn Mu'attib ibn Malik

He was in the delegation of Thaqif who came to the Messenger of Allah 鬱 when they became Muslim.

Ghaylan ibn Salama

Ghaylan ibn Salama ibn Mu'attab ibn Malik ibn Ka'b ibn 'Amr ibn Sa'd ibn 'Awf ibn Thaqif. The mother was Salama ibn Mu'attab was Kunna bint Kusayra ibn Thumala of Azd. His half-brother by the mother was Aws ibn Rabi'a ibn Mu'attab. They were the sons of Kunna and are ascribed to her. Ghaylan ibn Salama was a poet and went to Chosroes. He asked him to build him a fortess in Ta'if and he built him a fortress there. Then Islam came and Ghaylan became Muslim while having ten wives. The Messenger of Allah 鬱 said to him, "Choose four of them and divorce the rest." He said, "I did not know which of them to prefer. He will know that tomorrow." So he chose four of them and said to those he wanted of them, "Accept." He said to those he did not want, "Withdraw," until he had chosen four and divorced the rest.

Al-Walid ibn Muslim said from Ibn Lahi'a from Yazid ibn Abi Habib from Ghaylan ibn Salama from his father that Nafi' belonged to Ghaylan ibn Salama and fled to the Prophet 鬱 and became Muslim while Ghaylan was an unbeliever. Then Ghaylan became Muslim and the Messenger of Allah 鬱 restored his *wala'*.

Shurahbil ibn Ghaylan

He was the son of Ghaylan ibn Salama ibn Mu'attab. He was in the delegation which came to the Messenger of Allah 鬱. Shurahbil died in 60 AH.

'Abd Yalil ibn 'Amr

'Abd Yalil ibn 'Amr ibn 'Umayr ibn 'Awf ibn 'Uqda ibn Ghiyara ibn 'Awf ibn Thaqif. The head of the delgation was of Thaqif who went to the Messenger of Allah ﷺ and became Muslim. 'Abd Yalil was the same age as 'Urwa ibn Mas'ud.

Kinana ibn Yalil

The son of Yalil ibn 'Amr ibn 'Umayr ibn 'Uqda ibn 'Awf. He was a noble and became Muslim with the delegation of Thaqif.

Al-Harith ibn Kalada ibn 'Amr ibn 'Ilaj

His name was 'Umayr ibn Abi Salama ibn 'Abd al-'Uzza ibn Ghiyara ibn 'Awf ibn Thaqif. He was the physician of the Arabs. The Prophet ﷺ commanded those who had an illness to go to him to ask him about his illness. Sumayya was the mother of al-Harith's son, Ziyad.

Nafi' ibn Kalada

The son of al-Harith ibn Kalada. He was Abu 'Abdullah who moved to Basra and foddered the horses.

Al-'Ala' ibn Jariya

Al-'Ala' ibn Jariya ibn 'Abdullah ibn Abi Salama ibn 'Abd al-'Uzza ibn Ghiyara ibn 'Awd ibn Thaqif. He was the ally of the Banu Zuhra.

'Uthman ibn Abi al-'As

'Uthman ibn Abi al-'As ibn Bishr ibn 'Abd Duhman ibn 'Abdullah ibn Hammam ibn Aban ibn Yasar ibn Malik ibn Hutayt ibn Jutham ibn Thaqif. He went to the Messenger of Allah ﷺ with the delgation of Thaqif. He was the youngest of the delegation. They used to leave him with their baggage to keep watch over them. When they returned from the Messenger of Allah ﷺ and slept at midday, 'Uthman would go to the Messenger of Allah ﷺ and became Muslim secretly before them and concealed that from them. He began to question the Messenger of Allah ﷺ about the *deen* and asked for him to recite the Qur'an and he recited some *sura*s. When he found the Messenger of Allah ﷺ asleep, he went to Abu Bakr and questioned him and asked for him to recite, and to Ubayy ibn Ka'b and questioned him and asked him to recite. The Messenger of Allah 🌼 admired and loved him. When the delegation became Muslim and the Messenger of Allah 🌼 wrote for them the document of agreement and they wanted to return to their land, they said, "Messenger of Allah, appoint one of us to be in charge of us." He appointed 'Uthman ibn Abi al-'As over them although he was the youngest of them because of what the Messenger of Allah 🌼 saw of his eagerness for Islam.

'Uthman said, "The last instruction the Messenger of Allah 🌼 gave me was to take a *mu'adhdhin* who should not take a wage for giving the *adhan*. He said, 'When you lead your people in the prayer, take account of their weak ones. When you pray for yourself, then you can pray accordingly.'"

Muhammad ibn 'Abdullah al-Asadi reported from 'Abdullah ibn 'Abd ar-Rahman ibn Ya'la ibn Ka'b ath-Thaqafi that 'Abdullah ibn al-Hakam heard 'Uthman ibn al-'As say, "The Messenger of Allah 🌼 appointed me over Ta'if. The last instruction the Messenger of Allah 🌼 gave me was: 'Lighten the prayer for people.'"

Hisham Abu al-Walid at-Tayalasi reported from Za'ida from 'Abdullah ibn 'Uthman ibn Khuthaym who said that Dawud ibn Abi 'Asim related that 'Uthman ibn Abi al-'As said, "The last of the words which the Messenger of Allah 🌼 said to me was when he appointed me over Ta'if were: 'Lighten the prayer for people.' He stopped or paused and then said, *'Recite in the Name of your Lord who created'* (96) and similar *suras* of the Qur'an."

Muhammad ibn 'Umar reported from Muhammad ibn Salih that Musa ibn 'Imran ibn Mannah said, "The Messenger of Allah 🌼 died while 'Uthman ibn Abi al-'As was his governor of Ta'if."

Musa ibn Isma'il reported from Abu Hilal that Qatada related from Mutarrif that 'Uthman ibn Abi al-'As had the *kunya* Abu 'Abdullah.

Muhammad ibn 'Umar said, "'Uthman ibn Abi al-'As remained in charge of Ta'if until the Messenger of Allah 🌼 died and through the caliphate of Abu Bakr as-Siddiq and 'Umar ibn al-Khattab until 'Umar wanted to appoint someone over Bahrayn and they named 'Uthman ibn Abi al-'As to him. He said, 'That is a governor which the Messenger of Allah 🌼 appointed over Ta'if. I will not dismiss him.' They said to him, 'Amir al-Mu'minin, you can command him to delegate to his office whomever he wishes and help him by that.

Then it will be as if you have not dismissed him.' He said, 'I will do this.' He wrote to him to delegate whomever he wished to his position and then go to him. He delegated his brother, al-Hakam ibn al-'As, over Ta'if and he went to 'Umar ibn al-Khattab who appointed him over Bahrayn. When he was dismissed from Bahrayn, he settled in Basra along with the people of his house and they were honoured there. The place in Basra called Shatt 'Uthman is ascribed to him."

Al-Hakam ibn Abi al-'As

His brother, al-Hakam ibn Abi al-'As ibn Bishr ibn 'Abd Duhman. He was a Companion of the Prophet 鸞.

Aws ibn 'Awf ath-Thaqafi

One of the Banu Malik. He is the one who shot 'Urwa ibn Mas'ud ath-Thaqafi and killed him.

Then after that he came in the delegation of Thaqif to the Messenger of Allah 鸞 and became Muslim before the agreement was made with the Messenger of Allah 鸞 with Thaqif, fearing Abu Malih ibn 'Urwa and Qarib ibn al-Aswad ibn Mas'ud. They complained about that to Abu Bakr as-Siddiq and he forbade them to touch him. He said, "Are they not Muslims?" They answered, "Yes." He said, "You took the blood revenge of idolatry when this man has come desiring Islam and he has security and safe conduct. If he had become Muslim, then his blood would be unlawful to you two." Then he brought them together to shake hands and they let him be. Aws ibn 'Awf died in 59 AH.

Aws ibn Hudhayfa ath-Thaqafi

Ad-Dahhak ibn Makhlad, al-Fadl ibn Dukayn, 'Abd al-Malik ibn 'Amr Abu 'Amr and Muhammad ibn 'Abdullah al-Asadi reported from 'Abdullah ibn 'Abd ar-Rahman ath-Thaqafi from 'Uthman ibn 'Abdullah ibn Aws that al-Fadl ibn Dukayn and Muhammad ibn 'Abdullah and Abu 'Amr related from his grandfather Aws ibn Hudhayfa, and ad-Dahhak ibn Makhlad from his uncle, 'Amr ibn Aws, from his father: "We came to the Messenger of Allah 鸞 in the delegation of Thaqif and those with alliances stayed with al-Mughira ibn Shu'ba and the Messenger of Allah ﷺ put the Malikis in his tent. He would go to them after the *'Isha'* prayer and speak to them while standing. He shifted between his feet when he was tired of standing. He often spoke to them of the complaints of the people of Makka and Quraysh. He said, 'The war between us and them has ups and downs. Sometimes it is for us and sometimes against us.' He stayed away from us one night and we said, 'Messenger of Allah, what kept you from us in the night?' He said, 'Some of the jinn came to me and I still had some of my *hizb* to do and so I disliked to leave the mosque until I recited it.'"

Muhammad ibn 'Abdullah al-Asadi said in his *hadith*, "In the morning, we said to his companions, 'The Messenger of Allah ﷺ related to us that a group of the jinn came upon him and he still had some of his *hizb* to do. So how do you reckon a *hizb* of the Qur'an?' They answered, 'We make a *hizb* consist of three *sura*s, five *sura*s, seven *sura*s, nine *sura*s, eleven *sura*s, or thirteen *sura*s. The *hizb* of the *Mufassal* covers *Surat Qaf* and what is after it.'"

Yusuf ibn al-Ghariq reported from 'Abdullah ibn 'Abd ar-Rahman at-Ta'ifi from 'Abd Rabbih and 'Uthman ibn 'Abdullah both that Aws ibn Hudhayfa said, "We set out from Ta'if as seventy men of the allies and the Banu Malik. The allies stayed with al-Mughira ibn Shu'ba and the Messenger of Allah ﷺ put us in his tent between his house and the mosque." Then he mentioned the same as the first *hadith*.

Muhammad ibn 'Umar said that Aws died in the nights of the Battle of al-Harra.

Aws ibn Aws ath-Thaqafi

Abu Janab said in his *hadith* that he heard the Messenger of Allah ﷺ say, "On the Day of *Jumu'a*, whoever washes or has a *ghusl* in the morning and goes early and sits close to the imam, listens and is silent will have the reward of a year of fasting and praying at night for every step he takes."

Hisham Abu al-Walid and 'Abd al-Malik ibn 'Amr Abu 'Amr reported that Shu'ba from an-Nu'man ibn Salim said, "I heard a man whose grandfather was Aws ibn Aws say, 'While he was praying, my grandfather indicated to me to hand him his sandals. I handed them to him and he said, "I saw the Messenger of Allah 鐵 pray in his sandals.""

Al-Fudayl ibn Dukayn reported from Qays ibn ar-Rabi' from 'Umayr ibn 'Abdullah al-Khath'ami from 'Abd al-Malik ibn al-Mughira at-Ta'ifi that Aws ibn Aws or Uways ibn Aws said, "I stayed with the Messenger of Allah 鐵 for half a month and I saw him pray in sandals. I saw him spit to his right and to his left."

Muhammad ibn Sa'd said, "This is Aws ibn Aws. Shu'ba was sure about his name and did not doubt it as Qays did."

Al-Harith ibn 'Abdullah ibn Aws ath-Thaqafi

'Affan ibn Muslim and Yahya ibn Hammad reported from Abu 'Awana from Ya'la ibn 'Ata' from al-Walid ibn 'Abd ar-Rahman that al-Harith ibn 'Abdullah ibn Aws ath-Thaqafi said, "I asked 'Umar ibn al-Khattab about a woman who menstruates before returning to Makka. He replied, 'The last of her business should be *tawaf* of the House.'" He said to 'Umar, 'That is indeed the decision given to me by the Messenger of Allah 鐵.' 'Umar said to him, 'May your hand fall off! You asked me about something and I asked the Messenger of Allah 鐵 about it so that I might not diverge.'"

Muhammad ibn 'Umar said that Abu Ghassan Malik ibn Isma'il an-Nahdi reported the *hadith* to him, and he erred about his name. He said, "'Abd as-Salam ibn Harb related to us from Hajjaj from 'Abd al-Malik ibn 'Abd ar-Rahman ibn al-Baylamani from 'Amr ibn Aws from 'Abdullah ibn al-Harith ibn Aws who said that he heard the Messenger of Allah 鐵 say, 'If he performs *hajj* or '*umra*, let the end of his business be his business with the House.'"

Muhammad ibn Sa'd said, "He is al-Harith ibn 'Abdullah ibn Aws as Abu 'Awana recorded it from Ya'la ibn 'Ata'."

Al-Harith ibn Abi Uways ath-Thaqafi

He accompanied the Prophet 鐵 and related from him.

Ash-Sharid ibn Suwayd ath-Thaqafi

'Affan ibn Muslim reported from Hammam from Qatada from 'Amr ibn Shu'ayb from ash-Sharid ibn Suwayd ath-Thaqafi that the Prophet 鐵 said, "The neighbour of a house is more entitled to the house than someone else." Ash-Sharid is Abu 'Amr ibn ash-Sharid and the Prophet ﷺ put him behind him and he asked him to recite some of the poetry of Umayya ibn Abi as-Salt. He said, "I began to recite and he began to remark, 'It is almost as if he was Muslim.'" Ash-Sharid ibn Suwayd died in the caliphate of Yazid ibn Mu'awiya ibn Abi Sufyan.

Numayr ibn Kharasha ath-Thaqafi

He was in the delegation of Thaqif who came to the Messenger of Allah ﷺ.

Sufyan ibn 'Abdullah ath-Thaqafi

He was appointed over Ta'if. He was also in the delegation who came to the Messenger of Allah ﷺ.

Abu Zuhayr ibn Mu'adh ath-Thaqafi

His *hadith* is: "The Messenger of Allah ﷺ gave us a speech containing the news from the land of Ta'if." His son, Abu Bakr ibn Abi Zuhayr related it from him.

Kardam ibn Sufyan ath-Thaqafi

Muhammad ibn 'Umar reported from Ibn Jurayj, "Kardam ibn Sufyan ath-Thaqafi came to the Messenger of Allah ﷺ and said, 'Messenger of Allah, I vowed to sacrifice ten of my camels at Buwana.' The Messenger of Allah ﷺ said, 'When you vowed that, did you have any of the business of the *Jahiliyya* in mind [i.e. sacrifice to idols)?' He answered, 'No, by Allah, Messenger of Allah.' He said, 'Then go and sacrifice them.'"

Wahb ibn Khuwaylid

Wahb ibn Khuwaylid ibn Zuwaylim ibn 'Awf ibn 'Uqda ibn Ghiyara ibn Thaqif. He became Muslim and was a Companion of the Prophet ﷺ. He died while the Messenger of Allah ﷺ was still alive, and the Banu Ghiyara disagreed about his inheritance. The Messenger of Allah ﷺ gave it to Wahb ibn Umayya ibn Abi as-Salt.

Wahb ibn Umayya

Wahb ibn Umayya ibn Abi as-Salt ibn 'Uqda ibn Ghiyara ibn Thaqif. He became Muslim and was a Companion of the Prophet ﷺ. His father was the poet, Umayya ibn Abi as-Salt.

Abu Mihjan ibn Habib

Abu Mihjan ibn Habib ibn 'Amr ibn 'Umayr ibn 'Awf ibn 'Uqda ibn Ghiyara ibn Thaqif. He was a poet and had *hadith*s.

Al-Hakam ibn Hazm al-Kulfi

One of the Banu Kulfa ibn 'Awf ibn Nasr ibn Mu'awiya ibn Bakr ibn Hawazin.

Sa'id ibn Mansur reported that Shihab ibn Khirash ibn Hawshab related that Shu'ayb ibn Zurayq at-Ta'ifi said, "I sat with a man who had been a Companion of the Prophet ﷺ called al-Hakam ibn Hazn al-Kulfi. He said, 'I came to the Messenger of Allah ﷺ as one of seven or nine men. He gave us permission and we went into him. We said, "Messenger of Allah, we have visited you so that you can pray for good for us." He commanded that we be lodged and ordered some dates for us. Things at that time were meagre. We remained with him for some days in which we attended *Jumu'a* with the Messenger of Allah ﷺ. He stood leaning on his bow (or his staff) and praised Allah with some excellent short blessed words and then said, 'O people, you will not be able (or will not do) all that you are commanded. So act correctly and receive good news.'"'"

Zufar ibn Hurthan

Zufar ibn Hurthan ibn al-Harith ibn Hurthan ibn Dhakwan ibn Kulfa ibn 'Awf ibn Nasr ibn Mu'awiya ibn Bakr ibn Hawazin. He came to the Messenger of Allah ﷺ and became Muslim.

Mudarris ibn Sufyan

Mudarris ibn Sufyan ibn Khafaja ibn an-Nabigha ibn 'Utar ibn Habib ibn Wathila ibn Duhman ibn Nasr ibn Mu'awiya ibn Bakr ibn Hawazin. He came to the Messenger of Allah ﷺ and became Muslim and was present with him at Hunayn. Al-'Abbas ibn Mirdaws mentioned him in his poetry.

Yazid ibn al-Aswad al-'Amiri of the Banu Suwa'a

Yazid ibn Harun reported from Hisham from Ya'la ibn 'Ata' from Jabir ibn Yazid ibn al-Aswad as-Suwa'i from his father from Sulayman Abu Dawud at-Tayalisi from Shu'ba from Ya'la ibn 'Ata' from Jabir ibn Yazid ibn al-Aswad as-Suwa'i that his father said, "We prayed *Fajr* with the Prophet 🌸 in the mosque of Mina in the Farewell *Hajj*. When he finished the prayer, he turned and there were two men who had not prayed. He said, 'Bring them to me.' They were brought trembling. He asked, 'What kept you from praying with us?' They answered, 'Messenger of Allah, we had already prayed in our baggage.' He said, 'When you come and the imam is praying, then pray with him. It is supererogatory for you.'"

Ma'n ibn 'Isa reported from Sa'id ibn as-Sa'ib at-Ta'ifi from his father from Yazid ibn al-Aswad that he was present at Hunayn with the idolators and then became Muslim and was a Companion of the Prophet 🌸. His *kunya* was Abu Hajiza.

'Ubaydullah ibn Mu'ayya as-Suwa'i

Waki' ibn al-Jarrah and Humayd ibn 'Abd ar-Rahman ar-Rawasi reported that Sa'id ibn as-Sa'ib at-Ta'ifi said, "I heard an old man of the Banu Suwa'a, one of the Banu 'Amir ibn Sa'sa'a called 'Ubaydullah ibn Mu'ayya."

Waki' said in his *hadith*: "He was born in the time of the Prophet 🌸 or close to that."

Humayd said, "He was alive in the *Jahiliyya*." He said, "Two of the Companions of the Messenger of Allah 🌸 were killed at the door of the Banu Salim of Ta'if on the day of the Siege of Ta'if. They were carried to the Messenger of Allah 🌸 and he heard about that and sent to have us ascertain where they were struck down or where they were found. We estimated where they died and informed the Messenger of Allah 🌸 and they were buried where they were found."

Abu Razin al-'Uqayli

His name was Laqit ibn 'Amr ibn al-Muntifiq.

'Affan ibn Muslim, Hisham Abu al-Walid at-Tayalisi and Yahya ibn 'Abbad reported from Shu'ba from an-Nu'man ibn Salim from 'Amr ibn Aws that Abu Razin went to the Messenger of Allah ﷺ and said, "Messenger of Allah, my father is an old man who cannot perform *hajj* or *'umra* even in a sedan." He said, "Perform *hajj* and *'umra* on behalf of your father."

Muhammad ibn Sa'd said, "Abu al-Walid did not mention 'a sedan'. 'Affan and Yahya ibn 'Abbad mentioned it."

Al-Hakam ibn Sufyan ath-Thaqafi and **Abu Tarif** were also part of this generation.

The *fuqaha'* and *hadith* scholars in Ta'if after them

'Asim ibn Sufyan ath-Thaqafi

He related from 'Umar ibn al-Khattab.

Abu Hindiyya

He related from 'Umar ibn al-Khattab. He was Abu Muhammad ibn Abi Hindiyya from whom Sa'id ibn al-Musayyab related.

'Amr ibn 'Aws

'Amr ibn 'Aws ibn 'Abdullah ibn Rabi'a ibn al-Harith ibn Hubayb ibn al-Harith ibn Malik ibn Huyayt ibn Jutham ibn Thaqif. His mother was Umm al-Hakam bint Abi Sufyan ibn Harb ibn Umayya. His uncle was Mu'awiya ibn Sufyan. He was the one who was called Ibn Umm al-Hakam. His grandfather was 'Uthman ibn 'Abdullah who carried the banner of the idolators in the Battle of Hunayn and 'Ali ibn Abi Talib killed him. The Messenger of Allah ﷺ said, "May Allah put him far! He used to hate Quraysh." He listened to 'Abd ar-Raman ibn 'Abdullah from 'Uthman ibn 'Affan. He was appointed over Kufa and Egypt. His children today live in Damascus.

Waki' ibn 'Udus

This is what Shu'ba said from Ya'la from 'Ata'. He is the nephew of Ibn Abi Razin. His *kunya* was Abu Mus'ab. He related from his uncle Abu Razin. Ya'la ibn Ata' related from him. Hammad ibn Salama and Abu 'Awana said "from Ya'la ibn 'Ata' from Waki' ibn Hudus."

Ya'la ibn 'Ata'

He went to Wasit and settled there at the end of the rule of the Umayyads. Shu'ba, Hushaym, Abu 'Awana and their Companions listened to him.

'Abdullah ibn Yazid at-Ta'ifi

He died in 120 AH.

Bishr ibn 'Asim ibn Sufyan ath-Thaqafi

He related from his father from the *hadith* of Waki' from Muhammad ibn 'Abdullah ibn Aflah at-Ta'ifi from Bishr ibn 'Asim ibn Sufyan ath-Thaqafi that 'Umar (i.e. ibn al-Khattab) used to send his *zakat* collectors at the beginning of summer.

'Utayf ibn Abi Sufyan

He died in 140 AH.

Sa'id ibn as-Sa'ib at-Ta'ifi

Waki', Humayd ar-Rawwasi and Ma'n ibn 'Isa related from him.

'Abdullah ibn 'Abd ar-Rahman ibn Ya'la ibn Ka'b ath-Thaqafi

Waki', Abu 'Asim an-Nabil, Abu Nu'aym, Muhmmad ibn 'Abdullah al-Asadi and others related from him.

Yunus ibn al-Harith at-Ta'ifi

Waki' ibn al-Jarrah, Abu 'Asim an-Nabil and others related from him.

Muhammad ibn 'Abdullah ibn Aflah at-Ta'ifi

Waki' and others listened to him.

Muhammad ibn Muslim ibn Sawsan at-Ta'ifi

He settled in Makka and Waki' ibn al-Jarrah, Abu Nu'aym, Ma'n ibn 'Isa and others listened to him.

Yahya ibn Sulaym at-Ta'ifi

He settled in Makka until he died there. He used to treat hides.

Also part of this generation are: **'Amr ibn ash-Sharid** ibn Suwayd ath-Thaqafi, **Ibrahim ibn Maysara, 'Ubayd ibn Sa'd, Muhammad ibn Abi Suwayd, Abu Bakr ibn Abi Musa** ibn Abi Shaykh, and **Muhammad ibn Abi Sa'id** ath-Thaqafi.

Chapter Three: Yemen

The Names of the Companions of the Messenger of Allah ﷺ who settled in Yemen

Abyad ibn Hammal al-Mazini of Himyar

Muhammad ibn Sa'd said: "'Abd al-Mun'im ibn Idris ibn Sinan said that he was from Azd among those who settled at Ma'rab among the children of 'Amr ibn 'Amir."

Musa ibn Isma'il reported from Muhammad ibn Yahya ibn Qays al-Mazini from his father from Thumama ibn Sharahil from Sumayy ibn Qays ibn Shumayr that Abyad ibn Hammal went to the Prophet ﷺ and asked him for a land grant of Milh (salt mines) and he gave it to him. When he left, a man said, "Messenger of Allah, do you know what you gave him? You have granted for him the [equivalent of] abundant spring water." He retracted the grant. He said, "I asked the Prophet ﷺ, 'What will be protected of arak trees?' He answered, 'That beyond the reach of the hooves of camels.'"

'Abdullah ibn az-Zubayr al-Humaydi reported from Faraj ibn Sa'id from his uncle Thabit from his father that his grandfather Abyad went to the Prophet ﷺ in Madina and became Muslim with three brothers from Kinda. They had been his slaves in the *Jahiliyya*. The Messenger of Allah ﷺ concluded a truce in exchange for seventy fine robes. Abyad asked the Messenger of Allah ﷺ for a grant of Milh. Milh is a distant salt source at Ma'rab. He granted it to him.and then cancelled and revoked it and the Messenger of Allah ﷺ then gave him some land and thickets at Jawf of Murad.

'Abdullah ibn az-Zubayr al-Humaydi reported from Faraj ibn Sa'id from his uncle Thabit from his father that his grandfather Abyad ibn Hammal had a marks on his face, i.e. pockmarks. The Prophet of Allah ﷺ prayed for him and wiped his face and removed that and there was no trace of it on his face.

Farwa ibn Musayk

Farwa ibn Musayk ibn al-Harith ibn Salama ibn al-Harith ibn ad-Du'ayb ibn Malik ibn Munabbih ibn Ghutayf ibn 'Abdullah ibn

Najiyya ibn Yuhabir, He was Murad ibn Udad. He was from the tribe of Madhhij.

Muhammad ibn 'Umar reported from 'Abdullah ibn Zuhayr that Muhammad ibn 'Umara ibn Khuzayma ibn Thabit said, "Farwa ibn Musayk al-Muradi came in 10 AH to the Messenger of Allah ﷺ, leaving Kinda to follow the Prophet ﷺ. He was a man with honour and he had him stay with Sa'd ibn 'Ubada. Then he went to the Messenger of Allah ﷺ who was sitting in the mosque and did not greet him. Then he said, 'Messenger of Allah, I represent those behind me of my people.' He asked, 'Where are you staying?' He answered, 'With Sa'd ibn 'Ubada.' He said, 'May Allah bless Sa'd.' He used to attend the gathering of the Messenger of Allah ﷺ whenever he sat and learned the Qur'an and the obligations and laws of Islam. Then the Messenger of Allah ﷺ appointed him over all of the tribes of Murad, Zubayd and Madhhij. He travelled in it and he sent with him Khalid ibn Sa'id ibn al-'As to be in charge of *zakat*. He continued to stay with him until the Messenger of Allah ﷺ died."

Muhammad ibn 'Umar reported from 'Abdullah ibn 'Amr from Mijhan ibn Wahb al-Khuza'i that his people said, "The Messenger of Allah ﷺ allowed Farwa ibn Musayk twelve *uqiya*s, mounted him on a noble camel and gave him a robe woven in 'Uman."

Muhammad ibn 'Umar reported from 'Abdullah ibn 'Amr ibn Zuhayr from Muhammad ibn 'Umara ibn Khuza'a ibn Thabit who said, "When the Messenger of Allah ﷺ died, he confirmed Farwa ibn Musayk in Islam to attack those who opposed him with those who obeyed him. He did not apostatise as others did."

Muhammad ibn Sa'd said that Hisham ibn Muhammad al-Kalbi said, "Farwa ibn Musayk was a poet."

Qays ibn Makshuh

The name of Makshuh was Hubayra ibn 'Abd Yaghuth ibn al-Ghuzayyal ibn Salama ibn Bada ibn 'Amir ibn 'Awabthan ibn Zahir ibn Murad. Hubayra ibn 'Abd Yaghuth was a master of Murad and branded on his hip by fire. It is said that Makshuh, a horseman of Madhhij, and his son Qays ibn Makshuh came to the Prophet ﷺ in a delegation. He is the one who killed al-Aswad al-'Ansi who claimed to be a prophet in Yemen.

'Amr ibn Ma'di Karib

'Amr ibn Ma'di Karib ibn 'Abdullah ibn 'Amr ibn 'Usm ibn 'Amr ibn Zubayd as-Saghir. He is Munabbih ibn Rabi'a ibn Salama ibn Mazin ibn Rabi'a ibn Munabbih. He is the Jima' Zubayd. He was from the tribe of Madhhij. 'Amr ibn Ma'di Karib was the outstanding horseman of the Arabs.

Muhammad ibn 'Umar reported from 'Abdullah ibn 'Amr ibn Zuhayr that Muhammad ibn 'Umara ibn Khuza'a ibn Thabit said, "'Amr ibn Ma'di Karib came in 10 AH from Zubayd to Madina. When he entered, he said while holding onto the reins of his mount, 'Who is the master of this area of the Banu 'Amr ibn 'Amir?' He was told, 'Sa'd ibn 'Ubada.' So he went forward leading his mount until it knelt at his door. Sa'd came out to him and welcomed him, commanded that his baggage be brought down, honoured him and then took him to the Prophet ﷺ. He became Muslim and stayed for some days. The Messenger of Allah ﷺ gave him and the delegation a gift. He left to return to his land.

When the Messenger of Allah ﷺ died, 'Amr ibn Ma'di Karib apostatised with those who apostatised in Yemen. Then he returned to Islam and emigrated to Iraq and was present at the victory of al-Qadisiyya and other battles and endured great affliction.

Surad ibn 'Abdullah al-Azdi

He used to live at Jurash.

Muhammad ibn 'Umar reported from 'Abdullah ibn 'Amr ibn Zuhayr from Munir ibn 'Abdullah al-Azdi: "Surad ibn 'Abdullah al-Azdi came with about ten of his people and they stayed with Farwa ibn 'Amr al-Bayadi. He honoured them and they stayed with him for ten days. Surad was the most decisive of them. He used to attend the gatherings of the Prophet ﷺ and the Messenger of Allah ﷺ liked him. He put him in command of those of his people who had become Muslim and ordered him to strive with those who became Muslim who were experiencing trial from the people of idolatry among the people of Yemen. He ordered him to keep the group who were good with him. He left at the command of the Messenger of Allah ﷺ and he settled at Jurash. At that time it was a gated fortified city and some of the tribes of Yemen were fortified there. Surad invited them to

Islam and he let those who became Muslim go their way and he him-self mixed with them, and he chopped off the heads of those who refused. Then he opposed them and defeated them and killed them in a long battle."

Muhammad ibn 'Umar reported from Muhammad ibn Saluh from Musa ibn 'Imran ibn Mannah: "The Messenger of Allah ﷺ died while his governor over Jurash was Surad ibn 'Abdullah al-Azdi."

Namat ibn Qays

Namat ibn Qays ibn Malik ibn Sa'd ibn Malik ibn La'yy ibn Salman ibn Mu'awiya ibn Sufyan ibn Arhab from Hamdan. He came to the Prophet ﷺ in Madina in 20 AH with a number of his people. The Messenger of Allah ﷺ fed him with a food which continues to feed them today.

Hudhayfa ibn al-Yaman al-Azdi

Muhammad ibn 'Umar reported from Muhammad ibn Salih that Musa ibn 'Imran ibn Mannah who said, "The Messenger of Allah ﷺ died while his governor of Daba was Hudhayfa ibn al-Yaman."

Qays ibn al-Husayn

Dhu al-Ghussa ibn Yazid ibn Shaddad ibn Qanan ibn Salama ibn Wahb ibn 'Abdullah ibn Rabi'a ibn al-Harith ibn Ka'b ibn Madhhij. He said, "Qays ibn al-Husayn came with Khalid ibn al-Walid to the Prophet ﷺ and the Messenger of Allah ﷺ put him in command of the Banu al-Harith and wrote a letter to him and gave him twelve *uqiya*s and a *nashsh*. He and those with him of his people went to their land of Najran of Yemen. It was only four months later that the Messenger of Allah ﷺ died."

'Abdullah ibn 'Abd al-Madan

His name was 'Amr ibn ad-Dayyan, whose name was Yazid ibn Qatan ibn Ziyad ibn al-Harith ibn Malik ibn Rabi'a ibn Ka'b ibn al-Harith ibn Ka'b ibn Madhhij. 'Abdullah came with Khalid ibn al-Walid to the Messenger of Allah ﷺ. His name was 'Abd al-Hijr. The Messenger of Allah ﷺ asked him, "Who are you?" He replied, "I am 'Abd al-Hijr.' He said, "You are 'Abdullah."

Yazid ibn 'Abd al-Madan

His brother, Yazid ibn 'Abd al-Madan ibn ad-Dayyan ibn Qatan ibn Ziyad ibn al-Harith ibn Malik. He was noble, a poet, and he was part of the delegation.

Hisham ibn al-Kalbi said that ad-Dayyan means 'the judge'.

Yazid ibn al-Muhajjal

Al-Muhajjal's name was Mu'awiya ibn Hazn ibn Mawa'la ibn Mu'awiya ibn al-Harith ibn Malik ibn Ka'b ibn al-Harith ibn Ka'b ibn Madhhij. He was in the delegation which came with Khalid ibn al-Walid from Najran and Khalid lodged them in his home. His father was called 'al-Muhajjal' (white-footed) because of some whiteness he had.

Shaddad ibn 'Abdullah al-Qanani

One of the Banu al-Harith ibn Ka'b. He was in the delegation which came with Khalid ibn al-Walid.

'Abdullah ibn Qurad

One of the Banu al-Harith ibn Ka'b. He was in the delegation which came with Khalid ibn al-Walid from Najran. The Messenger of Allah ﷺ granted him ten *uqiya*s. Then he and those with him of his people left with him to their lands. That was only four months before the Messenger of Allah ﷺ died.

Zur'a Dhu Yazin of Himyar

Muhammad ibn 'Umar reported from 'Umar ibn Muhammad ibn Suhban from Zamil ibn 'Amr from Shihab ibn 'Abdullah al-Khawlani that Zur'a Dhu Yazin became Muslim and the Messenger of Allah ﷺ wrote to him: "Muhammad testifies that there is no god but Allah and that he is His slave and Messenger. Malik ibn Murara ar-Rahawi related to me that you became Muslim among the first of Himyar and killed the idolators. Take the good news of hope for what is good."

Al-Harith and Nu'aym, the sons of 'Abd Kalal and An-Nu'man, the Qayl Dhi Ru'ayn

Muhammad ibn 'Umar related from 'Umar ibn Muhammad ibn Suhban from Zamil ibn 'Amr from Shihab ibn 'Abdullah al-Khawlani that al-Harith and Nu'aym, the sons of 'Abd Kalal, and an-Nu'man, the Qayl Dhi Ru'ayn, Ma'afir and Hamdan became Muslim. The Messenger of Allah ※ summoned Ubayy ibn Ka'b and said, "Write to them: 'Following on: your Messenger has come to us from the land of the Greeks to Madina and conveyed what you sent and informed us that you have become Muslims and fought the idolators. Allah has guided you with His guidance if you do right, obey Allah and His Messenger, establish the prayer, pay the *zakat* and give the fifth of the booty of Allah and the share of the Prophet and its pick, and what has been prescribed for the Muslims of *sadaqa*.'"

Malik ibn Murara ar-Rahawi

Raha' is a sub-tribe of Madhhij. The Messenger of Allah ※ sent him with his letter to the kings of Himyar. He was with Mu'adh ibn Jabal when the Messenger of Allah ※ sent him to Yemen and wrote to instruct them.

'Uqba ibn Namir

He was also one of the messengers of the Messenger of Allah ※ whom he sent with Mu'adh ibn Jabal to Yemen. He wrote to Zur'a Dhi Yazin to instruct them and command them to collect the *zakat* and give it to his messengers.

'Abdullah ibn Zayd

He was also one of the messengers of the Messenger of Allah ※ whom he sent with Mu'adh ibn Jabal to Yemen.

Zurara ibn Qays

Zurara ibn Qays ibn al-Harith ibn 'Adda' ibn al-Harith ibn 'Awf ibn Jusham ibn Ka'b ibn Qays ibn Sa'd ibn Malik ibn an-Nakha' of the tribe of Madhhij. He was in the delegation of an-Nakha' which came to the Messenger of Allah ※ in the middle of Muharram 10

AH. They were two hundred men. They stayed in the house of Ramla bint al-Hadath and then went to the Messenger of Allah ﷺ affirming Islam. They had given their allegiance to Mu'adh ibn Jabal in the Yemen. Zurara said to him, "Messenger of Allah, I had an extraordinary dream in this journey." He asked, "What did you see?" He said, "I saw a donkey which I left in the quarter which seemed to have given birth to a dark-brown goat." The Messenger of Allah ﷺ asked him, "Did you leave a slavegirl of yours with a camel with scant milk who was pregnant?" He replied, "Yes, Messenger of Allah, I left a slave-girl who was pregnant." He said, "She has given birth to a boy who is your son." He asked, "Why is he dark brown?" He said, "Come close." He went close to him and he asked, "Do you have any white leprosy which you have concealed?" "Yes," he answered, "by the One Who sent you with the truth. No one knew it or was aware of it but you," He said, "So it is like that."

He said, "Messenger of Allah, I also saw an-Nu'man ibn al-Mundhir wearing earrings and bracelets." He said, "That is the king of the Arabs who has returned to the best of his adornment and splendour." He said, "And I saw an old grey-haired woman who came out of the earth." He said, "That is what remains of this world." He said, "I saw a fire emerging from the earth which came between me and and a son of mine called 'Amr. It was saying, 'Blaze, blaze! Seeing and blind! Feed me! I will consume your family and wealth!'" The Messenger of Allah ﷺ said, "That is a trial which will occur at the end of time." He asked, "Messenger of Allah, what is the trial?" He answered, "People will kill their leader and fall into conflict with one another," and the Messenger of Allah ﷺ moved his fingers alternately, "reckoning the evildoer among them is good and a believer considers the blood of a believer more lawful than drinking water. If your son dies, you will experience the trial. If you die, your son will experience the trial." He said, "Messenger of Allah, pray to Allah that I do not meet it." The Messenger of Allah ﷺ said, "O Allah, do not let him meet it!" He died and his son 'Amr lived and was one of those who deposed 'Uthman in Kufa.

Arta'a ibn Ka'b

Arta'a ibn Ka'b ibn Sharahil ibn Ka'b ibn Salaman ibn 'Amir ibn Haritha ibn Sa'd ibn Malik ibn an-Nakha'. He came to the Messenger of Allah ﷺ and became Muslim and had a banner under which he was martyred at al-Qadisiyya. He was killed that day and his brother Durayd ibn Ka'b took up the banner and was also killed.

Al-Arqam ibn Yazid

Al-Arqam ibn Yazid ibn Malik ibn al-Harith ibn Bishr ibn Yasir ibn Jushum ibn Malik ibn Bakr ibn 'Awf ibn an-Nakha'. He came to the Messenger of Allah ﷺ and became Muslim.

Wabr ibn Yuhannas

He was one of the *abna'* in Yemen. He came to the Prophet ﷺ and became Muslim. He came from the Prophet ﷺ to the *abna'* in Yemen. He stayed with the daughters of an-Nu'man ibn Burzraj and they became Muslim. He sent to Fayruz ibn ad-Daylami and he became Muslim, and to Markabudh who became Muslim. His son, 'Ata' ibn Markabudh, was the first to compile the Qur'an in Sana'a. Badhan became Muslim in Yemen and he sent his Islam to the Messenger of Allah ﷺ in 10 AH.

Fayruz ibn ad-Daylami

He was one of the *abna'* of the people of Persia whom Chosroes sent to Yemen with Sayf ibn Dhi Yazin. They drove out the Abyssinians from Yemen and conquered it. When the news about the Messenger of Allah ﷺ reached them, Fayruz ibn ad-Daylami went in a delegation to the Prophet ﷺ and became Muslim. He listened to him and related *hadith*s from him. Some of the people of *hadith* say 'Fayruz ibn ad-Daylami' and some of them simply say 'ad-Daylami'. It is the same person: they mean Fayruz ibn ad-Daylami. So the *hadith* which he related is the same.

Abu 'Asim ad-Dahhak ibn Makhlad ash-Shaybani reported from 'Abd al-Hamid ibn Ja'far from Yazid ibn Abi Habib from Marthad ibn 'Abdullah al-Yazini that ad-Daylami said, "I said, 'Messenger of Allah, we are in a cold land and we fortify outselves with a drink made from wheat.' He asked, 'It is an intoxicant?' 'Yes,' I replied. He said, 'Do not drink it.' I asked again and he asked, 'Is it an intoxi-cant?' I answered, 'Yes' and he said, 'Do not drink it.' I said, 'They cannot bear to be without it.' He said, 'If they cannot bear it, then kill them.'"

Muhammad ibn 'Umar reported from Ibn Abi Sabra from Ishaq ibn 'Abdullah from Abu Wahb al-Jayshani from Abu Khirash from ad-Daylami al-Himyari, Fayruz ibn ad-Daylami related a *hadith* about *qadar* from the Prophet ﷺ. Fayruz's *kunya* was Abu 'Abdullah.

'Abd al-Mun'im ibn Idris said, "His son was ascribed to the Banu Dabba and they said, 'Saba' attacked us in the *Jahiliyya*.'" Fayruz was one of those who killed al-Aswad ibn Ka'b al-'Ansi in Yemen when he claimed to be a prophet in Yemen. The Messenger of Allah ﷺ said, "The righteous man, Fayruz ibn ad-Daylami, killed him." Fayruz died in Yemen while 'Uthman ibn 'Affan was caliph.

Dadhawayh

He was one of the *abna'*. He was a very old man. He became Muslim in the time of the Messenger of Allah ﷺ. He was one of those who killed al-Aswad ibn Ka'b al-'Ansi who claimed to be a prophet in Yemen. Qays ibn Makshuh feared the people of al-'Ansi and claimed that Dadhawayh killed him. Then he attacked Dadhawayh and killed him in order to placate the people of al-'Ansi. Abu Bakr as-Siddiq wrote to al-Muhajir ibn Abi Umayya to send Qays ibn Makshuh to him in chains. He was sent to him in chains. He said, "The righteous man Dadhawayh killed him!" He intended to execute him. Qays spoke to him and swore that he had not done it. He said, "Successor of the Messenger of Allah, let me live for your war. I have insight into war and devices against the enemy." Abu Bakr let him live and sent him to Iraq and commanded that he not be giving any authority but to consult him about war.

An-Nu'man

He was a Jew from the people of Sheba. He came to the Messenger of Allah ﷺ and became Muslim. Then he returned to the land of his people. He heard about al-Aswad ibn Ka'b al-'Ansi and seized him and cut him limb by limb.

Hadith Scholars in Yemen after them First Generation

Mas'ud ibn al-Hakam ath-Thaqafi

He met 'Umar ibn al-Khattab and related from him.

Sa'd al-A'raj

One of the Companions of Ya'la ibn Munya. He met 'Umar ibn al-Khattab.

'Abd ar-Rahman ibn al-Baylamani

One of the *akhmas* of 'Umar ibn al-Khattab.

'Abd al-Mun'im ibn Idris

He was one of the *abna'* who were in Yemen. He used to live in Najran and died in the governorship of al-Walid ibn 'Abd al-Malik.

Hujr al-Madari of Hamdan

He related from Zayd ibn Thabit and Tawus related from him.

Ad-Dahhak ibn Fayruz ad-Daylami

One of the *abna'*. He related from his father.

Abu al-Ash'ath as-San'ani

Sharahil ibn Shurahbil ibn Kulayb ibn Udda of the *abna'*. He settled in Damascus at the end of it. The Syrians related from him and he died early on in the governorship of Mu'awiya ibn Abi Sufyan.

Hanash ibn 'Abdullah as-San'ani

He was one of the *abna'*. Then he moved to Egypt. The Egyptians related from him and he died there.

Wahb adh-Dhimari

He lived in Dhimar, one of the provinces of Yemen. He used to recite the Book.

Second Generation

Tawus ibn Kaysan

Sufyan ibn 'Uyayna reported from Ibn Abi Najih from al-Walid ibn 'Uqba from Hamza az-Zayyat from Habib ibn Abi Thabit that Tawus's *kunya* was Abu 'Abd ar-Rahman.

Muhammad ibn 'Umar reported that Tawus was a *mawla* of Bahir ibn Raysan al-Himyari. He lived in al-Janad.

Al-Fadl ibn Dukayn and others said that he was a *mawla* of Hamdan.

'Abd al-Mun'am ibn Idris said that he was a *mawla* of Ibn Hawda al-Hamdani. The father of Tawus was one of the people of Persia. He made alliance with the people of this house. He used in live in al-Janad.

'Affan ibn Muslim and Ahmad ibn 'Abdullah ibn Yunus reported from Muhammad ibn Talha from Humayd ibn Wahb al-Qurashi that the sons of Tawus said, "Tawus used to dye his hair yellow."

Sulayman ibn Harb reported that Jarir ibn Hazim said, "I saw Tawus using henna which was very red."

'Ubaydullah ibn Musa reported that Hanzala said, "I saw Tawus dyeing his head and beard with henna."

Al-Fadl ibn Dukayn reported that Fitr said, "I saw Tawus using henna."

Al-Fadl ibn Dukayn reported that Fitr said, "I saw Tawus was one of those who often used to wear a veil. I asked Fitr, 'Did he often wear a veil?' 'Yes,' he answered."

'Ubaydullah ibn Musa reported that Hani' ibn Ayyub al-Ju'fi said, "Tawus used to wear a veil and did not stop doing it."

'Ubaydullah ibn Musa reported that Kharija ibn Mas'ab said, "Tawus used to wear a veil. In the night, he would uncover."

'Ubaydullah ibn Musa reported that Yunus ibn al-Harith said, "I saw Tawus praying in a veil."

Hafs ibn Ghiyath reported that Layth said that Tawus used to use a lot of fine cloth and traded in it.

Yahya ibn 'Abbad reported that 'Umara ibn Zadhan said, "I saw Tawus al-Yamani wearing two stained garments."

'Amr ibn al-Haytham Abu Qatan reported that Abu al-Ashhab said that he saw Tawus wearing two garments stained with mud when he was in *ihram*.

Qabisa ibn 'Uqba reported from Sufyan from Ma'mar from Ibn Tawus that his father used to dislike wearing a turban, and did not put any of it under his chin.

Ahmad ibn Muhammad ibn al-Walid al-Azraqi reported that Muslim heard Ayyub as-Sakhtiyani ask 'Abdullah ibn Tawus, "What did your father wear on journeys?" He answered, "He used to wear two long shirts and did not wear a waist-wrapper under them."

Ma'n ibn 'Isa reported that 'Abd ar-Rahman ibn Abi Bakr al-Mulayki said, "I saw Tawus with the mark of prostration between his eyes."

Muhammad ibn 'Abdullah al-Ansari reported that Isma'il ibn Muslim said, "They mentioned Tawus in the presence of al-Hasan and he said, 'Tawus! Tawus! If only his people had been able to give him a different name or one better than this!'" [as it means peacock].

'Abdullah ibn Ja'far ar-Raqqi reported from Ibn al-Mubarak from Ma'mar from Ibn Tawus that when he had letters collected with him, he would command that they be burned.

Qabisa ibn 'Uqba reported from Sufyan that Habib ibn Abi Thabit said, "Tawus said to me: 'When I relate the *hadith* to you, I make it firm for you, so do not ask anyone about it.'"

Ahmad ibn 'Abdullah ibn Yunus reported from Abu Shihab from Humayd at-Tawil that Tawus came from Yemen while the people were at 'Arafa and he began at 'Arafa rather than Makka.

Ahmad ibn Muhammad ibn al-Walid al-Azraqi reported from Muslim ibn Khalid who heard 'Abd al-Karim ibn Abi al-Makhariq say, "Tawus said to us, 'When I am in *tawaf*, do not ask me about anything. *Tawaf* is prayer.'"

Al-Hajjaj ibn Muhammad reported from Ibn Jurayj from 'Ali ibn Abi Humayrd that Tawus used to not leave a black slave-girl of his or anyone else without commanding them to use henna on their hands and feet on the days of the *'Id al-Fitr* and *al-Adha*. He said, "It is *'Id*."

Muhammad ibn Humayd al-'Abdi reported that Hanzala said, "I used to walk with Tawus and he passed by some people selling copies of the Qur'an and said, 'We belong to Allah and to Him we return!'"

Qabisa ibn 'Uqba reported from Sufyan that Muhammad ibn Sa'id said, "Part of the supplication of Tawus was, 'O Allah, deprive me of wealth and children and provide me with faith and action.'"

Al-'Ala' ibn 'Abd al-Jabbar al-'Attar reported from Muhammad ibn Muslim from 'Amr ibn Dinar that Tawus said, "I do not know a worse companion than one with wealth and honour."

Isma'il ibn 'Abdullah ibn Khalid as-Sakkari reported from Yahya ibn Sulaym at-Ta'ifi that Zam'a ibn Salih heard 'Abdullah ibn Tawus say that he heard Tawus say, "When a Jew or Christian greets you, say to him, ''*Alaak as-salam* (peace is above you)'.''

Ahmad ibn 'Abdullah ibn Yunus reported from Mindhal from Zam'a ibn Salih that Salama ibn Wahram said, "They brought a thief past Tawus and he ransomed him with a *dinar* and sent him on his way."

Qabisa ibn 'Uqba reported from Sufyan from Layth that Tawus said, "It was mentioned from Ibn 'Abbas, '*Khul'* is divorce.' Sa'id ibn Jubayr objected to it and Tawus met him and said, 'I read the Qur'an before you were born. I heard it while you were concerned with morsels of stew.'"

Qabisa ibn 'Uqba reported from Sufyan from Ma'mar from the son of Tawus that his father said, "I would like our brothers among the people of Iraq to call al-Hajjaj a believer."

Qabisa ibn 'Uqba reported from Sufyan from Layth that Tawus said, "I studied and taught myself. People have lost trustworthiness." He said, "He used to count *hadith*s letter by letter."

'Arim ibn al-Fadl reported from Hammad ibn Zayd from Sa'id ibn Abi Sadaqa that Qays ibn Sa'd said, "Tawus among us was like Ibn Sirin among you."

'Affan ibn Muslim reported from Hammad ibn Zayd that Ayyub said, "A man asked Tawus about something and he said, 'Do you want to put a rope around my neck and lead me around by it?'"

'Affan ibn Muslim reported from Hammad ibn Zayd from Ayyub that a man asked Tawus about a question and he rebuffed him. He said, "'Abu 'Abd ar-Rahman, I am your brother," He said, "My brother is the one who is below the Muslims."

Al-Fadl ibn al-Dukayn and Qabisa ibn 'Uqba reported from Sufyan from Abu Umayya that Dawud ibn Shabur said, "A man said to Tawus, 'Pray for us.' He said, 'I do not find any reckoning now for that.'"

Rawh ibn 'Ubada reported from Ibn Jurayj from Ibrahim ibn Maysara that Muhammad ibn Yusuf appointed Tawus over some of the collectors. Ibrahim said, "I asked him, 'What did you do?' He said, 'We used to say to the man, "Pay *zakat*, may Allah have mercy on you, from what Allah has given you." If he gives to us, we take it. If he turned away, we did not say, "Come."'"

Al-Fadl ibn Dukayn reported from Abu Ishaq as-San'ani who said, "Tawus and Wahb ibn Munabbih visited Muhammad ibn Yusuf, the brother of al-Hajjaj, our governor, on a cold morning. He had Tawus sit on the chair. Muhammad said, 'Boy, bring that tall cap and put it on Abu 'Abd ar-Rahman.' They put it on him and he continued to move his shoulders until the cap fell off him. Muhammad ibn Yusuf became angry and Wahb said to him, 'By Allah, you would stop him being angry with us if you were to accept the cap and sell it and give its price to the poor.' He said, 'Yes, were it not that it would be said after me that Tawus took it and he would do with it what I do if I were to do it.'"

Al-Fadl ibn Dukayn reported from Ibrahim ibn Nafi' from 'Imran ibn 'Uthman that 'Ata' used to say what Tawus said about that and I said, "Abu Muhammad, from whom did you take it?" He said, "From the trustworthy Tawus."

Hisham Abu al-Walid at-Tayalisi reported from Abu 'Awana that Abu Bishr said, "Tawus said to some young men of Quraysh who were doing *tawaf* of the Ka'ba, 'You are wearing clothes which your fathers did not wear and walk in a manner which is not good for dancers to walk.'"

Al-Fadl ibn Dukayn reported from Mis'ar that 'Abd al-Malik said, "Tawus came performing *qiran* and did not go to Makka until he had gone to 'Arafat."

'Arim ibn al-Fadl reported from Hammad ibn Zayd from Humayd ibn Tarkhan that 'Abdullah ibn Tawus said, "We travelled to Makka with my father for a month. When we returned, he travelled with us for two months. We spoke to him and he told us, 'It reached me that a man continues in the Path of Allah until he reaches his house.'"

'Affan ibn Muslim reported from 'Abd al-Wahid ibn Ziyad that Layth said, "I saw Tawus when he was in his final illness and he prayed on his bed standing and prostrated on it."

Muhammad ibn 'Umar reported that Sayf ibn Sulayman said, "Tawus died in Makka a day before the Day of *Tarwiya*. Hisham ibn 'Abd al-Malik performed *hajj* that year. He was the caliph in 106 AH. He prayed over Tawus. On the day he died he was about ninety."

Wahb ibn Munabbih

He was one of the *abna'*. His *kunya* was Abu 'Abdullah.

Isma'il ibn 'Abd al-Karim ibn Ma'qil ibn Munabbih as-San'ani said that al-Walid ibn Muslim related from Marwan ibn Salim ad-Dimishqi from al-Ahwas ibn Hakim ibn Khalid ibn Ma'dan that 'Ubada ibn as-Samit said, "I heard the Messenger of Allah ﷺ say, 'There will be in my community two men. One is Wahb to whom Allah will give wisdom, and the other is Ghaylan whose trial for this community will be worse than the trial of Shaytan.'"

Isma'il ibn 'Abd al-Karim reported from Muhammad ibn Dawud that his father Dawud ibn Qays as-San'ani said, "I heard Wahb ibn Munabbih say, 'I saw ninety-two books all of which were revealed from heaven: seventy-two of them were in covers and in the hands of people, and only a little is known of twenty. I found in all of them that the one who ascribes something to himself of walking has disbelieved.'"

Ahmad ibn Muhammad ibn al-Walid al-Azraqi reported from Muslim ibn Khald that al-Muthanna ibn as-Sabbah said, "Wahb ibn Munabbih remained for forty years not cursing anything which was alive. He remained for twenty years in which he did not perform *wudu'* between *'Isha'* and *Subh*. Wahb said, 'I read thirty books revealed to thirty Prophets.'"

Muhammad ibn 'Umar and 'Abd al-Mun'im ibn Idris reported that Wahb ibn Munabbih died in San'a' in 110 AH at the beginning of the caliphate of Hisham ibn 'Abd al-Malik.

Hammam ibn Munabbih

One of the *abna'*. He was older than his brother, Wahb ibn Munabbih. He met Abu Hurayra and related a lot from him. He died before Wahb. He died in 101 or 102 AH. His *kunya* was Abu 'Uqba.

Ma'qil ibn Munabbih

One of the *abna'*. His *kunya* was Abu 'Uqayl. He died before his brother Wahb. He was related from.

'Amr ibn Munabbih

One of the *abna'*. His *kunya* was Abu Muhammad. He also was related from.

'Ata' ibn Markabudh

One of the *abna'*. He was also related from. He recited the Qur'an and he is the first of those who collected it in Yemen. Wahb ibn Munabbih was clear.

Al-Mughira ibn Hakim as-San'ani

One of the *abna'*.

Simak ibn al-Fadl al-Khawlani

One of the people of San'a.

Ziyad ibn ash-Shaykh

One of the *abna'* of the people of San'a.

Third Generation

'Abdullah ibn Tawus

His *kunya* was Abu Muhammad. He died at the beginning of the caliphate of Abu al-'Abbas as-Saffah, the Amir al-Mu'minin.

Al-Hakam ibn Aban

One of the people of Aden. He died in 154 AH.

Salm as-San'ani

He used to relate from 'Ata'.

Isma'il ibn Sharus

He was related from.

Ma'mar ibn Rashid

His *kunya* was Abu 'Urwa. Rashid's *kunya* was Abu 'Amr and he was a *mawla* of Azd. He was from the people of Basra and then moved to Yemen. When Ma'mar left Basra, Ayyub accompanied him and gave him travel provisions. Ma'mar was a man with forbearance, manliness and nobility.

Muhammad ibn Sa'd said that 'Abdullah ibn Ja'far al-Ju'fi that 'Ubaydullah ibn 'Amr reported: "I was in Basra waiting for the arrival of Ayyub from Makka. He came to us with Ma'mar accompanying him. Ma'mar had come to visit his mother. I went to him and began to ask him about the *hadith* of 'Abd al-Karim and he related it."

Muhammad ibn 'Umar said that he died in Ramadan 153 AH. 'Abd al-Mun'im ibn Idris said that he died at the beginning of 150 AH.

'Abd ar-Rahman ibn Yunus reported that he heard Sufyan ibn 'Uyayna ask 'Abd ar-Razzaq, "Tell me what people say about Ma'mar. He died while with you." 'Abd ar-Razzaq said, "Ma'mar died with us and we were present when he died and appointed our qadi, Mutarrif ibn Mazin, to look after his wife."

Yusuf ibn Ya'qub

Yusuf ibn Ya'qub ibn Ibrahim ibn Sa'd ibn Dadhayh of the *abna'*. His *kunya* was Abu 'Abdullah. He was the qadi of San'a and gave *fatwa* there.

Muhammad ibn 'Umar said that he died in 153 AH.

'Abd al-Mun'im ibn Idris said that he died in 151 AH.

Bakkar ibn 'Abdullah ibn Sahuk

One of the *abna'*. He lived in al-Janad. 'Abdullah ibn al-Mubarak and others related from him.

'Abd as-Samad ibn Ma'qil ibn Munabbih

He related from Wahb ibn Munabbih.

Fourth Generation

Rabah ibn Zayd

A *mawla* of the family of Mu'awiya ibn Abi Mu'awiya.

Muhammad ibn 'Umar said, "I saw him and he had excellence and knowledge of the *hadith*s of Ma'mar ibn Rashid."

Mutarrif ibn Mazin

His *kunya* was Abu Ayyub. He was the qadi at San'a.

Muhammad ibn 'Umar said that he was a *mawla* of Kinana and died at Manbaj. 'Abd al-Mun'im ibn Idris said that he was a *mawla* of Qays and died in Raqqa in the caliphate of Harun ar-Rashid.

Hisham ibn Yusuf

His *kunya* was Abu 'Abd ar-Rahman. He was one of the *abna'*. He was appointed qadi in Yemen. He related a lot from Ma'mar and from Ibn Jurayj and others. He died in Yemen in 197 AH.

'Abd ar-Razzaq ibn Hammam ibn Nafi'

His *kunya* was Abu Bakr, a *mawla* of Himyar. He died in Yemen in the middle of Shawwal 211 AH. Hammam ibn Nafi' had transmission. He related from Salim ibn 'Abdullah and others.

Isma'il ibn 'Abd al-Karim ibn Ma'qil ibn Munabbih

His *kunya* was Abu Hisham. He died in Yemen in 210 AH.

Ibrahim ibn al-Hakam ibn Aban and **Ghawth ibn Jabir** are also from this generation.

Chapter Four: Yamama
The Names of the Companions of the Messenger of Allah ﷺ who settled in Yamama

Mujja'a ibn Murara

Mujja'a ibn Murara ibn Sulma ibn Zayd ibn 'Ubayd ibn Tha'laba ibn Yarbu' ibn Tha'laba ibn ad-Dawl ibn Hanifa ibn Lujaym ibn Sa'b ibn 'Ali ibn Bakr ibn Wa'il ibn Rabi'a. He was in the delegation of the Banu Hanifa who came to the Messenger of Allah ﷺ and became Muslim.

Muhammad ibn 'Umar reported from Hisham ibn Sa'd from ad-Dakhil ibn Abi Mujja'a ibn Murara that his father said, "When Khalid ibn al-Walid alighted at al-'Ird making for Yamama, he sent ahead about two hundred of the cavalry. He said, 'Seize whomever you come upon.' They went and seized Mujja'a ibn Murara al-Hanafi with twenty-three men of his people who had gone out seeking a man of the Banu Numayr. He questioned Mujajja'a who said, 'By Allah, how near Musaylima is! I went to the Messenger of Allah ﷺ and became Muslim and I have not changed or altered.' Khalid went to the people and struck off their heads and did not kill Mujja'a. He was a noble. It used to be said, 'Mujjaja of Yamama.' Sariya ibn 'Amr said to Khalid ibn al-Walid, 'You have a need of the people of Yamama, so let this one live (meaning Mujja'a ibn Murara).' So he did not kill him and bound him in iron chains and handed him to his wife Umm Tamim and she gave him protection from killing and Mujja'a gave her protection from him if Hanifa were victorious. They made an alliance on that basis.

"Khalid used to summon him and speak to him and question him about the business of Yamama and the Banu Hanifa and Musaylima. Mujja'a said, 'By Allah, I have not followed him. I am a Muslim.' He said, 'Did you not come out to me and speak to me the like of what Thumama ibn Uthal said?' He said, 'I thought you would pardon all of this, so do it.' He said, 'I did it.' He is the one with whom Khalid ibn al-Walid made peace for Yamama and what was in it after killing Musaylima. Khalid ibn al-Walid brought him in the delegation to Abu Bakr as-Siddiq and mentioned his Islam and what had happened. Abu Bakr pardoned him and gave him security and wrote for him and his delegation safe conduct and returned them to their land of Yamama."

Thumama ibn Uthal

Thumama ibn Uthal ibn an-Nu'man ibn 'Ubayd ibn Tha'laba ibn Yarbu' ibn Tha'laba ibn ad-Dul ibn Hanifa al-Hanafi. The Messenger of Allah ﷺ passed by him and Thumama wanted to kill him. His uncle prevented him from doing that. The Messenger of Allah ﷺ declared Thumama's blood lawful. Then after that Thumama went on *'umra*. When he approached Madina, the messengers of the Messenger of Allah ﷺ took him without contract or pledge and they brought him to the Messenger of Allah ﷺ. He said, "If you punish, that is someone with a sin, and if you pardon, you pardon one who is thankful." The Messenger of Allah ﷺ pardoned his sin and he became Muslim. The Messenger of Allah ﷺ gave him permission to go out to Makka for *'umra* and went out and performed *'umra*. Then he left. He constricted Quraysh and did not allow a single grain to come to them from Yamama. When Musaylima appeared and claimed to be a prophet, Thumama ibn Uthal stood up among his people and admonished them and reminded them. He said, "Two Prophets are not joined in the same business. Muhammad is the Messenger of Allah and there will be no Prophet after him and no Prophet to share with him." He recited to them, *"HaMim. The revelation of the Book from Allah, the Almighty, the All-Knowing, the Forgiver of wrong action, the Accepter of repentance, the Severe in retribution, the Possessor of abundance. There is no god but Him. He is the final destination."* (40:1-3) He said, "These are the words of Allah. See where this is in relation to 'Frog, croak. You do not deny the drink nor muddy the water.' By Allah, you see that these words are not from a deity." When Khalid ibn al-Walid came to Madina, he thanked him for that and acknowedged his sound companionship.

'Ali ibn Shayban

'Ali ibn Shayban ibn 'Amr ibn 'Abdullah ibn 'Amr ibn 'Abd al-'Uzza ibn Suhaym ibn Murra ibn ad-Duwal ibn Hanifa.

Sa'id ibn Sulayman reported from Mulazim ibn 'Amr al-Yamani from 'Abdullah ibn Badr from 'Abd ar-Rahman ibn 'Ali that his father, who was in the delegation, said, "We prayed behind the Messenger of Allah ﷺ. He saw behind him a man who did not make his back straight in *ruku'* and prostration. When he finished his prayer, he said, 'Company of Muslims, there is no prayer for someone who does not make his back straight in *ruku'* and prostration.' Then we prayed behind him in another prayer and he performed the prayer and a man prayed on his own behind the row. When he finished the prayer, the Messenger of Allah ﷺ stopped by him until the man finished the prayer and said, 'Begin your prayer. There is no prayer for someone who prays alone behind the row.'"

Abu an-Nadr Hashim ibn al-Qasim reported from Ayyub ibn 'Utba from 'Abdullah ibn Badr from 'Abd ar-Rahman ibn 'Ali ibn Shayban from his father that the Messenger of Allah ﷺ said, "Allah does not look at a man who does not make his back straight in *ruku'* and prostration."

Talq ibn 'Ali al-Hanafi

He is the father of Qays ibn Talq.

Sa'id ibn Sulayman reported from Mulazim ibn 'Amr from 'Abdullah ibn Badr ibn Qays ibn Talq that his father Talq said, "We went out in delegation to the Prophet ﷺ. We went to him and gave him our allegiance and we prayed with him and reported to him that in our land we had a church' and we asked him to give us his excess *wudu'* water. He called for water and performed *wudu'* with it and rinsed his mouth and then poured it for us into a vessel. Then he said, 'Take it and when you reach your land, break your allegiance and sprinkle the place with this water and make a mosque there.' We said, 'Messenger of Allah. The heat is intense and our land is far and water is scarce.' He said, 'Seek help with some of the water. It will only increase it in goodness.' So we left and when we arrived, we broke the church and sprinkled its place and built a mosque there and we called the prayer there."

Muhammad ibn Sa'd said that someone other than Sa'id ibn Sulayman said in another *hadith* that Talq said, "I went to the Messenger of Allah ﷺ while he was building his mosque and the

Muslims were working on it with him. I was a person who knew the method of mixing mud. So I took a shovel to mix the mud while the Messenger of Allah ﷺ was looking at me and saying, 'This Hanafi is a master of mud.'"

Abu an-Nadr Hashim ibn al-Qasim reported from Ayyub ibn 'Utba from Qays ibn Talq from his father that the Messenger of Allah ﷺ said, "A woman should not refuse her husband, even if she is on the back of a saddle." The Prophet ﷺ said, "There are not two *witr*s in the night." A man came and said, "Prophet of Allah, should one of us do *wudu'* after he touches his penis?" He said, "Is it other than a part of you or your body?" A man came after *Zuhr* and said, "Prophet of Allah, can one of us pray in a single garment?" He was silent until the time of *'Asr* came and untied his waist-wrapper while Tariq had his mantle and waist-wrapper. Then he put them on his shoulders. When he finished the *'Asr* prayer, he said, "Where is the one who asked about praying in a single garment?" A man said, "It is me, Prophet of Allah?" He said, "Does everyone own two garments?"

Al-Hirmas ibn Ziyad al-Bahili

Hisham Abu al-Walid at-Tayalisi reported from 'Ikrima ibn 'Ammar that al-Hirmas ibn Ziyad said, "I saw the Messenger of Allah ﷺ while my father had me riding behind him on a camel of his. I was a young boy. I saw the Prophet ﷺ speaking to people while mounted on his she-camel al-'Adba' on the Day of *al-Adha* at Mina."

Abu an-Nadr Hashim ibn al-Qasim reported from 'Ikrima ibn 'Ammar that al-Hirmas ibn Ziyad al-Bahili said, "I was riding behind my father on the Day of *Adha* while the Prophet of Allah ﷺ was speaking to people on his she-camel at Mina."

Jariya Abu Nimran al-Hanafi

Ahmad ibn 'Abdullah ibn Yunus reported from Abu Bakr ibn 'Ayyash from Dahsham ibn Qarran al-Yamami from Nimran ibn Jariya al-Hanafi from his father that some people disagreed about a hut. They took the case to the Prophet ﷺ and he sent Hudhayfa who judged in favour of those who were next to the reeds. He returned to the Prophet ﷺ and mentioned that to him and he allowed it.

The *fuqaha'* and *hadith* scholars in Yamama after them

Damdam ibn Haws al-Hiffani

He related from Abu Hurayra and from 'Abdullah ibn Hanzala. 'Ikrima ibn 'Ammar and others related from him.

Hilal ibn Siraj ibn Mujja'a al-Hanafi

Yahya ibn Abi Kathir related from him.

Abu Kathir al-Ghubari

His name was Yazid ibn 'Abd ar-Rahman ibn Udhayna as-Suhaymi. He met Abu Hurayra and related from him. Al-Awza'i and 'Ikrima ibn 'Ammar related from this Abu Kathir.

Abu Sallam

His name was Mamtur. He related from Yahya ibn Abi Kathir.

Yahya ibn Abi Kathir

A *mawla* of Tayy'. He was one of the people of Basra and moved to Yamama.

Yahya ibn Abi Kathir ibn Yahya ibn Abi Kathir al-Yamani reported: "I saw my uncle Nasr ibn Yahya ibn Abi Kathir, and by him he has the *kunya* Yahya ibn Abi Kathir al-Yamami." Someone else said, "The *kunya* of Yahya ibn Abi Kathir."

Musa ibn Isma'il reported that he heard Wuhayb ibn Khalid say that he heard Ayyub as-Sakhtiyani say, "There is no one on the surface of the earth like Yahya ibn Abi Kathir."

Muhammad ibn Sa'd said that Isma'il ibn 'Ulayya said, "I saw Ayyub write to Yahya ibn Abi Kathir."

Sufyan ibn 'Uyayna said, "We used to wait for his coming to us."

I heard Abu Nu'aym al-Fadl ibn Dukayn say, "Yahya ibn Abi Kathir died in 129."

A man of the Banu Tamim of the people of knowledge said that the name of Abu Kathir was Dinar.

'Ikrima ibn 'Ammar al-'Ijli

He related from Iyas ibn Salama ibn al-Akwa', al-Hirmas ibn Ziyad al-Bahili and 'Asim ibn Shunaykh al-Ghaylani, one of the Banu Tamim, and from 'Ata' ibn Abi Rabah, Damdam ibn Jaws, al-Hadrami ibn Lahiq, Yahya ibn Abi Kathir, Abu an-Najashi, the *mawla* of Rafi' ibn Khudayj, Tariq ibn 'Abd ar-Rahman al-Qurashi and Simak al-Hanafi Abi Zumayl. He listened to al-Qasim ibn Muhmmad, Salim ibn 'Abdullah, Nafi', the *mawla* of 'Abdullah ibn 'Umar, Tawus, Abu Kathir al-'Ubri and Yazid ar-Raqqashi.

Ayyub ibn 'Utba

His *kunya* is Abu Yahya. He was appointed qadi in Yamama. He related from Iyas ibn Salama ibn al-Akwa', Qays ibn Talq, and 'Abdullah ibn Badr. He listened to Abu Bakr ibn Muhammad ibn 'Amr ibn Hazm, Taysaka ibn 'Ali and Abu Kathir al-'Ghubari, who is as-Suhaymi, and from an-Najashi, the *mawla* of Rafi' ibn Khadij, Yahya ibn Abi Kathir and Yazid ibn 'Abdullah ibn Qusayt.

'Abdullah ibn Yahya ibn Abi Kathir

He related from his father.

Khalid ibn al-Haytham

His *kunya* was Abu al-Haytham. He was a *mawla* of the Banu Hashim. He related from Yahya ibn Abi Kathir and Muhammad ibn 'Umar related many *hadith*s from him.

Muhammad ibn Jabir al-Hanafi

He grew up in Kufa and listened to 'Umayr ibn Sa'id.

Ayyub ibn an-Najjar al-Yamani

He related from Yahya ibn Abi Kathir and others.

'Amr ibn Yunus al-Yamani

He related from 'Ikrima ibn 'Ammar.

Chapter Five: Bahrayn

The Names of the Companions of the Messenger of Allah ﷺ in Bahrayn

Ashajj 'Abd al-Qays

Muhammad ibn Sa'd said, "We disagree about his name."

Muhammad ibn 'Umar reported from Qudama ibn Musa from 'Abd al-'Aziz ibn Rumana that 'Urwa ibn az-Zubayr said, "The Messenger of Allah ﷺ wrote to the people of Bahrayn and twenty of their men came to him from them. Their leader was 'Abdullah ibn 'Awf al-Ashajj. There were three from the Banu 'Ubayd, three from the Banu Ghanm, and eleven from the Banu 'Abd al-Qays. One of their men was al-Jarud who was a Christian."

Muhammad ibn 'Umar reported from 'Abd al-Hamid ibn Ja'far that his father said, "It was said to the Messenger of Allah ﷺ when they came, 'Messenger of Allah, the delegation of 'Abd al-Qays.' He said, 'Welcome to them. The 'Abd al-Qays are an excellent people.' Their leader at this time was 'Abdullah ibn 'Awf al-Ashajj. They all came when they were told that the Messenger of Allah ﷺ was sitting in the mosque and said, 'We greet the Messenger of Allah ﷺ.' They came in their garments and made their camels kneel at the door of the house of Ramla bint al-Hadath. That is what delegations used to do. They greeted the Messenger of Allah ﷺ and the Messenger of Allah ﷺ began to question them, 'Which of you is 'Abdullah al-Ashajj?' They said, 'He has come to you, Messenger of Allah.' 'Abdullah had removed his travelling clothes and brought out good garments and put them on. He was an ugly man. When he came, the Messenger of Allah ﷺ saw an ugly man. 'Abdullah said, 'Messenger of Allah. Water is not carried in men's skins. What is needed in a man is his two small things: his tongue and heart.' The Messenger of Allah ﷺ said, 'You have two qualities which Allah loves.' 'Abdullah asked, 'What are they, Messenger of Allah?' He answered, 'Forbearance and steadiness.' 'Abdullah said, 'Messenger of Allah. Is that acquired or an innate trait?' He answered, 'An innate trait.'"

Muhammad ibn 'Umar said that someone other than 'Abd al-Hamid ibn Ja'far said in this *hadith*: "The hospitality of the Messenger of Allah ﷺ was given to the delegation of 'Abd al-Qays for ten days. 'Abdullah al-Ashajj used to ask the Messenger of Allah ﷺ about *fiqh* and the Qur'an and the Messenger of Allah ﷺ used to bring him close to him when he sat. He also used to go to Ubayy ibn Ka'b and recite to him. The Messenger of Allah ﷺ commanded gifts for the delegation and gave more to 'Abdullah al-Ashajj: twelve *uqiya*s and a *nashsh*. That was more than the Messenger of Allah ﷺ allotted the delegation."

As for Hisham ibn Muhammad as-Sa'ib al-Kalbi, he mentioned from his father that Ashajj 'Abd al-Qays's name was al-Mundhir ibn al-Harith ibn 'Amr ibn Ziyad ibn 'Asar ibn 'Awf ibn 'Amr ibn 'Awf ibn Jadhima from 'Awf ibn Bakr ibn 'Awf ibn Anmar ibn 'Amr ibn Wadi'a ibn Lukayz ibn Afsa ibn 'Abd al-Qays ibn Afsa ibn Dumiyy ibn Jadila ibn Asad ibn Rabi'.

'Ali ibn Muhammad ibn 'Abdullah ibn Abi Sayf al-Mada'ini said that his name was al-Mundhir ibn 'A'idh ibn al-Harith ibn al-Mundhir ibn an-Nu'man ibn Ziyad ibn 'Asar.

'Abd al-Wahhab ibn 'Ata' reported from 'Awf that al-Hasan said, "We heard that the Messenger of Allah ﷺ said to 'A'idh ibn al-Mundhir al-Ashajj." Muhammad ibn Bishr al-'Abdi said, "I asked our shaykh al-Buhtari about the name of al-Ashajj and he said that his name was al-Mundhir ibn 'A'idh."

Al-Jarud

His name was Bishr ibn 'Amr ibn Hanash ibn al-Mu'alla who is al-Harith ibn Zayd ibn Haritha ibn Mu'awiya ibn Tha'laba ibn Jadhima ibn 'Awf ibn Bakr ibn 'Awf ibn Anmar.

He said, "He was called al-Jarud because the land of 'Abd al-Qays was lost until only Shalliyya remained for al-Jarud. Ash-Shalliya is the remnant. He hastened there to his maternal uncles of the Banu Hind of the Banu Shayban and he and his camels got mange and their camels returned and died. People said, "He stripped (*jarrada*) them and so he was called al-Jarud." The poet said:

We stripped them with the sword on every side
like al-Jarud stripped Bakr ibn Wa'il.

Al-Jarud's mother was Darmaka bint Ruwaym, the sister of Yazid ibn Ruwaym, the father of Hawshab ibn Yazid ash-Shaybani. Al-Jarud was a noble in the *Jahiliyya*. He was a Christian who came to the Messenger of Allah ﷺ in a delegation. The Messenger of Allah ﷺ invited him to Islam and presented it to him. Al-Jarud said, "I was following a religion and if I leave my religion for your religion, will you guarantee my religion for me?" The Messenger of Allah ﷺ said, "I guarantee for you that Allah has guided you to what is better than it." Then al-Jarud became a good Muslim. He was not undervalued. He wanted to return to his land and asked the Prophet ﷺ for mounts. He said, "I do not have anything on which to mount you." He said, "Messenger of Allah, there are stray camels between me and my land. Can I ride them?' The Messenger of Allah ﷺ said, "They are the burning of the Fire. Do not go near them." Al-Jarud lived until the Ridda. When he returned to his people with al-Ma'rur ibn al-Mundhir ibn an-Nu'man, al-Jarud stood and testified with the true testimony and called people to Islam. He said, "People! I testify that there is no god but Allah and that Muhammad is His Messenger ﷺ. Refrain from the one who does not testify." He said:

> We are pleased with the *deen* of Allah in the face of every event
> and are pleased with Allah, the All-Merciful as a Lord.

Muhammad ibn 'Umar reported from Ma'mar, Muhammad ibn 'Abdullah, and 'Abd ar-Raman ibn 'Abd al-'Aziz related from az-Zuhri from 'Abdullah ibn 'Amir ibn Rabi'a that 'Umar ibn al-Khattab put Qudama ibn Maz'un in charge of Bahrayn and Qudama went out to his office and stayed in it and in it there was no complaint of injustice nor release other than him not attending the prayer. Al-Jarud, the master of 'Abd al-Qays, came to 'Umar ibn al-Khattab and said, "Amir al-Mu'minin! Qudama drinks and I thought that it was a duty for me to present one of the *hudud* of Allah to you." 'Umar said, "Who will testify to what you say?" Al-Jarud said, "Abu Hurayra will testify." 'Umar wrote to Qudama to come to him. He came and al-Jarud went forward to speak to 'Umar and said, "Carry out the punishment of the Book of Allah on this one." 'Umar said, "Are you a witness or a litigant?" Al-Jarud answered, "Indeed I am a witness." 'Umar said, "You have given your testimony." Al-Jarud was silent.

Then he went to him the following day and said, "Carry out the *hadd* punishment on this man!" 'Umar said, "I think that you are a litigant. Only one man has testified. By Allah, you will control your tongue or I will treat you badly!" Al-Jarud said, "By Allah, it is not right that your cousin drinks and you are bad to me!" 'Umar detained him.

Muhammad ibn 'Umar reported from 'Abdullah ibn Ja'far from 'Uthman ibn Muhammad that 'Abd ar-Rahman ibn Sa'id ibn Yarbu' said, "When al-Jarud al-'Abdi came, 'Abdullah ibn 'Umar met him, he said, 'By Allah, the Amir al-Mu'minin will flog you!' Al-Jarud said, 'By Allah, he will flog your uncle or your father sins against his Lord. Will you break me with this, 'Abdullah ibn 'Umar?' Then al-Jarud went in to 'Umar and said, 'Impose the Book of Allah on someone.' 'Umar chided him and said, 'By Allah, were it not for Allah, I would do something to you!' Al-Jarud said, 'By Allah, were it not for Allah, I would not care about that.' 'Umar said, 'You spoke the truth. By Allah, you are far from the house with a lot of relatives.' Then 'Umar summoned Qudama and flogged him."

Muhammad ibn Sa'd said as did 'Ali ibn Muhammad: "Al-Jarud used to say, 'I fear testifying against a Qurashi after 'Umar has gone.'"

Al-Hakam ibn Abi al-'As put al-Jarud in charge of fighting on the Battle of Suhrak and he was killed at 'Aqaba at-Tin as a martyr in 20 AH. It was then called 'Aqaba al-Jarud. Al-Jarud's *kunya* was Abu Ghiyath. It is also said that his *kunya* was Abu al-Mundhir. His children were al-Mundhir, Habib and Ghiyath whose mother was Umama bint an-Nu'man of Jadhima, 'Abdullah and Salm whose mother was the daughter of al-Jadd, one of the Banu 'A'ish of 'Abd Shams, and Muslim and al-Hakam who had no descendants and was killed in Sijistan. His sons were nobles. Al-Mundhir ibn al-Jarud was a generous chief whom 'Ali ibn Abi Talib appointed over Istakhr. No one came to him but that he gave to him. Then 'Ubaydullah ibn Ziyad appointed him over the frontier of India. He died there in 61 or the beginning of 62 AH. At that time he was sixty.

Suhar ibn 'Abbas al-'Abdi

One of the Banu Murra ibn Zafar ibn ad-Dil. His *kunya* was Abu 'Abd ar-Rahman. He was in the delegation of 'Abd al-Qays.

Sa'id ibn Sulayman reported from Mulazim ibn 'Amr from Siraj ibn 'Uqba that his aunt Khalida bint Talq said, "My father said to us, 'We were sitting with the Messenger of Allah ﷺ when Suhar of 'Abd al-Qays came and asked, 'Messenger of Allah, what do you think that a drink which we make from our dates?' The Prophet ﷺ turned away from him until he had asked him three times.' He led us in the prayer and when he had finished the prayer, he said, 'Who is the one who asked about the intoxicant? You ask me about the intoxicant which your brother does not drink nor provide. By the One Who has the soul of Muhammad in His hand, if a man does not drink it at all seeking the pleasure of its intoxiation he will be given wine to drink on the Day of Rising.'" Suhar was one of those who sought revenge for 'Uthman.

Sufyan ibn Khawla

Sufyan ibn Khawla ibn 'Abd 'Amr ibn Khawla ibn Hammam ibn al-'Atik ibn Jabir ibn Hidrijan ibn 'Isas ibn Layth ibn Huddad ibn Zalim ibn Dhuhl ibn 'Ijl ibn 'Amr ibn Wadi'a ibn Lujayz ibn Afsa ibn 'Abd al-Qays. He came in a delegation to the Prophet ﷺ.

Muharib ibn Muzida

Muharib ibn Muzida ibn Malik ibn Hammam ibn Mu'awiya ibn Shabbaba ibn 'Amir ibn Hutama ibn 'Amr ibn Muharib ibn 'Abd al-Qays. He came in a delegation to the Prophet ﷺ.

'Ubayda ibn Malik

'Ubayda ibn Malik ibn Hammam ibn Mu'awiya ibn Shabbaba. He came in a delegation to the Prophet ﷺ.

Az-Zari' ibn al-Wazza' al-'Abdi

He was in the delegation of 'Abd al-Qays. He later lived in Basra.

Aban al-'Abdi

He was in the delegation. One of them said in a *hadith* that he is Ghassan.

Munqidh ibn Hayyan al-'Abdi

He was the nephew of al-Ashajj. He is the one whose face the Prophet ﷺ stroked.

'Amr ibn al-Marjum

The name of al-Marjum was 'Abd al-Qays ibn 'Amr ibn Shihab ibn 'Abdullah ibn 'Asar ibn 'Awf of 'Abd al-Qays. He was in the delegation which 'Abd al-Qays sent to Basra.

Shihab ibn al-Matruk

The name of al-Matruk was 'Abbad ibn Shihab ibn 'Abdullah ibn 'Asr from the 'Abd al-Qays. He was in the delegation.

'Amr ibn 'Abd Qays

One of the Banu 'Amir ibn 'Asar. He was the nephew of al-Ashajj. He married his daughter, Umama bint al-Ashajj. He wanted to learn about the Messenger of Allah ﷺ and so he made him carry dates as if he wanted to sell them, and he took a guide from the Banu 'Amir ibn al-Harith called al-Urayqit. He said to him, "It has reached me that he consumes gifts but does not consume *sadaqa*. And there is a sign between his shoulder-blades. Get me knowledge of that."'Amr ibn 'Abd al-Qays went out to Makka in the year of the Hijra and went to the Prophet ﷺ and gave him some dates, saying, 'This is *sadaqa*.' He did not accept them. So he sent some others to him and said, 'This is a gift,' and he accepted it. He leaned so as to look between his shoulder-blades and the Prophet ﷺ called him to Islam and he became Muslim. He taught him the *Fatiha* and *"Recite in the Name of your Lord"* (96). He told him, "Invite your uncle [to Islam]." He returned and his guide stayed in Makka. He went to Bahrayn and entered his house giving the greeting of Islam. His wife went to her father, showing her aversion, and said, "By the Lord of the Ka'ba, 'Amr has become a heretic!" Her father chided her and said, "I hate a woman who differs from her husband." Al-Ashajj came to him and told him the news and so al-Ashajj became Muslim and concealed his Islam for a time. Then he left concealing his Islam with seventeen men in a delegation to the Prophet ﷺ from the people of Hajar. One of them said that there were twelve men and they went to the Prophet 🌸 and became Muslim.

Tarif ibn Aban

Tarif ibn Aban ibn Salama ibn Jariya of the Banu Jadila ibn Asad ibn Rabi'a. He went in a delegation to the Prophet 🌸.

'Amr ibn Shu'ayb

One of the Banu 'Asar of 'Abd al-Qays. He went in a delegation to the Prophet 🌸.

Jariya ibn Jabir

One of the Banu 'Asar. He was in the delegation.

Hammam ibn Rabi'a

One of the Banu 'Asar. He was in the delegation.

Khuzayma ibn 'Abd al-Qays

One of the Banu 'Asar. He was in the delegation.

'Amir ibn 'Abd al-Qays

One of the Banu 'Amir ibn 'Asar. He was in the delegation. He was the brother of 'Amr ibn 'Abd al-Qays whom al-Ashajj sent to learn the knowledge of the Messenger of Allah 🌸.

'Uqba ibn Jirwa

One of the Banu Subah ibn Lukayz ibn Afsa ibn 'Abd al-Qays. He was in the delegation.

Matar

A brother of 'Uqba ibn Jirwa by his mother. He was an ally of them from 'Anaza.

Sufyan ibn Hammam

One of the Banu Zafr ibn Zafar ibn Muharib ibn 'Amr ibn Wadi'a ibn Lukayz ibn Afsa ibn 'Abd al-Qays. He went in delegation to the Prophet 🌸.

'Amr ibn Sufyan

The son of Sufyan ibn Hammam in whose house al-Ash'ath stayed in when he came to Basra and then went out to az-Zawiya.

Al-Harith ibn Jundub

One of the Banu 'A'ish ibn 'Awf ibn ad-Dil. He went in delegation to the Prophet ﷺ.

Hammam ibn Mu'awiya

Hammam ibn Mu'awiya ibn Shabbaba ibn 'Amir ibn Hutama of 'Abd al-Qays. He went in delegation to the Prophet ﷺ.

Chapter Six: Kufa
Generations of the Kufans

The Names of the Companions of the Messenger of Allah ﷺ who lived in Kufa and those there after them of the Tabi'un and others of the people of *fiqh* and knowledge

Waki' ibn al-Jarrah reported from Sufyan from Habib ibn Abi Thabit from Nafi' ibn Jubayr that 'Umar ibn al-Khattab said, "The notable people are in Kufa."

Waki' ibn al-Jarrah reported, and Yunus ibn Abi Ishaq added that he heard that ash-Sha'bi said, "'Umar ibn al-Khattab wrote to the people of Kufa: 'To the head of the people of Islam.'"

Waki' ibn al-Jarrah reported from Isra'il from Jabir that 'Amir said, "'Umar ibn al-Khattab wrote to the people of Kufa, 'To the head of the Arabs.'"

Waki' ibn al-Jarrah reported from Qays from Shamir ibn 'Atiyya that an old man of the Banu 'Amir said, "'Umar ibn al-Khattab said when he mentioned the people of Kufa: 'The spear of Allah, treasure of faith and skull of the Arabs. They protect their frontiers and help the cities.'"

'Ubaydullah ibn Musa reported from Sufyan from al-A'mash from Shamir ibn 'Atiyya that 'Umar ibn al-Khattab said, "In Iraq is found the treasure of faith, and they are the spear of Allah. They protect their frontiers and help the cities."

'Ubaydullah ibn Musa reported from Sa'd ibn Tarif from al-Asbagh ibn Nubata that 'Ali said, "Kufa is the skull of Islam, treasury of faith and the sword and spear of Allah which he puts where He wishes. By Allah, Allah will help its people in the east and west of the lands as He helped Hijaz."

Al-Fadl ibn Dukayn reported from Sharik from 'Ammar ad-Dajni from Salim that Salman said, "Kufa is the dome of Islam and the people of Islam."

Al-Fadl ibn Dukayn reported from Musa ibn Qays al-Hadrami from Salama that Salman said, "That which defended the land after the tent of Muhammad ﷺ is what will defend Kufa. No one heads for it intending to ruin it but that Allah destroys him and there will come a day when nothing but a believer will be there or his desire will be there."

Waki' ibn al-Jarrah reported from Mis'ar from ar-Rukayn al-Fazari that his father said that Hudhayfa said, "There is no tent after the tent of the Prophet ﷺ at Badr which will defend what this place (Kufa) defends."

'Ubaydullah ibn Musa reported from Isra'il from Simak from Mughith al-Bakri that Hudhayfa said, "By Allah, nothing defends the people of a town as this is defended (i.e. Kufa) except the Companions of the Messenger of Allah ﷺ who followed him."

Muhammad ibn 'Ubayd at-Tanafisi reported from Yusuf ibn Suhayb from Musa ibn Abi al-Mukhtar from Yalal, a man of the Banu 'Abs that Hudhayfa, said, "There is no tent after the tent of the Messenger of Allah ﷺ at Badr which defends them as it defends the people of this tent. An evil people do not intend to attack them that something distracts them from it."

Al-Fadl ibn Dukayn reported from Sufyan from Salama ibn Kuhayl from Abu Sadiq that 'Abdullah said, "I know the first of the people of houses whom the Dajjal will strike." They asked, "Who is it, Abu 'Abd ar-Rahman?" He answered, "You, people of Kufa."

Sufyan ibn 'Uyayna reported from Bayan from ash-Sha'bi that Qaraza ibn Ka'b al-Ansari said, "We wanted to go to Kufa and 'Umar accompanied us to Sirar and did *wudu'* and washed twice. He asked, 'Do you know why I accompanied you?' We replied, 'Yes. We are the Companions of the Messenger of Allah ﷺ.' He said, 'You are going to the people of a town in which the sound of the humming of the Qur'an is like the humming of bees. Do not counter them with *hadiths* so to distract them. Unleash the Qur'an and have few transmissions from the Messenger of Allah ﷺ. Carry it out and I will be your partner.'"

Sulayman ibn Dawud at-Tayalisi reported from Shu'ba that Salama ibn Kuhayl heard Habba al-'Arabi say, "'Umar ibn al-Khattab wrote to the people of Kufa: 'People of Kufa, you are the head of the Arabs and their skull and my arrow which I shoot if someone comes to me from here and there. I have sent 'Abdullah to you and I have chosen for you and preferred him for you over myself.'"

Wahb ibn Jarir ibn Hazim and Yahya ibn 'Abbad reported from Shu'ba from Abu Ishaq that Haritha ibn al-Mudarrib said, "I read the letter of 'Umar ibn al-Khattab to the people of Kufa: 'I have sent 'Ammar to you as governor and 'Abdullah as a teacher and helper (*wazir*). They are among the nobles of the Companions of the Messenger of Allah ﷺ, so listen to them and obey them. I have preferred you with 'Abdullah over myself.'"

'Ubaydullah ibn Musa reported from Isra'il from Abu Ishaq that Haritha said, "The letter of 'Umar was read to us: 'I have sent you 'Ammar ibn Yasar as governor and 'Abdullah ibn Mas'ud as a teacher and a helper. They are among the nobles of the Companions of the Messenger of Allah ﷺ, the people of Badr. I have put 'Abdullah ibn Mas'ud in charge of your treasury. Learn from them and obey them. I have preferred you with 'Abdullah ibn Mas'ud over myself.'"

Haritha said, "Hudhayfa was sent as governor of al-Mada'in. Their provision was a sheep: 'Ammar had half of it, Ibn Mas'ud had a fourth and Hudhayfa had a fourth."

Waki' ibn al-Jarrah, al-Fadl ibn Dukayn and Qabisa ibn 'Uqba reported from Sufyan from Abu Ishaq that Haritha ibn Mudarrib said, "'Umar ibn al-Khattab wrote to the people of Kufa." (Waki' has: "The letter of 'Umar was read to us"): 'I have sent you 'Ammar ibn Yasir as governor and Ibn Mas'ud as a teacher and helper.'"

Abu Nu'aym and Qabisa said, "A teacher and helper. They are among the nobles of the Companions of Muhammad ﷺ from the people of Badr. Imitate them and listen to their words. I have preferred you to myself by giving you 'Abdullah."

Waki' added, "I have appointed Ibn Mas'ud over your treasury and put 'Uthman ibn Hunayf in charge of the Sawad and provided them with a sheep every day. I appoint half of it and its valley for 'Ammar ibn Yasir and the other half is shared between you."

'Affan ibn Muslim and Musa ibn Isma'il reported from Wuhayb from Dawud from 'Amir that the Muhajir 'Abdullah ibn Mas'ud was at Hims and 'Umar sent him to Kufa and wrote to them: "By Allah – there is no god but He – I have preferred you with him over himself, so take him."

Qabisa ibn 'Uqba reported from Sufyan from al-Ajlah from Abu Hamza from Ibrahim that 'Alqama said, "I heard 'Umar say, 'I have preferred the people of Kufa with 'Abdullah before myself.'"

Muhammad ibn 'Ubayd at-Tanafisi reported from Jubaybir that ad-Dahhak said that 'Umar said, "I preferred the people of Makka with Ibn Umm 'Abd to myself. He is the most superior of you, an enclosure filled with knowledge."

Ma'n ibn 'Isa reported from Mu'awiya ibn Salih from Asad ibn Wada'a that 'Umar ibn al-Khattab mentioned Ibn Mas'ud and said, "An enclosure filled with knowledge which I have preferred for the people of al-Qadisiyya."

Waki' reported from al-A'mash from Malik ibn al-Harith that Abu Khalid, one of the companions of 'Umar, said, "We came to 'Umar and he gave us a stipend and gave a greater to the people of Syria than to us and so we said, 'Amir al-Mu'minin, do you give more to the people of Syria than to us?' He answered, 'People of Kufa, are you annoyed that I have given more to the people of Syria than you because of the distance of your journey? I have preferred you by giving you Ibn Umm 'Abd.'"

Ahmad ibn 'Abdullah ibn Yunus reported from al-Hasan ibn Salih from 'Ubayda that Ibrahim said, "Three hundred of the people of the Tree and seventy of the people of Badr stayed in Kufa. We do not know of any of them who shortened or prayed two *rak'at*s before *Maghrib*."

'Ubaydullah ibn Musa reported from Isra'il that 'Uthman ibn al-Mughira said, "I was sitting with Salim when a woman came to him to ask him for a *fatwa*. She related to us: 'The head of 'A'isha was in my lap which I was delousing and she said, 'There is no mosque which I would have liked to pray four *rak'at*s in more than the mosque of Kufa.'"

Al-Fadl ibn Dukayn reported from Sufyan from al-A'mash from Khaythama that 'Abdullah ibn 'Amr said, "There is no day but that some of the blessing of the Garden descends in your Euphrates."

Al-Fadl ibn al-Dukayn reported from Isra'il from 'Ammar ad-Dahni from Salim ibn Abi al-Ja'd that 'Abdullah ibn 'Amr said, "The happiest of people with the Mahdi will be the people of Kufa."

Al-Fadl ibn al-Dukayn and Ishaq ibn Yusuf al-Azraq reported from Malik ibn Mighwal that al-Qasim that 'Ali said, "The companions of 'Abdullah are the lamps of this town."

Shihab ibn 'Abbad al-'Abdi reported from Ibrahim ibn Humayd ar-Rawasi from Isma'il ibn Abi Khalid that 'Amir said, "None of the Companions of the Prophet 爨 had more *fiqh* than our companion 'Abdullah (i.e. Ibn Mas'ud)."

Ahmad ibn 'Abdullah ibn Yunus reported from Abu Bakr ibn 'Ayyash that al-Mughira said, "The most truthful of people with people about 'Ali are the companions of 'Abdullah."

Qabisa ibn 'Uqba reported from Sufyan from al-'Ala' ibn al-Musayyab that Abu Ya'la said, "There were thirty men in the Banu Thawr and there was no man in them less than ar-Rabi' ibn Khuthaym."

Ishaq ibn Yusuf al-Azraq and Qabisa ibn 'Uqba reported from Sufyan ath-Thawri from Mansur that Ibrahim said, "The companions of 'Abdullah who used to recite and give *fatwa* were six: 'Alqama, al-Aswad, Masruq, 'Abida, al-Harith ibn Qays and 'Amr ibn Shurahbil.

'Affan ibn Muslim reported from Hammad ibn Salama from Ayyub that Muhammad said, "The companions of 'Abdullah ibn Mas'ud were five. Some of them advanced 'Abida and some of them advanced 'Alqama. They do not disagree that Shurayh was the last of them." It was said to Hammad, "Count them," He said, "'Abida, 'Alqama, Masruq, al-Hamdhani and Shurayh."

Hammad said, "I do not know if he began with al-Hamdhani or Shurayh."

Rawh ibn 'Ubada reported from Hisham that Muhammad said, "The companions of 'Abdullah ibn Mas'ud are those who preserved his *hadith*s are five. All of them made Shurayh the last of them." He said, "Some of them began with al-Harith, then 'Abida, and some began with 'Abida and then al-Harith and then 'Alqama ibn Masruq."

'Ubaydullah ibn Musa reported from 'Abd al-Jabbar ibn 'Abbas that his father said, "I sat with 'Ata' and began to question him. He said to me, 'Where are you from?' I answered, 'From the people of Kufa.' 'Ata' said, 'Knowledge has only come to us from you.'"

Muhammad ibn 'Abdullah al-Asadi reported from Sufyan that 'Umara ibn al-Qa'qa' said that he heard Shubruma say, "I have not see anyone alive with more worship and *fiqh* than the Banu Thawr."

'Arim ibn al-Fadl reported from Hammad ibn Zayd from Ibn 'Awn that Muhammad said, "I have not seen a people with more knowledge than a people whom I left in Kufa from a people in whom is boldness."

Muhammad ibn Sa'd said that he was informed that Sufyan ibn 'Uyayna said, "A man asked al-Hasan, 'Abu Sa'id, the people of Basra or the people of Kufa?" He said, "'Umar began with the people of Kufa and all the houses of the Arabs are there but not in Basra."

Ibn Sa'd said that he was informed from Ibn Idris that Malik ibn Mighwal said that ash-Sha'bi said, "None of the Companions of Muhammad ﷺ entered it with more beneficial knowledge or more *fiqh* than one of his Companions (meaning Ibn Mas'ud)."

Muhammad ibn Sa'd said that Sufyan ibn 'Uyayna said that ash-Sha'bi said, "I have not seen anyone with greater forbearance or more knowledge or more reluctance to shed blood than the companions of 'Abdullah except for the Companions of the Messenger of Allah ﷺ."

Muhammad ibn Sa'd said that Sufyan ibn 'Uyayna said that Mis'ar said, "I asked Habib ibn Abi Habib, 'Do these or those have more knowledge?' He said, 'Those.'"

'Ali ibn Abi Talib

'Ali ibn Abi Talib ibn 'Abd al-Malik ibn Hashim ibn 'Abd Manaf ibn Qusayy. His *kunya* was Abu al-Hasan. His mother was Fatima bint Asad ibn Hashim ibn 'Abd Manaf ibn Qusayy. He was present at Badr. He settled in Kufa in the square which was called Rahba 'Ali in special parts there. He did not stay in the fortress where the governors before him had stayed. He was murdered, may Allah have mercy on him, on the morning of Jumu'a night 19 Ramadan 40 AH when he was sixty-three. He was buried in Kufa at the Jumu'a mosque in the governor's fortress. The one who murdered him was 'Abd ar-Rahman ibn Muljam al-Muradi. He was a Kharijite – may Allah curse him. 'Ali related from Abu Bakr as-Siddiq. We wrote his report under those who were present at Badr.

Sa'd ibn Abi Waqqas

Abu Waqqas's name was Malik ibn Uhayb ibn 'Abd al-Manaf ibn Zuhra ibn Kilab. His *kunya* was Abu Ishaq. His mother was Hamna bint Sufyan ibn Umayya ibn 'Abd Shams ibn 'Abd Manaf ibn Qusayy. He was present at Badr. He is the one who was victorious at al-Qadisiyya. He founded Kufa and laid out its areas for the Arab tribes and built houses there. He was its governor for both 'Umar ibn al-Khattab and 'Uthman ibn 'Affan. Then he was dismissed and al-Walid ibn 'Uqba ibn Abi Mu'ayt was appointed after him and Sa'd returned to Madina and he died in his fortress at al-'Aqiq which is about ten miles from Madina. He was carried to Madina on the shoulders of men and buried in al-Baqi' in 55 AH. Marwan ibn al-Hakam prayed over him. At that time Marwan was the governor of Madina for Mu'awiya. On the day he died, Sa'd was over seventy. He had gone blind. That is what Muhammad ibn 'Umar said at the time of his death. Others said that he died in 50 AH. We recorded his reports among those who were present at Badr.

Sa'id ibn Zayd

Sa'id ibn Zayd ibn 'Amr ibn Nufayl ibn 'Abd al-'Uzza ibn Rabah ibn 'Abdullah ibn Qurt ibn Razzah ibn 'Adi ibn Ka'b. His *kunya* was Abu al-A'war. His mother was Fatima bint Ba'ja ibn Umayya ibn Khuwaylid ibn Khalid ibn al-Ma'mur ibn Hayyan ibn Ghanm ibn Mulayh of Khuza'a. He was present at the Battle of Badr. He was at Kufa and lived there and then returned to Madina and died at al-'Aqiq. He was carried on the shoulders of men and buried in Madina. Sa'd ibn Abi Waqqas and Ibn 'Umar went down into his grave. That was in 50 AH and he was over seventy at that time. That is what Muhammad ibn 'Umar said about the time of his death. Others said that he died in Kufa in the caliphate of Mu'awiya and al-Mughira ibn Shu'ba, the governor of Kufa at that time for Mu'awiya, prayed over him. We wrote his reports under those who were present at Badr.

'Abdullah ibn Mas'ud al-Hudhali

An ally of the Banu Zuhra ibn Kilab. His *kunya* was Abu 'Abd ar-Rahman. He was present at Badr. He emigrated to Hims and 'Umar ibn al-Khattab sent him to Kufa and wrote to the people of Kufa, "I have sent you 'Abdullah ibn Mas'ud as a teacher and helper. I have preferred you for him over myself, so take him." He went to Kufa and settled there and built a house there beside the mosque. Then he went to Madina in the caliphate of 'Uthman ibn 'Affan and died there and was buried in al-Baqi' in 32 AH while he was over sixty. We wrote his reports with those who were at Badr.

'Ammar ibn Yasir

Of 'Ans from Yemen. He was the ally of the Banu Makhzum. His *kunya* was Abu al-Yaqzan. He settled in Kufa and remained with 'Ali ibn Abi Talib and was present at his battles with him. He was killed at Siffin in 37 AH and was buried there at the age of ninety-three. He was present at Badr and his reports are among those who were present at Badr.

Khabbab ibn al-Aratt

A *mawla* of Umm Anmar bint Siba' ibn 'Abd al-'Uzza al-Khuza'iyya, the allies of the Banu Zuhra ibn Kilab. His *kunya* was Abu 'Abdullah. He was present at Badr.

Muhammad ibn Sa'd said that he heard those some say that he was a man of the Arabs from the Banu Sa'd ibn Zayd Manat ibn Tamim. He was taken captive and Umm Anmar bought him and set him free. He settled in Kufa and built a house there in the crossroads of Khunays. He died there while returning with 'Ali from Siffin in 37 AH and 'Ali prayed over him and buried him outside Kufa. On the day he died he was seventy-three. We wrote his reports among those who were present at Badr.

Sahl ibn Hunayf

Sahl ibn Hunayf ibn Wahib ibn 'Ukaym of the Banu Jusham ibn 'Awf ibn 'Amr ibn 'Awf of Aws. His *kunya* was Abu 'Adi. He was present at Badr. When 'Ali ibn Abi Talib left Madina, appointed him over Madina and wrote to him to join him. He joined him and remained with it and was present at Siffin with him. Then he returned to Kufa and remained there until he died in 38 AH. 'Ali ibn Abi Talib prayed over him and said the *takbir* over him six times. He said that he is one of the people of Badr. We wrote his reports among those who were present at Badr.

Hudhayfa ibn al-Yaman

Al-Yaman is Husayl ibn Jabir of the Banu 'Abs, the allies of the Banu 'Abd al-Ashhal. His *kunya* was Abu 'Abdullah. He was present at Uhud and the battles after that. He died in al-Mada'in in 36 AH. He had come to announce the death of 'Uthman there. He lived in Kufa and al-Mada'in and has descendants in Mada'in. We wrote his reports among those who were present at Uhud.

Abu Qatada ibn Rib'i al-Ansari

Then one of the Banu Salama of Khazraj. He was present at Uhud. His name, according to Muhammad ibn Ishaq, was al-Harith ibn Rib'i.

'Abdullah ibn Muhammad ibn 'Umara al-Ansari and Muhammad ibn 'Umar said that his name was an-Nu'man ibn Rib'i. Others said that he was 'Amr ibn Rib'i. He settled in Kufa and died there while 'Ali was there and he prayed over him. Muhammad ibn 'Umar denied that and said that Yahya ibn 'Abdullah ibn Abi Qatada related to him that Abu Qatada died in Madina in 54 AH at the age of seventy.

Abu Mas'ud al-Ansari

His name was 'Uqba ibn 'Amr of the Banu Khudara ibn 'Awf ibn al-Harith ibn al-Khazraj. He was present at the night of the Pledge of 'Aqaba while a child. He was not present at Badr or Uhud and he settled in Kufa. When 'Ali left for Siffin, he put him in charge of Kufa. Then he dismissed and Abu Mas'ud returned to Madina and died there at the end of the caliphate of Mu'awiya ibn Abi Sufyan. His descendants ended and none of them are left.

Abu Musa al-Ash'ari of Madhhij

His name was 'Abdullah ibn Qays.

Muhammad ibn Sa'd said that he heard someone who mentioned that he became Muslim in Makka and emigrated to Abyssinia and the first event he attended was Khaybar. 'Umar ibn al-Khattab appointed him over Basra and then dismissed him and he settled in Kufa and built a house there and has descendants there. 'Uthman ibn 'Affan appointed him over Kufa and 'Uthman was murdered while Musa was in charge of it. Then 'Ali came to Kufa and Abu Musa remained with him and was one of the two arbiters. He died in Kufa in 42 AH. Muhammad ibn 'Umar reported from Khalid ibn Ilyas that Abu Bakr ibn 'Abdullah ibn Abi Jahm said, "Abu Musa was not one of those who emigrated to Abyssinia. He died in 52."

Salman al-Farisi

His *kunya* was Abu 'Abdullah. He became Muslim when the Prophet ﷺ came to Madina. Before that he had read Scriptures and sought religion. He was a slave of one of the Banu Qurayza. He gave him a *kitaba* and the Messenger of Allah ﷺ settled his *kitaba*. He was freed and his *wala'* connected to the Banu Hashim. The first battle he attended was the Ditch. He settled in Kufa and died in al-Mada'in while 'Uthman ibn 'Affan was caliph.

Al-Bara' ibn 'Azib

Al-Bara' ibn 'Azib ibn al-Harith al-Ansari from the Banu Haritha ibn al-Harith of Aws. His *kunya* was Abu 'Umara. He lived in Kufa and built a house there.

Muhammad ibn 'Umar said that he went to Madina and died there. Someone else said that he died in the time of Mus'ab ibn az-Zubayr and has descendants in Kufa. He related from Abu Bakr.

'Ubayd ibn 'Azib

The brother of al-Bara'. He was one of the ten Ansar whom 'Umar ibn al-Khattab sent with 'Ammar ibn Yasir to Kufa. He has descendants in Kufa.

Qaraza ibn Ka'b al-Ansari

One of the Banu al-Harith ibn al-Khazraj, the ally of the Banu 'Abd al-Ashhal of Aws. His *kunya* was Abu 'Amr. He was one of the ten Ansar whom 'Umar ibn al-Khattab sent to Kufa and he settled there and built a house there in the Ansar. He died there in the caliphate of 'Ali ibn Abi Talib. He prayed over him in Kufa.

Zayd ibn Arqam al-Ansari

One of the al-Harith ibn al-Khazraj.

Muhammad ibn 'Umar said that his *kunya* was Abu Sa'd. Another said that his *kunya* was Abu Unays. The first battle he attended with the Prophet 鬱 was al-Muraysi'. He settled in Kufa and built a house there in the Ansar.

'Abdullah ibn Yazid

'Abdullah ibn Yazid ibn Zayd al-Khatmi of the Ansar. He settled in Kufa and built a house there and died there in the caliphate of 'Abdullah ibn az-Zubayr. 'Abdullah appointed him over Kufa.

An-Nu'man ibn 'Amr

An-Nu'man ibn 'Amr ibn Muqarrin ibn 'A'idh ibn Mija ibn Hujayr ibn Nasr ibn Hubshiyya ibn Ka'b ibn 'Abd ibn Thawr ibn Hudhma ibn Latim ibn 'Uthman ibn Muzina. His *kunya* was Abu 'Amr. The first of his battles was the Ditch. He settled in Kufa and 'Umar ibn al-Khattab appointed him over Kaskar and then dismissed him and sent him against the people in the Battle of Nihawand.

Muhammad ibn 'Umar reported from Kathir ibn 'Abdullah al-Muzani from his father from his grandfather who was present at Nihawand, said, "The commander of the people on that day was an-Nu'man ibn 'Amr ibn Muqarrin. When Allah defeated them, the first to be slain was an-Nu'man ibn Muqarrin."

Muhammad ibn 'Umar said that Nihawand took place in 21 AH.

Sulayman Abu Dawud at-Tayalisi reported from Shu'ba that Iyas ibn Abi Mu'awiya said, "Sa'id ibn al-Musayyab asked me, 'Who are you from?' I answered, 'I am a man of the tribe of Muzayna.' Sa'id ibn al-Musayyab said, 'I remember the day when the death of 'Umar ibn al-Khattab was announced by an-Nu'man ibn Muqarrin on the minbar.'"

Ma'qil ibn Muqarrin

His brother. He is Abu 'Abdullah ibn Ma'qil. They have descendants in Kufa.

Sinan ibn Muqarrin

Their brother. He was present at the Ditch.

Suwayd ibn Muqarrin

Their brother. His *kunya* was Abu 'Ali.

'Abd ar-Rahman ibn Muqarrin

Their brother.

'Aqil ibn Muqarrin

Their brother. His *kunya* was Abu Hakim.

'Abd ar-Rahman ibn 'Aqil ibn Muqarrin

Muhammad ibn 'Umar reported from Ishaq ibn Yahya ibn Talha that Mujahid said, "The weepers were the Banu Muqarrin. They were seven."

Muhammad ibn 'Umar said, "I heard that they were present at the Ditch."

Al-Mughira ibn Shu'ba

Al-Mughira ibn Shu'ba ibn Abi 'Amir ibn Mas'ud ibn Mu'attib ibn Malik ibn Ka'b ibn 'Amr ibn Sa'd ibn 'Awf ibn Thaqif. His *kunya* was Abu 'Abdullah. The first of his expeditions was al-Hudaybiya. 'Umar ibn al-Khattab put him in charge of Basra and then dismissed him and after that appointed him over Kufa. 'Umar was murdered while he was in charge of Kufa. 'Uthman ibn 'Affan dismissed him from that post and appointed Sa'd ibn Abi Waqqas. When Mu'awiya became caliph, he appointed al-Mughira ibn Shu'ba over Kufa and al-Mughira died there.

'Abd ar-Rahman ibn Muhammad al-Muharibi said that he heard 'Abd al-Malik ibn 'Umayr say, "I saw al-Mughira ibn Shu'ba speaking to people on the *'Id* on a camel and I saw him using yellow dye."

Muhammad ibn 'Umar reported from Muhammad ibn Abi Musa ath-Thaqafi that his father said, "Al-Mughira ibn Shu'ba died in Kufa in Sha'ban 50 in the caliphate of Mu'awiya. He was seventy. He was a tall man, blind in one eye which had been wounded in the Battle of Yarmuk."

Waki' ibn al-Jarrah reported from Mis'ar that Ziyad ibn 'Ilaqa said that he heard Jarir ibn 'Abdullah say when al-Mughira ibn Shu'ba died, "Ask for well-being for your governor. He used to love well-being."

Khalid ibn 'Urfuta

Khalid ibn 'Urfuta ibn Abraha ibn Sinan al-'Udhri from Quda'a, an ally of the Banu Zuhra ibn Kilab. He was a Companion of the Prophet ﷺ. He related from him. Sa'd ibn Abi Waqqas was put in charge of the fighting at al-Qadisiyya. He is the one who killed the Kharijites in the Battle of an-Nukhayla. He settled in Kufa after that and built a house there and still has descendants today.

'Abdullah ibn Abi Awfa

His name was 'Alqama ibn Khalid ibn al-Harith ibn Abi Usayd ibn Rifa'a ibn Tha'laba ibn Hawazin ibn Aslam ibn Afsa of Khuza'a. His *kunya* was Abu Mu'awiya.

Hisham ibn 'Abd al-Malik Abu al-Walid at-Tayalisi reported from Shu'ba that 'Amr reported: "I listened to 'Abdullah ibn Abi Awfa and he was one of the people of the Tree (al-Hudaybiya)."

Muhammad ibn 'Umar said that 'Abdullah ibn Abi Awfa remained in Madina until the Prophet ﷺ died and he moved to Madina and settled there when the Muslims settled there and built a house there among Aslam. He lost his sight and died in Kufa on 86 AH.

Muhammad ibn 'Umar reported from Khulayd ibn Da'laj from Qatada that al-Hasan said, "'Abdullah ibn Abi Awfa was the last of the Companions of the Prophet ﷺ to die in Kufa."

'Adi ibn Hatim at-Ta'ifi

One of the Banu Thu'al. His *kunya* was Abu Tarif. He settled in Kufa and built a house there among Tayy'. He remained with 'Ali ibn Abi Talib and was present with him at the Camel and Siffin. He lost his eye in the Battle of the Camel. He died in Kufa in the time of al-Mukhtar in 68 AH.

Jarir ibn 'Abdullah al-Bajali

His *kunya* was Abu 'Amr. He became Muslim in the year in which the Prophet ﷺ died and the Messenger of Allah ﷺ sent him to [the idol] Dhu al-Khalasa and he destroyed it. He settled in Kufa after that and built a house there among the Bajila. He died at Sarat while ad-Dahhak ibn Qays was governor of Kufa. Ad-Dahhak was the governor for two and a half years after Ziyad ibn Abi Sufyan.

Al-Ash'ath ibn Qays ibn Ma'di Karib al-Kindi

One of the Banu al-Harith ibn Mu'awiya. His *kunya* was Abu Muhammad. He came to the Prophet 爨 and then returned to Yemen. When the Prophet 爨 died, he apostatised and Ziyad ibn Labid al-Bayadi laid siege to him at an-Nujayr until he came down to him. He took him and sent him to Abu Bakr as-Siddiq. He was gracious to him and married him to his sister. When the people went out to Iraq, he went with them and settled in Kufa and built a house there among Kinda and died there. Al-Hasan ibn 'Ali ibn Abi Talib was at Kufa when he made peace with Mu'awiya and he prayed over him.

Waki' ibn al-Jarrah reported from Isma'il ibn Abi Khalif from Abu Khalid that Hakim ibn Jabir said, "When al-Ash'ath ibn Qays died while his daughter was married to al-Hasan ibn 'Ali, he said, 'When you wash him, do not hurry to bury him until you tell me.' They told him and he came and performed *wudu'* for him using *hanut*."

Sa'id ibn Hurayth

Sa'id ibn Hurayth ibn 'Amr ibn 'Uthman ibn 'Abdullah ibn 'Umar ibn Makhzum. He is the brother of 'Amr ibn Hurayth. He was older than his brother 'Amr. They say that he was present at the Conquest of Makka with the Prophet 爨 when he was fifteen. Then he moved to Kufa with his brother 'Amr ibn Hurayth.

'Amr ibn Hurayth

His brother, 'Amr ibn Hurayth ibn 'Amr ibn 'Uthman ibn 'Abdullah ibn 'Umar ibn Makhzum. His *kunya* was Abu Sa'id.

Muhammad ibn 'Umar said, "The Prophet 爨 died when 'Amr was twelve."

Al-Fadl ibn al-Dukayn Abu Nu'aym said: "''Amr ibn Hurayth settled in Kufa and built a house there beside the mosque. It is large and famous and contains people of rough silk today."

Muhammad ibn Sa'd said, "When Ziyad ibn Abi Sufyan went to Basra he put 'Amr ibn Hurayth in charge of Kufa."

Al-Fadl ibn al-Dukayn said, "''Amr ibn Hurayth died in Kufa in 85 in the caliphate of 'Abd al-Malik ibn Marwan." He has descendants there.

Samura ibn Junada

Samura ibn Junada ibn Jundub ibn Hujayr ibn Ribab ibn Habib ibn Suwa ibn 'Amir ibn Sa'sa'a. He was a Companion of the Prophet ※ and related from him.

Jabir ibn Samura as-Suwa'i

His son. They were the allies of the Banu Zuhra ibn Kilab. His *kunya* was Abu 'Abdullah. He settled in Kufa and built a house there in the Banu Suwa'a. He died there at the beginning of the caliphate of 'Abd al-Malik ibn Marwan while Bishr ibn Marwan was governor of Kufa.

Hudhayfa ibn Asid al-Ghifari

His *kunya* was Abu Surayha. The first expedition which he attended with the Prophet ※ was al-Hudaybiya. He related from Abu Bakr as-Siddiq. He settled in Kufa after that.

Al-Walid ibn 'Uqba

Al-Walid ibn 'Uqba ibn Abi Mu'ayt ibn Abi 'Amr ibn Umayya ibn 'Abd Shams. His *kunya* was Abu Wahb. His mother was Arwa bint Kurayz ibn Habib ibn 'Abd Shams. He was the brother of 'Uthman ibn 'Affan by the mother. 'Uthman ibn 'Affan appointed him governor of Kufa and he built a large house there beside the mosque. Then 'Uthman dismissed him from Kufa and appointed Sa'id ibn al-'As over it. Al-Walid returned to Madina and remained there until 'Uthman was murdered. When what happened between 'Ali and Mu'awiya happened, al-Walid ibn 'Uqba withdrew from both of them to Raqqa and did not take the side of either of them until the matter was decided. He died in Raqqa and has descendants there and also some children in Kufa. His house in Kufa is the great house, the House of the Fullers.

'Amr ibn al-Hamiq

'Amr ibn al-Hamiq ibn al-Kahin ibn Habib ibn 'Amr ibn al-Qin ibn Razzah ibn 'Amr ibn Sa'd ibn Ka'b ibn 'Amr of Khuza'a. He was a Companion of the Prophet ※ and settled in Kufa and attended the battles of 'Ali with him. He was one of those who travelled to 'Uthman and helped to kill him. Then 'Abd ar-Rahman ibn Umm al-Hakam killed him in Jazira.

Muhammad ibn 'Umar reported from 'Isa ibn 'Abd ar-Rahman that ash-Sha'bi said, "The first head carried in Islam [to the ruler] was that of 'Amr ibn al-Hamiq."

Sulayman ibn Surd ibn al-Jawn

Al-Jawn is 'Abd al-'Uzza ibn Munqidh ibn Rabi'a ibn Asram ibn Dabis ibn Haram ibn Hubaysha ibn Salul ibn Ka'b of Khuza'a. His *kunya* was Abu Mutarrif. His name was Yasar. When he became Muslim, the Messenger of Allah ﷺ named him Sulayman. He was old and settled in Kufa and built a house there among Khuza'a. He was present at Siffin with 'Ali. He was one of those who wrote to al-Husayn to ask him to come to them in Kufa. When al-Husayn came to Kufa, he withdrew from him and was not with him.

When al-Husayn was killed, those who had disappointed him regretted that and repented of their disappointment and they went out and formed an army at an-Nukhayla to seek revenge for the blood of al-Husayn and so they were called the Penitents. They put Sulayman ibn Surd in charge of them and then set out for Syria. When they were at 'Ayn al-Warda in Jazira, the Syrian cavalry under the command of al-Husayn ibn Numayr met them and fought them and most of them were killed, and only a few of them survived. Sulayman ibn Surd was killed on that day in the month of Rabi' al-Akhir 65 AH. He was ninety-three on the day he was killed.

Hani' ibn Aws al-Aslami

He settled in Kufa and built a house there among Aslam. He died in the caliphate of Mu'awiya ibn Abi Sufyan while al-Mughira ibn Shu'ba was governor.

'Ubaydullah ibn Musa reported from Isra'il from Majza'a from Hani' ibn Aws. He was one of those who had been at the Tree. He had something wrong with his knee and when he prostrated, he put a pillow under his knee.

Wa'il ibn Hujr al-Hadrami

Musa ibn Mas'ud Abu Hudhayfa reported from Sufyan ibn Sa'id ath-Thawr from 'Asim ibn Kulayb from his father that Wa'il ibn Hujr said, "I went to the Prophet ﷺ and I had some poetry. He said, 'Flies,' and I went and took from my poetry and then came to him. He said, 'Why have you taken some of your poetry?' I said, 'I heard you say, "Flies" and I thought you meant me.' He said, 'I did not mean you. This is better."

He said that *dhabab* is a Yamani word.

Safwan ibn 'Assal al-Muradi

He was from the Banu ar-Rabad ibn Zahir ibn 'Amir ibn 'Awbathan ibn Zahir ibn Murad and their numbers in Jamal.

'Amr ibn 'Asim al-Kilabi reported from Hammam ibn Yahya from 'Asim that Zirr ibn Hubays said, "I met Safwan ibn 'Assal al-Muradi and asked him, 'Did you see the Messenger of Allah ﷺ?' He replied, 'Yes, and I went on twelve expeditions with him.'"

Muhammad ibn Sa'd said that 'Abd as-Samad ibn 'Abd al-Warith related this *hadith* from Hammam and in it he quoted from Zirr: "I came in the caliphate of 'Uthman and was carried on a cushion. I met Ubayy ibn Ka'b and the Companions of the Messenger of Allah ﷺ. I met Safwan ibn 'Assal al-Muradi."

Usama ibn Sharik ath-Tha'labi

One of Qays 'Aylan. His *hadith* is: "I was with the Messenger of Allah ﷺ when the desert Arabs came to ask him."

Malik ibn 'Awf

Malik ibn 'Awf ibn Nadla ibn Khadij ibn Habib ibn Hadid ibn Ghanm ibn Ka'b ibn 'Usayma ibn Jusham ibn Mu'awiya ibn Bakr ibn Hawazin of Qays 'Aylan. He was the father of Abu al-Ahwas, the companion of 'Abdullah ibn Mas'ud.

'Affan ibn Muslim reported from Shu'ba from Abu Ishaq who heard Abu al-Ahwas relate that his father said, "I went to the Prophet ﷺ when I had a coarse appearance. He asked, 'Do you not have wealth?' I answered, 'Yes.' He asked, 'What is your wealth?' I answered, 'Every sort: horses, camels, slaves and sheep.' He said, 'When Allah gives you wealth, it should be seen on you.'"

'Amir ibn Shahr al-Hamdani

Muhammad ibn Sa'd said that Abu Usama said that Mujalid related from ash-Sha'bi that 'Amir ibn Shahr said, "Hamdan fortified themselves in the mountain of al-Haql against the army. Allah protected them by it until the Persians came against Hamdan. They continued to fight them until the people were averse to war and the business seemed too long for them and the Messenger of Allah 鬄 came across them. Hamdan [the tribe] said to me, "Amir ibn Shahr, you have been a close companion of kings for a long time. Go to this man and explore things for us. If you are pleased with something for us, we will accept it. If you dislike something for us, we dislike it.' I said, 'I will do it.' I went to the Messenger of Allah 鬄 in Madina and I sat with him. A group went to him and said, 'Messenger of Allah, command us.' He said, 'I command you to have *taqwa* of Allah and to listen to the words of Quraysh and let them act.' I was content, by Allah, with what he was asked and I was satisfied by what he said. Then it seemed to me proper that I should not return to my people until I had gone by the Negus who was a friend of mine. So I went by him and while I was sitting with him, a young son of his passed by him. He asked him to read a tablet he had and the boy read it and I laughed. The Negus said, 'What are you laughing at?' I said, 'At what the boy just read.' He said, 'By Allah, it is part of what was revealed on the tongue of Jesus son of Mary. The curse will be in the earth when its rulers are children.' I returned having heard these words from the Prophet 鬄 and these words from the Negus. My people became Muslim and descended to the plains. The Messenger of Allah 鬄 wrote this letter to 'Umayr Dhu Murran."

He said, "The Messenger of Allah 鬄 sent Malik ibn Murara ar-Rahawi to all of Yemen and 'Akk Dhu Khaywan became Muslim. He went to the Messenger of Allah 鬄 and received security from him for his village and property. He had a village which contained slaves and property. He went to the Messenger of Allah 鬄 and said, 'Messenger of Allah, Malik ibn Murara ar-Rahawi came to us to invite us to Islam and we became Muslim. I have land which contains slaves and wealth, so write a document for me.' The Messenger of Allah 鬄

wrote: 'In the Name of Allah, the All-Merciful, Most Merciful. From Muhammad, the Messenger of Allah to 'Akk Dhu Khaywan: if he is truthful in his land, property and wealth, he has the security of Allah and the *dhimma* of His Messenger.' Khalid ibn Sa'id wrote it.'"

Nubayt ibn Shurayt al-Ashja'i

He was one of Qays 'Aylan. He is Abu Salama ibn Nubayt.

Al-Fadl ibn Dukayn reported that Salama ibn Nubayt said, "My father said, 'I went on *hajj* with my father and uncle and my father said to me, "Do you see the one on the red camel who is speaking? That is the Messenger of Allah.""'

Malik ibn Isma'il reported from Musa ibn Muhammad al-Ansari from Abu Malik al-Ashja'i that Nubayt ibn Shurayt said, "I was riding behind my father on the rump of the camel while the Prophet ﷺ was speaking at the *Jamra*. He said, 'Praise be to Allah. We seek help and ask His forgiveness and we bear witness that there is no god but Allah and Muhammad is His slave and Messenger. I command you to have *taqwa* of Allah. Which day is sacred?' They answered, 'This one.' He said, 'What month is sacred?' They replied, 'This month.' He said, 'What land is sacred?' They answered, 'This land.' He said, 'Your blood and property are sacrosanct to you like the sanctity of this day in this month in this land.'"

Mu'ammil ibn Isma'il reported that Sufyan that Salama ibn Nubayt said, "I said to my father who was present with the Prophet ﷺ and saw him and listened to him, 'Father, if you deceive this ruler, I will attack him and your people will take on your side.' He said, 'My son, I fear to take a position with them that will bring me to Hell.' I heard my father say, 'I saw the Prophet ﷺ giving a *khutba* on the Day of Sacrifice on a red camel.'"

Salama ibn Yazid

Salama ibn Yazid ibn Mashja'a ibn al-Mujamma' ibn Malik ibn Ka'b ibn Sa'd ibn 'Awf ibn Harim ibn Ju'fi ibn Sa'd al-'Ashira of Madhhij. He came in a delegation to the Prophet ﷺ and became Muslim. He related from that when the Prophet ﷺ was speaking, he stood up and said, "Messenger of Allah, do you think that we will have rulers after you who ask the right of us while they deny it to us?"

'Arfaja ibn Shurayh al-Ashja'i

He was called Ibn Durayh.

Sakhr ibn al-'Ayla

Sakhr ibn al-'Ayla ibn 'Abdullah ibn Rabi'a ibn'Amr ibn 'Amir ibn 'Ali ibn Aslam ibn Ahmas from Bajila. His *kunya* was Abu Hazim. He belonged to a house of [the tribe of] Ahmas.

Waki' and al-Fadl ibn Dukayn reported from Aban ibn 'Abdullah al-Bajali from 'Uthman ibn Abi Hazim that Sakhr ibn al-'Ayla said, "I took the aunt of al-Mughira ibn Shu'ba to the Messenger of Allah ﷺ. They said, 'Al-Mughira has come.' The Messenger of Allah ﷺ questioned his aunt and she said that she was with me. The Messenger of Allah ﷺ summoned me and said, 'Sakhr, when the people become Muslim, protect their property and lives. Give it to him.' The Messenger of Allah ﷺ had given me water for the Banu Sulaym. They went to the Prophet of Allah ﷺ and asked him for water and so the Prophet of Allah ﷺ summoned me and said, 'Sakhr, when the people become Muslim, protect their property and lives. Give it to them.' So I gave it to them."

'Urwa ibn Mudarris

'Urwa ibn Mudarris ibn Aws ibn Haritha ibn Lam at-Ta'i. He became Muslim and was a Companion of the Prophet ﷺ. He settled in Kufa after that. He is the one who sent Khalid ibn al-Walid with him with 'Uyayna ibn Hisn when he was captured on the Day of Butah as an apostate to Abu Bakr as-Siddiq. He said that Butah is a water source of the Banu Tamim.

Al-Fadl ibn Dukayn reported from Zakariyya' from 'Amir that 'Urwa ibn Mufarris ibn Aws ibn Haritha ibn Lam related that he went on *hajj* in the time of the Messenger of Allah ﷺ and only joined the people at night at Jam'. He went to the Messenger of Allah ﷺ to 'Arafat at night and went on from it and then returned to Jam' and went to the Messenger of Allah and said, "Messenger of Allah, I worked myself and made my camel lean. Do I have any of the *hajj*?"

He said, "If someone performs the Evening Prayer with us at Jam' and stands with us until we pour on and he also pours on from 'Arafat before that at night or day, he has completed his *hajj* and finished his dishevelled state."

Al-Hulb ibn Yazid

Al-Hulb ibn Yazid ibn 'Adi ibn Qunafa ibn 'Adi ibn 'Abd Shams ibn 'Adi ibn Akhzam at-Ta'i. His name was Salama. He went in a delegation to the Prophet ﷺ. He was bald. The Prophet ﷺ stroked his head and his hair grew and so he was called al-Hulb [hairy]. Abu Qabisa ibn Hulb related from him.

Zahir Abu Mijza'a ibn Zahir al-Aslami

He was one of those who gave allegiance under the Tree and he settled in Kufa.

Nafi' ibn 'Utba

Nafi' ibn 'Utba ibn Abi Waqqas ibn Uhayb ibn 'Abd Manaf ibn Zuhra. He was the brother of Sa'd ibn Abi Waqqas.

Labid ibn Rabi'a

Labid ibn Rabi'a ibn Malik ibn Ja'far ibn Kilab ibn Rabi'a ibn 'Amir ibn Sa'sa'a the poet. His *kunya* was Abu 'Aqil. He came to the Messenger of Allah ﷺ and became Muslim and returned to the land of his people and then he emigrated to Kufa and settled there with some of his sons. He died there on the night that Mu'awiya camped at an-Nukhayla to make peace with al-Hasan ibn 'Ali, may Allah have mercy on both of them. He was buried in the desert of the Banu Ja'far ibn Kilab and his sons returned to the desert. Labid did not compose any poetry in Islam and said, "Allah has given me the Qur'an to replace it."·

Habba and Sawa'

The sons of Khalid al-Asadi from Asad ibn Khuza'a.

'Affan ibn Muslim reported from Jarir ibn Hazim from al-A'mash from Sallam ibn Shurahbil that Habba ibn Khalid and Sawa' ibn Khalid said, "We came to the Messenger of Allah ﷺ while he was

113

building a structure of his and we helped him with it until he finished it. He taught us and part of what he taught us was that we should not despair of good as long as our heads move. Every child is born is born red with no covering and then Allah provides for him and gives to him."

Salama ibn Qays al-Ashja'i

He was a Companion of the Prophet ﷺ who settled in Kufa.

Tha'laba ibn al-Hakam al-Laythi

He became Muslim and was present with the Messenger of Allah ﷺ at Hunayn.

'Urwa ibn Abi al-Ja'd al-Bariqi of Azd

Al-Fadl ibn Sukayn reported from al-Hasan ibn Salih from Ash'ath that ash-Sha'bi said, "Before Shurayh the qadi of Kufa was 'Urwa ibn Abi al-Ja'd al-Bariqi and Salman ibn Rabi'a."

Muhammad ibn Sa'd said in other than this *hadith*, "'Urwa was a *murabit* at Baraz ar-Ruz. He had a horse in it which he got for twenty thousand dirhams."

Sa'id ibn Mansur reported from Sufyan that Shabib ibn Gharqada said, "I saw that 'Urwa al-Bariqi had about seventy horses." 'Urwa is the one who related from the Prophet ﷺ, "Good is found in the forelocks of horses until the Day of Rising."

Samura ibn Jundub

Samura ibn Jundub ibn Hilal ibn Kharij ibn Murra ibn Hazn ibn 'Amr ibn Jabir ibn Khushayn ibn La'yy ibn 'Usaym ibn Shamkh ibn Fazara. He had an alliance with the Ansar and was a Companion of the Prophet ﷺ. Ziyad ibn Abi Sufyan appointed him over Basra when he went to Kufa.

Wahb ibn Jarir ibn Hazim reported I think from his father that he heard Abu Yazid al-Mada'ini say, "When Samura ibn Jundub was in his final illness, he experienced great cold and so I kindled a fire for him and put a fire-pot before him, one behind him, one to his right and one to his left. That did not help him and he said, 'What will I do with what is in my belly?' He continued like that until he died."

Jundub ibn Sulaym

Jundub ibn Sulaym ibn al-Harith ibn 'Awf ibn Tha'laba ibn 'Amir ibn Dhuhl ibn Mazin ibn Dhubyan ibn Tha'laba ibn ad-Dul ibn Sa'd Manat ibn Ghamid of Azd. It is the house of Azd in Kufa. He became Muslim and was a Companion of the Prophet 襐 and settled in Kufa after that his son Abu Makhnaf Lut ibn Yahya.

Al-Harith ibn Hassan al-Bakri

'Affan ibn Muslim reported from Sallam Abu al-Mundhir from 'Asim ibn Bahdala from Abu Wa'il that al-Harith ibn Hassan said, "We went out making for the Messenger of Allah 襐. We entered the mosque and he was involved with the people. There was a black banner fluttering. I think that he said that Bilal was wearing a sword, I asked, 'What are the people doing today?' They answered, 'The Messenger of Allah 襐 is intending to send out 'Amr ibn al-'As.'"

Jabir ibn Abi Tariq al-Ahmasi

One of Bajila. He is Abu Hakim ibn Jabir. He related from the Prophet 襐.

Abu Hazim

His name was 'Awf ibn 'Abd al-Harith ibn 'Awf ibn Hushaysh ibn Hilal ibn al-Harith ibn Razzah ibn Kalb ibn 'Amr ibn Lu'ayy ibn Ruhm ibn Mu'awiya ibn Aslam ibn Ahmas from Bajila. He is Abu Qays ibn Abi Hazim.

Hisham Abu al-Walid reported from Shu'ba from Isma'il from Qays ibn Abi Hazim that the Messenger of Allah 襐 saw Abu Hazim in the sun while he was speaking and he commanded him or was commanded to move [to the shade].

Qutba ibn Malik

One of the Banu Tha'laba. He was the uncle of Ziyad ibn 'Ilaqa.

Ma'n ibn Yazid

Ma'n ibn Yazid ibn al-Ahmas ibn Habib ibn Jirw ibn Zi'b ibn Malik ibn Khufaf ibn 'Usayya ibn Khufaf ibn Imru' al-Qays ibn Buhtha ibn Sulaym ibn Mansur.

Yahya ibn Hammad reported from Abu 'Awana from Abu al-Juwayriya that Ma'n ibn Yazid said, "I gave allegiance to the Messenger of Allah ﷺ as did my father and grandfather. I argued with him and he defeated me and asked someone to marry me and carried out my marriage." Ma'n ibn Yazid settled in Kufa and was present at the Battle of Marj Rahit with ad-Dahhak ibn Qays al-Fihri.

Tariq ibn al-Ashyam al-Ashja'i

He is the son of Abu Malik. The name of Abu Malik is Sa'd. Tariq related from Abu Bakr as-Siddiq, 'Umar, 'Uthman and 'Ali.

Abu Maryam as-Sululi

His name of Malik ibn Rabi'a. He is Abu Barid ibn Abi Maryam. He related *hadith* from the Prophet ﷺ from the *hadith* of 'Ata' ibn as-Sa'ib.

Hubshi ibn Junada

Hubshi ibn Junada ibn Nasr ibn Usama ibn al-Harith ibn Mu'ayt ibn 'Amr ibn Jandal ibn Murra ibn Sa'sa'a ibn Mu'awiya ibn Bakr ibn Hawazin. The mother of Jandal ibn Murra was Salul bint Dhuhl ibn Shayban ibn Tha'laba. They are known by it. Hubshi became Muslim and was a Companion of the Prophet ﷺ and was present with 'Ali in his battles.

Malik ibn Isma'il reported from Isra'il from Qurra ibn 'Abdullah as-Sahuli that Hubshi ibn Junada visited a man and asked, "Are you afraid of anything except your going with 'Ali?" He answered, "None of my actions are more hopeful in my view than it."

Dukayn ibn Sa'id al-Khush'ami

Some of them said Ibn Su'ayd. Qays ibn Abi Hazim related from him.

Burma ibn Mu'awiya

Burma ibn Mu'awiya ibn Sufyan ibn Munqidh ibn Wahb ibn 'Umayr ibn Nasr ibn Qu'ayn ibn al-Harith ibn Tha'laba ibn Dudan ibn Asad ibn Khuzayma. Abu Qabisa ibn Burma related *hadith* from him.

Khuraym ibn al-Akhram

Khuraym ibn al-Akhram ibn Shaddad ibn 'Amr ibn al-Fatik ibn al-Qulayb ibn 'Amr ibn Asad ibn Khuzayma.

'Ubaydullah ibn Musa reported from Isra'il from Abu Ishaq from Shamir ibn 'Atiyya from Khuraym ibn Fatik, and Muhammad ibn 'Abdullah al-Asadi reported from Yunus ibn Abi Ishaq from Shamir that Khuraym ibn Fatik came to the Prophet 🌿 and he said to him, "Khuraym, were it not for two qualities in you, you would be a man." He asked, "What are they? One will be sufficient for me." He said "You let your hair grow full and wear your waist-wrapper low." He said, "He shortened his hair and raised his wrapper."

Muhammad ibn Sa'd said that his son Ayman ibn Khuraym was a noble Persian poet. He is the one who said:

I did not kill a man who prays
    for power of another Qurayshi.
He has his power and I have my sin.
    I seek refuge with Allah from ignorance and rashness!
Will I kill a Muslim without right?
    I would not benefit for as long as I live.

He said that ash-Sha'bi related from Ayman ibn Khuraym who said, "My father and uncle were present at Badr."

In the transmission of Muhammad ibn Ishaq, Musa ibn 'Uqba, Abu Ma'shar and Muhammad ibn 'Umar: only Quraysh, the Ansar and their allies and *mawla*s attended.

Dirar ibn al-Azwar

The name of al-Azwar was Malik ibn Aws ibn Jadhima ibn Rabi'a ibn Malik ibn Malik ibn Tha'laba ibn Dudan ibn Asad ibn Khuzayma. He was a horseman and became Muslim. He related the *hadith* about the fecundation of palm trees from the Prophet 🌿. Dirar ibn al-Azwar fought fiercely in the Battle of Yamama until both his legs were severed and be began to crawl on knees fighting and the horses trod on him until death overtook him.

Muhammad ibn 'Umar said that 'Abdullah ibn Ja'far said, "Dirar ibn al-Azwar remained wounded in Yamama until Khalid ibn al-Walid travelled on the day he died."

Muhammad ibn 'Umar said that he thought that this was firmer than other reports.

Furat ibn Hayyan

Furat ibn Hayyan ibn Tha'laba ibn 'Abd al-'Uzza ibn Habib ibn Habba ibn Rabi'a ibn Sa'd ibn 'Ijl. He was an ally of the Banu Sahm. He settled in Kufa and built a house there among the Banu 'Ijl and he has descendants in Kufa.

Ya'la ibn Murra

Ya'la ibn Murra ibn Wahb ibn Jabir ibn 'Attab ibn Malik ibn Ka'b ibn 'Amr ibn Sa'd ibn 'Awf ibn Thaqif. He is the one who is called Ya'la ibn Siyaba. Siyaba was his mother or grandmother.

Rawh ibn 'Ubada reported from Shu'ba from 'Ata' ibn as-Sa'ib who said that Abu Hafs ibn 'Amr or Abu 'Amr ibn Hafs ath-Thaqafi said that he heard Ya'la ibn Murra ath-Thaqafi say, "The Messenger of Allah ﷺ saw me ragged and he asked, 'Do you have a wife?' 'No,' I answered. He said, 'Wash it, then wash it, and then wash it and then do not repeat this.'"

Muhammad ibn 'Umar said that Ya'la ibn Murra was present with the Messenger of Allah ﷺ at the Homage of Ridwan, Khaybar, the Conquest of Makka, the Ta'if expedition, and Hunayn.

'Umara ibn Ruwayba ath-Thaqafi

He related from the Prophet ﷺ about praying before sunset.

'Abd ar-Rahman ibn Abi 'Aqil ath-Thaqafi

One of the tribe of al-Hajjaj ibn Yusuf.

Ahmad ibn Yunus reported from Zuhayr from Abu Khalid Yazid al-Asadi from 'Awn ibn Abi Juhayfa as-Suwa'i from 'Abd ar-Rahman ibn 'Alqama ath-Thaqafi that 'Abd ar-Rahman ibn Abi 'Aqil said, "I went to the Messenger of Allah ﷺ in a delegation and our camels knelt at the door. There was no man among the people more hateful to us than a man we went to. We did not leave until there was no man among the people we loved more than a man who we had come to. There is a story we mentioned."

'Utba ibn Farqad

He is Yarbu' ibn Habib ibn Malik ibn As'ad ibn Rifa'a ibn Rabi'a ibn Rifa'a ibn al-Harith ibn Buhtha ibn Sulaym ibn Mansur. He was a Companion of the Prophet ☆. He was a noble who settled in Kufa. The family is called al-Faraqida.

Ahmad ibn 'Abdullah ibn Yunus reported from Isra'il from Jabir that 'Amir said, "'Umar wrote to his governors: 'If you find a ring with Arabic writing on it, break it.' A ring of 'Utba's was found with "Utba the governor' on it and it was broken."

Yazid ibn Harun reported from Hammad ibn Salama from al-Juwayri from Abu 'Uthman an-Nahdi that 'Umar ibn al-Khattab saw 'Utba ibn Farqad wearing a shirt with long sleeves. He called for a knife to cut it at the ends of his fingers. 'Utba said, "Amir al-Mu'minin, I am ashamed to have you cut it. I will cut it." So he let him be.

'Ubaydullah ibn Khalid as-Sulami

He related from the Prophet ☆ that he made brotherhood between two men. One of them died before the other.

Tariq ibn 'Abdullah al-Muharibi

He related from the Prophet ☆ that when one of you spits, he should not spit in front of him or to his right.

Al-Fadl ibn Dukayn reported from Abu Janab from Abu Sakhra that a man of the people of Tariq ibn 'Abdullah said, "I was at the Dhu al-Majaz market when a young man passed by me wearing a streaky red robe, saying, 'O people, say: "There is no god but Allah" and you will have success.' A man behind him was throwing stones at him until his heels and legs bled. He said, 'He is a liar, so do not obey him!' I asked, 'Who is this?' They said, 'A lad of the Banu Hashim who claims that he is the Messenger of Allah. This is his uncle, 'Abd al-'Uzza.' When Muhammad ☆ emigrated to Madina and people became Muslim, we travelled from ar-Rabadha with a sedan which we had. When we came to Madina to the lowest of its walls, we stopped to change our clothes. There was a man in the road. He asked, 'From where are you people coming?' We replied, 'From ar-Rabadha. He asked, 'Where are you going?' We answered, 'Madina.' He asked, 'What do you want?' We said, 'We will supply our people with some of its dates. We have red camels with halters ready.' He asked, 'Will you sell your camels?' 'Yes,' we answered. 'For how much?' he inquired. We said, 'For a certain number of *sa*'s of dates.' He did not investigate what we said to him at all. Then he made the deal and took the halters of the camels and turned back. When he turned back from us with the halters, we said, 'By Allah, we have not done anything and we have sold to someone we do not know!' A woman who was sitting said, 'I saw a man whose face was like half of the full moon. He will not wrong you or cheat you. I will guarantee the price of your camels.' A man came to us and said, 'I am the messenger of the Messenger of Allah ﷺ to you. These are your dates, so eat, fill yourselves and measure.' We ate and had enough and were full. Then we entered Madina and went to the mosque and he was speaking on the minbar. We heard those who said, 'Give *sadaqa*. *Sadaqa* is good for you. The upper hand is better than the lower hand. Begin with those you support: your mother, your father, your sister and your brother, and then the next closest relatives to you and so on.' A man of the Banu Yarbu' entered and a man of the Ansar stood up and said, 'Messenger of Allah, those are the Banu Yarbu' who killed one of our men in the *Jahiliyya*! Help us against them!' The Messenger of Allah ﷺ said, 'Unless you should not wrong a child' three times."

Ibn Abi Shaykh al-Muharibi

Al-Fadl ibn Dukayn and Hisham Abu al-Walid at-Tayalisi reported from Qays ibn ar-Rabi' from Imru'l-Qays al-Muharibi from 'Asim from Buhayr that Ibn Abi Shaykh said, "The Messenger of Allah ﷺ came to us and said, 'Company of Muharib! Allah has helped you. Do not give me the milk of a woman to drink.'"

'Abida ibn Khalid al-Muharibi

He was the uncle of the aunt of al-Ash'ath ibn Sulaym.

Hisham Abu al-Walid at-Tayalisi reported from Shu'ba from al-Ash'ath ibn Sulaym who said that he heard his aunt relate that her uncle said, "While I was walking in Madina, someone said, 'Raise your waist-wrapper. Let your garment last and purify for your Lord.' I turned and it was the Messenger of Allah ﷺ. I said, 'Messenger of Allah, it is a fine cloak.' He said, 'Do you have an example in me?' I looked and his waist-wrapper reached the middle of his leg.'"

Abu al-Walid said that Abu al-Ahwas said that his name was 'Abida ibn Khalid, (i.e. his uncle).

Salim ibn 'Ubayd al-Ashja'i

He related from Abu Bakr as-Siddiq about *sahur*. He settled in Kufa later.

Nawfal al-Ashja'i

He related that the Prophet ﷺ said, "When you want to sleep, then recite, *'Say: "O unbelievers..."'* It is freedom from idolatry." He is Abu Suhaym ibn Nawfal.

Salama ibn Nu'aym al-Ashja'i

He was a Companion of the Prophet ﷺ. He listened to him and later settled in Kufa. He related from the Prophet ﷺ: "Whoever meets Allah and has not associated anything with Him will enter the Garden."

Shakal ibn Humayd al-'Absi

He is Abu Shutayr ibn Shakal.

His *hadith* is: "I heard the Prophet ﷺ said, 'O Allah, I seek refuge with you from the evil of my hearing, the evil of my sight and the evil of my sperm.'"

Al-Aswad ibn Tha'laba al-Yarbu'i

He said, "I was present with the Prophet ﷺ in the Farewell *Hajj*. He said, 'Someone who does wrong only wrongs himself.'"

Rushayd ibn Malik as-Sa'di

His *kunya* was Abu 'Amira.

Al-Fadl ibn Dukayn related from Mu'arrif ibn Wasil as-Sa'di from Hafsa bint Talq, a woman of the tribal quarter, in 90 AH that his grandfather Abu 'Amira Rushayd ibn Malik said, "I was with the Messenger of Allah ﷺ one day and a man came with a plate of dates. He asked, 'What is this? *Sadaqa* or a gift?' The man answered, '*Sadaqa*.' He said, 'Give it to the people.' Al-Hasan was playing in the dust before him and took a date and put it in his mouth. The Messenger of Allah ﷺ saw him and put his finger in his mouth and removed the date and threw it aside. He said, 'We, the family of Muhammad, do not consume *sadaqa*.'"

Al-Fuji' ibn 'Abdullah

Al-Fuji' ibn 'Abdullah ibn Hundaj ibn al-Bakka' ibn 'Amir ibn Rabi'a ibn 'Amir ibn Sa'sa'a al-'Amiri

Al-Fadl ibn Dukayn reported from 'Uqba ibn Wahb ibn 'Uqba al-'Amiri al-Bakka'i who heard his father relate that al-Fuji' al-'Amiri went to the Messenger of Allah ﷺ and asked, "What carrion is lawful for us?" He asked, "What is your food?" He replied, "We drink in the evening and then go to sleep." 'Uqba explained it to me: he had a cup in the morning and one in the evening. He said, "That, by my father, is hunger. Carrion is lawful for you in such a situation."

'Attab ibn Shumayr

Al-Fadl ibn Dukayn reported from 'Abd as-Samad ibn Jabir ibn Rabi'a ad-Dabbi from Mujamma' ibn 'Attab ibn Shumayr that his father said, "I said to the Prophet ﷺ, 'Messenger of Allah, I have a very old father and brothers. Should I go to them and perhaps they will become Muslim and I will bring them?' He said, 'If they become Muslim, it is better for them. If they stay, Islam is wide.'"

Dhu al-Jawshan ad-Dabbabi

Hisham ibn Muhammad ibn as-Sa'ib al-Kalbi said that his name was Shurahbil ibn al-A'war ibn 'Amr ibn Mu'awiya. He is ad-Dabbab ibn Kilab ibn Rabi'a ibn 'Amir ibn Sa'sa'a.

Someone else said that his name was Jawshan ibn Rabi'a al-Kilabi. He is Abu Shamir ibn Dhi al-Jawshan who was present at the killing of al-Husayn ibn 'Ali. Shamir's *kunya* was Abu as-Sabigha.

Yazid ibn Harun reported from Jarir ibn Hazim from Abu Ishaq as-Sabi'i who said, "Jawshan ibn Rabi'a al-Kilabi came to the

Prophet ﷺ and he gave him a horse. At that time he was an idolater. The Messenger of Allah ﷺ refused to accept it and said, 'If you wish, I will purchase it in exchange for the best of the armour of Badr.' Then he said to him, 'Dhu al-Jawshan, would you like to be one of the first of this business?' 'No,' he answered. He asked, 'What stops you?' He said, 'I saw that your people denied you and expelled you and fought you. I will wait. If you defeat them, then I will believe in you and follow you. If they defeat you, then I will not follow you.' The Messenger of Allah ﷺ told him, 'Dhu al-Jawshan, perhaps if you remain nearby, you will see my defeat of them.' He said, 'By Allah, I was at Dariyya when a rider came to us from the direction of Makka and we said, 'What is the news?' He answered, 'Muhammad has defeated the people of Makka.'" Dhu al-Jawshan used to be pained by not accepting Islam when the Messenger of Allah ﷺ offered it to him.

'Abdullah ibn Muhammad ibn Abu Shayba reported from 'Isa ibn Yunus from his father from his grandfather that Dhu al-Jawshan ad-Dabbabi said, "I went to the Prophet ﷺ after Badr and said, 'Messenger of Allah, I have brought you the colt of al-Qarha', so take him.' The Messenger of Allah ﷺ said, 'No, but if you wish, I will buy him from you in exchange for the best of the armour of Badr.' I said, 'I would not sell you a horse for armour today.'"

Someone other than 'Abdullah ibn Muhammad ibn Abi Shayba related this *hadith* in a more complete form from 'Isa ibn Yunus from his father that Dhu al-Jawshan said, "I went to the Messenger of Allah ﷺ after he had finished with the people of Badr with a foal of a horse of mine called al-Qarha'. I said, 'Muhammad, I have brought you the colt of al-Qarha' for you to take.' He said, 'I have no need of it.' Then he said, 'Dhu al-Jawshan, will you not become Muslim and be the first in this business?' He said, 'No.' Then he said, 'I see that your people have attacked you.' He said, 'What has reached you of their losses at Badr?' I answered, 'I have heard.' He said, 'You will have this if you overcome the Ka'ba and its land.' He said, 'Perhaps if you live, you will see that.' Then he said, 'Bilal, take the bag of the man and provide him with the best dates.' When I turned back, he said, 'The best horses are those of the Banu 'Amir.' He said, 'By Allah, I was with my family at al-'Awd when a rider came and I asked, "What have the people done?" He answered, 'By Allah,

Muhammad has defeated the Ka'ba and its people.' I said, 'May my mother lose me! If only I had become Muslim that day! Then I would have asked him to give me Hira as a fief.'"

Ghalib ibn Abjar al-Muzani

'Ubaydullah ibn Musa reported from Isra'il from Mansur from 'Ubaydullah ibn Abi al-Hasan that 'Abd ar-Rahman said that Ghalib ibn Abjar said, "We were afflicted by famine and I had nothing in my property to eat except for a fat red donkey. The Messenger of Allah ﷺ had made the flesh of domestic donkeys unlawful and so I went to the Messenger of Allah ﷺ and said, 'Messenger of Allah, we are suffering from famine and there is nothing in my property with which to feed my family except for a fat donkey. You have forbidden the flesh of domestic donkeys.' He said, 'Feed your family from the flesh of your donkey. I forbade it for the sake of the travellers of the town.'"

Al-Agharr al-Muzani It is said that he is al-Juhani

'Affan ibn Muslim reported from Shu'ba that 'Amr ibn Murra reported that he heard Abu Burda say, "I heard a man from Juhayna called al-Agharr who was one of the Companions of the Prophet ﷺ, say that he heard the Prophet ﷺ say, 'O people, repent to your Lord. I repent a hundred times a day.'"

Hani' ibn Yazid

Hani' ibn Yazid ibn Nahik ibn Durayd ibn Sufyan ibn ad-Dabbab of the Banu al-Harith ibn Ka'b.

Al-Fadl ibn Dujayn reported from Qays ibn ar-Rabi' from al-Miqdam ibn Shurayh from his father that his grandfather Hani' ibn Yazid came to the Prophet ﷺ in the delegation of the Banu al-Harith. His *kunya* was Abu al-Hakam. He said they began to use the *kunya* Abu Hakam for him. He said, "The Prophet ﷺ asked, 'Why do those people call you Abu al-Hakam?' He said, 'Because there was a quarrel between them. They came to me and I judged between them.' He asked, 'Do you have a child?' He answered, 'Yes.' He said, 'Which of them is oldest?' 'Shurayh,' I replied. He said, 'Then you are Abu Shurayh.'"

Abu Sabra

His name was Yazid ibn Malik ibn 'Abdullah ibn adh-Dhu'ayb ibn Salama ibn 'Amr ibn Dhuhl ibn Marran ibn Ju'fi ibn Sa'd al-'Ashira of Madhhij. He was the grandfather of Khaythama ibn 'Abd ar-Rahman ibn Abi Sabra.

'Ubaydullah ibn Musa reported from Isra'il from Abu Ishaq that Khaythama said, "My grandfather came to Madina and my father was born. He named him 'Aziz. That was mentioned to the Prophet ﷺ. He said, 'He is 'Abd ar-Rahman.'"

Hisham Abu al-Walid at-Tayalisi reported from Shu'ba that Abu Ishaq said that he heard Khaythama say, "When my father was born 'Aziz, my grandfather went to the Prophet ﷺ and mentioned that to him. He said that his name was 'Abd ar-Rahman."

Al-Miswar ibn Yazid al-Asadi

'Abdullah ibn az-Zubayr al-Humaydi reported from Marwan ibn Mu'awiya al-Fazzari from Yahya ibn Kathir al-Kahili al-Asadi that Miswar ibn Yazid al-Asadi said, "I was present when the Messenger of Allah ﷺ was reciting in the prayer and he left something which he did not recite. A man said, 'Messenger of Allah, you omitted such-and-such an *ayat*.' He said, 'Why did you not remind me then?'"

Bashir ibn al-Khassasiyya

His name was Zahm ibn Ma'bad as-Sadusi.

'Affan ibn Muslim reported from 'Ubaydullah ibn Iyad as-Sadusi that he heard Abu Iyad ibn Laqit as-Sadusi relate: "I heard Layla, the wife of Bashir ibn al-Khassasiya say, 'The Messenger of Allah ﷺ named him Bashir. His name before that had been Zahm.'"

Numayr Abu Malik al-Khuza'i

Waki' ibn al-Jarrah reported from 'Isam ibn Qudama from Malik ibn Numayr al-Khuza'i that his father said, "I saw the Messenger of Allah ﷺ putting his right hand on his left thigh to point with his finger in the prayer."

Abu Rimtha at-Taymi

His name was Habib ibn Hayyan.

Abu Umayya al-Fazari

Al-Fadl ibn Dukayn reported from Sharik that Abu Ja'far al-Farra' heard Abu Umayya al-Fazari said, "I saw the Messenger of Allah ﷺ being cupped."

Khuzayma ibn Thabit

Khuzayma ibn Thabit ibn al-Fakih al-Khatmi of the Ansar. His *kunya* was Abu Umara. He is the one with two *shahada*s. He came to Kufa with 'Ali ibn Abi Talib. He remained with him until he was killed at Siffin in 37 AH. He has descendants.

Mujamma' ibn Jariya

Mujamma' ibn Jariya ibn 'Amir ibn Mujamma' ibn al-'Attaf ibn Dubay'a ibn Zayd of the Banu 'Amr ibn 'Awf. He is the one whom the Kufans related compiled the Qur'an in the time of the Prophet ﷺ except for one or two *suras*. He died in the caliphate of Mu'awiya ibn Abi Sufyan and has no descendants.

Thabit ibn Wadi'a ibn Khidham

One of the Banu 'Amr ibn 'Awf. He related *hadith*s from the Messenger of Allah ﷺ. He settled at Kufa in the end.

Sa'd ibn Bujayr ibn Mu'awiya

He is the one called Sa'd ibn Habta. He was from Bajila, the ally of the Banu 'Amr ibn 'Awf. He was considered too young to fight on the Day of Uhud. He settled in Kufa and died in Kufa and the prayer was performed over him by Zayd ibn Arqam and he said five *takbir*s. One of his children was Khunays ibn Sa'd ibn Habta, the owner of the crossroads of Khunays at Kufa. One of his children was Qadi Abu Yusuf. His name was Ya'qub ibn Ibrahim ibn Habib ibn Sa'd ibn Habta.

Qays ibn Sa'd

Qays ibn Sa'd ibn 'Ubada ibn Dulaym of the Banu Sa'ida ibn Ka'b ibn al-Khazraj. His *kunya* was Abu 'Abd al-Malik. 'Ali ibn Abi Talib appointed him over Egypt and then dismissed him from his post. Qays went to Madina and then joined 'Ali at Kufa and remained with him. He was in charge of the Shurta al-Khamis.

Ya'la ibn 'Ubayd reported from al-Ajlah from Abu Ishaq that Yuraym ibn Sa'd said, "I saw Qays ibn Sa'd in charge of the Shurta al-Khamis. Then he went to the Tigris and performed *wudu'* and wiped over his leather socks. It is as if I could see the marks of his toes in the sock. Then he went and led the people in the prayer."

Muhammad ibn 'Umar said, "Qays ibn Sa'd remained with 'Ali until 'Ali was killed and then he went with al-Hasan ibn 'Ali ﷺ. He sent him with his vanguard to make for Syria. Then al-Hasan ibn 'Ali made peace with Mu'awiya and Qays returned to Madina and remained there until he died at the end of the caliphate of Mu'awiya."

An-Nu'man ibn Bashir ibn Sa'd

One of the Banu al-Harith ibn al-Khazraj. His mother was 'Amra bint Rawaha, the sister of 'Abdullah ibn Rawaha of the Banu al-Harith ibn al-Khazraj. His *kunya* was Abu 'Abdullah. He was the first of the Ansar to be born in Madina after the Hijra of the Messenger of Allah ﷺ. He was born in Rabi' al-Akhir at the beginning of the fourteenth month of the Hijra of the Messenger of Allah ﷺ. This is in the transmission of the people of Madina. As for the people of Kufa, they relate much from him, including: "I heard the Messenger of Allah ﷺ." It indicates that he was older than what the people of Madina relate about his birth. He was put in charge of Kufa for Mu'awiya ibn Abi Sufyan and stayed there. He was a partisan of 'Uthman. Then Mu'awiya dismissed him and he went to Syria. When Yazid ibn Mu'awiya died, an-Nu'man called people to Ibn az-Zubayr and was governor of Homs. When ad-Dahhak ibn Qays was slain at Marj Rabit in Dhu al-Hijja in 64 AH in the caliphate of Marwan ibn al-Hakam, an-Nu'man ibn Bashir fled from Hims and the people of Homs sought him, caught him, killed him and took his head and put it in the lap of his Kalbi wife.

'Abdullah ibn Bakr as-Sahmi reported from Hatim ibn Abi Saghira from Simak ibn Harb that Mu'awiya appointed an-Nu'man ibn Bashir over Kufa. He said, "By Allah, he was one of the most eloquent of those I heard speaking of the people of this world."

Abu Layla

His name was Bilal ibn Bulayl ibn Uhayha ibn al-Jallah of the Banu 'Amr ibn 'Awf. He was the father of Abu 'Abd ar-Rahman ibn Abi Layla. Abu Layla had a house in Kufa among Juhayna.

'Amr ibn Bulayl

His brother, 'Amr ibn Bulayl ibn Uhayha ibn al-Jallah of the Banu 'Amr ibn 'Awf.

Shayban, the grandfather of Abu Hubayra

He was one of the Ansar.

Al-Fadl ibn Dukayn reported from Hafs ibn Ghiyath from Ash'ath from Abu Hubayra Yahya ibn 'Abbad that his grandfather Shayban said, "I came and entered the mosque and sat by a stone of it." He heard the Prophet ﷺ clear his throat and he said, "Abu Yahya?" I said, "Abu Yahya." He said, "Come to lunch." I answered, "I am fasting." He said, "I was intending to fast. Our *mu'adhdhin* gave the *adhan* before dawn. There was something wrong with his eye."

Hanzala ibn ar-Rabi'

The scribe of the Banu Tamim, then the Banu Usayd ibn 'Amr ibn Tamim.

Muhammad ibn 'Umar said, "He once wrote a letter for the Prophet ﷺ and so because of that he was called 'the scribe'. There were few who could write among the Arabs."

Ribah ibn ar-Rabi'

His brother. He related from the Prophet ﷺ.

Ma'qil ibn Sinan al-Ashja'i

He was killed in the Battle of al-Harra in Dhu al-Hijja 63 AH.

'Adi ibn 'Umayra al-Kindi

He settled in Kufa and related from the Prophet ﷺ. Qays ibn Abi Hazim related from him. He is Abu 'Adi ibn 'Adi ibn 'Umayra, the companion of 'Umar ibn 'Abd al-'Aziz.

Mirdas ibn Malik al-Aslami

Qays ibn Abi Hazim related from him.

'Abdullah Abu al-Mughira

'Ubaydullah ibn Musa reported from Isra'il from Abu Ishaq from al-Mughira ibn 'Abdullah that his father said, "I went to a man who was relating to the people and he said that he described the Prophet ﷺ to me and I had not seen him. I went until I stopped on the road at 'Arafat and the mounts began to pass by me until the caravan of a lot of people moved and I looked and recognised the Prophet ﷺ in the middle of them by the description. When he came near to me, a man of the people called out and then said, 'Leave the faces of the mounts.' The Messenger of Allah ﷺ said, 'Leave the man to see what he wants.' I went and took hold of the halter or reins of his she-camel. I said, 'Tell me about an action which will admit me into the Garden and put me far from the Fire.' He said, 'That is what you will do?' I said, 'Yes.' He said, 'Understand then. You should worship Allah and not associate anything with him, establish the prayer, pay *zakat*, fast Ramadan and make *hajj* to the House and do to people what you want them to do to you and dislike to do to them what you dislike for yourself. Let the mount go.'"

Abu Shahm

Al-'Ala' ibn 'Abd al-Jabbar reported from Yazid ibn 'Ata' from Bayan from Qays ibn Abi Hazim from Abu Shahm. He was an idle man and a girl passed by him in Madina and he put his hand to her hip. He said, "I went to the Prophet ﷺ in the morning when he was taking the allegiance of people. He took my hand and asked, 'Is this the one who was bold yesterday?' I said, 'Messenger of Allah, I will not do it again.' He said, 'Yes,' and then took my allegiance."

Abu al-Khattab

Al-Fadl ibn Dukayn reported from Isra'il that Thubayr said, "I heard a man from the Companions of the Messenger of Allah ﷺ called Abu al-Khattab. He was asked about the *witr*. He said, 'I want to perform the *witr* in the middle of the night. Allah descends from the seventh heaven to the lowest heaven and says, "Is there any wrongdoer who asks for forgiveness? Is there anyone who supplicates?" and continues to do so until dawn rises.'"

Hariz or Abu Hariz

Al-Fadl ibn Dukayn reported from Qays ibn ar-Rabi from 'Uthman ibn al-Mughira that Abu Layla al-Kindi said, "The lord of this house, Hariz or Abu Hariz, said, 'I went to the Messenger of Allah ﷺ while he was standing and speaking at Mina. I put my hands on his skin and it was like musk.'"

Ar-Rasim

'Ubaydullah ibn Muhammad ibn Abi Shayba al-'Absi reported from 'Abd ar-Rahim ibn Sulayman ar-Razi from Yahya ibn Ghassan from ar-Rasim's son that his father said, "We came in a delegation to the Prophet ﷺ and asked him about drinks in certain vessels and he forbade them. Then we returned to him and said, 'Messenger of Allah, our land is unhealthy.' The Messenger of Allah ﷺ said, 'Drink from whatever you wish.'"

Ibn Saylan

'Abdullah ibn Muhammad ibn Abi Shayba reported from Muhammad ibn al-Hasan al-Asadi from Khalid at-Tahhan from Bayan from Qays that Ibn Saylan said, "I was with the Prophet ﷺ when he raised his head to heaven and said, 'You are blessed. You release trials on us.'"

Abu Tayba

He was the keeper of the milk camels of the Messenger of Allah ﷺ.

Abu Salma, the shepherd of the Messenger of Allah ﷺ

Sulayman ibn 'Abd ar-Rahman ad-Dimishqi reported from al-Walid ibn Muslim from 'Abdullah ibn al-'Ala' and Ibn Jabir from Abu Sallam al-Aswad from Abu Salma, the shepherd of the Messenger of Allah ﷺ, who said in a mosque in Kufa, "I heard the Messenger of Allah ﷺ say, 'Excellent! Excellent! How heavy these are in the balance! 'There is no god but Allah,' 'Allah is greater,' 'Praise be to Allah' and 'Glory be to Allah.' The righteous child gives a full share to the Muslim and he is reckoned for it.'"

A man of the Banu Taghlib

He was the grandfather of Harb ibn Hilal ath-Thaqafi by his mother.

Sa'id ibn Mansur reported from Jarir ibn 'Abd al-Hamid from 'Ata' ibn as-Sa'ib from Harb ibn Hilal ath-Thaqafi from his father to whom a man of Taghlib said, "I went to the Messenger of Allah ﷺ and he taught me the laws of Islam and I only remembered the tenth [due on land]. I said, 'Is it their tenth?' He said, 'There is no tenth for the Muslims. There it's a tenth for the Jews and Christians. He said that the tenth is *jizya*."

The grandfather of Talha ibn Musarrif al-Iyami

Yazid ibn Harun reported from 'Uthman ibn Miqsam al-Burri from Layth from Talha ibn Musarrif al-Iyyami from his father than his grandfather said, "I saw the Messenger of Allah ﷺ wipe his head like that." Yazid illustrated all of that with his hands. He began to wipe the front of his head and pulled his hands to the back of his neck until he passed them over his temples on the inside of his beard.

Yazid said, "That is how I took it."

Abu Marhab

Muhammad ibn 'Umar reported from ath-Thawri from Isma'il ibn Abi Khalid from ash-Sha'bi that Abu Marhab said, "I can still see 'Abd ar-Rahman ibn 'Awf as one of four men in the grave of the Messenger of Allah ﷺ."

Muhammad ibn 'Umar said, "This *hadith* is not known with us nor is Abu Marhab known. What is firm with us and with the people of our land is what Ma'mar related from az-Zuhri that Sa'id ibn al-Musayyab said, "There are four who undertook to wash him and shroud him ※: al-'Abbas, 'Ali, al-Fadl and Shuqran. May Allah have mercy on all of them."

Qays ibn al-Harith al-Asadi

He is the grandfather of Qays ibn ar-Rabi'.

Bakr ibn 'Abd ar-Rahman reported from 'Isa ibn al-Mukhtar from Muhammad ibn 'Abd ar-Rahman ibn Abi Layla from Humayda ibn ash-Shamardal that Qays ibn al-Harith became Muslim. He had eight wives and the Messenger of Allah ※ commanded him to choose four of them.

Al-Falatan ibn 'Asim al-Jarmi

He is the uncle of 'Asim ibn Kilab al-Jarmi.

'Amr ibn al-Ahwas

He is Abu Sulayman. Sulayman's mother was Umm Jundub al-Azdiyya who related from the Messenger of Allah ※ about the pebbles of the *jamra*s being like small pebbles.

Nuqada al-Asadi

He is ibn 'Abdullah ibn Khalaf ibn 'Amir ibn Murri ibn Sa'd ibn Malik ibn Malik ibn Tha'laba ibn Dudan ibn Asad.

He related from that the Prophet ※ sent him to a man to ask him for the milk of a camel and the man refused him.

Al-Mustawird ibn Shaddad ibn 'Amr

One of the Banu Muharib ibn Fihr.

'Abdullah ibn Numayr and Muhammad ibn 'Ubayd reported from Isma'il ibn Abi Khalid that Qays ibn Abi Hazim said that al-Mustawird, the brother of Banu Fihr, reported that he heard the Messenger of Allah ※ say, "This world in relation to the Next World is only like one of you putting his finger into the sea. Let him see what he brings back of it."

'Abdullah ibn Numayr said that he meant the finger next to the index finger.

Muhammad ibn Sa'd said that al-Mustawird ibn Shaddad related *hadith*s from the Messenger of Allah 鐕.

Muhammad ibn 'Umar said, "Al-Mustawird was a boy the day the Messenger of Allah 鐕 died. He settled in Kufa and the Kufans related from him.

Muhammad ibn Safwan

He related from the Prophet 鐕. He related from him the *hadith* of ash-Sha'bi a *hadith* about rabbits.

Muhammad ibn Sayfi

He related from the Prophet 鐕 the *hadith* about 'Ashura'.

Malik ibn 'Abdullah al-Khuza'i

He said in his *hadith*, "I prayed behind the Prophet 鐕 and I did not pray behind an imam who did a shorter prayer than him."

'Affan ibn Muslim reported from 'Abd al-Wahid ibn Ziyad from Mansur ibn Hayyan al-Asafi from Sulayman ibn Bishr al-Khuza'i that his uncle, Malik ibn 'Abdullah al-Khuza'i, said, "I went on an expedition with the Messenger of Allah 鐕. I never prayed behind an imam who led the prayer with a lighter prayer than the Messenger of Allah 鐕."

Abu Kamil al-Ahmasi of Bajila

His name was Qays ibn 'A'idh.

He said, "I saw the Prophet 鐕 speaking on a she-camel while an Abyssinian was holding its reins."

Malik ibn 'Umayr

His *kunya* was Abu Safwan.

Yazid ibn Harun and 'Amr ibn al-Haytham Abu Qatan reported from Shu'ba that Simak ibn Harb heard Abu Safwan Malik ibn 'Umayr al-Asadi say, "I went to Makka before the Messenger of Allah 鐕 emigrated."

'Umayr Dhu Murran

He is the grandfather of Mujalid ibn Sa'id al-Hamdani. He is the one to whom the Messenger of Allah ﷺ wrote. He settled in Kufa.

Abu Juhayfa as-Suwa'i

His name was Wahb ibn 'Abdullah of the Banu Suwa'a ibn 'Amir ibn Sa'sa'a. He related *hadith*s from the Prophet ﷺ.

Muhammad ibn Sa'd said that he heard someone mention that the Prophet ﷺ died when Abu Juhayfa had not reached puberty. He saw the Prophet ﷺ and listened to him. He died in Kufa while Bishr ibn Marwan was governor.

Tariq ibn Ziyad al-Ju'fi

Al-Fadl ibn Dukayn reported from Sharik from Simak from 'Alqama ibn Wa'il that Tariq ibn Ziyad al-Ju'fi said, "I said, 'Messenger of Allah, we have palm trees and vines. Can we press?' 'No,' he answered. I said, 'We use it for medicine.' He said, 'It is an illness.'"

'Affan ibn Muslim reported from Hammad ibn Salama with this *isnad*, but said it is Tariq ibn Suwayd.

Abu at-Tufayl 'Amr ibn Wathila al-Kinani

Muhammad ibn Sa'd said that he reported from Thabit ibn al-Walid ibn 'Abdullah ibn Jumay' that his father said, "Abu at-Tufayl said to me, 'I experienced eight years of the life of the Messenger of Allah ﷺ.'" He was born on the day of Uhud.

Al-Juhduma

Muhammad ibn as-Salt related from Mansur ibn Abi al-Aswad from Abu Janab from Iyad that al-Juhduma said, "I saw the Messenger of Allah ﷺ go out to the prayer and there was henna on his head."

Yazid ibn Nu'ama ad-Dabbi

Hatim ibn Isma'il reported from 'Imran ibn Muslim from Sa'id ibn Salman that Yazid ibn Nu'ama ad-Dabbi said that he meant the

Messenger of Allah ﷺ said, "When one man made brotherhood with another man he should ask about his name and the name of his father and where he is from. It connects love."

Abu Khallad

He was a Companion.

Yahya ibn Sa'id ibn Aban reported from Abu Farwa from Abu Khallad who was a Companion that the Messenger of Allah ﷺ said, "When you see a believing man who is given asceticism in this world and has few words, draw near to him. He gives wisdom."

Mikhnaf ibn Sulaym

Mikhnaf ibn Sulaym ibn al-Harith ibn 'Awf ibn Tha'laba ibn 'Amir ibn Dhuhl ibn Mazin ibn Dhubyan ibn Tha'laba ibn ad-Dul ibn Sa'd Manat ibn Ghamid of Azd. It was the house of Azd of Kufa. He became Muslim and was a Companion of the Prophet ﷺ. After that one of his sons, Abu Mikhaf Lut ibn Yahya, resided in Kufa.

First Generation of the people of Kufa after the Companions of the Messenger of Allah ﷺ who related from Abu Bakr as-Siddiq, 'Umar ibn al-Khattab, 'Uthman ibn 'Affan, 'Ali ibn Abi Talib, 'Abdullah ibn Mas'ud and others

Tariq ibn Shihab

Tariq ibn Shihab ibn 'Abd Shams ibn Salama ibn Hilal ibn 'Awf ibn Jusham ibn Nuqr ibn 'Amr ibn Luayy ibn Ruhm ibn Mu'awiya ibn Aslam ibn Ahmas ibn al-Ghawth ibn Anmar ibn Bajila. She was the daughter of Sa'b ibn Sa'd al-'Ashira by which they are known.

Yahya ibn 'Abbad and Sulayman Abu Dawud at-Tayalisi reported from Shu'ba that Qays ibn Muslim said that he heard Tariq ibn Shihab say, "I saw the Messenger of Allah ﷺ and I went on an expedition while Abu Bakr was caliph."

Yahya ibn 'Abbad added in the *hadith*, "He went on about forty expeditions and sorties."

Rawh ibn 'Ubada said with this *isnad*: forty-three. Tariq related from Abu Bakr, 'Umar, 'Uthman, 'Ali, 'Abdullah, Khalid ibn al-Walid, Hudhayfa ibn al-Yaman, Salman al-Farisi, Abu Musa al-Ash'ari and Abu Sa'id al-Khudri and from his brother Abu 'Azara. He was older. He used to often mention Salman.

Qays ibn Abi Hazim

His name was 'Awf ibn 'Abd al-Harith ibn 'Awf ibn Hushaysh ibn Hilal ibn al-Harith ibn Razzah ibn Kalb ibn 'Amr ibn Lu'ayy of Ahmas. He related from Abu Bakr, 'Umar, 'Uthman, 'Ali, Talha, az-Zubayr, Sa'd ibn Abi Waqqas, 'Abdullah ibn Mas'ud, Khabbab, Khalid ibn al-Walid, Hudhayfa, Abu Hurayra, 'Uqba ibn 'Amir, Jarir ibn 'Abdullah, 'Adi ibn 'Amira, and Asma' bint Abi Bakr. He was present at al-Qadisiyya.

'Abdullah ibn az-Zubayr al-Humaydi reported from Sufyan ibn 'Uyayna that Isma'il ibn Khalid said that he heard Qays say that he was present at al-Qadisiyya. He said, "Khalid ibn al-Walid addressed us at Hira and I was among them."

Muhammad ibn Sa'd said, "He meant that he was present with Khalid ibn al-Walid at the beginning of the business of Iraq when Khalid made peace with the people of Hira. All of this is ascribed to the event of al-Qadisiyya."

'Amr ibn 'Asim al-Kilabi reported that 'Umar ibn Abi Za'ida said, "I saw Qays ibn Abi Hazim used to use yellow dye."

Muhammad ibn 'Umar said that Qays ibn Abu Hazim died at the end of the caliphate of Sulayman ibn 'Abd al-Malik.

Rafi' ibn Abi Rafi' at-Ta'i

He is Rafi' ibn 'Amr. It is said Ibn Ghamira ibn Jabir ibn Haritha ibn 'Amr ibn Mihdab ibn Hizmir ibn Labid ibn Sinbis ibn Mu'awiya ibn Jarwal ibn Thu'l of Tayy'. He is called Rafi' al-Khayr. He went with 'Amr ibn al-'As on the expedition of Dhat as-Salasil when the Messenger of Allah ﷺ sent him. He accompanied Abu Bakr as-Siddiq and related from him. He returned to the land of his people and did not see the Prophet ﷺ. He was the guide of Khalid ibn al-Walid when he went from Iraq to Syria and travelled with them through the desert. It was said of him:

How excellent is Rafi'! How was he guided
    to the oath from Quraqir to Suwa?
When it had travelled for five days, the army wept:
    'No human has travelled it before you!'

Then in the time Rafi' became the *'arif* of his people. Tariq ibn Shihab related from him.

Suwayd ibn Ghafala

Suwayd ibn Ghafala ibn 'Awsaja ibn 'Amr ibn Wada' ibn Mu'awiya ibn al-Harith ibn Malik ibn 'Awf ibn Sa'd ibn 'Awf ibn Harim ibn Ju'fi ibn Sa'd al-'Ashira from Madhhij. He was alive in the time of the Prophet ﷺ and went to him in a delegation. He found that he had died and so he kept the company of Abu Bakr, 'Umar, 'Uthman and 'Ali. He was present with 'Ali at Siffin. He listened to

'Abdullah ibn Mas'ud but did not listen at all to 'Uthman. His *kunya* was Abu Umayya.

Al-Fadl ibn Dukayn and Hisham Abu al-Walid at-Tayalisi reported from Sharik from 'Uthman ath-Thaqafi from Abu Layla al-Kindi that Suwayd ibn Ghafala said, "The *zakat* collector of the Messenger of Allah ﷺ came to us and I took his hand and read in his instructions that he was to not separate flocks which are together nor to combine separate ones. A man brought an immense she-camel and he refused to take it. Another brought a smaller she-camel and he refused to take it. Then he said, 'What heaven will shade me and what earth will carry me if I go to the Messenger of Allah ﷺ having taken the best camels of a Muslim?'"

'Ubaydullah ibn Musa reported from Isra'il from Ibrahim ibn 'Abd al-A'la that Suwayd ibn Ghafala said, "I took the hand of 'Umar ibn al-Khattab and he said, 'Abu Umayya.'"

Al-Qasim ibn Malik al-Muzani reported that Nufa'a ibn Muslim said, "I saw Suwayd ibn Ghafala praying wearing a burnous."

Al-Fadl ibn Dukayn reported from Hanash ibn al-Harith from 'Ali ibn Mudrik that Suwayd ibn Ghafala used to give the *adhan* at midday and al-Hajjaj heard it while he was at Dabar. He said, "Bring me this *mu'adhdhin*." Suwayd ibn Ghafala was brought. He said, "What made you pray at midday?" He answered, "I prayed it with Abu Bakr and 'Umar." He said, "Do not give the *adhan* to your people or lead them in the prayer."

Abu Bakr ibn 'Ayyash used to relate this *hadith* also from Abu Husayn from Suwayd and he added in it that al-Hajjaj said, "Remove him from the *adhan* and leading the prayer."

'Affan ibn Muslim reported from Abu 'Awana from one of his companions that Suwayd ibn Ghafala concealed himself in the time of al-Hajjaj. They used to pray *Zuhr* on Friday in a group.

Al-Fadl ibn Dukayn reported from Hanash ibn al-Harith ibn Laqit that Suwayd ibn Ghafala passed by them in the mosque going to a woman of the Banu Asad there who was aged one hundred and twenty-seven. Sometimes he prayed and sometimes did not.

Ahmad ibn 'Abdullah reported from Zuhayr from 'Urwa ibn 'Abdullah ibn Qushayr that Suwayd ibn Ghafala shrouded al-Abayriq ibn Malik in two cloths.

'Abd ar-Rahman ibn Muhammad al-Muharibi reported from Layth from Khaythama: "Suwayd ibn Ghafala instructed me: 'When I die, do not announce it to anyone. Do not bring any gypsum or white-wash near my grave nor branches. Do not let a woman accompany me. Only shroud me in two cloths.'"

Muhammad ibn 'Umar reported that Suwayd ibn Ghafala died in Kufa in 81 or 82 AH in the caliphate of 'Abd al-Malik ibn Marwan.

Al-Fadl ibn Dukayn said that Suwayd ibn Ghafala died at the age of one hundred and twenty-eight.

Al-Aswad ibn Yazid

Al-Aswad ibn Yazid ibn Qays ibn 'Abdullah ibn Malik ibn 'Alqama ibn Salaman ibn Kahl ibn Bakr ibn 'Awf ibn an-Nakha' of Madhhij. His *kunya* was Abu 'Amr. He was the nephew of 'Alqama ibn Qays. Al-Aswad ibn Qays was older than 'Alqama. He mentioned that he sent the dowry of Umm 'Alqama to her. He sent his grandfather with it. Al-Aswad related from Abu Bakr as-Siddiq that he did the *hajj* with him. He related from 'Umar, 'Ali, 'Abdullah ibn Mas'ud and Mu'adh ibn Jabal. He listened to him in Yemen before he made *hijra* when the Prophet ﷺ sent Mu'adh to Yemen. He related from Salman, Abu Musa and 'A'isha and did not relate anything from 'Uthman."

Hisham Abu al-Walid at-Tayalisi reported from Shu'ba that al-Hakam said that al-Aswad used to fast all the time.

'Ubaydullah ibn Musa reported from Hasan ibn Salih from Mansur that one of his companions said, "Al-Aswad used to fast in the very hot day in which the red camels swayed from the heat."

Wahb ibn Jarir reported from ad-Dastuwa'i from Hammad from Ibrahim that al-Aswad used to fast in the very hot day until his tongue was black from the heat.

Al-Fadl ibn Dukayn reported from Hanash ibn al-Harith that Riyah an-Nakha'i said, "Al-Aswad used to fast in the journey until his colour changed due to thirst on a hot day. One of us would drink several times before finishing his camel outside of Ramadan."

Al-Fadl ibn Dukayn reported from Hanash ibn al-Harith from 'Ali ibn Mudrik that 'Alqama used to say to al-Aswad, "Why do you punish this body?" He answered, "I desire rest for it."

Al-Fadl ibn Dukayn reported from Hanash ibn al-Harith, "I saw al-Aswad who had lost an eye from fasting."

Al-Fadl ibn Dukayn reported from Hanash ibn al-Harith ibn Laqit that Riyah ibn al-Harith an-Nakha'i said, "I travelled with al-Aswad to Makka. When it was time for the prayer, he dismounted whatever the situation, even if he was on rough ground and prayed. If the foot of the camel was rising or falling, he made it kneel without waiting."

Wahb ibn Jarir reported from ad-Dastuwa'i from Hammad from Ibrahim that when the time for the prayer came, al-Aswad made his camel kneel, even on stone.

Al-Fadl ibn Dukayn reported from Abu Isra'il from Abu Ishaq that al-Aswad did *tawaf* of the House eighty times in *hajj* or *'umra*.

Al-Fadl ibn Dukayn and Muhammad ibn 'Abdullah al-Asadi reported from Sufyan from Mansur that Ibrahim said, "Al-Aswad assumed *ihram* from his house. 'Alqama used to enjoy his clothes."

Al-Fadl ibn Dukayn reported from Sufyan from Ash'ath ibn Abi ash-Sha'tha', "I saw al-Aswad and 'Amr ibn Maymun assuming *ihram* from Kufa."

Al-Fadl ibn Dukayn reported from Hammad ibn Zayd from as-Saq'ab ibn Zuhayr from 'Abd ar-Rahman ibn al-Aswad that his father used to leave Kufa in *ihram* with gummed hair.

Al-Fadl ibn Dukayn reported from Sufyan that Abu al-Juwayriya said, "I saw al-Aswad ibn Yazid assume *ihram* from Bajumayra."

'Arim ibn al-Fadl reported from Hammad ibn Zayd that 'Ata' ibn as-Sa'ib said, "I saw al-Aswad ibn Yazid on a mount and they put a coverlet around him on a saddle. We took him in *tawaf* while he was in *ihram*. He said, 'Do not take this from me. I am a very old man.'"

Ahmad ibn 'Abdullah ibn Yunus reported from Sharik from Mughira that Ibrahim said, "Sometimes al-Aswad assumed *ihram* from Jabbana 'Arzam [in Kufa]."

Malik ibn Isma'il reported from Sharik that Jabir that al-Aswad said, "Sometimes al-Aswad entered Makka at night."

Ahmad ibn 'Abdullah ibn Yunus reported from Zuhayr from Jabir al-Ju'fi that 'Abd ar-Rahman ibn al-Aswad said, "When he went into *ihram*, I did not hear al-Aswad stipulate *hajj* or *'umra*. He used to say, 'Allah knows my intention.'"

Al-Fadl ibn Dukayn reported from Abu al-Ahwas that Abu Ishaq said that al-Aswad added to his *talbiya*, "At Your service, Forgiver of sins."

Al-Fadl ibn Dukayn reported from Sarik from al-A'mash that Khaythama said, "Al-Aswad used to say in his *talbiya*: 'At Your service and kindness.'"

Yahya ibn 'Abbad reported from Malik ibn Mighwal from Muhammad ibn Suqa that his father went on *hajj* with al-Aswad and when the time for the prayer came, he used to make his camel kneel, even on stone. He added that he performed about seventy *hajjs*.

Yahya ibn 'Abbad reported from Malik ibn Mighwal who said that he heard Abu Mughith mention that Ibrahim said, "Al-Aswad did not pray the funeral prayer over anyone if he was wealthy and had died without performing *hajj*."

Muhammad ibn 'Abdullah al-Asadi reported from Sufyan from Mansur from Ibrahim and from Sufyan from al-A'mash that 'Umara said, "There was a wealthy man of Nakha' called Miqlas who had not performed *hajj*. Al-Aswad said, 'If he were to die, I would not pray over him.'"

Rawh ibn 'Ubada reported from Shu'ba from Sulayman from Ibrahim that al-Aswad performed *hajj* and 'Abdullah said, "If you meet 'Umar, give him the greeting."

'Arim ibn al-Fadl reported from Hammad ibn Zayd from Ayyub from Abu Ma'shar that 'Umar used to cling to 'Umar and 'Alqama used to cling to 'Abdullah. The two used to meet and not differ.

Al-Fadl ibn Dukayn, Muhammad ibn 'Abdullah al-Asadi and Abu al-Mundhir Isma'il ibn 'Umar reported from Sufyan from Mansur from Ibrahim that al-Aswad used to recite the entire Qur'an in the month of Ramadan every two nights. He used to sleep between *Maghrib* and *'Isha'*.

Muhammad ibn 'Abdullah al-Asadi reported from Sufyan from al-A'mash that Ibrahim said, "Al-Aswad used to recite the entire Qur'an over six nights."

Wahb ibn Jarir ibn Hazim reported that his father that he heard Abu Ishaq relate from 'Abd ar-Rahman ibn Yazid that 'A'isha said, "There is no man in Iraq more respected by me than al-Aswad."

Al-Fadl ibn Dukayn reported from Mandal that 'Ata' ibn as-Sa'ib said, "I was with Abu 'Abd ar-Rahman as-Sulami when al-Aswad ibn Yazid entered and asked him about something. They said, 'This is al-Aswad ibn Yazid,' and he embraced him."

Abu Mu'awiya reported from al-A'mash that Ibrahim said, "'Alqama said to al-Aswad, 'Abu 'Amr,' Al-Aswad said to him, 'At your service.' 'Alqama said to him, 'At the service of your hands.'"

Al-Fadl ibn Dukayn reported from Yunus ibn Abi Ishaq that Abu Ishaq said, "I and al-Aswad were in the police with 'Amr ibn Hurayth in difficult nights."

Hafs ibn Ghiyath reported from ash-Shaybani from 'Abd ar-Rahman ibn al-Aswad from his father that he used to prostrate in a burnous while his hands were in it or in his clothing."

Hafs ibn Ghiyath reported that al-Hasan ibn 'Ubaydullah said, "I saw al-Aswad ibn Yazid prostrate in a burnous."

Waki' and Muhammad ibn 'Ubayd reported that Abu Khalid said, "I saw al-Aswad ibn Yazid wearing a black turban."

Al-Fadl ibn Dukayn reported from Sharik that Abu Khalid said, "I saw al-Aswad ibn Yazid wearing a turban and it hung down behind him." He said that he saw him praying in his sandals.

Al-Fadl ibn Dukayn reported from Sharik that Abu Khalid said, "I saw al-Aswad with a yellow head and beard."

'Abd ar-Rahman ibn Muhammad al-Muharibi reported that al-Hasan ibn 'Ubaydullah said, "Al-Aswad had a yellow beard."

Muhammad ibn 'Abdullah al-Asadi reported from Sufyan from Mansur from Ibrahim that al-Aswad used to hurry to the prayer.

Al-Hasan ibn Musa reported from Abu 'Awana that Abu Balj said, "I saw al-Aswad ibn Yazid and 'Amr ibn Maymun meet and embrace."

Malik ibn Isma'il reported from Shark ibn Abi Ziyad that Ibrahim said, "Al-Aswad had a clean rag which he used to dry himself after doing *wudu'*."

'Amr ibn al-Haytham Abu Qatan reported from Shu'ba from Salama ibn Kuhayl that Ibrahim said, "I used to hold al-Aswad during his final illness. When he finished recitation, he made supplication."

Abu Qatan said that Shu'ba said, "This is the capital of the people of Kufa."

Waki' ibn al-Jarrah, Muhammad ibn 'Abdullah al-Ansari and 'Abd al-Wahhab ibn 'Ata' reported from Ibn 'Awn from Ibrahim that al-Aswad ibn Yazid said to a man when he was dying. "If you are able to instruct me so that the last that I say is: 'There is no god but Allah,' do so. Do not put bricks in my grave."

Waki' and Muhammad ibn 'Abdullah al-Ansari said that Ibn 'Awn said in his final instructions, "Do not follow me with sound (or wailing)."

Muhammad ibn 'Umar reported from Qays ibn ar-Rabi' that Ibn Ishaq said that al-Aswad ibn Yazid died in Kufa in 75 AH. He was trustworthy and had sound *hadiths*.

Masruq ibn al-Ajda'

He is 'Abd ar-Rahman ibn Malik ibn Umayya ibn 'Abdullah ibn Murr ibn Sulayman ibn Ma'mar ibn al-Harith ibn Sa'd ibn 'Abdullah ibn Wada'a ibn 'Amr ibn 'Amir ibn Nashih of Hamdan.

Hisham ibn al-Kalbi said that his father said, "Al-Ajda' came to 'Umar ibn al-Khattab. He was a poet. 'Umar asked him, 'Who are you?' He answered, 'Al-Ajda'.' He said, 'Al-Ajda' is a shaytan. You are 'Abd ar-Rahman.'"

Yazid ibn Harun reported from Hisham ad-Dastuwa'i from Hammad from Abu ad-Duha that Masruq said, "I prayed behind Abu Bakr as-Siddiq and he greeted to his right and to his left. When he said the *salam*, it was as if he was on the hot stones until he stood up.'"

'Abd ar-Rahman ibn Muhammad al-Muharibi reported from ash-Shaybani from Abu ad-Duha that Masruq's *kunya* was Abu Umayya.

Muhammad ibn Sa'd said that this is an error. I think that he meant Suwayd ibn Ghafala.

'Ubaydullah ibn Musa reported from Zakariyya from ash-Sha'bi that Masruq's *kunya* was Abu 'A'isha.

Muhammad ibn Sa'd said, "This is the sounder than what 'Abd ar-Rahman ibn Muhammad al-Muharibi related. Masruq also related from 'Umar, 'Ali, 'Abdullah, Khabbab ibn al-Aratt, Ubayy ibn Ka'b, 'Abdullah ibn 'Amr, 'A'isha, and 'Ubayd ibn 'Umayr and he did not relate anything from 'Uthman."

Muhammad ibn Rabi' al-Kilabi reported from Abu Hanifa from Ibrahim ibn Muhammad ibn al-Muntashir that his father said, "The engraving on the ring of Masruq was: 'In the Name of Allah, the All-Merciful, Most Merciful.'"

Waki' ibn al-Jarrah and al-Fadl ibn Dukayn reported from Isra'il that Abu Ishaq said, "Masruq used to pray in his burnous and fur-coat and did not take his hand out of them."

Yahya ibn Hammad reported from Abu 'Awana from Sulayman that Muslim ibn Subayh said, "Masruq had a head wound, i.e. he had a blow to his head. He said, 'It would not delight me to not have it.'"

Abu Shihab said that he thought that he meant in the armies.

Hisham ibn Muhammad ibn as-Sa'ib al-Kalbi reported that his father said, "Masruq ibn al-Ajda' was present at al-Qadisiyya with three of his brothers: 'Abdullah, Abu Bakr and al-Muntashir, the sons of al-Ajda'. They were killed on that day at al-Qadisiyya and Masruq was wounded and his brother became semi-paralysed and received a head injury."

'Abdullah ibn Ja'far ar-Raqqi reported from 'Ubaydullah ibn 'Amr from Zayd ibn Unaysa from 'Amr ibn Murra that ash-Sha'bi said, "When Masruq was told, 'You stayed behind 'Ali and his battles. You were not present at any of his battles.' He wanted to move their speech and said, 'I remind you by Allah. Do you think that when you form rows against one another and assault one another with weapons, killing one another, that a gate to heaven will be opened while you are looking and then angels will descend from it until they are behind the ranks? *'O you who believe, do not consume one another's property by false means, but only by means of mutually agreed trade. And do not kill yourselves. Allah is Most Merciful to you.'* (4:29) Is that not a barrier between you?' They answered, 'Yes.' He said, 'By Allah, Allah has opened a door from heaven and a noble angel descended with it on the tongue of your Prophet ﷺ. It gives judgements in the copies of the Qur'an which nothing has copied.'"

'Abdullah ibn Idris reported that he heard Mutarrif mention that 'Amir said, "Masruq said to me, 'Do you think that if there were two rows of believers lined up to fight one another and then an angel opened from the heaven and called, *'O you who believe, do not consume one another's property by false means, but only by means of mutually agreed trade. And do not kill yourselves. Allah is Most Merciful to you.* (4:29)' Do you think that they would stop?' I answered, 'Yes, unless they were dumb stones.' He said, 'His friend among the people of the heaven brought it down to His friend among the people of the earth but they did not stop and because believing it in the unseen is better than believing it by seeing it with the eyes.'"

'Arim ibn al-Fadl reported from Hammad ibn Zayd that 'Asim said, "It was mentioned that Masruq ibn Ajda' came to Siffin and stopped between the rows and said, 'People, be silent!' Then he said, 'Do you think that if a caller from heaven were to call you that you would listen to his words and see him? Allah has forbidden you what you are doing. Will you obey Him?' They said, 'Yes.' He said, 'By Allah, Jibra'il brought that down on Muhammad ﷺ. He continues to bring this: *'O you who believe, do not consume one another's property by false means, but only by means of mutually agreed trade. And do not kill yourselves. Allah is Most Merciful to you. (4:29)'* Then he slipped into the people and left."

Al-Fadl ibn Dukayn reported from Malik ibn Mighwal from Abu as-Safar that Murra said, "No Hamdani like Masruq has ever been born."

Hisham Abu al-Walid at-Tayalisi and 'Affan ibn Muslim reported from Shu'ba that Abu Ishaq said, "Masruq went on *hajj* and he did not sleep or prostrate except on his face."

'Abida ibn Humayd reported from Abu al-Harith Yahya ibn 'Abdullah al-Jabir from Hibal ibn Rufayda that Masruq ibn al-Ajda' said, "We went to the Umm al-Mu'minin 'A'isha and she said, 'Pour honey for my son.' Then she said, 'Let him eat it. If you doubt any of it, then give him more honey. If I were not fasting. I would taste it.' We said, 'Umm al-Mu'minin, we are fasting.' She asked, 'What sort of fast is it?' We said. 'We fast this day and if it is part of Ramadan, we have caught it. If it is not, then it is voluntary.' She said, 'The fast is the fast of the people and breaking it is when the people break it. The sacrifice is the sacrifice of the people. But I have fasted this month and it coincides with Ramadan.'"

Al-Hajjaj ibn Muhammad reported from Yunus ibn Abi Ishaq from his father who said, "One day Masruq had no provision for his family and so his wife went to him and said, 'Abu 'A'isha, there is no provision for your family today.' He smiled and said, 'By Allah, Allah will bring them provision.'"

Yazid ibn Harun reported from Shu'ba from Ibrahim ibn Muhammad ibn al-Muntashir from his father that Khalid ibn Usayd went to Masruq ibn al-Ajda' with thirty thousand and he refused to accept it. He said, "We said to him, 'You should take it and use it for relatives and give it as *sadaqa* and other such things.' He still refused to accept it."

Muslim ibn Ibrahim reported from Qurra ibn Khalid that Muhammad said: "When Masruq went out with a brick on which to prostrate in the ship."

Qabisa ibn 'Uqba reported from Sufyan from Jabir from ash-Sha'bi that Masruq ransomed with his right hand for fifty dirhams.

Al-Fadl ibn Dukayn and Muhammad ibn 'Abdullah al-Asadi reported from Sufyan that 'Ali ibn al-Aqmar said, "Masruq led us in the prayer in Ramadan and recited *Surat al-'Ankabut* in one *rak'at*."

Muhammad ibn 'Abdullah al-Asadi and Musa ibn Mas'ud an-Nahdi reported from Sufyan from al-A'mash from Abu ad-Duha that Masruq was asked about a verse of poetry and he said, "I dislike to find poetry on my page."

'Affan ibn Muslim reported from Abu 'Awana from Mughira fom 'Amir that a man used to sit with Masruq. He recognised his face without knowing his name and he accompanied him. The last of his farewell was to say, "You are the chief of the reciters and their master. Your adornment is adornment for them and your disgrace is their disgrace so do not relate yourself to poverty nor to a long life."

Al-Fadl ibn Dukayn reported from Ibn 'Uyayna from Ibrahim ibn Muhammad ibn al-Muntashir that his father said, "Masruq and his wife liked for one of them to go to the Euphrates to get water and sell it and give its price as *sadaqa*."

Al-Fadl ibn Dukayn reported from Hafs from al-A'mash from Abu ad-Duha that Masruq bought a ram and sacrificed it. Its owner came to him and said, "You gave us something and we give you something."

Al-Fadl ibn Dukayn reported from Sufyan from Abu Ishaq that Sa'id ibn Jubayr said, "Masruq met me and said, 'Sa'id, nothing remains which is desired except that we rub our faces in this dust.' He said, 'There was a curtain between him and his wife.'"

Ahmad ibn 'Abdullah ibn Yunus reported from Za'ida from al-A'mash from Muslim that Masruq said, "It is enough knowledge for a person that he fears Allah and it is enough ignorance for a man that he is proud of his actions."

Masruq said, "A person should have gatherings in which he can withdraw and remember his sons and ask Allah to forgive him."

'Arim ibn al-Fadl reported from Hammad ibn Zayd that Anas ibn Sirin said, "We heard in Kufa that Masruq fled from the plague and Muhammad objected to him doing that. He said, 'Let us go to his wife and ask her.' We went to her and asked her about that and she said, 'No, by Allah. He did not flee the plague. He used to say, 'On the days when people are busy, I want to withdraw for worship.' So he used to go aside and withdraw for worship. She said, 'Sometimes I sat behind him weeping because of what I saw he was doing to himself. He used to pray until his feet were swollen. I heard him say, "The plague, abdominal illness, lochia and drowning. If any Muslim dies in them, he has achieved martyrdom."'"

'Affan ibn Muslim reported from 'Abd al-Wahid ibn Ziyad from 'Asim al-Ahwal from ash-Sha'bi that Masruq said that he heard a beggar mentioning those who were ascetic in this world and desired the Next World. He said, "Masruq disliked to give him anything for that and feared that they would not do it. He said to him, 'Ask. Allah gives to you, both pious and impious.'"

Musa ibn Isma'il reported from Hafs ibn Ghiyath from Isma'il from Abu Ishaq that Masruq said, "Were it not for certain circumstances, I would establish a milk-camel for the Umm al-Mu'minin."

'Amr ibn al-Haytham Abu Qatan reported from al-Mas'udi from Bukayr ibn Abi Bukayr from Abu ad-Duha that Masruq interceded for a man who then gave him a slave-girl. He became angry. He said, "If I had known that you would do this, I would not have spoken in the case nor will I ever speak in what remains of it! I heard 'Abdullah ibn Mas'ud say, 'If someone intercedes in order to restore a right or to repel an injustice and then is given something and accepts it, that is theft.'" They said, "We only thought that theft was taking something for judgement." He said, "Taking for judgement is disbelief."

Qabisa ibn 'Uqba reported from Sufyan from Abu Ishaq that Masruq married his daughter to as-Sa'ib ibn al-Aqra' and he stipulated ten thousand for himself.

'Abd al-Wahhab ibn 'Ata' reported from Isra'il from Abu Ishaq that Masruq married his daughter to as-Sa'ib for ten thousand which he stipulated for himself and said, "Prepare your wife from your money." He said that Masruq used it for those doing *jihad*, the poor and *mukatib*s.

Sa'id ibn Mansur reported from Ya'qub ibn 'Abd ar-Rahman az-Zuhri from Hamza ibn 'Abdullah ibn 'Utba ibn Mas'ud who said, "It reached me that Masruq ibn al-Ajda' took the hand of a nephew of his and he showed a rubbish heap in Kufa. He said, 'Will I show you this world? They have consumed this world and made it vanish. They wore it and wore it out. They rode it and wore it out. They spilled their blood in it and made lawful what is unlawful and cut off their kin.'"

Muhammad ibn 'Abdullah al-Asadi reported from Yunus ibn Abi Ishaq that ash-Sha'bi said, "Masruq was a qadi."

Al-Fadl ibn Dukayn and 'Amr ibn al-Haytham reported from al-Mas'udi that al-Qasim said, "Masruq did not accept any pay for being a qadi."

'Arim ibn al-Fadl reported from Hammad ibn Zayd from Mujalid from ash-Sha'bi that Masruq said, "I prefer to judge a case and agree with the truth or grant a right to *ribat* in the Way of Allah for a year."

Muhammad ibn 'Abdullah al-Asadi and Qabisa ibn 'Uqba reported from Sufyan from Ibn Abjur that ash-Sha'bi said, "Masruq had more knowledge of *fatwa* than Shurayh but Shurayh had more knowledge of judgement. Shurayh used to consult Masruq."

'Abdullah ibn Numayr reported from al-A'mash that Shaqiq said, "Masruq was in charge of the chain of justice for two years: he used to pray *rak'at*s in twos intending to perform the *sunna*."

Abu Mu'awiya reported from al-A'mash that Shaqiq said, "I asked Masruq, 'What moved you to accept this post?' He said, 'Three would not leave me alone – Ziyad, Shurayh and Shaytan – pushed me into it.'"

Yahya ibn Hammad reported from Abu 'Awana from Sulayman that Shaqiq said, "I was with Masruq who was in charge of the chain of justice for two years: he used to pray *rak'at*s in twos intending to perform the *sunna*. I heard him say, 'I did not do an action at all which I more fear for myself than admitting me to the Fire than this action. I would not take a dirham or dinar nor did I wrong a Muslim or person with a treaty, but I did not know what this rope is which neither the Messenger of Allah ﷺ nor Abu Bakr nor 'Umar prescribed.' I said, 'What made you return to it when you left it?' He said, 'Ziyad, Shurayh and Shaytan obliged me and they continued to make it attractive it to me until they pushed me into it.'"

Hisham Abu al-Walid at-Tayalisi reported from Abu 'Awana from Husayn from Abu Wa'il that when Masruq was dying, he said, "O Allah, I will not die on a business that Messenger of Allah ﷺ has not prescribed nor Abu Bakr or 'Umar. By Allah, I have not left gold or silver with anyone except what is on this sword of mine. So shroud me with it."

Ya'la and Muhammad, the sons of 'Ubayd, and al-Fadl ibn Dukayn reported from Muti' al-Burjumi that ash-Sha'bi said, "Masruq died and did not leave enough to pay for his shroud. He said, 'Borrow the price of my shroud. Do not borrow it from a farmer or receiver. Look to someone with livestock or someone who sells livestock and borrow it from them.'"

Ahmad ibn 'Abdullah ibn Yunus reported that he heard Abu Shihab mention that Mallaha reported to him: "A Nabatean idolatress used to carry salt for him. She said, 'When there was a drought, we would go to Masruq's grave. Her house was at the chain. We would pray for rain and be given rain. We sprinkled his grave with wine and he came to us in a dream and said, 'If you must do it, then with water.' He died at the chain at Wasit."

He was told that Sufyan ibn 'Uyayna said, "Masruq lived longer than 'Alqama and no one was better than him."

Someone other than Sufyan ibn 'Uyyana said that Masruq died in 63 AH. He was trustworthy and had sound *hadith*s.

Sa'id ibn Nimran ibn Nimran an-Na'iti of Hamdan

'Umar ibn Sa'd Abu Dawud al-Hafari reported from Sufyan from Abu Ishaq from 'Amir ibn Sa'd from Sa'id ibn Nimran from Abu Bakr: "'*Those who say, "Our Lord is Allah" and then go straight.*' It means that they do not associate others with Allah."

Hisham ibn Muhammad reported from his father that Sa'id ibn Nimran was one of the companions of 'Ali ibn Abi Talib. He connected him to 'Ubaydullah ibn al-'Abbas ibn 'Abd al-Muttalib when he appointed him over Yemen. His son, Musafir ibn Sa'id, was one of the followers of al-Mukhtar.

An-Nazzal ibn Sabra al-Hilali

Al-Fadl ibn Dukayn and Khallad ibn Yahya reported from Mis'ar from 'Abd al-Malik ibn Maysara that an-Nazzal said, "The Messenger of Allah 鑁 said to us, 'We and you are the Banu 'Abd Manaf. You are the Banu 'Abdullah and we are the Banu 'Abdullah.'"

Abu Nu'aym said that the Messenger of Allah 鑁 said to the people of an-Nazzal, and Khallad ibn Yahya reported in his *hadith* that Mis'ar said: "We are from the Banu 'Abd Manaf ibn Hilal ibn 'Amir ibn Sa'sa'a and the Prophet 鑁 was from the Banu 'Abd Manaf ibn Qusayy of Quraysh."

Muhammad ibn 'Umar said that an-Nazzal ibn Sabra related from Abu Bakr, 'Umar, 'Uthman, 'Ali, 'Abdullah ibn Mas'ud, Abu Mas'ud al-Ansari and Hudhayfa ibn al-Yaman.

Muhammad ibn 'Abdullah al-Asadi reported from Mis'ar from 'Abd al-Malik ibn Maysara that ad-Dahhak said, "An-Nazzal said to me, 'When you put me in my grave, say, "O Allah, bless this grave and the one who enters it."'" An-Nazzal was trustworthy and had *hadith*s.

Zuhra ibn Humaysa

Zuhra said, "I rode behind Abu Bakr as-Siddiq and he did not meet anyone without greeting him." He had few *hadith*s.

Ma'di Karib

Al-Fadl ibn Dukayn reported from Sufyan from his father that Abu ad-Duha said, "Abu Bakr asked Ma'di Karib to recite and he said, 'You are the first to ask me to recite in Islam.'"

Those in this generation who related from 'Umar ibn al-Khattab, 'Ali ibn Abi Talib and 'Abdullah ibn Mas'ud and others

'Alqama ibn Qays

'Alqama ibn Qays ibn 'Abdullah ibn Malik ibn 'Alqama ibn Salaman ibn Kahl ibn Bakr ibn 'Awf ibn an-Nakha' of Madhhij. His *kunya* was Abu Shibl. He is the uncle of al-Aswad ibn Yazid ibn Qays. He related from 'Umar ibn al-Khattab, 'Uthman ibn 'Affan, 'Ali, 'Abdullah ibn Mas'ud, Hudhayfa, Salman, Abu Mas'ud, and Abu ad-Darda'.

Abu Mu'awiya reported from al-A'mash from Ibrahim that 'Alqama said, "'Abdullah resembled the Prophet ﷺ in his guidance, direction and aspect." 'Alqama resembled 'Abdullah.

Muhammad ibn 'Ubayd reported from al-A'mash from 'Umara that Abu Ma'mar said, "We visited 'Amr ibn Shurahbil and he said, 'Let us go to the person who most resembles the guidance and aspect of 'Abdullah.' We went to 'Alqama."

Al-Fadl ibn Dukayn reported from Abu al-Ahwas from Mughira from Ibrahim that 'Alqama recited to 'Abdullah and he said, "Recite slowly. By my mother and my father, that is the adornment of the Qur'an."

Muhammad ibn 'Abdullah al-Asadi reported from Sufyan from Mansur that Ibrahim said, "It was said to 'Alqama, 'Are you a believer, Abu Shibl?' He replied, 'I hope so.'"

Al-Fadl ibn Dukayn reported from Sufyan from Mughira from Ibrahim that 'Abdullah gave 'Alqama the *kunya* Abu Shibl when he had no children.

Muhammad ibn 'Umar al-Asadi reported from Sufyan from al-A'mash that Ibrahim said, "'Alqama used to recite the Qur'an over five days."

Al-Fadl ibn Dukayn reported from Sharik that Mansur said, "I asked Ibrahim, 'Was 'Alqama present at Siffin?' 'Yes,' he answered, 'and he fought until his sword was dark with blood. His brother Ubayy ibn Qays was killed.'"

Al-Fadl ibn Dukayn reported from 'Abd as-Salam ibn Harb who heard an old man while we were sitting at the door of the mosque for more than thirty years on Friday. He said, "'Alqama ibn Qays came while the imam was speaking on Friday and it was said to him, 'Abu Shibl, will you not enter?' He said, 'This is the manner of sitting of someone imprisoned.' He said, 'He sat at the door of the mosque.'"

'Abd al-Hamid ibn 'Abd ar-Rahman al-Himmani reported from al-A'mash from Ibrahim from 'Alqama said, "I remember when I was a lad and it was as if I was reading it on a page."

Al-Fadl ibn Dukayn and Muhammad ibn 'Abdullah al-Asadi reported from Sufyan from al-A'mash from Ibrahim that 'Alqama and al-Aswad one called the other he said, "At your service" and the other said, "At the service of your hands."

Muhammad ibn 'Abdullah al-Asadi reported from Sufyan from Mansur from Ibrahim that 'Alqama used to not have a *ghusl* on a journey on Friday and did not pray *Duha*.

Muhammad ibn 'Abdullah al-Asadi reported from Sufyan from Mansur from Ibrahim that 'Alqama used to say to his wife, "Feed me from that pleasurable enjoyment." He used to interpret the words of Allah Almighty, *'But if they are happy to give you some of it, make use of it with pleasure.'* (4:4)"

Muhammad ibn 'Abdullah al-Asadi reported from Sufyan from Mansur that Ibrahim said, "We were with 'Alqama when he put his foot in the stirrup and said, 'In the Name of Allah.' When it was upright, he said, 'Praise be to Allah. *"Glory be to Him who has subjected this to us. We could never accomplished it by ourselves. Indeed we are returning to our Lord."'* (43:13-14)"

Al-Fadl ibn Dukayn reported from Hafs ibn Ghiyath from al-A'mash that Ibrahim said, "I went out with 'Alqama and when he put his foot in the stirrup, he said, 'O Allah, I am intending *hajj* if it is feasible. Otherwise it is *'umra.'* I did not see him have a *ghusl* on Friday until he had entered Makka. I saw him take a garment and wrap himself in it and then sit in it while he was in *ihram* and he covered the end of his nose and mouth."

Muhammad ibn 'Abdullah al-Asadi reported from Sufyan from Husayn from Ibrahim that 'Alqama shortened the prayers at an-Najaf and al-Aswad at al-Qadisiyya when they went out to Makka.

Muhammad ibn 'Abdullah al-Asadi reported from Sufyan from Husayn from Ibrahim that 'Alqama had a mule he used to pawn.

Al-Fadl ibn Dukayn and Muhammad ibn 'Abdullah al-Asadi reported from Sufyan from Mansur from Ibrahim that 'Alqama came to Makka at night and did the *tawaf* of seven circuits and recited the long *suras*. Then he did *tawaf* seven times and recited the *Mathani*. Then he did *tawaf* again and recited the rest.

Yahya ibn Hammad reported from Abu 'Awana from al-A'mash from Malik ibn al-Harith that 'Abd ar-Rahman ibn Yazid said, "We said to 'Alqama, 'You should pray in the mosque and sit so that we could sit with you and ask. He said, 'I dislike for it to be said, "This is 'Alqama." They said, 'You should visit the governors and they would acknowledge your honour.' He said, 'I fear that they will diminish me more than I am diminished by them.'"

Talq ibn Ghannam reported from Sharik that Mansur said, "I asked Ibrahim, 'Was 'Alqama present at Siffin?' He answered, 'Yes, and his sword was dark and his foot was lame and his brother Ubayy as-Salat was struck down.'"

Talq said, "He was called Ubayy as-Salat because of the great number of his prayers."

Ahmad ibn 'Abdullah ibn Yunus reported from Isra'il from Mansur from Ibrahim that 'Alqama used to recite to 'Abdullah while there was a copy of the Qur'an in 'Abdullah's room. 'Alqama had a good voice. He said to 'Alqama, "Recite slowly, may my father and mother be your ransom!"

Qabisa ibn 'Uqba reported from Sufyan from Mansur from Ibrahim that Abu Burda wrote the books of 'Alqama in the expedition to Mu'awiya and 'Alqama wrote to him, "Erase me! Erase me!"

'Affan ibn Muslim reported from Azhar as-Samman from Ibn 'Awn: "I asked ash-Sha'bi, 'Was 'Alqama better or al-Aswad?' He replied, "'Alqama. Al-Aswad performed many *hajj*s and 'Alqama caught the swift while he was with the slow.'"

Hisham Abu al-Walid at-Tayalisi reported from Shu'ba from al-Hakam that Abu Wa'il said, "When Ibn Ziyad was in charge of both Basra and Kufa, he said, 'Accompany me when I go.' I went to 'Alqama and asked him about that and he said, 'Know that you will not get anything from them but that they will get what is better from you.'"

Ahmad ibn 'Abdullah ibn Yunus reported from Abu Shihab from al-A'mash from Ibrahim that when 'Alqama was told that 'Abdullah had died, he said, "If you were to sit for people, you could teach the *sunna*." He said, "Do you want to tread on my neck?" It was said to him, "You should go to the governor and command him to do good." He said, "I will not get anything from their world but that they will get better from my *deen*."

Ahmad ibn 'Abdullah ibn Yunus reported from Abu Shihab from al-A'mash from Ibrahim from 'Alqama that 'Abdullah said, "Recite *Surat al-Baqara* for me." When he recited it, he said, "Did you leave any of it?" I said, "One letter." He said, "Such-and-such?" I said, "Yes."

Ahmad ibn 'Abdullah ibn Yunus reported from Abu Shihab from al-A'mash from Ibrahim that 'Alqama said, "'Abdullah said to me, 'Recite.' 'Alqama had a good voice and he recited. 'Abdullah said, 'Recite slowly, may my father and mother be your ransom.'"

Muslim ibn 'Ibrahim reported that Sa'id ibn Zarbi said that Hammad related from Ibrahim that 'Alqama ibn Qays said, "I was a man to whom Allah gave a good voice in the Qur'an. 'Abdullah used to ask me to recite and would say, 'Recite, may your father and mother be your ransom. I heard the Prophet ﷺ say, "A good voice adorns the Qur'an."'"

'Abida ibn Humayd reported from Mansur that Ibrahim said, "'Alqama recited the Qur'an over six days and al-Aswad recited it over seven."

Muhammad ibn Rabi'a al-Kilabi reported from Fitr that a man said that he heard 'Alqama say, "Remind each other of knowledge. Its life is its remembrance."

Al-Hasan ibn Musa reported from Zuhayr from Abu Ishaq that Sa'id ibn Dhi Hamdan said, "We asked 'Alqama, 'What does a man say when he enters the mosque.' He replied, 'Peace be upon you, O Prophet and the mercy of Allah and His blessing. May Allah and His angels bless Muhammad. Peace be upon him.'"

Muhammad ibn 'Abdullah al-Ansari reported from Sa'id ibn Abi 'Aruba from Abu Mash'ar from an-Nakha'i that 'Alqama bought a camel from a man or a riding beast from a man and disliked it and wanted to return it with some dirhams. 'Alqama said, "This is our mount, so what is our right to your dirhams?" He accepted his animal and returned the dirhams.

Al-Fadl ibn Dukayn and Muhammad ibn 'Abdullah al-Asadi reported from Sufyan that Abu Qays said, "I saw Ibrahim take the stirrup of 'Alqama when he was a one-eyed boy."

Al-Fadl ibn Dukayn reported from al-Hasan ibn Salih from Ibrahim ibn Muhajir from Ibrahim that 'Alqama went out with 'Ali.

'Ubaydullah ibn Musa and al-Fadl ibn Dukayn reported from Isra'il that Ghalib Abu al-Hudhayl said, "I asked Ibrahim about 'Alqama and al-Aswad and who was better. He answered, "Alqama. He was present at Siffin.'"

Al-Fadl ibn Dukayn reported from Abu al-Ahwas from Abu Ishaq that 'Abd ar-Rahman ibn al-Aswad said, "'Alqama and al-Aswad said that the completion of the greeting was the handshake. Part of the completion of the *hajj* is to be present at the two prayers with the imam at 'Arafa."

Al-Fadl ibn Dukayn reported from Hanash ibn al-Harith from our shaykhs that when 'Abdullah heard 'Alqama recite, he said, "Recite, 'Alqama. May my father and mother be your ransom." He used to command that he recite after it.

Al-Fadl ibn Dukayn reported from Muhammad ibn Sa'd I think from Hanash from our shaykhs that 'Amr ibn Maymun said, "I was a baker for 'Alqama for ten years in residence."

'Ubaydullah ibn Musa and Ahmad ibn Yunus reported from Isra'il from Abu Ishaq from al-Aswad that 'Alqama commanded that he instruct him [when he was dying] with: 'There is no god but Allah' and that no one announce his death.

Al-Fadl ibn Dukayn and Muhammad ibn 'Abdullah al-Asadi reported from Sufyan from Husayn from Ibrahim that 'Alqama said, "Instruct me with 'There is no god but Allah' and take me quickly to my grave. Do not follow me. I fear that it will be like the death announcement of the *Jahiliyya*."

Ishaq ibn Mansur reported from Zuhayr from Abu Ishaq that 'Alqama said to al-Aswad and 'Amr ibn Maymun, "Remind me of 'There is no god but Allah' at death and do not announce me to anyone. It is the death announcement of the *Jahiliyya* (or the call of the *Jahiliyya*)."

Waki' ibn al-Jarrah reported from Muhammad ibn Qays from 'Ali ibn Mudrik an-Nakha'i from Ibrahim that 'Alqama instructed, "If you are able to instruct me at the end with 'There is no god but Allah alone with no partner,' do so. Do not announce my death to anyone. I fear that it will be like the death announcement of the *Jahiliyya*. When you take me out, close the door on me and women should not follow me."

'Ubaydullah ibn Musa reported from Isra'il from Jabir that 'Amir said, "I stood with 'Alqama at Marw for two years praying two *rak'at*s."

Muhammad ibn Sa'd and another said, "He went to Khwarazm and stayed there for two years."

Al-Fadl ibn Dukayn reported from Sufyan from al-Hasan that Ibrahim said, "I used to stand behind 'Alqama until the *mu'adhdhin* descended."

Waki' and al-Fadl ibn Dukayn reported from Isra'il that Abu Ishaq said, "'Alqama prayed in a burnous and fur-coat and did not remove his hand from it."

Al-Fadl ibn Dukayn reported that 'Alqama died in Kufa in 62 AH. He was trustworthy and had a lot of *hadith*s.

'Abida ibn Qays as-Salmani from Murad

'Abdullah ibn Bakr ibn Habib as-Sahmi reported from Hisham ibn Hassan from Muhammad ibn 'Abida that he became Muslim two years before the Prophet ﷺ died but did not meet him.

'Arim ibn al-Fadl reported from Hammad ibn Zayd from Hisham from Muhammad that 'Abida prayed two years before the Prophet ﷺ died, but did not actually see the Prophet ﷺ.

Muhammad ibn Sa'd said that Muhammad ibn 'Umar said: "'Abida emigrated in the time of 'Umar. He related from 'Umar, 'Ali and 'Abdullah."

Al-Fadl ibn Dukayn, Abu 'Amir al-'Aqadi and Muslim ibn Ibrahim all reported from Qurra ibn Khalid that Muhammad ibn Sirin said, "'Abida was the *'arif* (supervisor) of his people."

Muhammad ibn 'Abdullah al-Ansari reported from Hisham ibn Hassan from Muhammad ibn Sirin that 'Abida was the *'arif* of his people and he divided a gift to them between them. There was a dirham left over and he commanded that there be lots between them for that dirham. A man came close to him and said, "This is not proper." He said, "Is this not what we used to do in our expeditions?" He said, "If you do that, you divide between the people and then draw lots between them and no one removes the one who gets a share. If you draw lots between them in this, then one of them will have it rather than his companions." He said, "You spoke the truth." So he ordered that something be purchased with that dirham and then it was divided between them.

'Affan ibn Muslim reported from Hammad ibn Zayd from Ayyub and Hisham from Muhammad that 'Ali said, "People of Kufa, are you unable to be like as-Salmani and al-Hamdani? (meaning al-Harith ibn al-Azma', not al-A'war). They are two halves of a man."

Hammad said that 'Abida was one-eyed.

'Affan ibn Muslim reported from Hammad ibn Salama from Ayyub that Muhammad said, "The companions of 'Abdullah ibn Mas'ud were five. Some of them advanced 'Abida, and some of them advanced 'Alqama. They do not disagree that Shurayh was the last of them. It is said that Hammad had their number." He said, "'Abida, 'Alqama, Masruq, al-Hamdani and Shurayh."

Hammad said, "I do not know whether he began with al-Hamdani or Shurayh."

'Affan ibn Muslim and Hisham Abu al-Walid and 'Amr ibn al-Haytham Abu Qatan reported from Shu'ba from al-Hakam that Ibrahim said, "'Abida said, 'Do not make a book abide for me.'"

Qabisa ibn 'Utba reported from Sufyan that an-Nu'man ibn Qays said, "'Abida called for his books when he died and erased them. He said, 'I fear someone will follow me and put them other than in their proper place.'"

Ahmad ibn Ishaq al-Hadrami reported from 'Abd al-Wahid ibn Yazid from 'Asim that Muhammad ibn Sirin said, "Some people brought a dispute to 'Abida so that he could mediate between them. He said, 'I will not speak until you command me.' It is as if he thought that the ruler had in that what neither the qadi nor anyone else had."

Muhammad ibn 'Abdullah al-Ansari reported from Hisham from Muhammad that 'Abida said, "Two boys brought him two tablets on which there was writing in which they were competing and he said, 'It is judgement,' and refused."

Muhammad ibn 'Abdullah reported from Ibn 'Awn that Muhammad said, "I asked 'Abida about an *ayat* and he said, 'You must have fear of Allah and do what is correct. Those people believed that they were teaching what the Qur'an revealed.'"

Muhammad ibn 'Abdullah al-Asadi reported from Sufyan from Hisham from Muhammad that 'Abida said, "People disagreed with me about drinks. I have not had anything to drink for thirty years except for honey, milk and water."

Sulayman ibn Harb reported from Hammad ibn Zayd from Ayyub and Yahya ibn 'Atiq that Muhammad said, "I asked 'Abida and he said, 'People have discussed drinks. I have not had anything to drink for twenty years except for water, milk and honey.'"

Muhammad ibn 'Abdullah al-Ansari reported from Hisham ibn Hassan, i.e. from Muhammad: "I said to 'Abida, 'We have some of the hair of the Messenger of Allah ﷺ from Anas.' 'Abida said, 'I would prefer to have a hair from him than to have all of gold and silver on the surface of the earth.'"

Musa ibn Isma'il reported from 'Abd al-Wahid ibn Ziyad from an-Nu'man ibn Qays who said that his father said, "I said to 'Abida, 'It reached me that you will die and then return before the Day of Rising carrying a banner and you will conquer what no one before you has conquered and none after you will conquer.' 'Abida said, 'If Allah brings me to life twice and makes me die twice before the Day of Rising, He does not desire good for me.'"

Waki' ibn al-Jarrah reported from Mis'ar from Abu Husayn that 'Abida left instructions that al-Aswad ibn Yazid should pray over him.

Sulayman Abu Dawud at-Tayalisi reported from Shu'ba that Abu Hasin said, "''Abida as-Salmani left instructions. Al-Aswad said, 'Make haste with him before the Liar comes (meaning al-Mukhtar).' He prayed over him before sunset." 'Abida died in 72 AH.

Abu Wa'il

His name was Shaqiq ibn Salama al-Asadi, one of the Banu Malik ibn Malik ibn Tha'laba ibn Dudan ibn Asad ibn Khuzayma.

Waki' ibn al-Jarrah reported that Abu al-'Anbas 'Amr ibn Marwan asked Abu Wa'il, "Were you alive while the Prophet ﷺ was alive?" He answered, "Yes, I was a beardless boy, but I did not see him."

Abu Mu'awiya reported that al-A'mash that Shaqiq said, "The letter of Abu Bakr reached us when we were at al-Qadisiyya and 'Abdullah ibn al-Arqam wrote."

Abu Mu'awiya reported from al-A'mash that Shaqiq said, "He said to me, 'Sulayman, if you could have seen us when we were fleeing from Khalid ibn al-Walid in the Battle of Buzakha. I fell off my camel and my neck almost snapped. If I had died on that day, I would have been in the Fire.'"

Sa'id ibn Mansur reported from Hushaym from Mughira that Abu Wa'il said, "The *zakat*-collector of the Prophet ﷺ came to us and he used to take a she-camel from every fifty she-camels. I brought him a

ram of mine and said to him, 'Take the *zakat* due on this.' He said,
'There is no *zakat* on this.'"

Waki' ibn al-Jarrah reported from al-A'mash that Abu Wa'il was
asked, "Were you present at Siffin?" He said, "Yes, and the rows
were wretched as they were."

'Abd ar-Rahman ibn Mahdi reported from Shu'ba that Yazid ibn
Abi Ziyad said, "I asked Abu Wa'il. 'Who is older: you or Masruq?'
He answered, 'I am older than Masruq.'"

'Abd ar-Rahman reported from Sufyan from his father from Abu
Wa'il who said, "He was asked, 'Who is older: you or Rabi' ibn
Khuthaym?' He said, 'I am a year older than him, but he is greater
than me in intelligence.'"

Ya'la and Muhammad, the sons of 'Ubayd reported from Salih ibn
Hayyan that Shaqiq ibn Salama said, "'Amr gave me four gifts by his
own hand and said, 'One *takbir* is better than this world and what it
contains.'"

'Affan ibn Muslim reported from Abu al-Ahwas from Muslim al-
A'war that Abu Wa'il said, "I went on an expedition to Syria with
'Umar ibn al-Khattab. He said, 'I heard the Messenger of Allah

say, "Do not wear silk or brocade. Do not drink from gold or silver
vessels. They are for them in this world and for us in the Next
World."'"

'Affan ibn Muslim and Sa'id ibn Mansur reported from Abu
'Awana from Muhajir Abu al-Hasan who said, "I went to Abu Burda
and Shaqiq who were in charge of the treasury with my *zakat* and
they took it."

Sa'id said in his *hadith*, "Then I came another time and found
Abu Wa'il alone and he said to me, 'Take it back and distribute it in
its places.' I asked, 'What do I do with the portion of 'those whose
hearts are to be reconciled'?" He said, 'Give it to the others.'"

'Affan ibn Muslim reported from Shu'ba from al-Hakam who said
that he heard Abu Wa'il say, "There was recognition between me and
Ziyad. When he controlled both Kufa and Basra, he said to me,
'Accompany me whatever you get from me.' I went to 'Alqama and
asked him and he said, 'You will not get anything from them but that
he will get better from you.' He said, 'Yes, from my *deen*.'" Ziyad
appointed Abu Wa'il over the treasury and then dismissed him.

Al-Fadl ibn Dukayn reported from Abu Bakr ibn 'Ayyash from 'Asim that Abu Wa'il said, "When Mu'awiya appointed Yazid ibn Mu'awiya, Abu Wa'il said, 'Do you think that Mu'awiya will return to Yazid after his death and see him in his kingdom?'"

Sa'id ibn Mansur reported from Abu 'Awana from 'Asim ibn Bahdala that Abu Wa'il said, "Al-Hajjaj sent for me and I went to him and he asked, 'What is your name?' I answered, 'The governor would not send for me without knowing my name.' He asked, 'When did you arrive in this land?' I replied, 'The night its people fell.' He said, 'It seems that you recite the Qur'an?' I replied, 'I recite from it that which, if I follow it, will be enough for me.' He said, 'We want to employ you in a post.' I asked, 'What post, governor?' He replied, 'As-Silsila [the chain across the Euphrates].' I said, 'As-Silsila will only be put right by men who stand over it and work on it. If you seek my help, you are seeking the help of an old man, tattered and weak, who fears evil helpers. I prefer for the governor to excuse me. If the governor pushes me, I will embark on it. By Allah, I am restless in bed at night, remembering the governor and could not sleep until morning. I did not work for the governor, so how will it be when the governor appoints me over a task? By Allah, I only know people who have fled the governor out of awe of you, governor.' He liked what I said and said, 'Repeat to me.' I repeated to him. He said, 'As for your words "I prefer for the governor to excuse me. If the governor pushes me, I will embark on it," if we do not find someone other than you, we will press you. If we do find someone else, we will not press you. As for your words, "I only know people who have fled the governor out of awe of you, governor," by Allah, I do not know today of a man on the surface of the earth who has shed more blood than me. I mastered matters which the people feared, so leave me with them. Go. May Allah have mercy on you.' I left his presence and turned aside from the road deliberately as if I could not see. He said, 'Guide the old man. Guide the old man' until a man came and took my hand and took me out. I did not return to him again."

Qabisa ibn 'Uqba reported from Sufyan that Ibn 'Awn said, "A man took me to Abu Wa'il and he asked, 'Abu Wa'il, what did you testify to against al-Hajjaj?' He answered, 'Will you command me to judge against Allah?'"

Muhammad ibn 'Abdullah al-Asadi reported from Sufyan that Abu Hashim said, "I saw Abu Wa'il making indications in the time of al-Hajjaj."

Muhammad ibn 'Ubayd reported from al-A'mash, "Ibrahim said to me, 'You must have Shaqiq. I was alive in the time of the companions of 'Abdullah who were many and they counted him among the best of them.'"

Jarir ibn 'Abd al-Hamid reported that Mughira said, "Ibrahim at-Taymi was reminding in the house of Abu Wa'il. Abu Wa'il used to tremble like a bird."

Al-Fadl ibn Dukayn reported from Abu Bakr from 'Ayyash that 'Asim said, "Abu Wa'il did not turn about in a prayer nor in the road."

Musa ibn Isma'il reported from 'Abdullah ibn Bakr from 'Asim ibn Bahdala who said that he heard Shaqiq ibn Salama say that Abu Wa'il said while he was prostrating, "O Allah, pardon me and forgive me. If You pardon me, You pardon a lot. If You punish me, You punish me without wronging."

Qabisa ibn 'Uqba reported from Sufyan that al-'Amash said, "When Abu Wa'il was asked about something of the Qur'an, he said, 'Allah gave him that which he wanted.'"

'Ali ibn 'Abdullah ibn Ja'far reported from Sufyan ibn 'Uyayna from 'Ata' ibn as-Sa'ib that Abu Wa'il disliked to say a letter. He said, '*ism* (word)' meaning in the Qur'an.

'Arim ibn al-Fadl reported from Hammad ibn Zayd that 'Asim said, "I met some people who took burdens on this night. They used to drink the *nabidh* made in jars and wear saffron-dyed garments and did not see any harm in that. They included Abu Wa'il and another man."

Ahmad ibn 'Abdullah ibn Yunus reported from Abu Bakr ibn 'Ayyash that 'Asim said, "When 'Abdullah saw Abu Wa'il, he said, 'The penitent.'"

'Affan ibn Muslim and 'Arim ibn al-Fadl reported from Abu 'Awana from Mughira from Abu Wa'il that when he was called, he said, "At the service of Allah."

'Affan said in his *hadith*, "He did not say, 'At Your service.'"

'Arim said, "And he did not say, 'At the service of Your hands.'"

Khallad ibn Yahya and Ahmad ibn 'Abdullah ibn Yunus reported from Mu'arraf ibn Wasil: "Abu Wa'il used to say to his boy when the sun set, 'Boy, are we in evening yet?'"

Ahmad ibn 'Abdullah said in his *hadith*, "Shaqiq lost his eyesight."

Ahmad ibn 'Abdullah ibn Yunus reported from Mu'arraf ibn Wasil: "I saw Ibrahim at-Taymi with Abu Wa'il while his hand was in mine. When Ibrahim reminded, Abu Wa'il wept as if he was frightened."

Sa'id ibn Muhammad ath-Thaqafi reported that az-Zibriqan said, "Shaqiq commanded me: 'Do not sit with the people of "I think, I think."'"

Muhammad ibn 'Abdullah al-Asadi reported from Mindal from Sufyan from 'Amr ibn Qays from 'Asim that Abu Wa'il said, "I prefer one dirham from trade to ten from my stipend." Qays reported the like of it from Abu Wa'il.

Al-Fadl ibn Dukayn reported from Hafs that al-A'mash said, "I saw that the waist-wrapper of Abu Wa'il reached the middle of his calves and his shirt was above that and his cloak was above that. Mujahid was the same."

Al-Fadl ibn Dukayn reported that Sa'id ibn Salih al-Asadi said, "Abu Wa'il used to wear cut Yemeni garments."

'Ubaydullah ibn Musa reported from Shayban that al-A'mash said, "I saw Shaqiq dyeing his beard yellow."

Al-Fadl ibn Dukayn reported that Fitr said, "I saw Abu Wa'il dyeing his beard yellow."

'Amr ibn al-Haytham Abu Qatan reported: "I asked Mu'arrif ibn Wasil: 'Did you see Abu Wa'il dyeing his hair yellow?' I answered, 'Yes, Abu Wa'il used to dye his beard yellow."

Zuhayr ibn Harb reported from 'Ali ibn Thabit that Sa'id ibn Salih said, "I saw Abu Wa'il hear mourning and he wept."

'Affan ibn Muslim reported from 'Abdullah ibn Bakr al-Muzani said, "I heard 'Asim ibn Bahdala say, 'Abu Wa'il went to al-Aswad ibn Hilal to visit him.' Abu Wa'il said, 'By Allah, I only came to you because I wanted to meet you.' He asked, 'Why, Abu Wa'il?' He said, 'Because I would refrain you from life and I fear trials for you. I know that what is with Allah is better.' He said, 'No, do not do it, Abu Wa'il. I have not forgone fifty prayers every day. When I die, my action stands and I do not increase in prayer or in a good action for a good action nor in fasting for a fast.'"

'Affan ibn Muslim reported from Hammad ibn Salama that 'Asim ibn Bahdala said, "When Abu Wa'il died Abu Burda faced him."

Al-Fadl ibn Dukayn and others said that Abu Wa'il died in the time of al-Hajjaj after al-Jamajim. Abu Wa'il related from 'Amr, 'Ali, 'Abdullah, Usama ibn Zayd, Hudhayfa, Abu Musa, Ibn 'Abbas and 'Azra. He went to Syria and listened to Abu ad-Darda'. He related from Ibn az-Zubayr and Salman ibn Rabi'a. He attended the expedition to Balanjar with Salman ibn Rabi'a. He related from Ibn Mu'ayyiz as-Sa'di who related from 'Abdullah. Abu Wa'il also related from Masruq, Kurdus, 'Amr ibn Shurahbil, Yasar ibn Numayr, Salama ibn Sabra and 'Amr ibn al-Harith who related from Zaynab, the wife of 'Abdullah. He was trustworthy and had a lot of *hadiths*.

Waki' ibn al-Jarrah reported from al-A'mash from Abu Wa'il from ad-Dabbi ibn Ma'bad al-Juhani.

Zayd ibn Wahb al-Juhani

One of the Banu Hisl ibn Nasr ibn Malik ibn 'Adi ibn at-Tawl ibn 'Awf ibn Ghatafan ibn Qays ibn Juhayna of Quda'a. His *kunya* was Abu Sulayman. Zayd related from 'Amr, 'Ali, 'Abdullah and Hudhayfa. He was present with 'Ali ibn Abi Talib in his battles.

Al-Fadl ibn Dukayn reported from Ibn Abi Ghaniyya from al-Hakam that Zayd ibn Wahb said, "We went on an expedition to Azerbaijan in the rule of 'Umar. On that day az-Zubayr ibn al-'Awwam was among us. 'Umar's letter reached us: 'You are in a land in which carrion is mixed in its food and carrion in its garments. Only eat what is slaughtered and wear what is slaughtered.'"

Al-Fadl ibn Dukayn reported that the *mawla* of Zayd ibn Wahb said, "On that day Zayd was in a garment wrapped in it. He used to do four *takbir*s in the funeral prayer. When he said the *salam*, he said, 'Peace be upon you and the mercy of Allah and His blessings and forgiveness and His excellent prayers.'"

Abu Mu'awiya ad-Darir reported from al-A'mash who said, "I saw Zayd ibn Wahb dyeing his beard yellow."

Our companions say that Zayd ibn Wahb died while al-Hajjaj was governor after al-Jamajim.

'Abdullah ibn Sakhbara al-Azdi

His *kunya* was Abu Ma'mar. He related from 'Umar, 'Ali, 'Abdullah, Khabbab, Abu Mas'ud and 'Alqama. He related from the *hadith* of Isra'il from Abu Ma'mar that he heard Abu Bakr as-Siddiq who said, "Disbelief in Allah is claiming lineage not known." I do not consider that to be firm.

Ya'la ibn 'Ubayd reported from al-A'mash from Ibrahim that Abu Ma'mar said, "When 'Umar went into *ruku'*, he put his hands on his knees."

'Abd al-Hamid ibn 'Abd ar-Rahman al-Himmani reported from al-A'mash from 'Umara ibn 'Umayr from Abu Ma'mar that he used to relate *hadith* and used ungrammatical Arabic in it to imitate what he heard.

Our companions said that Abu Ma'mar died in Kufa while 'Ubaydullah ibn Ziyad. He was trustworthy and had *hadith*s.

Yazid ibn Sharik at-Taymi

He is Abu Ibrahim at-Taymi. He related from 'Umar, 'Ali, 'Abdullah ibn Mas'ud, Sa'd ibn Abi Waqqas, Hudhayfa and Abu Dharr. He was the *'arif* of his people. He was trustworthy and had *hadith*s.

Abu 'Amr ash-Shaybani

His name was Sa'd ibn Iyas. He was present at al-Qadisiyya. He related from 'Umar, 'Ali, 'Abdullah, Hudhayfa and Abu Mas'ud al-Ansari. He was old and reached an advanced age. He was trustworthy and had *hadith*s.

Al-Fadl ibn Dukayn reported from 'Isa ibn 'Abd ar-Rahman as-Salami who heard Abu 'Amr ash-Shaybani said, "I remember that I heard the Messenger of Allah ﷺ while I was herding some camels for my people at Kazima."

'Abdullah ibn az-Zubayr al-Humaydi reported from Sufyan ibn 'Uyayna from Isma'il ibn Abi Khalid who heard Abu 'Amr ash-Shaybani. He lived for one hundred and twenty years. He used to say, "My youth came to an end on the Day of al-Qadisiyya. I was forty."

Zirr ibn Hubaysh al-Asadi

One of the Banu Ghadira ibn Malik ibn Tha'laba ibn Dudan ibn Asad ibn Khuzayma. His *kunya* was Abu Maryam. He related from 'Umar, 'Ali, 'Abdullah, 'Abd ar-Rahman ibn 'Awf, Ubayy ibn Ka'b, Hudhayfa and Abu Wa'il.

'Abdullah ibn Idris reported that Isma'il ibn Abi Khalid said, "I saw Zirr ibn Hubaysh opening his jaws a lot."

He said, "I heard him say, "Ubayy ibn Ka'b said that the Night of Power was the 27th.""

Muhammad ibn 'Ubayd at-Tanafisi reported that Isma'il ibn Abi Khalid said, "I saw Zirr ibn Hubaysh. He went to him when he was one hundred and twenty. His beard was trembling due to old age."

Someone other than Muhammad ibn 'Ubayd at-Tanafisi said that he died when he was one hundred and twenty-two.

Yahya ibn Adam said from Abu Bakr ibn 'Ayyash that 'Asim said, "Zirr ibn Hubaysh had the most Arabic among the people. 'Abdullah used to ask him about Arabic."

Yahya ibn Adam said from Abu Bakr that 'Asim said, "Zirr ibn Hubaysh was older than Abu Wa'il. When they met together, Abu Wa'il did not relate in the presence of Zirr. Zirr used to like 'Ali while Abu Wa'il liked 'Uthman. They used to sit together and I did not hear them reminding one another about anything all."

'Ubaydullah ibn Musa reported from 'Asim ath-Thaqafi that 'Asim ibn Abi an-Nujud said, "Often I saw Zirr ibn Hubaysh come in a single garment that he folded on his shoulder until he joined the row with the people."

Al-Fadl ibn Dukayn reported from Qays ibn ar-Rabi' that 'Asim ibn Abi an-Nujud said, "A man of the Ansar passed by Zirr ibn Hubaysh while he was giving the *adhan* and said, 'Abu Maryam, I used to honour you for that (or for the *adhan*). Then I will not say a word to you until you meet Allah.'" He was trustworthy, with many *hadith*s.

'Amr ibn Shurahbil

He is Abu Maysara al-Hamdani then al-Wafa'i. He related from 'Umar, 'Ali and 'Abdullah.

'Abd al-Malik ibn 'Amr Abu 'Amir al-'Aqadi reported from Shu'ba from Ibrahim ibn Muhammad ibn al-Muntashir that his father said, "'Amr ibn Shurahbil was the imam of the mosque of the Banu Wadi'a."

Ahmad ibn 'Abdullah ibn Yunus reported from Zuhayr from Jabir from 'Amir that Abi Maysara said, "Ibn Mas'ud said, 'Abu Maysara, what do you say about *"the planets with their retrograde motion, swiftly moving, self-concealing"* (81:115-6)?' He said, 'I only think that they are wild cows.' He said, 'I only know about it what I said.'"

Al-Fadl ibn Dukayn reported that he heard Isra'il ibn Yunus say, "When Abu Maysara received his stipend, he gave some of it as *sadaqa*. When he went to his people and they counted it, they found it to be the same. He said to his nephews, 'Will you not do the like of this?' They replied, 'If we knew that it would not decrease, we would do it.' Abu Maysara said, 'I do not stipulate this for my Lord.'"

Abu Mu'awiya ad-Darir reported from al-A'mash that Shaqiq said, "I have not seen a Hamdani in whose skin I would more like to be than 'Amr ibn Shurahbil."

Al-Fadl ibn Dukayn reported from Sharik from 'Asim that Abu Wa'il said, "No Hamdaniya woman has had the like of Abu Maysara." He was asked, "Not Masruq?" He said, "Not Masruq."

Al-Hasan ibn Musa reported from Zuhayr from Abu Ishaq that Abu Maysara said, "Allah is only mentioned in a good place."

Al-Hasan ibn Musa and Ahmad ibn 'Abdullah ibn Yunus reported from Zuhayr from Abu Ishaq that Abu Maysara used to feed people after he prayed, i.e. the *zakat al-fitr*.

Al-Hasan ibn Musa reported from Zuhayr that Abu Ishaq said, "Abu Maysara used to feed a *sa'* and did not give less than that."

Al-Hasan ibn Musa reported from Zuhayr from Abu Ishaq that Abu Maysara ordered his wife: "If you bear a boy, call him ar-Rahin. If you have a girl, call her Umm ar-Rahin." She had a girl and named her Umm Rahin."

Qabisa ibn 'Uqba reported from Sufyan from Abu Ishaq that Abu Maysara said, "It was said to him, 'What will be enough for you in the Rising?' He answered, 'I perform the *witr*.'"

Al-Fadl ibn Dukayn reported from Sharik from 'Asim from Abu Wa'il: "Abu Maysara ordered: 'Do not announce my funeral to anyone as was done in the *Jahiliyya*. Do not make my grave high. Put a bundle of reeds on my grave. I saw that the Muhajirun liked that.'"

Al-Fadl ibn Dukayn reported from Abu al-Ahwas that Abu Ishaq said, "Abu Maysara ordered that a bundle of reeds be put on his grave. They put together four branches against one another and put them on his grave."

Al-Hasan ibn Musa reported Zuhayr that Abu Ishaq said, "Abu Maysara commanded that they put a bundle of reeds or branches on his grave. He said, 'It cheers me that I leave no debt and do not leave children.'"

'Affan ibn Muslim reported from Hammad ibn Zayd from 'Asim ibn Bahdala that Abu Wa'il said, "''Amr ibn Shurahbil said when he was dying, 'I am going to die now. I think so.' He said, 'I only have terror of the presentation. I do not leave wealth and I have no debts and I do not leave dependents to worry me after me. When I die, do not announce my death to anyone. Walk quickly and put some reeds on my grave. I saw that the Muhajirun liked that. Do not elevate my grave. I saw that the Muhajirun dislike that.'"

Waki' and al-Fadl ibn Dukayn reported from Sufyan that Abu Ishaq said, "Abu Maysara ordered that Shurayh, the Qadi of the Muslims, pray over him."

Al-Fadl ibn Dukayn reported from Yunus that Abu Ishaq said, "Abu Maysara ordered his brother al-Arqam, 'Do not announce my death to any of the people and have Shurayh, the Qadi of the Muslims and their imam, pray over me. Hurry with my bier walking and only put reeds over my grave.'"

Ishaq ibn Mansur and al-Hasan ibn Musa reported from Zuhayr that Abu Ishaq said, "Abu Maysara commanded his brother al-Arqam, 'I only think that I will die tonight. In the morning, take me out and do not announce my death to anyone. It is the *Jahiliyya* (or the summons of the *Jahiliyya*).'"

Al-Hasan ibn Musa reported the like and he said that Zuhayr said that Abu Ishaq said, "That is what 'Alqama said to al-Aswad and 'Amr ibn Maymun. He said to them, 'Remind me of 'There is no god but Allah' when I die.'"

'Affan ibn Muslim reported from Shu'ba from Abu Ishaq that 'Amr ibn Shurahbil ordered that when he died his funeral should not be announced to anyone. He gave 'Alqama those instructions.

Wahb ibn Jarir reported from Shu'ba from Abu Ishaq that 'Amr ibn Shurahbil ordered that his brother not announce his death to anyone. He gave those instructions to 'Alqama.

Waki' ibn al-Jarrah reported from al-A'mash from 'Umara ibn 'Umayr that Abu Ma'mar said, "When Abu Maysara died, the companions of 'Abdullah said, 'Walk behind Abu Maysara. He used to like for people to walk behind the bier.'"

Waki' ibn al-Jarrah reported from Malik ibn Mighwal that Abu Ishaq said, "I saw Shurayh riding in the funeral of Abu Maysara."

Waki' and Abu Dawud at-Tayalisi reported from Isra'il that Abu Ishaq said, "I saw Abu Juhayfa in the funeral of Abu Maysara holding onto the post of the bed until he was brought out. Then he began to say, 'May Allah forgive you, Abu Maysara.' He did not leave him until he reached the grave."

Muhammad ibn Sa'd said that they said that Abu Maysara died in Kufa while 'Ubaydullah ibn Ziyad was governor.

'Abd ar-Rahman ibn Abi Layla

His name was Yasar ibn Bilal ibn Bulayl ibn Uhayha ibn al-Jallah ibn al-Harish ibn Jahjaba ibn Kulfa ibn 'Awf ibn 'Amr ibn 'Awf of Aws. His *kunya* was Abu 'Isa. He related from 'Amr, 'Ali, 'Abdullah, Ubayy ibn Ka'b, Sahl ibn Hunayf, Khawwat ibn Jubayr, Hudhayfa, 'Abdullah ibn Zayd, Ka'b ibn 'Ujra, al-Bara' ibn 'Azib, Abu Dharr, Abu ad-Darda', Abu Sa'id al-Khudri, Qays ibn Sa'd and Zayd ibn Arqam. He also related from his father and said, "I met one hundred and twenty of the Ansar from the Companions of the Prophet 纂."

Al-Fadl ibn Dukayn and Muhammad ibn 'Abdullah al-Asadi reported from Sufyan from 'Ata' ibn as-Sa'ib that he heard Ibn Abi Layla say, "I met one hundred and twenty of the Ansar from the Companions of the Messenger of Allah 纂 in this mosque. None of them related a *hadith* but that he wished that his brother would spare him giving *fatwa*."

Malik ibn Isma'il reported from Isra'il from 'Abd al-A'la that 'Abd ar-Rahman ibn Abi Layla said, "I was sitting with 'Umar ibn al-Khattab when a rider came to him and claimed that he had seen the new moon. He said, 'People! Break the fast!' Then he went to a bowl filled with water and did *wudu'* and wiped over his socks. Then he prayed *Maghrib*. The rider said, 'I only came to ask you about this. Is it something you have seen someone else do?' He answered, 'Yes. Good from me and good of the community. Abu al-Qasim, the Messenger of Allah ﷺ, used to do that. I saw him do it.'"

Shihab ibn 'Abbad reported from Sufyan ibn 'Uyayna from Ibn Abi Najih that Mujahid said, "''Abd ar-Rahman ibn Abi Layla had a room in which copies of the Qur'an were collected. Then they only finished with some food. I went to him and had some gold nuggets. He asked, 'Will you adorn a sword with it?' I answered, 'No.' He asked. 'Will you adorn a copy of the Qur'an with it?' I replied, 'No.' He said, 'Perhaps you will estimate it. It is disliked.'"

Muslim ibn Ibrahim reported from Hammam ibn Yahya that Thabit al-Bunani said, "When 'Abd ar-Rahman ibn Abi Layla had prayed *Subh*, he opened the copy of the Qur'an and recited until sunrise."

Hammam said, "Thabit used to do it."

Muslim said, "Hammad ibn Salama used to do it."

Hajjaj ibn Muhammad reported from Shu'ba that Abu Firwa said, "I saw 'Abd ar-Rahman ibn Abi Layla doing *wudu'*. A towel was brought and he threw it aside."

Qabisa ibn 'Uqba reported from Sufyan that Muslim al-Juhani said, "I saw 'Abd ar-Rahman ibn Abi Layla indicate with a finger at Muhammad ibn Sa'd to be silent in *Jumu'a*, i.e. while the imam was speaking."

Muhammad ibn as-Salt reported from Abu Kudayna that Abu Firwa said, "''Abd ar-Rahman ibn Abi Layla commanded me to make the rows straight and that none should spit in front of him in the prayer place, but should spit under his left foot."

Muhammad ibn al-Fadl ibn Ghazwan reported that Yazid ibn Abi Ziyad said, "I saw 'Abd ar-Rahman ibn Abi Layla wearing a gown of rough silk and he wore it until it was cut up and then he shortened it another time and it was done for him. He said to his companion, 'Do not put silk in it. Make its edge linen or cotton.' It was said to him, 'But you used to wear it.' He said, 'That was done by someone else.'"

Abu al-Walid at-Tayalisi reported from Abu 'Awana from Yazid ibn Abi Ziyad that 'Abd ar-Rahman ibn Abi Layla said that the life of *hadith* is to remember it. He said, "'Abdullah ibn Shaddad said, 'May Allah have mercy on you. How many *hadith*s have you brought to life in my breast which were dead!'"

Muhammad ibn 'Abdullah al-Asadi reported from as-Sabbah ibn Yahya al-Muzani that Yazid ibn Abi Ziyad heard 'Abd ar-Rahman ibn Abi Layla say to 'Abdullah ibn 'Ukaym, "Come so we can remind one another of *hadith*. Its life is its remembrance."

Al-Fadl ibn Dukayn reported from Isra'il from 'Abd al-A'la ath-Tha'labi that 'Abd ar-Rahman's *kunya* was Abu 'Isa.

Waki' related from Mis'ar from al-Hakam that the *kunya* of 'Abd ar-Rahman ibn Abi Layla was Abu 'Isa.

Al-Fadl ibn Dukayn reported from Qays that Abu Husayn said, "When al-Hajjaj came, he wanted to appoint 'Abd ar-Rahman ibn Abi Layla as qadi. Hawshab said to him, 'If you want to put 'Ali ibn Abi Talib in charge of the qadiship, then do it.'"

Qabisa ibn 'Uqba reported that Hammam ibn 'Abdullah at-Taymi said, "I saw 'Abd ar-Rahman ibn Abi Layla beaten and he was wearing trousers. Al-Hajjaj beat him." He said, "Hawshab was in charge of the police for al-Hajjaj. He is Abu al-'Awwam ibn Hawshab."

Abu Mu'awiya ad-Darir reported that al-A'mash said, "I saw 'Abd ar-Rahman ibn Abi Layla. Al-Hajjaj stopped him and said to him, 'Curse the liars: 'Ali ibn Abi Talib, 'Abdullah ibn az-Zubayr and al-Mukhtar ibn Abi 'Ubayd.' 'Abd ar-Rahman said, 'May Allah curse the liars.' Then he began and said, "'Ali ibn Abi Talib, 'Abdullah ibn az-Zubayr and al-Mukhtar ibn Abi 'Ubayd.'"

Abu Mu'awiya ad-Darir reported from al-A'mash from 'Amr ibn Murra that when 'Abd ar-Rahman ibn Abi Layla heard them mentioning 'Ali and what they said about him, he said, "We sat with 'Ali and accompanied him and we did not hear him say anything that those people say. Is it not enough that 'Ali was the cousin of the Messenger of Allah ﷺ and his son-in-law who was married to his daughter, and the father of Hasan and Husayn, and was present at Badr and al-Hudaybiya?" They all agreed that 'Abd ar-Rahman ibn Abi Layla went out with those who went out against al-Hajjaj with 'Abd ar-Rahman ibn Muhammad ibn al-Ash'ath and was killed at Dujayl.

'Abdullah ibn 'Ukaym al-Juhani

His *kunya* was Abu Ma'bad. He related from 'Umar, 'Uthman, 'Ali and 'Abdullah. He was old and had been alive in the *Jahiliyya*.

Ya'la ibn 'Ubayd reported from al-Ajlah from al-Hakam ibn 'Utba from 'Abd ar-Rahman ibn Abi Layla that 'Abdullah ibn 'Ukaym said, "The Messenger of Allah ﷺ wrote to us not to use carrion for tanning nor sinews."

Wahb ibn Jarir reported from Shu'ba from al-Hakam from 'Abd ar-Rahman ibn Abi Layla that 'Abdullah ibn 'Ukaym said, "The letter of the Messenger of Allah ﷺ was read to us while I was a young lad in the land of Juhayna telling us not to use carrion for tanning or sinews."

'Affan ibn Muslim reported from Shu'ba that Hilal al-Wazzan heard 'Abdullah ibn 'Ukaym say, "I gave allegiance to 'Umar with this hand of mine to hear and obey as much as I could."

Muhammad ibn al-Fudyal ibn Ghazwan reported from 'Abd ar-Rahman ibn Ishaq from 'Abdullah al-Qurashi from 'Abd ar-Rahman ibn Abi Layla and 'Abdullah ibn 'Ukaym that when the *mu'adhdhin* said, 'I testify that there is no god but Allah and I testify that Muhammad is the Messenger of Allah,' 'Ali said, 'Those who denied Muhammad are deniers.'"

Muhammad ibn 'Abdullah al-Asadi reported from Sufyan that Muslim al-Juhani said, "I saw 'Abd ar-Rahman ibn Abi Layla and 'Abdullah ibn 'Ukaym. This one liked 'Ali and that one liked 'Uthman." The mother of 'Abd ar-Rahman ibn Abi Layla died and 'Abdullah ibn 'Ukaym went forward to pray over her. He was the Imam of the mosque of Juhayna in Kufa.

'Abd ar-Rahman ibn Mahdi related from Musa al-Juhani that the daughter of 'Abdullah ibn 'Ukaym said, "'Abdullah ibn 'Ukaym loved 'Uthman. Ibn Abi Layla loved 'Ali. They were brotherly. She said, "I did not hear them discussing anything at all but that I heard them say to 'Abd ar-Rahman ibn Abi Layla, 'If your companion has patience, people will come to him.'"

'Amr ibn al-Haytham Abu Qatan reported from al-Mas'udi from al-Hakam who said that 'Abdullah ibn 'Ukaym did not tie up a bag. He said, "I heard Allah say, *'He amassed and hoarded.'*" (70:18)

'Abdullah ibn Idris reported from Muhammad ibn Abi Ayyub that Hilal ibn Abi Humayd heard 'Abdullah ibn 'Ukaym say, "I will not help against a caliph ever after 'Uthman." It was said to him, "Abu Ma'bad, did you help against his blood?" He said, "I was prepared to mention his evil qualities to help against his blood."

Sufyan ibn 'Uyayna said that Abu Firwa said, "I washed 'Abdullah ibn 'Ukaym." He said that someone other than Sufyan said that 'Abdullah ibn 'Ukaym died in Kufa while al-Hajjaj ibn Yusuf was governor.

'Abdullah ibn Abi Abi al-Hudhayl al-'Anazi of Rabi'a. His *kunya* was Abu al-Mughira. He related from 'Umar, 'Ali, 'Abdullah ibn Mas'ud, 'Ammar ibn Yasir, Ibn 'Abbas, 'Abdullah ibn 'Amr and Abu Zur'a ibn 'Amr ibn Jarir.

Ya'la ibn 'Ubayd reported from al-Ajlah that Ibn Abi al-Hudhayl said, "I was sitting with 'Umar when an old man was brought drunk in Ramadan. He said, 'Woe to you! When young men are fasting?' He gave him eighty lashes."

Muhammad ibn 'Abdullah ibn Numayr reported from Yahya ibn Adam from al-Ashja'i from Sufyan from Sinan that 'Abdullah ibn Abi al-Hudhayl heard 'Umar say, "Men travel only to the Ancient House."

Shu'ayb ibn Harb reported from Shu'ba from al-Hakam that 'Abdullah ibn Abi al-Hudhayl said, "The people of Kufa presented questions to me about which I questioned Ibn 'Abbas. There were questions about what was in all of my book." He had *hadith*s.

Haritha ibn Mudarrib al-'Abdi

He related from 'Ali, 'Abdullah, 'Ammar, Abu Musa al-Ash'ari, Furat ibn Hayyan al-'Ajli and al-Walid ibn 'Uqba.

Muhammad ibn 'Abdullah al-Asadi reported that Yunus ibn Abi Ishaq said, "I saw Haritha ibn Mudarrib dyeing with *wars* and saffron."

'Abdullah ibn Salama al-Jamali of Murad

He related from 'Umar, 'Ali, 'Abdullah, Sa'd ibn Abi Waqqas and 'Ammar ibn Yasar and Salman.

Ishaq ibn Mansur reported from Zuhayr from Abu Ishaq from Abu al-'Aliya, who is 'Abdullah ibn Salama.

Sulayman Abu Sawud at-Tayalisi reported from Shu'ba that 'Amr ibn Murra said, "'Abdullah ibn Salama said the *takbir* and he would relate and we would acknowledge or disacknowledge."

Murra ibn Sharahil al-Hamdani

He is Murra al-Khayr and Murra at-Tayyib. He related from 'Umar, 'Ali and 'Abdullah.

Yazid ibn Harun reported from al-Hajjaj ibn Arta'a from 'Amr ibn Murra that Murra al-Hamdani said, "I heard 'Umar ibn al-Khattab say, 'By Allah, I will return it to you until a man of you returns with a hundred camels (i.e. the *zakat*).'" He was trustworthy.

'Ubayd ibn Nudayla al-Khuza'i

His *kunya* was Abu Mu'awiya. He related from 'Umar and 'Abdullah. He related from 'Ali about the shares of inheritance.

Yahya ibn Adam said from al-Hasan ibn Salih said, "Yahya ibn Waththab recited to 'Ubayd ibn Nudayla. 'Ubayd ibn Nudayla recited to 'Alqama and 'Alqama recited to 'Abdullah. Which recitation is sounder than this?"

Someone other than Yahya ibn Adam said that 'Ubayd ibn Nudayla recited to 'Abdullah ibn Mas'ud. Then he recited to 'Alqama after that. They said that 'Ubayd ibn Nudayla was in Kufa when Bishr ibn Marwan was governor.

Among this generation those who related from 'Umar ibn al-Khattab and 'Abdullah ibn Mas'ud but did not relate from 'Ali ibn Abi Talib

'Amr ibn Maymun

'Amr ibn Maymun al-Asadi Awd ibn Sa'b ibn Sa'd al-'Ashira of Madhhij. He related from 'Umar and 'Abdullah. He listened to Mu'adh in Yemen while the Messenger of Allah ﷺ was alive. He related from Abu Mas'ud al-Ansari, 'Abdullah ibn 'Amr, Salman ibn Rabi'a and ar-Rabi' ibn Khuthaym.

'Ubaydullah ibn Musa reported from Isra'il from Abu Ishaq in the *hadith* he related from 'Amr ibn Maymun that his *kunya* was Abu 'Abdullah.

Muhammad ibn 'Umar said that 'Amr ibn Maymun died in 74 or 75 AH at the beginning of the caliphate of 'Abd al-Malik ibn Marwan.

Qabisa ibn 'Uqba reported from Yunus ibn Abi Ishaq that his father said, "When 'Amr ibn Maymun entered the mosque, he was seen remembering Allah."

Al-Ma'rur ibn Suwayd al-Asadi

One of the Banu Sa'd ibn al-Harith ibn Tha'laba ibn Dudan ibn Asad. He related from 'Umar, 'Abdullah and Abu Dharr.

Abu Nu'aym said that al-Ma'rur ibn Suwayd reached the age of one hundred and twenty.

'Abd ar-Rahman ibn Mahdi said from Shu'ba that Wasil said, "Al-Ma'rur ibn Suwayd used to say to us, 'Sons of my brother, learn from me.'" He had a lot of *hadith*s.

Hammam ibn al-Harith an-Nakha'i

He related from 'Umar, 'Abdullah, Abu Mas'ud al-Ansari, Abu ad-Darda', 'Adi ibn Hatim, Jarir ibn 'Abdullah and 'A'isha. He died in Kufa while al-Hajjaj was governor.

Muhammad ibn al-Fadl reported from Husayn from Ibrahim from

Hammam that he used to say, "O Allah, heal me from my sleep a little and make my wakefulness in obeying You." He only slept a little while he was sitting.

Al-Fadl ibn Dukayn reported from Hafs ibn al-Hajjaj that it was related to him from someone who saw Hammam in *i'tikaf* in the mosque of his people.

Al-Harith ibn al-Azma'

Al-Harith ibn al-Azma' ibn Abi Buthayna ibn 'Abdullah ibn Murr ibn Malik ibn Harb ibn al-Harith ibn Sa'd ibn 'Abdullah ibn Wada'a of Hamdan. He is al-Harith al-A'raj. He and his brother Shaddad ibn al-Azma' were nobles at Kufa. He listened to 'Umar, 'Abdullah and 'Amr ibn al-'As. He had few *hadith*s. He died in Kufa at the end of Mu'awiya ibn Abi Sufyan while an-Nu'man ibn Bashir was in charge of Kufa at that time.

Al-Aswad ibn Hilal

Al-Aswad ibn Hilal al-Muharibi Muharib ibn Khasfa ibn Qays ibn 'Aylan ibn Mudar. He related from 'Umar, 'Abdullah and Mu'adh ibn Hanbal.

Sa'id ibn Mansur reported from Sharij ibn 'Abdullah from al-Ash'ath ibn Sulaym that al-Aswad ibn Hilal said, "I emigrated in the time of 'Umar ibn al-Khattab and entered Madina with some camels of mine. I entered the mosque and there was 'Umar ibn al-Khattab addressing the people. He was saying, 'O people, perform *hajj* and sacrifice. Allah loves the sacrifices.' I went out and a man was holding the reins of every camel and they bartered with me for them and I found a market."

Al-Fadl ibn Dukayn reported from Mis'ar that Abu Sakhr said, "Al-Aswad ibn Hilal was wearing a long brocade shawl." He said that al-Aswad ibn Hilal died in the time of al-Hajjaj after the time of Dayr al-Jamajim.

Sulaym ibn Hanzala al-Bakri

He related from 'Umar, 'Abdullah and Ubayy ibn Ka'b.

An-Nu'man ibn Humayd al-Bakri

He related from 'Umar and 'Abdullah. He also related from Salman. He said, "I visited him with my uncle at al-Mada'in and he shook my hand."

'Ubaydullah ibn Musa reported from Isra'il from Simak in a *hadith* which he related from an-Nu'man ibn Humayd that his *kunya* was Abu Qudama. He had few *hadith*s.

'Abdullah ibn 'Utba ibn Mas'ud al-Hudhali

An ally of the Banu Zuhra ibn Kilab. He related from 'Umar ibn al-Khattab and 'Abdullah ibn Mas'ud.

Yazid ibn Harun reported from Hisham ibn Hassan that Muhammad ibn Sirin said, "I was with 'Abdullah ibn 'Utba. He was the qadi of the people of Iraq."

Al-Fadl ibn Dukayn reported from Qays that Abu Hasin said, "I saw 'Abdullah ibn 'Utba wearing rough silk."

Abu Nu'aym said that 'Abdullah ibn 'Utba was Qadi for Mus'ab ibn az-Zubayr. He was trustworthy.

Abu 'Atiyya al-Wadi'i of Hamdan

His name was Malik ibn 'Amir and he is Abu Humra al-Hamdani. He related from 'Umar and 'Abdullah. He died in Kufa while Mus'ab ibn az-Zubayr was governor. He was trustworthy and had *hadith*s.

'Amir ibn Matar ash-Shaybani

He related from 'Umar, 'Abdullah and Hudhayfa. He had few *hadith*s.

'Abdullah ibn Khalifa at-Ta'i

He related from 'Umar and 'Abdullah.

'Ubaydullah ibn Musa reported from Isra'il from Abu Ishaq from 'Abdullah ibn Khalifa that 'Umar and 'Abdullah said, "The prayer of '*Asr* is that in which a rider travels for two parasangs and a walker one parasang."

Abu Qatan said from Shu'ba from Abu Ishaq from 'Abdullah ibn Khalifa that the sandal strap of 'Umar broke and he said, "To Allah we return." I said, "Amir al-Mu'minin!"

'Abd ar-Rahman ibn Yazid

'Abd ar-Rahman ibn Yazid ibn Qays ibn 'Abdullah ibn Malik ibn 'Alqama ibn Salaman ibn Kahl ibn 'Awf ibn an-Nakha' of Madhhij. He was the brother of al-Aswad ibn Qays. He related from 'Umar and 'Abdullah.

Muhammad ibn 'Ubayd reported from Isma'il ibn Abi Khalid from Muhammad ibn 'Abd ar-Rahman that his father said, "We went to 'Umar wanting to ask him about wiping over leather socks. He rose and urinated and then performed *wudu'* and wiped over his leather socks. We said, 'We came to you to ask about wiping over leather socks.' He said, 'I did this for your sake.'"

'Abd ar-Rahman ibn Muhammad al-Muharibi reported that al-Hasan ibn 'Ubaydullah said, "''Abd ar-Rahman ibn Yazid used to dye his beard yellow."

Hafs ibn Ghiyath reported that al-Hasan ibn 'Ubayd said, "I saw 'Abd ar-Rahman ibn Yazid prostrating in a Syrian burnous."

Abu Mu'awiya ad-Darir and Yahya ibn 'Ubayd reported from al-A'mash that Muslim said, "I saw on 'Abd ar-Rahman ibn Yazid a turban with thick turns."

Ya'la said in his *hadith*: "I saw him prostrating and he prostrated on the curl of the turban."

Abu Mu'awiya said in his *hadith*: "It came between his brow and the ground."

Waki' and al-Fadl ibn Dukayn reported from Malik ibn Mighwal that Abu Sakhra said, "I saw 'Abd ar-Rahman ibn Yazid wearing a black turban." He said that they said that 'Abd ar-Rahman's *kunya* was Abu Bakr. He died in Kufa while al-Hajjaj was governor before the Battle of al-Jamajim. He was trustworthy and has *hadith*s.

❀❀❀

From this generation those who related from 'Umar ibn al-Khattab and 'Ali ibn Abi Talib

'Abis ibn Rabi'a an-Nakha'i from Madhhij

He related from 'Umar ibn al-Khattab and 'Ali ibn Abi Talib. He was trustworthy and had *hadith*s.

Ibn Sa'd said, "I saw them recommending his *hadith*s and using them as authoritative."

Zayd ibn Suhan

Zayd ibn Suhan ibn Hujr ibn al-Harith ibn al-Mujris ibn Sabra ibn Hidrijan ibn 'Isas ibn Layth ibn Hudad ibn Zalim ibn Dhulm ibn 'Ijl ibn 'Amr ibn Wadi'a ibn Afsa ibn 'Abd al-Qays ibn Afsa ibn Du'miy ibn Jadila ibn Asad ibn Rabi'a ibn Nizar. Sa'sa'a was his full brother.

Ya'la ibn 'Ubayd reported from al-Ajlah that 'Ubayd ibn Lahiq said, "The Messenger of Allah ﷺ was on a journey and a man of the people dismounted and drove them reciting *rajaz* poetry. Then another dismounted and then it seemed proper to the Messenger of Allah ﷺ to console his Companions. So he dismounted and began to say, 'Jundub! What is Jundub? And the one who most cuts good is Zayd.' Then he mounted and his Companions drew near him and said, 'Messenger of Allah, we heard you say in the night, "Jundub! What is Jundub? And the one who most cuts good is Zayd."' He replied, 'There are two men in this community. One of them will strike a blow which separates the truth from falsehood and the other will have his hand severed in the Way of Allah. Then Allah will make the rest of his body follow the first."

Ya'la said that al-Ajlah said, "Jundub killed the sorcerer with al-Walid ibn 'Utba and Zayd had his hand severed in the Battle of Jalula' and was killed in the Battle of the Camel."

Al-A'mash mentioned that Zayd's hand was severed in the Battle of Nihawand.

'Affan ibn Muslim reported from Hammad ibn Salama from Abu at-Tayyah from 'Abdullah ibn Abi al-Hudhayl that the delegation of the people of Kufa came to 'Umar. They included Zayd ibn Suhan. A man of the people of Syria came to him to ask for his help. He said, "People of Kufa, you are the treasure of the people of Islam. The people of Basra asked for your help and you helped them. The people of Syria asked for your help and you helped them." 'Umar appointed a man for Zayd and said, "People of Kufa, work by Zayd. Otherwise I will punish you."

Shihab ibn 'Abbad al-'Abdi reported from Muhammad ibn Fudayl ibn Ghazwan from al-Ajlah that Ibn Abi al-Hudhayl said, "'Umar ibn al-Khattab called Zayd ibn Suhan and followed him by his saddle as you do with your governors. Then he turned to the people and said, 'Do this with Zayd and Zayd's companions.'"

Hisham Abu al-Walid at-Tayalisi and Ya'qub ibn Ishaq al-Hadrami reported from Abu 'Awana from Simak that an-Nu'man ibn Qudama was in an army under the command of Salman al-Farisi. Zayd ibn Suhan led them in the prayer as Salman commanded that.

Yahya ibn 'Abbad reported from Shu'ba from Simak ibn Harb from Milhan ibn Tharwan that Salman used to say to Zayd ibn Suhan on Friday, "Rise and remind your people."

Hajjaj ibn Nusayr reported from 'Uqba ibn 'Abdullah ar-Rifa'i that Humayd ibn Hilal said, "Zayd ibn Suhan went to 'Uthman ibn 'Affan and said, 'Amir al-Mu'minin, you have deviated and your community has deviated. Be just and your community will be just three times. He asked, 'Are you an obedient listener?' He said, 'Yes.' He said, 'The truth is in Syria.' He left him immediately and divorced his wife and then went where he had commanded him. They used to think that obedience was their duty."

Shihab ibn 'Abbad reported from 'Abd al-Wahhab ath-Thaqafi from Ayyub that Ghaylan ibn Jarir said, "Zayd ibn Suhan was carried off wounded in the Battle of the Camel. Some of his companions came to him and said, 'Receive the good news, Abu Salman, of the Garden.' He said, 'Do you speak with power? Or will it be the Fire? You do not know. We raided some people in their lands and we killed their ruler and perhaps when we were wronged, we should have been patient.'"

Al-Fadl ibn Dukayn reported from Sufyan from Mukhawwal from al-'Ayzar ibn Hurayth that Zayd ibn Suhan said, "Do not wash the blood from me and do not remove from me any garment except for my leather socks. Put me in the ground. I am a man who is a litigant who will argue on the Day of Rising."

Muhammad ibn 'Abdullah al-Asadi reported from Sufyan from Mus'ab Abu al-Muthanna that Zayd ibn Suhan commanded him to bury him with his blood in his clothes.

Shihab ibn 'Abbad reported from Sufyan ibn 'Uyayna that 'Ammar ad-Dahani said, "Zayd said, 'Bury me, by my mother and father, in a grave and do not wash the blood from me. We are a litigant people.'"

Shihab ibn 'Abbad reported from Muhammad ibn 'Abdullah al-Kirmani from 'Ali ibn Hashim from his father that Zayd ibn Suhan commanded that his copy of the Qur'an be buried with him. He was trustworthy and had few *hadiths*.

'Abdullah ibn Shaddad ibn al-Hadi al-Laythi

He related from 'Umar and 'Ali.

Muhammad ibn 'Abdullah al-Ansari reported that Ibn 'Awn said, "'Abdullah ibn Shaddad was the brother of the daughter of Hamza by the same mother."

Hisham ibn 'Abdullah ibn as-Sa'ib said that the mother of 'Abdullah ibn Shaddad ibn al-Hadi was Sallami bint 'Umays al-Khath'amiyya, the sister of Asma' bint 'Umays. He was married to Hamza ibn 'Abd al-Muttalib and she bore him his daughter 'Umara and then Hamza ibn 'Abd al-Muttalib on the Day of the Battle of Uhud and Shaddad ibn al-Hadi married her and she bore him 'Abdullah ibn Shaddad from the companions of 'Ali. He related from 'Umar.

Sufyan ibn 'Uyayna reported from Isma'il ibn Muhammad ibn Sa'd ibn Abi Waqqas who listened to 'Abdullah ibn Shaddad ibn al-Hadi said, "I heard 'Umar weeping while I was at the end of the rows while he was reciting *Sura Yusuf* when he reached, *'I make complaint about my grief and sorrow to Allah alone.'* (12:86)"

Muhammad ibn 'Umar and others said that 'Abdullah ibn Shaddad went out with those reciters who went out against al-Hajjaj ibn Yusuf in the time of 'Abd ar-Rahman ibn Muhammad ibn al-Ash'ath. He was killed at the Battle of Dujayl. He was trustworthy, a *faqih* with a lot of *hadiths*, a Shi'ite partisan.

Rib'i ibn Hirash

Rib'i ibn Hirash ibn Jahsh ibn 'Amr ibn 'Abdullah ibn Bajjad ibn 'Abd ibn Malik ibn Ghalib ibn Qutay'a ibn 'Abs ibn Baghid ibn Rayth ibn Ghatafan ibn Sa'd ibn Qays ibn 'Aylan ibn Mudar.

Hisham ibn Muhammad ibn as-Sa'ib said that his father said that the Prophet ﷺ wrote to Hirash ibn Jahsh and he tore up his letter. He related from Hirash from 'Umar and 'Ali and Kharsha ibn al-Hurr.

Al-Hajjaj said, "I asked Shu'ba, 'Did Rib'i meet 'Ali?' He replied, 'Yes. He related from 'Ali.' He did not say, 'He listened.'"

Rib'i ibn Hirash died while al-Hajjaj ibn Yusuf was governor after the Battle of al-Jamajim and he left no descendants. His brother, Mas'ud ibn Hirash, had descendants. Mas'ud also related from 'Umar. Their brother Rabi' ibn Hirash spoke after his death.

Abu Nu'aym said that Rib'i died while 'Umar ibn 'Abd al-'Aziz was governor. He was trustworthy and has sound *hadith*s. He died in 101 AH.

'Ababa ibn Rib'i al-Asadi

He related from 'Umar and 'Ali ibn Abi Talib. He had few *hadith*s. May Allah have mercy on him and bless him.

Wahb ibn al-Adja' al-Hamdani, then al-Kharifi

He heard 'Umar say, "When a man comes on *hajj* he should perform *tawaf* of the House seven times." He also related from 'Ali. He had few *hadith*s.

Nu'aym ibn Dijaja al-Asadi

He related from 'Umar, 'Ali and Abu Mas'ud al-Ansari. He had few *hadith*s.

Shurayh ibn Hani'

Shurayh ibn Hani' ibn Yazid ibn Nahik ibn Durayd ibn Sufyan ibn ad-Dabbab of the Banu al-Harith ibn Ka'b. He related from 'Umar, 'Ali, Sa'd ibn Abi Waqqas and 'A'isha.

Ahmad ibn 'Abdullah ibn Yunus reported from Zuhayr from al-Hasan ibn al-Hurr that al-Qasim ibn Mukhaymira said that Shurayh ibn Hani' al-Harithi related to him. He said, "I did not think Harith was better than him." They said, "Shurayh was one of the companions of 'Ali ibn Abi Talib and was present at battles with him. He was trustworthy and had *hadith*s. He was old and was killed in Sijistan with 'Ubaydullah ibn Abi Bakr.

Abu Khalid al-Walibi

Waliba is a sub-tribe of the Banu Asad ibn Khuzayma. Abu Khalid related from 'Umar and 'Ali.

'Abdullah ibn Numayr reported from al-A'mash from Malik ibn Harith that Abu Khalid al-Walibi said, "I came in a delegation to 'Umar with my family and I camped and I raised my voice with the Qur'an."

Muhammad ibn 'Ubayd reported from Fitr that Abu Khalid al-Walibi said, "'Ali ibn Abi Talib came out to us while we were waiting for him to go forth." He said, "Why do I see you silent?"

Qays Abu al-Aswad ibn Qays al-'Abdi

He was present at the treaty of Hira with Khalid ibn al-Walid. He related a *hadith* from 'Umar about *Jumu'a*. He also related from 'Ali ibn Abi Talib.

Al-Mustazill ibn al-Husayn al-Bariqi from Azd

He related from 'Umar and 'Ali.

'Abd al-Malik ibn 'Amr Abu 'Amir al-'Aqadi related from Sufyan that Shabib ibn Gharqadha said: "Al-Mustazill ibn al-Husayn al-Bariqi of Azd related to me that he heard 'Umar ibn al-Khattab say, "I know, by the Lord of the Ka'ba when the Arabs will be destroyed: when their business is led by someone who was not a Companion of the Messenger and was not cured of the business of the *Jahiliyya*."

Al-Fadl ibn Dukayn related from Sharik ibn Shabub ibn Gharqada al-Mustazill, i.e. Ibn al-Husayn al-Bariqi who said, "A man of ours died and we sent for 'Ali who was slow in coming to us. So we prayed over him and buried him. 'Ali came after we had finished and stood at the grave with it in front of him and then made supplication for him." He was trustworthy and had few *hadith*s, may Allah have mercy on him.

Qays al-Kharifi of Hamdan

He related from 'Umar and 'Ali.

Al-Hasan ibn Musa, Ahmad ibn 'Abdullah ibn Yunus and Malik ibn Isma'il reported from Zuhayr from Abu Ishaq that Qays said, "He was the master of the Kharifis." He said, "I went to 'Umar and said that my family wanted to make *hijra* and he wrote to Ibn Abi Rabi'a that he carried them and prepared them." He said: "He transported them."

Yazid ibn Harun reported from Sufyan from Hashim al-Qasim ibn Kathir that Qays al-Kharifi said that he heard 'Ali say on the minbar, "The Messenger of Allah preceded and Abu Bakr prayed and the third was 'Umar. Then we had the affliction and it is what Allah wills."

Ziyad ibn Hudayr al-Asadi

One of the Banu Malik ibn Malik ibn Tha'laba ibn Dudan ibn Asad ibn Khuzayma. He related from 'Umar, 'Ali, and Talha ibn 'Ubaydullah.

Qabisa ibn 'Uqba and Yahya ibn Adam reported from Sufyan that Ibrahim ibn al-Muhajir said that he heard Ziyad ibn Hudayr say, "I was the first to take the tenth [*'ushr*, tax on land] in Islam."

Qabisa added in the *hadith*, "I asked, 'From whom did you take a tenth?' He answered, 'The Christians of the Banu Taghlib.'"

They said, "Ziyad ibn Hudayr had descendants in Kufa. One of his children was Abu Hawala al-Qari, the Imam of the community mosque in Kufa."

❀❀❀

From this generation those who related from 'Umar ibn al-Khattab but did not relate from 'Ali ibn Abi Talib and 'Abdullah ibn Mas'ud

Salman ibn Rabi'a

Salman ibn Rabi'a ibn Yazid ibn 'Amr ibn Sahm ibn Tha'laba ibn Ghanm ibn Qutayba ibn Ma'n ibn Malik ibn 'Asur. He is Munabbih ibn Sa'd ibn Qays ibn 'Aylan ibn Mudar. He related from 'Umar ibn al-Khattab. He appointed him qadi of Kufa.

Al-Fadl ibn Dukayn reported from Isma'il ibn Ibrahim ibn al-Muhajir: "I heard my father mention that ash-Sha'bi said, 'Salman ibn Rabi'a was sent as a qadi and I remained for forty days which I counted a day in which I did not return to my family except at noon.'" They said, "Salman ibn Rabi'a went on the expedition to Balanjar while Uthman ibn 'Affan was caliph. He was killed as a martyr. That was while Sa'id ibn al-'As was governor. He was trustworthy and had few *hadiths*.

Qadi Shurayh

Shurayh ibn al-Harith ibn Qays ibn al-Jahm ibn Mu'awiya ibn 'Amir ibn ar-Ra'ih ibn al-Harith ibn Mu'awiya ibn Muratti' of Kinda. He had no peer from the Banu ar-Ra'ish as the rest of the Banu ar-Ra'ish were in Hajar and Hadramawt. No one except for Shurayh went to Kufa. He said that his *kunya* is Abu Umayya.

Muhammad ibn 'Ubayd at-Tanafisi reported from al-A'mash that Ibrahim said that Shurayh was a poet.

Al-Fadl ibn Dukayn reported that he heard Sufyan say, "Shurayh was asked who he was from. He answered, 'From the people of Yemen and their numbers in Kinda.'"

'Affan ibn Muslim and 'Arim ibn al-Fadl reported from Hammad ibn Zayd from Ayyub that Muhammad ibn Sirin said, "Shurayh was a poet. He had a thin beard."

Muhammad ibn 'Ubayd and al-Fadl ibn Dukayn reported from Umm Dawud al-Wabishiyya that he took a case to Shurayh and said, "He did not have a beard."

'Arim ibn al-Fadl reported from Hammad ibn Zayd from 'Ata' ibn as-Sa'ib that a bedouin came to Shurayh one day and asked, "Who are you from?" He said, "I am from those whom Allah blessed with Islam." The Bedouin went out saying. "By Allah, I do not think that this qadi of yours knows who he is from!"

Musa ibn Isma'il reported from Abu Hilal from Humayd ibn Hilal that ash-Sha'bi said, "A man came and said, 'Who will direct me to Shurayh.' We said, 'That is Shurayh.' He went to him and asked, 'From whom are you, Abu 'Abdullah?' He said, 'I am from those whom Allah blessed with Islam and my register is in Kinda.' He returned to us and said, 'May Allah have mercy on you! You directed me to a man who is *mawla*?' We asked, 'What did he say to you?' He said, 'I am from those whom Allah has blessed with Islam and my register is in Kinda.' We said, 'All of us are from those whom Allah has blessed with Islam. That is your companion whom you wanted.'"

Jarir ibn 'Abd al-Hamid reported from Abu Ishaq ash-Shaybani that ash-Sha'bi said, "'Umar ibn al-Khattab bartered for a horse and rode it to test it and it was injured. He said to the man, 'Take your horse.' The man said, 'No.' He said, 'Put a judge between you and me.' The man said, 'Shurayh.' So they went to him for judgement and Shurayh said, 'Amir al-Mu'minin, take what you bought or return it as you took it.'" 'Umar said, 'Is there any other judgement like that? Go to Kufa.' He sent him as Qadi over it." He said, "It was the first day he recognised what he had."

Malik ibn Isma'il related from Ja'far ibn Ziyad from Hisham ibn Hassan that Ibn Sirin said, "The first to ask about what was secret was Shurayh. It was said to him, 'Abu Umayya, from whom did you relate?' He said, 'People related and so I related.' He used to say, 'Bring a clear proof' when he suspected them when they were considered just. He said, 'I will not leave you two and I will not forbid you two if you leave. There is judgement on this. When I fear for you, fear for yourselves.' They refused to do anything but testify and were considered just witnesses. He said to the one for whom he gave judgement, "By Allah, I judge for you but I think you are a wrongdoer. But I cannot judge by supposition. I judge by what is presented in the form of a clear proof. My judgement does not make anything lawful for you which Allah made unlawful for you. Go.'"

Muhammad ibn 'Umar al-Asadi reported from Sufyan from Abu Hashim that al-Bakhtari went to Shurayh and said, "What do you relate in judgement?" He said, "People have related, and so I related."

'Affan ibn Muslim and 'Ubaydullah ibn Muhammad al-Qurashi ibn 'A'isha reported from Hammad ibn Salama from Shu'ayb ibn al-Habhab from Ibrahim that Shurayh said, "I have not spoken severely to a litigant and I did not instruct any litigant in a proof at all."

'Affan ibn Muslim reported from Hammad ibn Zayd from Ayyub from Muhammad that Shurayh used to accept a man's oath when accompanied with his proof.

'Affan ibn Muslim reported from 'Abd al-Wahid ibn Ziyad from Furat ibn Ahnaf that his father said, "I was present with Shurayh when he judged against a man. The man said to him, 'Listen to me and do not be hasty against me.' He let him finish speaking. Then Shurayh said, "Leave him. It is too much and baseless. Bring me a proof of what you say.'"

'Affan ibn Muslim reported from 'Abd al-Wahid that Furat ibn Ahnaf said that his father saw Shurayh have when a man brought a case to him and he refused to accept it. He said, "I do not read the scrolls."

Al-Fadl ibn Dukayn reported from Sufyan that al-Ja'd ibn Dhakwan said, "Shurayh gave judgement in his house when it was a rainy day."

Muhammad ibn 'Abdullah al-Asadi reported from Sufyan from al-Ja'd ibn Dhakwan that when it was a cloudy day, Shurayh would judge in his house.

Muhammad ibn 'Abdullah al-Asadi reported from Sufyan from al-Ja'd ibn Dhakwan that a son of Shurayh asked him about something concerning a dispute. He said, "Do you want me to set you on your opponent?"

Musa ibn Isma'il reported from Wuhayb from Dawud from 'Amir that one of Shurayh's sons said to his father, "There is a dispute between me and some people. Investigate. If the right is mine, I will argue for it. If I do not have a right, I will not argue." He related the story to him and he said, "Go and litigate against them." He went to them and disputed with them before him and then he gave judgement against his son. When he returned to his family, he told him, "By Allah, if I had not gone first to you, I would not have broached it with you! You disgraced me." He said, "By Allah, you are dearer to me than the entire earth being filled with the like of you. But Allah is dearer to me than you. I feared that I would tell you that judgement would go against you and you would reconcile with them and take some of their right."

Al-Hasan ibn Musa and Ahmad ibn 'Abdullah ibn Yunus reported from Zuhayr from Jabir that 'Amir said, "The son of Shurayh acted as surety for a man who fled and so Shurayh imprisoned his son. He used to send food to him in prison."

'Affan ibn Muslim reported from Shu'ba from al-Hakam that Ibrahim said, "Shurayh almost did not retract a judgement that he had made until al-Aswad related to him that 'Umar said about a slave of his who was married to a free woman who had born him children and that slave was then set free that his *wala'* goes to the masters of the slave." Shurayh took that decision.

'Affan ibn Muslim and 'Arim ibn al-Fadl reported from Hammad ibn Zayd that Wasil, the *mawla* of Abu 'Uyayna, said, "Engraved on Shurayh's ring was 'The seal is better than supposition.'"

'Arim reported from Hammad ibn Zayd from Shu'ayb ibn al-Habhab from Ibrahim that Shurayh said when he went out to judge, "The wrongdoer will know a portion of decrease. The wrongdoer waits for punishment and the wronged waits for help."

'Arim ibn al-Fadl reported from Hammad ibn Zayd from Ayyub from Sa'id ibn Jubayr that a man sought to transgress against a man who was related to Shurayh and Shurayh commanded that he be secured to a pillar. When Shurayh rose, he spoke, and Shurayh turned from him and said, "I have not imprisoned you. The right has imprisoned you."

Qabisa ibn 'Uqba reported from Sufyan that Abu Husayn said, "Two men took a dispute to Shurayh and he judged against one of them and said, 'You know from where you came.' Shurayh said to him, 'May Allah curse the briber, the bribed and the liar.'"

Qabisa reported from Sufyan that Hisham ibn Muhammad said, "When Shurayh came to the land subject to *kharaj*, he would rise and not give judgement in *kharaj* land. He was brought a pearl and was told, 'When a pregnant woman looks at this, she will miscarry.' He got up."

Hushaym ibn Bashir reported from Ibn 'Awn and Hisham from Muhammad that a man confirmed something in the presence of Shurayh and then went to deny it. Shurayh said, "The son of your uncle's sister testified against you (i.e. that you admitted it against yourself.)"

Isma'il ibn Ibrahim al-Asadi reported from Ayyub from Muhammad that a man made witnesses stand with Shurayh and he asked him to swear an oath and he hesitated. He said, "Evil is how you praise your witnesses!"

Isma'il reported from Ayyub that Muhammad said, "Shurayh used to say to witnesses, 'I did not summon you two. If you stand, I will not prevent you. The judgement against this man is down to the two of you. I call on you to fear Allah, so fear Him.'"

Isma'il ibn Ibrahim reported from Ayyub that Muhammad said, "Shurayh used to say, 'Whoever claims my judgement, it is against him until the Ultimate Truth makes it clear whether the actual truth is truer than my judgement.'"

Isma'il reported from Ayyub that Muhammad said, "Shurayh used to say, 'Not permitted against you is the testimony of an adversary nor a partner nor someone suspicious nor someone who avoids a liability. Ask about him. If they say, 'Allah knows best,' then Allah knows best and they are afraid to say he is doubtful. If they say, 'This is what we know: a just Muslim,' then we allow his testimony, but no slave can testify for his master nor employee for his employer.'"

Isma'il reported from Ayyub from Muhammad that some of the spinners took a disagreement to Shurayh about something. One of them said, "It is a custom among us." He said, "Your custom is between you."

Isma'il reported from Ayyub from Muhammad that Shurayh asked people to swear in the *qasama* and they could not get a full fifty. So he made them take the oath again until they had done fifty oaths.

Isma'il reported from Ayyub from Muhammad that Shurayh used to say, "Slave of Allah, leave what gives you doubt for what does not give you doubt. By Allah, you do not find even a single *fa-qad* on anything which I left for the sake of Allah."

Isma'il ibn Ibrahim reported from Ayyub from Muhammad that a man asked an opponent of his to swear in the presence of Shurayh and then he brought clear evidence against him after that. Shurayh said, "The just clear proof is truer than the false oath."

Sa'id ibn Mansur related from Hushaym that Abu Ishaq al-Kufi reported from Abu Jarir al-Azdi from Shurayh that he got up when he was hungry or angry.

Sa'id ibn Mansur said that Abu 'Awana related that Ash'ath ibn Sulaym said, "A mother and grandmother brought a dispute to Shurayh. The grandmother said:

'Abu Umayya, we have come to you
    and you are someone to whom we come.
My son and his mother have come to you
    and both of us seek to obtain him

She has married, so give him to me.
  Do not become lost.
You should ask for an oath
  about the subject of our dispute
O Qadi, this
  is my story in it.

Then the mother said:

O Qadi, the grandmother
  has spoken to you,
So listen to my words
  and do not disregard me.
Give my soul solace in my son
  when my heart knows his.
When he was a weak orphan
  in my lap, all alone.
I married and hoped for good
  in someone who would spare me poverty:
Someone to show me love
  and satisfy my provision.

Shurayh said:

The Qadi has understood what you both said
  and judged between you and then uttered
The judgement between you.
  The Qadi strives if he understands.
He says to the grandmother, 'Bring me the child
  and take it from the one with defects.'
If she is patient, she will have
  a replacement she desires from her supplication."

Ahmad ibn 'Abdullah ibn Yunus reported from Zuhayr that 'Ata' ibn as-Sa'ib said, "Shurayh came walking to us. I said, 'Give me a *fatwa*.' He said, 'I do not give *fatwa*, but I judge.' I said, 'It is not something in which there is judgement.' He said, 'What is it?' He answered, 'A man made his house a prison for another relative of his.' He said, 'Command one he loves and say, "Listen to the man. There is no detention from the obligations of Allah."''

Qabisa ibn 'Uqba reported from Sufyan from Isma'il al-Asadi from ash-Sha'bi that Shurayh said, "I will not be both a qadi and witness."

Muhammad ibn 'Abdullah al-Asadi reported from Sufyan from Mughira from Ibrahim that a collector of Shurayh beat a man with his whip and Shurayh took retaliation from him.

Al-Fadl ibn Dukayn reported from al-Hasan ibn Salih that Ibn Abi Layla said, "It reached me (or us) that 'Ali provided Shurayh with five hundred dirhams."

Ahmad ibn 'Abdullah ibn Yunus reported from Abu Shihab from Hajjaj from 'Umar ibn Sa'id that Shurayh led the people in prayer in Ramadan.

Al-Fadl ibn Dukayn reported from Ibn 'Uyayna from 'Amr that Jabir ibn Zayd said, "Ziyad advanced Shurayh and he judged us for a year and none like him judged us before or after him (i.e. judging in Basra)."

Malik ibn Isma'il reported from al-Hasan ibn Salih from al-Ja'd ibn Dhakwan that Shurayh said, "It was said to a man, 'Rabi'a!' and he did not answer. He said, 'Rabi'a little unbeliever!' and he answered. He said, 'You have admitted disbelief. You have no testimony.'"

One of our companions reported from al-Walid ibn Muslim from 'Uthman ibn 'Atiyya al-'Ansi who heard Makhul say, "I frequented Shurayh for six months in which I did not ask about anything. I had enough in what I heard him judge."

'Affan ibn Muslim and 'Arim ibn al-Fadl reported from Hammad ibn Zayd that Wasil, the *mawla* of Abu 'Uyayna, said, "Engraved on the ring of Shurayh was; 'The seal is better than supposition.'"

Al-Fadl ibn Dukayn reported from Sharik ibn 'Abdullah from Jabir that al-Qasim said, "Engraved on the ring of Shurayh were two lions with a tree between them."

Ya'la ibn 'Ubayd at-Tanafisi reported that Isma'il said, "I saw Shurayh judging while wearing a shawl of rough silk and a burnous."

Al-Fadl ibn Dukayn reported from Sharik that the son of Abu Khalid said, "I saw Shurayh wearing a turban with one turn."

Shihab ibn 'Abbad reported from Ibrahim ibn Humayd ar-Rawasi that Isma'il ibn Abi Khalid saw Shurayh walking short and I saw him wearing a turban which tailed behind him.

Waki' ibn al-Jarrah reported that Isma'il said, "I saw Shurayh wearing a burnous of rough silk and I saw him wearing a turban which hung down behind him. I saw him come on Friday and sit in his place and not err."

Muhammad ibn Yazid al-Wasiti reported that Isma'il ibn Abi Khalid said, "I saw Shurayh wearing a shawl of rough silk and a burnous of rough silk."

Waki' reported from al-A'mash that Abu ad-Duha said, "I saw Shurayh prostrating in his burnous."

'Ubaydullah ibn Musa reported from al-A'mash from Abu ad-Duha that Shurayh used to pray in his fur-coat and did not remove his hands from it.

Abu Mu'awiya ad-Darir and Ya'la ibn 'Ubayd reported from al-A'mash that Muslim said, "I saw Shurayh prostrating wearing a burnous whose end came between his brow and the earth."

Waki', Wahb ibn Jarir, al-Fadl ibn Dukayn and Hisham Abu al-Walid at-Tayalisi reported from Shu'ba that al-Hakam said, "I saw Shurayh praying in his burnous."

'Ubaydullah ibn Musa reported from Isra'il from Abu Ishaq that Shurayh had a burnous of dusty rough silk.

Al-Fadl ibn Dukayn reported from Qays that Abu Hasin said, "I saw Shurayh wearing rough silk."

'Arim ibn al-Fadl reported from Hammad ibn Zayd that 'Asim said, "I saw Shurayh wearing a burnous of rough silk."

'Abdullah ibn Ja'far reported from 'Ubaydullah ibn 'Amr that Isma'il ibn Abi Khalid said, "I saw Shurayh judging in the mosque while bearing a rough silk burnous."

Al-Hasan ibn Musa reported from Zuhayr from 'Amir that Shurayh said, "Beware of those assistants!" He commanded that they be driven off, meaning those who accompanied with litigants.

Kathir ibn Hisham reported that Ja'far ibn Burqan heard Maymun ibn Mihran say, "Shurayh said in the civil war which occurred in the time of Ibn az-Zubayr, 'I did not ask about nor seek to be reported to.'"

Ja'far said, "I heard that he used to say, 'I fear that I will not be saved.'"

'Abdullah ibn Ja'far reported that Abu al-Malih said, "Shurayh remained for nine years in the civil war without reporting or seeking reports. He was told, 'You are safe.' He answered, 'And how much more desire?'"

Qabisa ibn 'Uqba reported from Sufyan that Mansur said, "When Shurayh went into *ihram*, he was like a silent snake."

Qabisa reported from Sufyan from al-A'mash that Khaythama said, "When Shurayh was asked how he was, he replied, 'In a blessing from Allah.'"

Al-Fadl ibn Dukayn reported from Zuhayr that Abu Ishaq was with Shurayh. When a man came to him and said, "Peace be upon you," Shurayh said, "Peace be upon you and the mercy of Allah." If the man said, "And the mercy of Allah," he added, "And His blessings."

Yahya ibn 'Abbad reported from al-Mas'udi that al-Qasim said, "No one beat Shurayh in giving the greeting. When he was greeted, he returned the like of what was said to him."

Rawh ibn 'Ubada reported from Ibn 'Awn that 'Isa ibn al-Harith said, "I was never able to give the greeting to Shurayh first. I used to meet him in the road and I would say, 'Now, now.' When he saw me, he ignored me but when he came near, he raised his head and said, 'Peace be upon you.'"

Rawh ibn 'Ubada reported from Ibn 'Awn from ash-Sha'bi that Shurayh said, "I have never met two men but that the one entitled of them with Allah is the one who gave the greeting first."

Ibn 'Awn said, "I mentioned that to Muhammad and he said, 'We related that they said, 'When two men meet, the better of them begins the greeting.'"

Al-Fadl ibn Dukayn reported from Sufyan from Mansur from Ibrahim or Tamim ibn Salama that Shurayh passed by a dirham and did not turn to it. One time he said that he did not pick it up.

Al-Fadl ibn Dukayn and Muhammad ibn 'Abdullah al-Asadi reported from Sufyan from Mansur that Ibrahim said, "Shurayh sent a she-camel to al-Aswad and he asked 'Alqama about it. 'Alqama said, 'Your brother sent it to you, so accept it.'"

'Affan ibn Muslim reported from Hammad ibn Salama from Ayyub from Muhammad ibn Sirin that Shurayh used to pray all the prayers with one *wudu'*.

'Affan ibn Muslim reported from Abu 'Awana from Husayn ibn 'Abd ar-Rahman that Abu Talha, the *mawla* of Shurayh, said, "When Shurayh returned from the prayer place, he entered his house and locked the door. He remained in it until the middle of the day or close to the middle of the day." He thought that he was praying.

'Affan reported from Shu'ba that al-Hakam said, "I saw Shurayh praying in burnouses and I saw him walking in front of the bier."

'Affan ibn Muslim and 'Arim ibn al-Fadl reported from Hammad ibn Zayd from Yahya ibn 'Atiq from Muhammad that a man spoke to Shurayh about a need he was asking for from Ibn Ziyad. He said, "Who has any power over Ibn Ziyad? Command a sparrow or a bird. That bird has more power over Ibn Ziyad than I do!'"

Al-Mu'alla ibn Asad reported from al-Harith ibn 'Ubayd from Harun ibn Abi Sa'id that Muhammad ibn Sirin said, "Shurayh used to swear by Allah that he would not leave a person in need of something if he found that he had what he lacked."

Yahya ibn 'Abbad reported from al-Mas'udi that al-Qasim said, "Shurayh used to put his drains inside his house."

'Abdullah ibn Ja'far reported from Abu al-Malih that Maymun said, "Shurayh did not refuse a gift until he returned its like."

Hajjaj ibn Nusayr reported from Qurra ibn Khalid from Budayl ibn Maysara al-'Uqayli that 'Abdullah ibn Shaqiq said that Jandal as-Sadusi related that he heard Shurayh say, "The blameworthy: the truly blameworthy is the one about whom it is said, 'This one is impious, so fear him.'"

Al-Fadl ibn Dukayn reported from Sharik that Ibn Abi Khalid said, "I saw Shurayh with a white beard."

Al-Fadl ibn Dukayn reported from Qays from Layth that Mujahid said, "Shurayh accepted gifts and returned their like."

Mu'ammil ibn Isma'il reported from Sufyan from Dawud from ash-Sha'bi that Shurayh buried his son at night.

Ishaq ibn Mansur reported from Isra'il from Ibrahim ibn Muhajir that Shurayh buried his son 'Abdullah at night.

'Affan ibn Muslim reported from 'Abd al-Wahid from 'Asim al-Ahwal that 'Amir said, "Shurayh used to bury those of his family who had died at night, taking advantage of that." He said, "He used to be asked about him when he had died and would say, 'He calmed himself and hoped that he would be relieved.'"

Waki' ibn al-Jarrah reported from Sharik from Yahya ibn Qays that Shurayh ordered that he be prayed over in the cemetery and that they not cover his grave with a cloth.

Ishaq ibn Mansur reported from al-Hasan ibn Salih and Sharik from Yahya ibn Qays that Shurayh ordered that a cloth not be stretched out on his grave.

Sharik added in his report, "and that he be buried at night."

Malik ibn Isma'il reported from Sharik from Yahya ibn Qays who said, "I attended the funeral of Shurayh. It was a hot day and he has ordered that no cloth be stretched on his grave."

Al-Fadl ibn Dukayn reported that Shurayh reached the age of one hundred and eight.

Al-Fadl ibn Dukayn reported from Sharik that Yahya ibn Qays al-Kindi said, "Shurayh ordered that the prayer be said over him at the cemetery and that no one announce it and that a woman shouter should not follow it and that no cloth should be placed on his grave and that a *lahd* grave be prepared for him."

Muhammad ibn 'Umar reported from Abu Sabra from 'Isa that ash-Sha'bi said that Shurayh died in 77 or 78 AH.

Al-Fadl ibn Dukayn reported that Shurayh died in 76 AH.

Another of the people of knowledge said it was 78 AH. He was trustworthy. May Allah have mercy on him and be pleased with him.

The rest of this generation who related from 'Umar ibn al-Khattab

As-Subayy ibn Ma'bad al-Juhani

He related that 'Umar asked him about the Qur'an and he said, "I was guided to the *sunna* of your Prophet."

Qabisa ibn Jabir

Qabisa ibn Jabir ibn Wahb ibn Malik ibn 'Amira ibn Hudhar ibn Murra ibn al-Harith ibn Sa'd ibn Tha'laba ibn Dudan ibn Asad ibn

Khuzayma. He related from 'Umar ibn al-Khattab and 'Abd ar-Rahman ibn 'Awf.

Muhammad ibn Qays ibn ar-Rabi' reported that his father said that Qabisa ibn Jabir died before al-Jamajim. He was trustworthy and had *hadith*s.

Yasar ibn Numayr

He was a *mawla* of 'Umar ibn al-Khattab. He was his store-keeper. He related from 'Umar and settled in Kufa. The Kufans related from him. He was trustworthy and had few *hadith*s.

'Ufayf ibn Ma'di Karib

He related from 'Umar.

Al-Fadl ibn Dukayn related from Ibn al-Ghasil from Harun ibn 'Abdullah that 'Ufayf ibn Ma'di Karib said, "We went out to people to inform Sa'd al-Ash'ath and others until we reached Madina. 'Umar ibn al-Khattab passed us on part of the road. He had a whip." It is a long *hadith*.

Husayn ibn Hudayr

He related from 'Umar ibn al-Khattab.

Qays ibn Marwan al-Ju'fi

Khaythama ibn 'Abd ar-Rahman related from him. Qays related that a man came to him and said, "Amir al-Mu'minin, I left a man copying out copies of the Qur'an." Qays was one of those who went to Jazira in the time of 'Ali. He was noble and respected by Mu'awiya. A poet said of him:

> I continued to ask about Ju'fi and its master
> until Qays ibn Marwan was pointed out.

Busayr ibn 'Amr as-Sakuni

One of the Banu Hind. He related from 'Umar ibn al-Khattab and Sa'd.

Al-Fadl ibn Dukayn reported from 'Amr ibn Qays ibn Busayr ibn 'Amr that he heard his father say, "Busayr ibn 'Amr was an *'arif* in the time of al-Hajjaj." Busayr ibn 'Amr said, "The Prophet ☀ died when I was ten." They said, "Busayr died while al-Hajjaj was governor before Dayr al-Jamajim." He was trustworthy and had *hadith*s.

'Abaya ibn Raddad

Isma'il ibn Ibrahim and Yazid ibn Harun reported from Shu'ba from Ibrahim ibn Muhammad ibn al-Muntashir from his father that 'Abaya ibn Raddad said that he heard 'Umar ibn al-Khattab say, "There is no prayer without the *Fatiha* of the Book and something with it." A man asked him, "And if you are behind the imam?" He replied, "Then recite to yourself."

Kharasha ibn al-Hurr

Kharasha ibn al-Hurr ibn Qays ibn Hisn ibn Hudhayfa ibn Badr al-Fazari. He related from 'Umar ibn al-Khattab, Hudhayfa, Abu Dharr, and 'Abdullah ibn Salam.

Hanzala ash-Shaybani

Abu 'Ali Hanzala. He related from 'Umar ibn al-Khattab.

Bishr ibn Qays

He related from 'Umar ibn al-Khattab about fasting.

Al-Husayn ibn Sabra

He related from 'Umar ibn al-Khattab.
He said, "'Umar led us in the *Fajr* prayer and recited *Sura Yusuf* in one *rak'at*."

Sayyar ibn Maghrur or Ma'rur

He heard 'Umar ibn al-Khattab say, "This mosque was founded by the Messenger of Allah ☀."

Hassan ibn al-Mukhariq

He related from 'Umar ibn al-Khattab.

Abu Qurra al-Kindi

He was the qadi in Kufa and his name was Fulan ibn Salama. He related from 'Umar ibn al-Khattab, Salman and Hudhayfa ibn al-Yaman. He was known and had few *hadiths*.

His son, 'Amr ibn Abi Qurra al-Kindi

He said, "The letter of 'Umar ibn al-Khattab came stating that some people take from this wealth in order to strive in the Cause of Allah but then stay back and do not go on *jihad*."

Ma'qil ibn Abi Bakr al-Hilali

He related from 'Umar ibn al-Khattab.

Kathir ibn Shihab ibn al-Husayn Dhu al-Ghussa

Dhu al-Ghussa was called that because of a choking fit (*ghussa*) which he experienced. He was Dhu al-Ghussa ibn Yazid ibn Shaddad ibn Qanan ibn Salama ibn Wahb ibn 'Abdullah ibn Rabi'a ibn al-Harith ibn Ka'b of Madhhij. Kathir's father was Shihab ibn al-Husayn. He killed the killer of his father al-Husayn in the Battle of ar-Razm. Kathir ibn Shihab was the master of Madhhij in Kufa. He was a miser. He related from 'Umar ibn al-Khattab. He was put in charge of Rayy for Mu'awiya ibn Abi Sufyan. His children included Muhammad ibn Zuhra ibn al-Harith ibn Mansur ibn Qays ibn Kathir ibn Shihab who settled in Masabadhan and was appointed governor of Masabadhan. He had power in Baghdad in the time of Harun ar-Rashid.

'Abdullah ibn Harun reported from al-Hajjaj from Abu Ishaq from Qarza ibn Arta'a al-'Abdi that Kathir ibn Shihab said, "We asked 'Umar about cheese. He said, "Say the Name of Allah over it and eat." He had few *hadiths*.

Mas'ud ibn Hirash

He was the brother of Rib'i ibn Hirash al-'Absi. He related from 'Umar ibn al-Khattab and he had few *hadiths*.

His brother, ar-Rabi' ibn Hirash

He spoke after his death and died before Rib'i ibn Hirash.

Muhammad ibn 'Ubayd reported from Isma'il ibn Abi Khalid that 'Abd al-Malik ibn 'Umayr said, "Rib'i was approached and was told that his brother had died. He hurried until he sat at his head praying for him and asking forgiveness for him. He uncovered his face and then he said, 'Peace be upon you.' I came to Rib'i after you and I met with rest and basil and a Lord who is not angry and He clothed me in brocade and rich brocade. I found the matter easier than you think. But do not speak. Carry me. I promised the Messenger of Allah ﷺ that I would not leave until the meeting."

Hisham ibn 'Abd al-Malik Abu al-Walid at-Tayalisi reported from Abu 'Awna from 'Abd al-Malik ibn 'Umar from Rib'i ibn Hirash that his brother ar-Rabi' was very ill and he became sluggish. He said, "I went out for a need and then returned and asked, 'What did my brother do?' They said, 'He died.' I said, *'We belong to Allah and to Him we return.'* (2:156) I went in and he was covered in a cloth and made to lie on his back as is done with the corpse. I commanded that he be perfumed with *hanut* and shrouded. While we were doing that he spoke with the cloth like that. He uncovered his face and then he reverted as the soundest he had ever been while he had been very ill before that. He said, 'Peace be upon you.' I said, 'And on you and the mercy of Allah.' Then I said, 'Glory be to Allah! Is this after death, my brother?' He said, 'I met my Lord after you and He gave me rest and enjoyment and a Lord who is not angry and He clothed me in green garments of brocade and rich brocade. I found the business easier than what is in yourselves. Do not be deluded. I asked my Lord for permission to give you good news. Carry me to the Messenger of Allah ﷺ. He promised me that he would not go ahead of me before I caught up to him. By Allah, I only compare his death after his words as pebbles which I threw into water and they disappeared.'"

Al-Harith ibn Laqit an-Nakha'i

He is Abu Hanash from whom Abu Nu'aym and others related. Al-Harith ibn Laqit was present at al-Qadisiyya. He related from 'Umar.

Al-Fadl ibn Dukayn reported from Hanash ibn al-Harith who said, "I saw my father and some of those who were at al-Qadisiyya dyeing their beards yellow."

Al-Fadl ibn Dukayn reported that Hanash ibn al-Harith said, "I saw my father and some of those who were at al-Qadisiyya wearing shawls."

Al-Fadl ibn Dukayn reported that Hanash ibn al-Harith said, "I saw my father wearing an iron ring." He had few *hadith*s.

Sulayk ibn Mishal al-'Absi

He related a *hadith* about *nabidh* from 'Umar ibn al-Khattab. He had few *hadith*s.

Ziyad ibn 'Iyad al-Ash'ari

He related from 'Umar and az-Zubayr.

'Ubaydullah ibn Musa reported from Isra'il from Jabir from 'Amir from Ziyad ibn 'Iyad who said, "'Umar ibn al-Khattab led us in the *'Isha'* prayer at al-Jabiya. I did not hear him recite in it." The *hadith* is long.

Abu Usama Hammad ibn Usama reported from ash-Sha'bi that al-Ash'ari, and not Abu Musa said, "'Umar ibn al-Khattab led us in the *Maghrib* prayer and did not recite to us anything in it. I said, 'Amir al-Mu'minin! You did not recite.'"

'Iyad al-Ash'ari

He related from 'Umar ibn al-Khattab. He had few *hadith*s.

Shubayl ibn 'Awf al-Ahmasi of Bajila

He related from 'Umar ibn al-Khattab.

Ya'la ibn 'Ubayd reported from Isma'il ibn Abi Khalid that Shubayl ibn 'Awf said, "'Umar ibn al-Khattab commanded us to give *sadaqa* and we said, 'We put a tenth each on our horses and slaves.' He said, 'I do not impose it on you.' Then he commanded two plots of land each for our slaves."

Shihab ibn 'Abbad reported from Ibn Idris from Isma'il ibn Abi Khalid who said that he heard Shubayl ibn 'Awf say, "I did not change my sandals in quest of this world at all nor did I sit at all in a seat except for a need or waiting for a bier and I did not consider any man ugly at all."

Shihab said, "I reckoned that he said, 'since I became a man, by the Lord of the House.'"

Muhammad ibn Sa'd said, "Shibl is in the *hadith*. Shubayl is the dimunitive of Shibl." He was trustworthy and had few *hadith*s.

Sa'id ibn Dhi La'wa the younger

He is Abu Karib ibn Zayd ibn Sa'id ibn al-Khasib ibn Dhi La'wa the elder. He is 'Amir ibn Malik ibn Mu'awiya ibn Duman ibn Bakil ibn Jusham ibn Khayran ibn Nawf ibn Hamdan. Sa'id ibn Dhi La'wa related from 'Umar ibn al-Khattab. His son Dawud ibn Sa'id also related.

'Ubaydullah ibn Musa reported from Isra'il from Kabir that 'Amir said, "I testify against Sa'id ibn Dhi La'wa that he related from 'Umar that raisins were steeped for him from the raisins of Ta'if. He put them in two threshing-floors and the camel churned them. In the morning he drank from it." The *hadith* is long.

Riyah ibn al-Harith an-Nakha'i

He related from 'Umar, 'Ammar, ibn Yasar, and Sa'id ibn Zayd ibn 'Amr ibn Nufayl.

Muhammad ibn al-Fudayl reported that Sadaqa ibn al-Muthanna an-Nakha'i heard Riyah ibn al-Harith say that 'Umar ibn al-Khattab used to judge according the observance of the Arabs between themselves before Islam and before the Prophet ﷺ was sent. If someone recognised that one of the people of his house was owned in one of the quarters of the Arabs a slave was ransomed by two slaves and a female slave by two female slaves.

'Abdullah ibn Shihab al-Khawlani

He related from 'Umar ibn al-Khattab.

'Affan ibn Muslim reported from Shu'ba from al-Hakam from Khaythama ibn 'Abd ar-Rahman that 'Abdullah ibn Shihab al-Khawlani said, "I saw 'Umar ibn al-Khattab when a man and woman came to him about a *khul'* which he allowed. He said, 'He has divorced you in exchange for your property.'"

Hassan ibn Fa'id al-'Absi

He related from 'Umar ibn al-Khattab that cowardice and bravery were innate qualities in men. He had few *hadith*s. Abu Ishaq as-Subay'i related from him.

His brother, Bukayr ibn Fa'id al-Absi

He related from 'Umar ibn al-Khattab and Hallam ibn Salih related from him.

Humayl Abu Jirwa

Muhammad ibn al-Fudayl and Yazid ibn Harun reported from Hajjaj from Zayd ibn Jubayr al-Asadi from Jirwa ibn Humayl that his father said, "I heard 'Umar ibn al-Khattab say, 'One of you hits with the like of something which eats the flesh and then thinks that there is no retaliation against him. By Allah, no one does that but that I will take retaliation from him.'"

Nabata al-Ju'fi

He related from 'Umar ibn al-Khattab.

Abu Jarir al-Bajali

He related from 'Umar ibn al-Khattab, 'Abd ar-Rahman ibn 'Awf and Sa'd.

Ishaq ibn Yusuf al-Azraq reported from Sufyan from Mansur from Abu Wa'il that Abu Jarir al-Bajali said, "I met a bedouin who had a gazelle he had caught. I bought it, took it and slaughtered it forgetting that I was in *ihram*. I went to 'Umar ibn al-Khattab and mentioned that to him. He said, 'Bring two just men who will judge you.'"

'Ubaydullah ibn Musa reported from Isra'il from Mansur from Shaqiq that Abu Jarir al-Bajali said, "We went out in *ihram* and I found a bedouin who had a gazelle with him. I bought it from him and slaughtered it and did not remember my *ihram*. I went to 'Umar ibn al-Khattab and recounted the story to him. He said, 'Go to some of your brothers so that they can judge you.' I went to 'Abd ar-Rahman ibn 'Awf and Sa'd ibn Malik and they judged that I owed a buck."

Salama

He saw 'Umar ibn al-Khattab go to the owner of the basin and hit him, saying, "Make a basin for men and a basin for women."

Hani' ibn Hizam

He related from 'Umar ibn al-Khattab.

Yahya ibn Adam reported from Sufyan from al-Mughira ibn an-Nu'man from Malik ibn Anas that Hani' ibn Hizam said, "I was sitting with 'Umar ibn al-Khattab when a man came to him and mentioned that he had found a man with his wife and had killed both of them. 'Umar wrote to his governor in al-'Alaniyya to take retaliation from him and he wrote to him in secret to take the blood money."

'Abdullah ibn Malik al-Azdi

Yazid ibn Harun reported from Sufyan from Abu Ishaq that 'Abdullah ibn Malik al-Azdi said, "I prayed with 'Umar ibn al-Khattab at Jam': three *rak'ats* for *Maghrib* and two *rak'ats* for *'Isha'*."

Maslama ibn Quhayf

One of the Bakr ibn Wa'il. He related from 'Umar.

Sulayman Abu Dawud at-Tayalisi reported from Shu'ba from Simak who heard the uncle of Abu Maslama ibn Quhayf say, "I was present with 'Umar ibn al-Khattab and he saw people praying *Duha*. He said, 'When you do that, then do it in the forenoon.'"

Ishaq ibn Yusuf al-Azraq reported from Zakariyya ibn Abi Za'ida from Simak ibn Harb that Maslama ibn Quhayf said, "I heard 'Umar ibn al-Khattab say, 'The slaves of Allah perform the *Duha* prayer.' I asked, 'Who said this?' They answered, "Umar ibn al-Khattab.'"

Bishr ibn Quhayf

He related from 'Umar.

Yazid ibn Harun reported from Shu'ba from Simak ibn Harb that Bishr ibn Quhayf said, "I went to 'Umar ibn al-Khattab while he was eating and there was a root in his hand. I said, 'Amir al-Mu'minin, I have come to give you allegiance.' He asked, 'Did you not give allegiance to my governor?' 'Yes,' I replied. He said 'When you gave allegiance to my governor, then you gave allegiance to me.'" It is a long *hadith*.

'Ubaydullah ibn Musa reported from Isra'il from Simak from Bishr ibn Quhayd that 'Umar said, "A man came and gave him allegiance and said, 'I give you allegiance both in what I am pleased and in what I dislike.' 'Umar said, 'No, rather as much as you are able.'"

Nuhayk ibn 'Abdullah

He related from 'Umar ibn al-Khattab.

'Ubaydullah ibn Musa reported from Isra'il from Mansur from Ibrahim from Nuhayk ibn 'Abdullah from 'Umar ibn al-Khattab that he moved on from 'Arafat while he was between him and al-Aswad ibn Yazid. He did not do more than one journey until he reached Mina. It is a long *hadith*.

Mudrik ibn 'Awf al-Ahmasi from Bajila

He related from 'Umar.

'Ubaydullah ibn Musa reported from Isra'il from Abu Ishaq from Mudrik ibn 'Awf al-Ahmasi that 'Umar said, "The lazy ones are those who perform the *witr* at the beginning of the night. The strong are those who perform the *witr* at the end of the night. It is better."

Usaym ibn Husayn al-'Absi

He related from 'Umar ibn al-Khattab and performed *hajj* with him.

Abu al-Malih

He related from 'Umar.

Al-Fadl ibn Dukayn reported from Sharik from 'Abd al-Malik ibn 'Umayr who said that Abu al-Malih said that he heard 'Umar say, "There is no Islam for someone who does not pray." It was said to Sharik, "On the minbar?" He said, "Yes, I heard it from him on the minbar."

Dihya ibn 'Amr

He related from 'Umar.

Al-Fadl ibn Dukayn reported from 'Atiyya ibn 'Uqba al-Asadi that Dihya ibn 'Amr said, "I went to 'Umar ibn al-Khattab and said, 'Peace be upon you, Amir al-Mu'minin and the mercy of Allah and His blessings.' He said, 'Peace be upon you, and the mercy of Allah and His blessings and forgiveness.'"

Hilal ibn 'Abdullah

He related from 'Umar.

'Uthman ibn 'Umar reported from Shu'ba from Simak ibn Harb that a man of his people called Hilal ibn 'Abdullah said, "I saw 'Umar ibn al-Khattab go between Safa and Marwa. When he reached the bottom of the valley, he ran (*tajawwaza*) and I asked Simak, 'What does '*tajawwaza*' mean?' He said, 'He ran.'"

Hamala ibn 'Abd ar-Rahman

He related from 'Umar ibn al-Khattab.

Usaq

A *mawla* of 'Umar ibn al-Khattab.

Hisham Abu al-Walid at-Tayalisi reported from Sharik from Abu Hilal at-Ta'i that Ishaq said, "I was a slave of 'Umar ibn al-Khattab and I was a Christian. He offered Islam to me and said, 'If you become Muslim, I will ask for help for my trust. It is not lawful for me to help you against the trust of the Muslims when you are not following their *deen*.' I refused him. He said, 'There is no compulsion in the *deen*.' When he was dying, he embraced me while I was a Christian and said, 'Go wherever you wish.' I said to Sharik, 'Abu Hilal heard it from Usaq.' He said, 'He claimed that.'"

Ar-Rubayya' ibn Ziyad

Ar-Rubayya' ibn Ziyad ibn Anas ibn ad-Dayyan, who is Yazid ibn Qatan ibn Ziyad ibn al-Harith ibn Malik ibn Rabi'a ibn Ka'b ibn al-Harith ibn Ka'b of Madhhij. He related from 'Umar ibn al-Khattab. 'Umar used to say, "Show me a man who is a prince when he is among the people." It was as if he was not a prince. When he was among them and was not a prince, it was as if he was like a prince.

They said, "We only know that to be ar-Rubayya' ibn Ziyad ibn Anas." He was humble and good. He was appointed governor of Khurasan and conquered most of it. He had a brother called al-Muhajir ibn Ziyad who was righteous and was killed with Abu Musa al-Ash'ari as a martyr in the Battle of Tustar.

In the Battle of Tustar, al-Muhajir wanted to sell himself for Allah. He was fasting and a brother of his went to Abu Musa and told him what he was. He said, "I resolve that someone who is fasting should break his fast." So al-Muhajir broke his fast and then went and was killed.

'Abdullah ibn 'Amr Abu Ma'mar al-Minqari reported from 'Abd al-Warith ibn Sa'id from al-Husayn ibn Dhakwan the teacher from Ibn Burayda a *hadith* which he related in which he described ar-Rubayya' ibn Ziyad al-Harithi. Then he said, "A white man, thin with a slight body."

Suwayd ibn Math'aba al-Yarbu'i of the Banu Tamim

He was one of the people who laid out the plots in Kufa in the time of 'Umar ibn al-Khattab. He was old and did not relate anything from 'Umar. He was a striving worshipper.

Ahmad ibn 'Abdullah ibn Yunus reported from Abu Shihab from Abu Hayyan at-Taymi that his father said, "I visited Suwayd ibn Math'aba. He was one of the people who laid out the plots. He had a cloth over him. If it had not been that I heard his wife say, 'My family be your ransom, what should we feed you and give you to drink?' I was not aware that there was anything under the cloth. He was rolled up to his face. When he saw me, he said, 'Nephew, the haunches and spine have turned back. There is no sleep except what you see. By Allah, I do not love to be deprived of the least victory.'"

Mi'dad ibn Yazid al-'Ijli

His *kunya* was Abu Yazid. He was also one of the worshipping strivers. He went out with a number of the companions of 'Abdullah to the cemetery (Jabbana) where they worshipped. 'Abdullah went to them and forbade them to do that. He went on an expedition to Azerbaijan when 'Uthman ibn 'Affan was caliph. Al-Ash'ath ibn Qays was in charge of it. He was killed as a martyr there.

Muhammad ibn 'Abdullah al-Asadi reported from Sufyan from Mansur that Ibrahim said, "Mi'dad used to say in his prayer, 'O Allah, heal me a little of sleep.' He was never again seen sleepy in the prayer." I asked to Ibrahim, "In the prescribed prayers?" He said, "No, not in the prescribed."

Sa'id ibn Mansur reported from Jarir ibn 'Abd al-Hamid from Mansur from Ibrahim that Hammam ibn al-Harith said, "Mi'dad al-'Ijli slept in his prostration and then got up and walked a time and said, 'O Allah, heal me of sleep a little.'" He was trustworthy and had few *hadith*s.

His brother, **Qays ibn Yazid**

He used to go to the Sawad and buy and sell. Mi'dad said, "Qays was better than me in buying and selling and spent on me."

Uways al-Qarani of Murad

He is Uways ibn 'Amr ibn Jaz' ibn Malik ibn 'Amr ibn Sa'd ibn 'Aswan ibn Qarn ibn Ridman ibn Nahiya of Murad. He is Yuhabir ibn Malik ibn Adad of Madhhij.

Hashim ibn al-Qasim reported from Sulayman ibn al-Mughira from Sa'id al-Jurayri from Abu Nadra that Usayr ibn Jabir said, "A *hadith* transmitter in Kufa related to us. When he finished his *hadith*, they separated and a group remained which contained a man who spoke words which I did not hear anyone say and I liked it and then I missed him. I asked my companions. 'Do you know a man who was sitting with us who was like such-and-such?' A man of the people said, 'Yes, I know him. That was Uways al-Qarani.' I said, 'Do you know his home?' He said, 'Yes.' I went with him until I knocked on his room and he came out to me. I said, 'My brother, what has kept you from us?' He replied. 'Nakedness.' His companions used to mock him and abuse him. I said, 'Take this cloak and wear it.' He said, 'Do not do it. When they see me wearing it they will abuse me.' I kept at him until he wore it and came out to us. They said, 'Do you see deceit from this cloak of his?' He came and put it down and said, 'Do you see?'" Usayr added, "I came to the gathering and said, 'What do you want from this man? You have abused him. A man is naked sometimes and clothed sometimes.'" He severely rebuked them.

Then it was decided that the people of Kufa should go to 'Umar and a man who was one of those who had mocked him went. 'Umar said, 'Are there any Qaranis here?' The man came and he said, 'The Messenger of Allah ﷺ said that a man called Uways would come to us from Yemen. He would not leave any women behind except his mother. He has some whiteness. He prayed to Allah and He removed that whiteness from him except for a spot the size of a dirham. If any of you meets him command him to ask for forgiveness for you.' He said, 'He came to us.' I asked, 'From where?' 'From Yemen,' he answered. I said. 'What is your name?' He replied, 'Uways.' I asked, 'Who did you leave in Yemen?' 'A mother of mine,' he answered. I asked, 'Did you have some whiteness which you prayed to Allah to remove?' 'Yes,' he answered. I said, 'Ask for forgiveness for me.' He said, 'Does someone like me ask for forgiveness for the like of you, Amir al-Mu'minin?' So he prayed for forgiveness for him. I said to him, 'You are my brother. Do not leave me.' He said, 'He left me and I was told that he came to you in Kufa.' That man who had mocked and demeaned him said, 'This man is not among us, Amir al-Mu'minin, and we do not know him.' 'Umar said, 'Yes, he is a man like that. It is as if he diminishes his importance.' He said, 'Amir al-Mu'minin, among us is a man called Uways whom we mock.' He said, 'Perceive. I do not think that you have perceived.' That man went until he went in where he was before going to his family. Uways said to him, 'This is not your custom. What has happened to you?' He replied, 'I heard 'Umar say such-and-such about you. So ask for forgiveness for me, Uways.' He said, 'I will not do it until you impose on me that you will not mock me again nor mention what you heard from 'Umar to anyone.' So he asked for forgiveness for him."

Usayr said, "It was not long before his business became widespread in Kufa. I went to him and visited him and said to him, 'My brother. I see you are a wonder while we are not aware of that.' He said, 'I do not have what is bandied among the people. A person is only rewarded for his actions.' Then he withdrew from them and left."

Al-Fadl ibn Dukayn reported from Sharik from Yazid ibn Abi Ziyad from 'Abd ar-Rahman ibn Abi Layla who said, "A man of the people of Syria called to us on the Day of Siffin, 'Is Uways al-Qarani among you?' They said, 'Yes.' He said, 'I heard the Messenger of Allah ﷺ say, 'Among the best of the Tabi'un is Uways al-Qarani.' Then he struck his camel and went in among them."

Muslim ibn Ibrahim reported from Sallam ibn Miskin that a man said that the Messenger of Allah ﷺ said, "My close friend of this community is Uways al-Qarani."

'Affan ibn Muslim reported from Hammad ibn Salama from Sa'id al-Jurayri from Abu Nadra that Usayr ibn Jabir ibn 'Umar said to Uways, "Ask forgiveness for me." He said, "How can I ask forgiveness for you when you are a Companion of the Messenger of Allah ﷺ?" He answered, "I heard the Messenger of Allah ﷺ say, 'The best of the Tabi'un is a man called Uways.'" It is a long *hadith* like that of Sulayman ibn al-Mughira.

Yahya ibn Khulayf ibn 'Uqba reported that Ibn 'Awn that Muhammad said, "'Umar was commanded to meet a man of the Tabi'un to ask him to ask forgiveness for him."

Muhammad said, "I was informed that 'Umar asked him in the festival (i.e. Uways)."

'Ali ibn 'Abdullah reported from Mu'adh ibn Hisham ad-Dastawa'i from his father from Qatada from Zurara ibn Awf that Usayr ibn Jabir said, "'Umar ibn al-Khattab had the reinforcements of Yemen come to him and he asked them, 'Is Uways ibn 'Amir among you?' until he came to Uways and said, 'Are you Uways ibn 'Amir?' 'Yes,' he answered. He said, 'From Murad and then from Qaran?' 'Yes,' he said. He said, 'Did you have some whiteness which was healed except for the size of a dirham?' 'Yes,' he answered. He asked, 'Do you have a mother?' He answered, 'Yes.' He said, 'I heard the Messenger of Allah ﷺ say, "Uways ibn 'Amir of Qaran will come to you. He will have whiteness which has healed except for the size of a dirham and he has a mother to whom he is dutiful. If he were to take an oath by Allah, He would fulfil it. If you are able to ask him to ask forgiveness for you, then do so." So ask for forgiveness for me.' He asked for forgiveness for him. Then he asked, 'Where are you going?' 'Kufa,' he answered. He said, 'Shall I write for you to its governor and give him commands about you?' 'No,' he answered, 'I prefer to be in the dust of the people.'

The next year a man of their nobles performed *hajj* and met 'Umar and he asked him about Uways and how he was. He replied, 'I left him with a ragged house and few goods.' He said, 'I heard the Messenger of Allah ﷺ say, 'Uways ibn 'Amir will come to you from the reinforcements of the people of Yemen from Murad and then Qaran. He will have whiteness which has healed except for the size of a dirham and he has a mother to whom he is dutiful. If he were to take an oath by Allah, He would fulfil it. If you are able to ask him to ask forgiveness for you, then do so.' When the man reached Kufa, he went to Uways and said, 'Ask forgiveness for me!' He said, 'You have come from a righteous journey! Ask forgiveness for me!' He said, 'You met 'Umar?' 'Yes,' he replied. So he asked for forgiveness for me."

Usayr said, "He gave him a cloak to wear. When someone saw him wearing it, they said, 'How does Uways have this cloak?'"

Qabisa ibn 'Uqba reported from Sufyan from Ibn Usayr ibn 'Amr that his father went to Uways al-Qarani and found him not covering from nakedness and clothed him.

Ahmad ibn 'Abdullah ibn Yunus reported from Abu al-Ahwas that a companion of his said, "A man of Murad went to Uways al-Qarani and said, 'Peace be upon you.' He replied, 'And on you.' He asked, 'How are you, Uways?' 'Good Praise be to Allah.' He asked, 'How is the time for you?' He said, 'You do not ask a man in the evening who may not see the morning nor ask a man in morning when he may not see the evening. Brother of Murad, death does not remain a joy for the believer. Brother of Murad, the recognition of the believer of the rights of Allah does not let gold or silver remain for him. Brother of Murad, a believer establishing the command of Allah does not leave any friend for him. By Allah, we command them the correct and forbid them the bad and they take us as enemies and find on that helpers from the impious so that, by Allah, they accuse me of terrible things. By Allah, that does not prevent me from standing for Allah by the truth.'"

Al-Fadl ibn Dukayn reported from Sayd ibn Harun al-Burjumi from Mansur from Muslim ibn Sabur from an old man of the Banu Haram that Harim ibn Hayyan al-'Abdi said, "I came from Basra and met Uways al-Qarani on the bank of the Euphrates without shoes. I said, 'How are you, brother? How are you, Uways?' He said to me, 'How are you, my brother?' I said, 'Relate to me.' He said, 'I dislike to open this door (i.e. to myself) that I be a *hadith* scholar or qadi or mufti.' Then he took my hand and wept. I said. 'Recite to me.' He said, 'I seek refuge with Allah, the All-Hearing, All-Knowing from the accursed Shaytan. *"Ha-Mim, by the Book which makes things clear. We sent it down in a blessed night. We are constantly giving warning."* (44:1-3) When he reached *'The All-Hearing. All-Knowing'* (6), he fainted. Then he recovered and said, 'I prefer solitude.'" Uways was trustworthy and does not have a *hadith* from anyone.

'Abda ibn Hilal ath-Thaqafi

'Umar ibn al-Khattab instructed him to break his fast on the Day of the *'Id al-Fitr* and *'Id ad-Adha*. He said, "My night will not ever testify to my sleep nor my day except to fasting." May Allah have mercy on him and be pleased with him.

Abu Ghadira ad-Dabbi

His name was 'Abd ar-Rahman ibn Khasafa.

Abu Khaythama Zuhayr ibn Harb reported from Jarir ibn Mughira that Abu Ghadira 'Abd ar-Rahman ibn Khasafa came to 'Umar ibn al-Khattab in the delegation of the Banu Dabba. They settled the needs of other than me. He said, "'Umar passed by me and I jumped up. When I was behind 'Umar on his camel he asked, 'Who is this man?' I answered, 'A Dabbi.' He said, 'Coarse.' I said, 'Against the enemy, Amir al-Mu'minin.' He said, 'And towards the friend.' He continued, 'Present your need.' He settled my need and then said, 'Leave us the back of our mount.'"

Sa'd ibn Malik al-'Absi

He related from 'Umar ibn al-Khattab. Hallam ibn Salih al-'Absi related from him.

Habib ibn Suhan al-Asadi

His *kunya* was Abu Malik. He related from 'Umar ibn al-Khattab. He was trustworthy and known, with few *hadith*s.

From this generation those who related from 'Ali ibn Abi Talib and 'Abdullah ibn Mas'ud

Al-Harith ibn Suwayd at-Taymi

One of Taym ar-Rabab. He related from 'Ali, 'Abdullah, Hudhayfa and Salman.

Qabisa ibn 'Uqba reported from Sufyan from al-A'mash from Ibrahim at-Taymi that al-Harith ibn Suwayd said, "If a man follows us to 'Abdullah, he would not accept him, but would send him back."

Isma'il ibn Ibrahim al-Asadi reported from Abu Hayyan at-Taymi from his father about a *hadith* which al-Harith ibn Suwayd reported it. His *kunya* was Abu 'A'isha. Muhammad ibn 'Umar and others said that al-Harith ibn Suwayd died in Kufa at the end of the time of 'Abdullah ibn az-Zubayr. He was trustworthy and had a lot of *hadith*s.

Al-Harith ibn Qays al-Ju'fi of Madhhij

He related from 'Ali and 'Abdullah.

Yahya ibn Adam reported from Sharik from Muhammad ibn 'Abdullah al-Muradi from 'Amr ibn Murra ibn Khaythama that Abu Musa al-Ash'ari prayed over al-Harith ibn Qays after the prayer had been performed over him.

Yahya ibn Adam said that he heard Sharik say that Abu Musa led the prayer over al-Harith ibn Qays after the prayer was said on him.

Al-Harith al-A'war

Al-Harith al-A'war ibn 'Abdullah ibn Ka'b ibn Asad ibn Khalid ibn Hawth. His name was 'Abdullah ibn Sab' ibn Sa'b ibn Mu'awiya ibn Kathir ibn Malik ibn Jusham ibn Hashid ibn Khayran ibn Nawf ibn Hamdan. Hawth is the brother of as-Subay', the group of Abu Ishaq as-Subay'i. He related from 'Ali and 'Abdullah ibn Mas'ud. He had bad words and he was weak in his transmission.

Muslim ibn Ibrahim reported from al-Mundhir ibn Tha'laba from 'Ilya' ibn Ahmar that 'Ali ibn Abi Talib addressed the people and said, "Who will purchase knowledge for a dirham?" Al-Harith ibn al-A'war bought some pages for a dirham and then brought them to 'Ali and 'Ali wrote a lot for him. 'Ali addressed the people after that and said, "People of Kufa, half a man has overcome me."

Al-Fadl ibn Dukayn reported from Sharik from Jabir that 'Amir said, "I saw al-Hasan and al-Husayn asking al-Harith al-A'war about the *hadith* of 'Amir. Jarir related from Mughira that ash-Sha'bi said, "Al-Harith al-A'war related to me, and he was a liar."

Al-Fadl ibn Dukayn reported from Zuhayr that Abu Ishaq said, "It used to be said there was no one in Kufa with more knowledge of the obligatory shares than 'Abida and al-Harith al-A'war."

Al-Fadl ibn Dukayn reported from Zuhayr ibn Mu'awiya that Abu Ishaq used to pray behind al-Harith al-A'war and he was the imam of his people. He used to lead the prayer in their funerals. When he prayed the funeral prayer, he said the *salam* once to his right.

Waki' reported from Isra'il from Abu Ishaq from al-Harith al-A'war that he instructed that 'Abdullah ibn Yazid al-Ansari pray over him.

'Ubaydullah ibn Musa reported from Isra'il from Abu Ishaq who said, "Al-Harith al-A'war ordered that 'Abdullah ibn Yazid al-Ansari pray over him. He prayed over him and said four *takbir*s. Then we took him to the grave and he said, 'Put him here at the end of it at his feet.' We put him down."

Wahb ibn Jarir reported from Shu'ba that Abu Ishaq said, "Al-Harith ordered that 'Abdullah ibn Yazid pray over him and put him in the grave from the side of the feet of the grave. He said, 'This is *sunna*.' He said, 'Remove the cloth from him. This is done with women.'"

Waki' reported from Sufyan that Abu Ishaq said, "I was present at the grave of al-Harith al-A'war. They stretched a cloth over his grave and 'Abdullah ibn Yazid al-Ansari removed it and said, 'It is a man.'"

Waki' ibn al-Jarrah reported from Sufyan that Abu Ishaq said, "I attended the funeral of az-Zubayr. 'Abdullah ibn Yazid al-Ansari al-Khatmi was the governor at that time for 'Abdullah ibn az-Zubayr over Kufa."

'Umayr ibn Sa'id an-Nakha'i

He related from 'Ali, 'Abdullah, 'Ammar and Abu Musa. He lived until he died in 115 AH while Khalid ibn 'Abdullah was gover-

nor in Kufa. Muhammad ibn Jabir al-Hanafi met him. He was trustworthy and had *hadiths*.

Sa'id ibn Wahb al-Hamdani

One of the Banu Yahmad ibn Mawhab ibn Sadiq ibn Yana' ibn
Duman. They are the Yana'iyyin of Hamdan. Sa'id related from 'Ali,
'Abdullah and Khabbab. He listened to Mu'adh ibn Jabal in Yemen
before he emigrated in the life of the Messenger of Allah 鬱. He clung
to 'Ali ibn Abi Talib and was called al-Qurad ('the tick') because of
his clinging to him. He related from Salman, Ibn 'Umar and Ibn az-
Zubayr and Shurayh.

Al-Fadl ibn Dukayn reported that Yunus ibn Abi Ishaq said, "I
saw Sa'id ibn Wahb come down from his upper room on Friday
when his son came. He did not attend *Jumu'a*. He was the *'arif* of his
people."

Muhammad ibn 'Abdullah al-Asadi reported from Yunus ibn Abi
Ishaq, "I saw Sa'id ibn Wahb using yellow dye. Sa'id died in Kufa in
86 AH in the caliphate of 'Abd al-Malik ibn Marwan." He was trustworthy and had *hadiths*.

Hubayra ibn Yarim ash-Shibbami of Hamdan

Shibbam is 'Abdullah ibn As'ad ibn Jusham ibn Hashid. Shibbam
was named after a mountain of theirs. He related from him also.
Hubayra showed weakness in the battle with al-Mukhtar.

'Affan ibn Muslim reported from Shu'ba that Abu Ishaq said, "I
heard Hubayra said that he heard 'Abdullah say, 'Fasting is a protection from the Fire.'"

'Amr ibn Salima

'Amr ibn Salima ibn 'Amira ibn Muqatil ibn al-Harith ibn Ka'b
ibn 'Alwi ibn 'Alyan ibn Arhab ibn Du'am of Hamdan. He related
from 'Ali and 'Abdullah and was a noble. He is the one whom al-
Hasan ibn 'Ali ibn Abi Talib sent with al-Ash'ath ibn Qays to make
peace with Mu'awiya. Mu'awiya liked what he saw of the openness,
eloquence and body of 'Amr. He asked, "Are you a Mudari?" "No,"
he replied. Then he said:

I am from a people whom the Prophet of Allah glorified
    over every Bedouin and settled person.
Our fathers were fathers of truthfulness
    by whom fathers of noble nature rose to glory.
Our mothers should be honoured as old women
    and they bequeathed height from proud man after proud man.
I am a man from Hamdan and then one of Arhab."

He was trustworthy and had few *hadith*s.

Abu az-Za'ra'

His name was 'Abdullah ibn Hani al-Hadrami and he is counted
as part of Kinda. He related from 'Ali and 'Abdullah ibn Mas'ud. He
was trustworthy and had *hadith*s.

Abu 'Abd ar-Rahman as-Sulami

His name was 'Abdullah ibn Habib. He related from 'Ali,
'Abdullah and 'Uthman.

Hajjaj ibn Muhammad related that Shu'ba said, "Abu 'Abd ar-
Rahman as-Sulami did not listen to 'Uthman but he listened to 'Ali.

Shabbaba ibn Sawwar related from Shu'ba from 'Alqama ibn
Martha from Sa'd ibn 'Ubayda from Abu 'Abd ar-Rahman as-Sulami
that 'Uthman said that the Messenger of Allah ﷺ said, "The best of
you is the one who learns the Qur'an and teaches it."

Abu 'Abd ar-Rahman said, "That one made me sit in this gathering."

'Affan ibn Muslim reported from Aban al-'Attar from 'Asim that
Abu 'Abd ar-Rahman said, "I took my recitation from 'Ali."

'Affan reported from Shu'ba from Mansur from Tamim ibn
Salama that Abu 'Abd ar-Rahman was the imam of the mosque and
he was carried through the mud on a rainy day.

Hafs ibn 'Umar al-Hawdi reported from Hammad ibn Zayd from
'Ata' ibn as-Sa'ib that Abu 'Abd ar-Rahman as-Sulami said, "We
took this Qur'an from some people who reported to us that when
they had learned ten *ayat*s, they did not go on to the next ten until
they had learned what was in them. We used to learn the Qur'an and

act by it. I will leave the Qur'an after us to people who will drink it like water and it will not go beyond their throats. Indeed, it will not go beyond here. He put his hand on his throat."

Shihab ibn 'Abbad reported from Ibrahim ibn Humayd from Isma'il ibn Abi Isma'il that Abu 'Abd ar-Rahman used to recite twenty *ayat*s in the morning and twenty in the evening. He would tell them the position of the ten and five and recite them in groups of five *ayat*s.

Malik ibn Isma'il reported from 'Abd al-Hamid ibn Abi Ja'far al-Farra' from his father that Abu 'Abd ar-Rahman as-Sulami said, "I came and found baskets and carrots in the house." They said, "'Amr ibn Hurayth sent this. You taught his son the Qur'an." He said, "Return it. We do not take a wage for the Book of Allah."

'Arim ibn al-Fadl reported from Hammad ibn Zayd that 'Asim ibn Bahdala said, "We used to go to Abu 'Abd ar-Rahman as-Sulami while we were young boys. He said, 'Do not sit with any story-teller except for Abu al-Ahwas. Do not sit with Shaqiq nor with Abu Wa'il nor Sa'd ibn Hayda.'"

Al-Hasan ibn Musa and Malik ibn Isma'il reported from Zuhayr from Abu Ishaq that 'Abdullah ibn Habib Abi 'Abd ar-Rahman as-Sulami said, "Abu al-Ahwas used to say, 'Take from him. He is a *faqih*.' He said, 'Do not take a cafiz of barley in exchange for a cafiz of wheat. That is disliked.'"

Al-Hasan ibn Musa reported from Zuhayr from Abu Ishaq that 'Abdullah ibn Habib said, "My father taught me the Qur'an. My father was one of the Companions of Muhammad ﷺ. He was present with him. I did not leave that which I could give as *sadaqa* for all I was seen. He said, 'Young or old, free or slave, of my people with a *sa'* of food of our best wheat for every person of my family for each breaking.'"

Ahmad ibn 'Abdullah ibn Yunus reported from Abu Shihab from Abu Ishaq ash-Shaybani from Sa'd ibn 'Ubayda Abu Hamza that Abu 'Abd ar-Rahman as-Sulami said, "If the one praying facing the *qibla* knew what he is in, he would not have faced it. If the one who prayed knew what he was in, he would not have faced it."

'Abd al-Hamid ibn 'Abd ar-Rahman al-Himmani reported from Mis'ar from 'Ata' ibn as-Sa'ib that Abu 'Abd ar-Rahman as-Sulami said to a man who had some barbaric Arabic, "Are you a believer or

Muslim?" He said, "Yes, if Allah wills." He said, "Do not say 'If Allah wills.'" I said to Mis'ar, "Abu Salama, should I say that I am truly a believer?" "Yes," he answered, "Are you falsely a believer? Is it good speech that a man says, 'This is the sky if Allah wills?'"

Ahmad ibn 'Abdullah ibn Yunus reported from Mindal from al-A'mash that Sa'd ibn 'Ubayda said, "Abu 'Abd ar-Rahman as-Sulami prayed in a shirt."

Al-Hasan ibn Musa reported from Zuhayr from Abu Ishaq that Abu Hamza Sa'd ibn 'Ubayda saw Abu 'Abd ar-Rahman praying in a single shirt without a cloak or a waist-wrapper.

Al-Hasan ibn Musa reported from Hammad ibn Salama from 'Ata' ibn as-Sa'ib that when Abu 'Abd ar-Rahman was asked, "How are you?" he would say, "In good. Praise be to Allah."

'Ata' said, "I mentioned that to Abu al-Bakhtari and he said, 'I take it! I take it!'"

Al-Fadl ibn Dukayn reported from 'Abd as-Salam ibn Harb that 'Ata' ibn as-Sa'ib said, "I visited Abu 'Abd ar-Rahman as-Sulami. He cauterised a slave of him and I said, 'Do you cauterise your slave?' He said, 'What will stop me when I heard 'Abdullah say that Allah has not sent down an illness while that He sent down a cure for it?'"

'Affan ibn Muslim reported from Hammad ibn Salama that 'Ata' ibn as-Sa'ib said, "I visited 'Abdullah ibn Habib while he was judging in his mosque. I said, 'May Allah have mercy on you! If you would go to your bed.' He said, 'It was related to me by someone who heard the Prophet ﷺ say, "A person is in the prayer as long as he is in his place of prayer, waiting for the prayer, and the angels say, 'O Allah, forgive him! O Allah, show mercy to him!'" I wanted to die while I am in my mosque.'"

'Arim ibn al-Fadl and Hafs ibn 'Umar al-Hawdi reported from Hammad ibn Zayd that 'Ata' ibn as-Sa'ib said, "We went to give Abu 'Abd ar-Rahman hope when he was dying. He said, 'I do not hope even when I have fasted eighty Ramadans.'"

Wahb ibn Jarir ibn Hazim reported from Shu'ba that Yazid ibn Abi Ziyad said, "Abu 'Abd ar-Rahman died and they took him by Abu Juhayfa who said, "Given rest and people given rest from.'"

Muhammad ibn 'Umar and others said that Abu 'Abd ar-Rahman as-Sulami died in Kufa while Bishr ibn Marwan was governor in the caliphate of 'Abd al-Malik ibn Marwan. He was trustworthy and had many *hadith*s.

'Abdullah ibn Ma'qil ibn Muqarrin al-Muzani

His *kunya* was Abu al-Walid. He related from 'Ali and 'Abdullah. Muhammad ibn 'Abdullah al-Asadi reported that Yunus ibn Abi Ishaq said, "'Abdullah ibn Ma'qil ibn Muqarrin was put in the expedition in which I also was."

Abu Bakr ibn 'Ayyash reported that Abu Ishaq said, "I attended the funeral of 'Abdullah ibn Ma'qil and he said that a man said, 'The person in this grave left instructions that he should quietly be buried and he has been.'" He was trustworthy and had many *hadith*s.

'Abd ar-Rahman ibn Ma'qil ibn Muqarrin al-Muzani

He was the brother of 'Abdullah ibn Ma'qil. He related from 'Ali and 'Abdullah. They spoke about his transmission from his father. They said that he was young.

Sa'd ibn 'Iyad ath-Thumali of Azd

He related from 'Ali and 'Abdullah. He had few *hadith*s.

Abu Fakhita

His name was Sa'id ibn 'Ilaqa, and he was a *mawla* of Ja'da ibn Hubayra al-Makhzumi. He related from 'Ali, 'Abdullah ibn Mas'ud, and 'Abdullah ibn 'Umar.

Ar-Rabi' ibn 'Umayla al-Fazari

Abu ar-Rujayn ibn ar-Rabi'. He related from 'Ali and 'Abdullah. Qabisa ibn 'Uqba reported from Sufyan from ar-Rukayn ibn ar-Rabi' that his father was with Salman ibn Rabi'a at Balanjar. He was trustworthy and had *hadith*s.

Qays ibn as-Sakan al-Asadi

One of the Banu Suwa'a ibn al-Harith ibn Sa'd ibn Tha'laba ibn Dudan ibn Asad. He related from 'Ali, 'Abdullah and Abu Dharr. He died in Kufa in the time of Mus'ab ibn az-Zubayr ibn al-'Awwam. He was trustworthy and had *hadith*s.

Al-Huzayl ibn Shurahbil al-Awdi of Madhhij

He related from 'Ali and 'Abdullah. He was trustworthy.

His brother, al-Arqam ibn Shurahbil al-Awdi

He listened to 'Abdullah. We do not know that he related anything from 'Ali. He said that his brother Huzayl related from him. He was trustworthy and had few *hadith*s.

Abu al-Kanud al-Azdi

His name was 'Abdullah ibn 'Awf. One of them said: 'Abdullah ibn 'Uwaymir. He related from 'Ali and 'Abdullah.

'Abd al-Malik ibn 'Amr Abu 'Amir al-'Aqadi reported from Shu'ba from al-Hakam that a man related to him that Abu al-Kanud prayed behind 'Ali. He said two *salam*s: 'Peace be upon you. Peace be upon you.' He was trustworthy and had a few *hadith*s.

Shaddad ibn Mi'qal al-Asadi, Asad of Banu Khuzayma

He related from 'Ali and 'Abdullah. He had few *hadith*s.

Habba ibn Juwayn al-'Urani of Bajila

He related from 'Ali and 'Abdullah. He died in 76 AH at the beginning of the caliphate of 'Abd al-Malik ibn Marwan. He has *hadith*s but he is weak.

Khumayr ibn Malik al-Hamdani

He related from 'Ali and 'Abdullah. He has two *hadith*s.

'Amr ibn 'Abdullah al-Asamm al-Wadi'i of Hamdan

He related from 'Ali, 'Abdullah and Masruq. He had few *hadith*s.

'Abdullah ibn Sinan al-Asadi

He was from Asad of the Banu Khuzayma. His *kunya* was Abu Sinan. He related from 'Ali, 'Abdullah and al-Mughira ibn Shu'ba.

He died in the time of al-Hajjaj before Dayr al-Jamajim. He was trustworthy and had *hadith*s.

Zadhan, Abu 'Umar

He was a *mawla* of Kinda. He related from 'Ali, 'Abdullah, Salman, al-Bara' ibn 'Azib and 'Abdullah ibn 'Umar.

'Abdullah ibn Idris reported that Shu'ba said, "I asked al-Hakam about Zadhan and he said, 'He had a lot.'"

Al-Fadl ibn Dukayn reported from 'Abdullah ibn 'Amr ibn Murra who heard 'Antara say, "Zadhan reported to me that he visited 'Abdullah when people had preceded him to the gathering. He said, "I went close to the people wearing rough silk and he said, 'Bring him near,' and he sat me beside him."

Qabisa reported from Sufyan from 'Abdullah ibn as-Sa'ib that Zadhan said, "I asked 'Abdullah ibn Mas'ud about things which I had not been asked about."

Al-Fadl ibn Dukayn reported from Muhammad ibn Talha ibn Musarrif from Zubayd that Zadhan said, "'Ali ibn Abi Talib provided the people with thickened grape juice and my master got from him a small earthen jar from which we used to eat and drink."

Al-Fadl ibn Dukayn reported from Muhammad ibn Talha that Muhammad ibn Juhada said, "Zadhan used to sell cloth and when the buyer came to him, he would open on it on the worse of the two sides."

They said that he died in Kufa in the time of al-Hajjaj ibn Yusuf after Dayr al-Jamajim. He was trustworthy and had few *hadith*s.

'Abbad ibn 'Abdullah al-Asadi

He related from 'Ali and 'Abdullah. He has *hadith*s.

Kumayl ibn Ziyad

Kumayl ibn Ziyad ibn Nahuk ibn Haytham ibn Sa'd ibn Malik ibn al-Harith ibn Suhban ibn Sa'd ibn Malik ibn an-Nakha' of Madhhij. He related from 'Uthman, 'Ali and 'Abdullah. He was present with 'Ali at Siffin. He was noble and obeyed among his people. When al-Hajjaj ibn Yusuf came to Kufa, he summoned him and killed him.

Qays ibn 'Abd al-Hamdani

He was an uncle of 'Amir ibn Sharahil ibn 'Abd ash-Sha'bi. He related from 'Ali and 'Abdullah. He had few *hadith*s.

Husayn ibn Qabisa al-Asadi

He was from Asad of Banu Khuzayma. He related from 'Ali, 'Abdullah and Salman.

Abu al-Qa'qa' al-Jarmi of Quda'a

He related from 'Ali and 'Abdullah.

Isma'il ibn Ibrahim al-Asadi reported from Abu 'Abdullah ash-Shaqari that Abu al-Qa'qa' al-Jarmi said, "I was present at al-Qadisiyya while I was a young lad."

Abu Razin

His name was Mas'ud, a *mawla* of Abu Wa'il.

Shaqiq ibn Salama al-Asadi

He related from 'Ali and 'Abdullah.

Yahya ibn Adam reported from Abu Bakr ibn 'Ayyash that 'Asim said, "Abu Wa'il said to me, 'Are you surprised at Abu Razin who is senile? He was a boy in the time of 'Umar ibn al-Khattab while I was a man.'" He has *hadith*s.

'Arfaja

He related from 'Ali and 'Abdullah.

'Ubaydullah ibn Musa reported from 'Uthman ibn al-Mughira that 'Arfaja said, "I prayed behind 'Ali and I did the *qunut* in both of the two *rak'at*s before *ruku'*."

Ma'di Karib al-Mishraqi from Hamdan

Mishraq is a place in Yemen to which he is attributed. He related from 'Ali and 'Abdullah. He had *hadith*s.

'Abd ar-Rahman ibn 'Abdullah ibn Mas'ud al-Hudhali

An ally of Banu Zuhra. He related from 'Ali and 'Abdullah.

Ishaq ibn Yusuf al-Azraq reported from Zakariyya' ibn Abi Za'ida from Simak ibn Harb that 'Abd ar-Rahman ibn 'Abdullah said that he heard 'Abdullah ibn Mas'ud say, "Making the lawful unlawful is like making the unlawful lawful." He was trustworthy and had few *hadiths*. They spoke about his transmission from his father. He was young.

Shutayr ibn Shakal ibn Humayd al-'Absi

He related from 'Ali and 'Abdullah and from his father. His father was a Companion, and from Hafsa. He died in Kufa in the time of Mus'ab ibn az-Zubayr. He was trustworthy and had few *hadiths*.

From this generation those who related from 'Abdullah ibn Mas'ud

Abu al-Ahwas

His name was 'Awf ibn Malik ibn Nadla al-Jushami of Hawazin. He related from 'Abdullah, Hudhayfa, Abu Mas'ud al-Ansari, Abu Musa al-Ash'ari and his father. He was a Companion, and related from Zayd ibn Suhan.

Sulayman Abu Dawud at-Tayalisi reported from Shu'ba that 'Ali ibn al-Aqmar heard Abu al-Ahwas say, "We were three brothers. The Haruriyya (Kharijites) killed one of them. Another was killed in such and such a battle. The third (meaning himself) does not know what Allah will do with him."

Abu Dawud reported that Shu'ba said, "I asked Abu Ishaq, 'How did Abu al-Ahwas relate?' He said, 'He gave it to us in the mosque and said, "'Abdullah said."'"

'Affan reported from Hammad ibn Zayd that 'Asim said, "We used to go to Abu 'Abd ar-Rahman as-Sulami when we were young lads. He used to tell us, 'Do not sit with any story-tellers other than Abu al-Ahwas. Beware of Shaqiq and Sa'id ibn 'Ubayda.'"

Hammad said, "Nor Abu Wa'il. This one used to relate the opinion of the Kharijites."

'Arim ibn al-Fadl reported to us from Hammad ibn Zayd that 'Asim said, "I saw Abu al-Ahwas wearing a robe of rough silk." He was trustworthy and had *hadith*s.

Ar-Rabi' ibn Khuthaym ath-Thawri

One of the Banu Tha'laba ibn 'Amir ibn Milkan ibn Thawr ibn 'Abd Manat ibn Add ibn Tabikha ibn Ilyas ibn Mudar. Thawr used to be called Thawr Athal. Athal was a mountain where he lived. Ar-Rabi' ibn Khuthaym's *kunya* was Abu Yazid. He related from 'Abdullah.

'Affan ibn Muslim reported from 'Abd al-Wahid ibn Ziyad from 'Abdullah ibn ar-Rabi' ibn Khuthaym that Abu 'Ubayda ibn 'Abdullah ibn Mas'ud said, "When ar-Rabi' ibn Khuthaym visited 'Abdullah, he did not at that time give permission to anyone until each of them had settled the needs of his companion. He said that 'Abdullah said to him, 'Abu Yazid, if the Messenger of Allah ﷺ had seen you, he would have loved you. I did not see you but that I remembered the humble.'"

Ahmad ibn 'Abdullah ibn Yunus reported from Abu Bakr ibn 'Ayyash that 'Asim said, "'Abdullah said when he saw ar-Rabi' ibn Khuthaym, 'Give good news to the humble.'"

Waki' related from Sufyan from 'Amr ibn Murra that Abu 'Ubayda said, "I did not see anyone finer in worship than Rabi' ibn Khuthaym."

Waki' and 'Abdullah ibn Numayr reported from Malik ibn Mighwal from ash-Sha'bi who said, "Rabi' ibn Khuthaym did not sit in a gathering. He used to say, 'I dislike to see something for which there will be testimony. I do not witness or see a pregnant woman whom I do not help or someone wronged whom I do not help.'"

'Abdullah ibn Numayr reported in his hadith, "He did not sit at a gathering or a road since he began to wear a waist-wrapper."

Another added, "Or I might see a man lies about another man and so I am obliged to testify against him or someone not lowering his eye or not guiding on the road."

Muhammad ibn al-Fudayl ibn Ghazwan reported from Abu Hayyan at-Taymi that his father said, "I never heard Rabi' ibn

Khuthaym mention anything of this world except that he asked one day, "How many mosques does Taym have?"

'Abdullah ibn Numayr reported from Fudayl ibn Ghazwan that Sa'id ibn Masruq related: "When Rabi' ibn Khuthaym was passing on the gathering which contained Bakr ibn Maghiz he said to him, 'Bakr ibn Maghiz, guard your tongue except from that which is for or against you. I suspect people are on my *deen*.'"

Muhammad ibn al-Fadl reported from Salim from Mundhir that Rabi' ibn Khuthaym said, "Slave of Allah! Speak good or do good and persevere in righteous deeds. Do not think time is long for you and they will not harden your heart. Do not be among those who say, *"'We hear," when they do not hear.'* (8:21) Slave of Allah! If you can do good, then follow good with more good. A day will come on you in which you will wish that you could have done more. If it has passed from you, then it is impossible. So do good. Allah says, *'Good actions eradicate bad actions. This is a reminder for people who pay heed.'* (11:114) Slave of Allah! Whatever knowledge Allah has taught you in His Book, praise Allah for it and if He has preferred someone else rather than you with any knowledge, entrust it to its Knower. Do not over-burden yourselves. He says, *'Say, "I do not ask you for any wage for it, nor am I a man of false pretensions. It is simply a reminder to all the worlds. You will come to know what it is talking about after a while."'* (38:86-88) Slave of Allah! Know that when the absence of the slave is long and his arrival is near, his people wait for him. When it comes, then often remember this death whose like those before you have not tasted and the secrets are the secrets which are hidden from people and they are clear to Allah."

'Abdullah ibn Numayr reported from al-A'mash that Ibrahim said, "Ar-Rabi' ibn Khuthaym used to visit 'Alqama. There was a group in the quarter and the road in the mosque. Some women entered the mosque and ar-Rabi' did not look about until they had left. He was asked, 'Why did you not visit 'Alqama?' He answered, 'His door was shut and I did not like to annoy him.'"

Yahya ibn 'Isa ar-Ramli reported that al-A'mash that Shaqiq said, "We went to visit ar-Rabi' ibn Khuthaym with a group of the companions of 'Abdullah. We passed by a man and he asked, 'Where are you going?' We answered, 'To ar-Rabi'.' He said, 'You are going to a man who will not lie when he relates something to you and will not break a promise he makes to you and will not betray you if you trust him.'"

'Ubaydullah ibn Musa and al-Fadl ibn Dukayn reported from Isra'il from Sa'id ibn Masruq that Abu Wa'il said, "We went to ar-Rabi' ibn Khuthaym in his house and a man said, 'You are going to a man who will not lie when he relates and will not betray you if you trust him.' We came in to him and he said, 'Praise be to Allah Who has not made you come to me so that I could fornicate and you fornicate with me, steal and so you steal with me or drink and you drink with me.'"

Al-Fadl ibn Dukayn reported from Sufyan from Mansur that Ibrahim said that a man said, "I do not see ar-Rabi' ibn Khuthaym speaking words for twenty years except for a word that ascended."

Al-Fadl ibn Dukayn reported from Sufyan from Nusayr ibn Dhu'luq that Ibrahim at-Taymi said, "I was told by someone who was a companion of ar-Rabi' ibn Khuthaym for twenty years that he did not hear him say anything which could be criticised."

Al-Fadl ibn Dukayn reported from Sufyan that Abu Qays said, "I sat with ar-Rabi' ibn Khuthaym who said, 'Speak good and do good and you will be rewarded with good.'"

Al-Fadl ibn Dukayn and Muhammad ibn 'Abdullah al-Asadi reported from Sufyan from his father that when Rabi' was asked, 'How are you this morning?' he would say, 'This morning we are weak sinners consuming our provision and waiting for our ends.'"

'Affan ibn Muslim reported from Abu Hayyan from his father that Rabi' ibn Khuthaym said, "Speak little except for nine: Glory be to Allah, Praise be to Allah, There is no god but Allah, Allah is greater, commanding the good and forbidding the bad, reciting the Qur'an, asking for good and seeking refuge from evil."

'Affan ibn Muslim reported from Abu 'Awana from Sa'id ibn Masruq from Mundhir ath-Thawri that when a man came to him, ar-Rabi' ibn Khuthaym, said, "Slave of Allah! Obey Allah in what you know and entrust to its Knower what others are preferred with because we fear more for you in what is deliberate than for me in error. The best of you is not the best because of his good. Good is the last of them in doing evil. You do not desire good truly and do not truly flee from evil. You have not grasped all that was sent down on Muhammad nor do you know what all you recite truly is. The secrets are the secrets which are concealed from people. They are evident to Allah. So seek their cure!" Then he added, "What is their cure? It is that you repent and do not revert."

Malik ibn Isma'il reported from Kamil Abu al-'Ala' that Mundhir ath-Thawri heard ar-Rabi' ibn Khuthaym say, "Sins are the sins of the secrets which are concealed from people but evident to Allah. What is their cure? That you repent and not revert."

Muhammad ibn as-Salt and Talq ibn Ghannam reported from ar-Rabi' ibn Mundhir from his father that ar-Rabi' ibn Khuthaym said, "All by which the Face of Allah is not desired will vanish."

Khalaf ibn Tamim reported from Sa'id ibn 'Abdullah ibn ar-Rabi' ibn Khuthaym reported that Nusayr ibn Du'luq said, "Ar-Rabi' ibn Khuthaym was asked, 'Abu Yazid, do you not censure people?' He replied, 'By Allah, I am not pleased with people so I censure people. People fear Allah for the sins of people but feel safe with Him with their own sins.'"

Talq ibn Ghannam an-Nakha'i reported from ar-Rabi' ibn Mundhir from his father that ar-Rabi' ibn Khuthaym said, "Some talk has a light like the light of the day which you recognise and some has a darkness like the darkness of the night which you dislike."

Ahmad ibn 'Abdullah ibn Yunus reported from Abu Bakr ibn 'Ayyash that 'Asim said, "It was said to ar-Rabi' ibn Khuthaym, 'If you were to utter a verse of poetry, your companions would quote it.' He said, 'No one speaks about something but that he finds it in front of him. I dislike to find poetry in front of me.'"

'Ali ibn Yazid as-Suda'i reported from 'Abd ar-Rahman ibn Nusayr ibn Dhu'luq that ar-Rabi' used to perform *tahajjud* in the darkness of the night and came to this *ayat*: *'Do those who perpetrate evil deeds suppose that We will make them like those who believe and do right actions, so that their lives and deaths will be the same? How bad their judgement is!'* (45:21) He continued to repeat in the night until morning.

Rawh ibn 'Ubada reported from Shu'ba from Muzahim ibn Zufar, who was among the people of Rabi' ibn Khuthaym, "A man said to ar-Rabi' ibn Khuthaym, 'Instruct me!' He said, 'Bring me a page.' He wrote on it, *'Say: "Come and I will recite to you what your Lord has forbidden you"'* (6:151) until the words, *'Perhaps you will be godfearing.'* (153) He said, 'I came to you so that you could instruct me.' He answered, 'Hold to these.'"

'Affan ibn Muslim reported from Sulaym ibn Akhdar from Ibn 'Awn that Muslim ibn Abi 'Abdullah said, "Rabi' ibn Khuthaym was in the mosque and a man was behind him. When they jumped up for the prayer, the man began to say, 'Go forward.' Rabi' did not find room before him. So the man raised his hand and pushed the neck of Rabi', not recognising Rabi'. Rabi' turned to him and said, 'May Allah have mercy on you! May Allah have mercy on you!' The man looked and wept when he recognised Rabi'."

Muhammad ibn 'Abdullah al-Asadi reported from Sufyan I think from his father who heard Abu Wa'il when a man asked him, "Who is older: you or Rabi'?" He said, "I am a year older than him and he is greater than me in intelligence."

'Ubaydullah ibn Musa reported from Isra'il from Sa'id ibn Masruq from Mundhir that Rabi' ibn Khuthaym said, "He used to say, 'Speak good and do good. Persist in the righteous of that. Do a lot of good and little evil. Do not make your hearts hard and do not think the time long. *'Do not be like those who say, "We hear," when they do not hear.'* (8:21)"

Al-Fadl ibn Dukayn reported from 'Abd ar-Rahman ibn 'Ajlan al-Burjumi from Nusayr Abu Ta'ma, a *mawla* of ar-Rabi' ibn Khuthaym that ar-Rabi' spent the night reciting a single *ayat* of the Qur'an and did not recite anything else until morning: *'Do those who perpetrate evil deeds...'* (45:21)

Muhammad ibn 'Abdullah al-Asadi reported from Sufyan that Nusayr ibn Dhu'luq said, "Ar-Rabi' ibn Khuthaym did not perform voluntary prayers in the mosque."

Al-Fadl ibn Dukayn reported from Sufyan that Nusayr ibn Dhu'luq said, "Ar-Rabi' ibn Khuthaym used to lead us in the prayer while leaning against a column when he was ill."

Waki' and 'Ubaydullah ibn Musa reported from al-A'mash from Mundhir ath-Thawri that ar-Rabi' ibn Khuthaym used to sweep the privy himself. It was said to him, "You are spared doing that." He replied, "I love to take my share of work."

Muhammad ibn Fudayl ibn Ghazwan reported from Abu Hayyan that his father said, "The daughter of ar-Rabi' ibn Khuthaym came to him and said, 'Father, can I go and play?' He said, 'Go and speak good.'"

Muhammad ibn 'Abdullah al-Asadi and Yahya ibn 'Abbad reported from Yunus ibn Abi Ishaq that Bakr ibn Ma'iz said, "The daughter of ar-Rabi' ibn Khuthaym went to him and said, 'Father, can I go and play?' He said, 'Go and speak good.' When she did that a lot to him, one of the people said to him, 'Let her go and play.' He said, 'I do not want for it to be written for me today that I ordered playing.'"

Muhammad ibn 'Ubayd at-Tanafisi reported from his father that Umm al-Aswad Surayya was married to ar-Rabi' ibn Khuthaym. Ar-Rabi' used to like to eat sugar. She said that when a beggar came, he gave it to him and she said, "What will he do with sugar? Bread is better for him." He said, "I heard Allah say, *'They give food in spite of their love for it.'* (76:8)"

Waki' and 'Ubaydullah ibn Musa reported from al-A'mash that Mundhir ath-Thawri said, "Ar-Rabi' ibn Khuthaym said to his family, 'Prepare *khabis* (a type of sweet made from dates) for us.' He almost did not like anything for them. He said, 'Make it.' He sent it to a neighbour who was suffering an affliction of insanity and began to feed it to him while his spittle was dripping it. When he went out, his family said to him, 'You imposed on us to make it and then you give it to this one to eat? He does not know what he is eating!' Ar-Rabi' said, 'But Allah knows.'"

Al-Fadl ibn Dukayn reported from Sufyan from Abu Hayyan that Abu 'Abd ar-Rahman ar-Rahhal said, "Ar-Rabi' used to repeat [the greeting], 'And on you.'"

'Ubaydullah ibn Musa reported from Sufyan that Nusayr ibn Dhu'luq said, "Ar-Rabi' ibn Khuthaym used to weep until his beard was dripping with tears. He said, 'We met some people for whom we were thieves in their pockets.'"

'Ubaydullah ibn Musa and Muhammad ibn 'Abdullah al-Asadi reported from Sufyan that Nusayr ibn Dhu'luq said, "''Azra said to ar-Rabi' ibn Khuthaym, 'Leave your copy of the Qur'an to me.' Ar-Rabi' looked at his son and said, *'Blood relations are closer to one another in the Book of Allah.'* (8:75)"

Al-Fadl ibn Dukayn reported from Sharik from Husayn from Hilal ibn Yasaf that ar-Rabi' ibn Khuthaym used to say, "O Allah, I have fasted for You and broken my fast on Your provision.'"

Muhammad ibn 'Abdullah al-Asadi reported from Sufyan from Husayn from Mu'adh that ar-Rabi' ibn Khuthaym used to say when he broke the fast, "O Allah, we have fasted for You and broken our fast on Your provision."

'Arim ibn al-Fadl reported from Hammad ibn Zayd that Abu Hayyan at-Taymi said, "Ar-Rabi' ibn Khuthaym went out to the prayer guided between two men and he was asked about that and said, 'When you hear 'Come to success,' then answer.'"

Al-Fadl ibn Dukayn reported from Sufyan from Abu Hayyan that his father said, "Ar-Rabi' ibn Khuthaym was led to the prayer when he was suffering from semi-paralysis. It was said to him, 'Abu Yazid! You have an allowance!' He said, 'I hear, 'Come to the prayer. Come to success.' If I can, I will come to it, even crawling.'"

Muhammad ibn 'Ubayd reported from Dawud al-Qattan, "Ar-Rabi' ibn Khuthaym was afflicted by semi-paralysis. Bakr ibn Ma'iz stood over him and oiled him and deloused his head and washed him. He said, 'Among us one day he washed the head of ar-Rabi' when the saliva of ar-Rabi' flowed and Bakr wept. Ar-Rabi' raised his head and asked, 'What is making you weep? By Allah, I do not want be the most presumptuous of the people of Daylam towards Allah.'"

Al-Fadl ibn Dukayn reported from Fitr from Mundhir that a beggar came to ar-Rabi' ibn Khuthaym and he said, "Make *sakkar* (a sweet) for him." His wife said to him, "What will this one do with *sakkar*?" He said, "I will make it." Ar-Rabi' said, "Fear that Allah call one of you a liar if he says, 'Allah says in His Book this and that,' and Allah says, 'You lied. I did not say it.' He says, 'Allah did not say this and that in His Book' and He says, 'You lied. I said it.'" Ar-Rabi' said, "What will one of you do with any words after nine? They are: Glory be to Allah, Praise be to Allah, There is no god but Allah, Allah is greater, commanding the good and forbidding the bad, reciting the Qur'an, asking Allah for good, and seeking refuge with Him from evil."

Muhammad ibn 'Abdullah al-Asadi reported from Sufyan from Nusayr ibn Dhu'luq that Hubayra ibn Khuzayma said, "When al-Husayn was killed, I went to ar-Rabi' ibn Khuthaym and told him. He recited this *ayat*: *'O Allah, Originator of the heavens and the earth, Knower of the Unseen and the Visible, You will judge between Your slaves regarding what they differed about.'* (39:46)"

Qabisa ibn 'Uqba reported from Sufyan from al-'Ala' ibn al-Musayyab that Abu Ya'la said, "There were thirty men among the Banu Thawr. There was no man among them less than Rabi' ibn Khuthaym."

Qabisa ibn 'Uqba reported from Sufyan from 'Umara ibn al-Qa'qa that Shubruma said, "In Kufa I did not see a quarter with a greater worshipping *faqih* shaykh than the Banu Thawr."

Qabisa ibn 'Uqba reported from Sufyan from Abu Bakr az-Zubaydi that his father said, "I have not seen a quarter with more people who sat in the mosque than the Thawris and 'Uranis.

'Abdullah ibn Ja'far reported from Abu al-Malih that Yusuf ibn al-Hajjaj al-Anmati who heard ar-Rabi' ibn Khuytham said, "I prefer to turn over pig fat in my hand than to turn dice over backgammon."

'Abd al-Wahhab ibn 'Ata' reported from Dawud ibn Abi Hind that ash-Sha'bi said, "We visited Rabi' ibn Khuthaym when he was ill. We said to him, 'Pray to Allah for us.' He said, 'O Allah, all praise is Yours and all good is in Your hand. The entire affair returns to You and You are the God of all creation. We ask You for all good and seek refuge with You from all evil.'"

Qabisa ibn 'Uqba reported from Sufyan from a man of the Banu Taym that his father said, "I sat with ar-Rabi' ibn Khuthaym for two years. He did not ask me about anything which people were engaged except that once he asked me, 'Is your mother alive? How many do you have in the mosque?'"

Qabisa ibn 'Uqba reported from Sufyan from his father from Abu Ya'la that ar-Rabi' ibn Khuthaym said, "How beloved is the entreaty of the slave of his Lord in saying, 'O Lord, You decreed mercy for Yourself. O Lord, You decreed mercy for Yourself!' I have not seen anyone yet say, 'I decreed what I owe, so decree what You owe.'"

Malik ibn Isma'il reported from Sayf ibn Harun from 'Abd al-Malik ibn Sal' that 'Abd Khayr said, "I was a companion of ar-Rabi' ibn Khuthaym in an expedition (which he mentioned). He returned with slaves and animals. After a few days I went to him and did not find any of those slaves or animals at all. I asked for permission to enter and no one answered. I entered and said, 'Where are your slaves and animals?' He did not answer me. I repeated the question and he said, *'You will not attain true goodness until you give of what you love.'* (3:92)"

229

'Umar ibn Hafs reported from Hawshab that al-Hasan said, "Ar-Rabi' ibn Khuthaym was told when he was afflicted by semi-paralysis, 'You should be treated.' He said, "Ad, Thamud, the people of ar-Rass and Qarun have gone among many more. Among them were those who described and were described by it. No describer or described remains who has not vanished.'"

Muhammad ibn 'Abdullah al-Asadi reported from Sufyan from Abu Hayyan from his father that ar-Rabi' ibn Khuthaym said, "Do not tell anyone about me and let me slip away to my Lord."

Waki' ibn Muhammad ibn 'Abdullah al-Asadi reported from Sufyan from his father from Mundhir ath-Thawri that ar-Rabi' ibn Khuthaym left instructions when he was dying: "This is what ar-Rabi' ibn Khuthaym says for himself: I testify to Allah on it and Allah is enough of a witness and repays His righteous slaves and affirms that I am pleased with Allah as a Lord, Muhammad as a Prophet and Islam as a *deen*. I am pleased for myself and whoever obeys me that I worship Him among the worshippers and praise Him among the praisers and I give good counsel to the Muslim community."

'Affan ibn Muslim and Sulayman ibn Harb reported from Shu'ba that Sa'id ibn Masruq said, "Rabi' ibn Khuthaym left a will." I said, "Did you hear it?" He said, "Our shaykhs and the quarter reported to me: 'This is what ar-Rabi' ibn Khuthaym says for himself: I testify to Allah on it and Allah is enough of a witness and repays His righteous slaves. I am pleased with Allah as a Lord, Islam as a *deen* and Muhammad as a Prophet. I am pleased for myself and any of the Muslims who follows me that we worship Allah among the worshippers and praise Him among the praisers and give good counsel to the Muslim community.'"

'Abd al-Wahhab ibn 'Ata' reported from Shu'ba and Isra'il ibn Yunus from Sa'id ibn Masruq that Mundhir ath-Thawri said, "Ar-Rabi' ibn Khuthaym ordered: 'This is what ar-Rabi' ibn Khuthaym instructs and calls on Allah to bear witness against himself (or for him, Shu'ba was unsure): Allah is enough of a witness and repays His righteous slaves and rewards His righteous slaves. I am pleased with Allah as a Lord, Islam as a *deen* and Muhammad as a Prophet and a Messenger and with the Discrimination (or he said the Qur'an) as an imam. I am pleased for myself and those who obey me that we worship Allah among the worshippers and praise Him among the praisers and give good counsel to the Muslim community.'"

They said that ar-Rabi' ibn Khuthaym died in Kufa when 'Ubaydullah ibn Ziyad was governor there.

Waki' ibn al-Jarrah reported from Sufyan from Abu Hayyan at-Taymi from his father that ar-Rabi' ibn Khuthaym ordered: "Release me to my Lord gently, i.e. do not harm anyone by me.'"

Abu al-'Ubaydayn

His name was Mu'awiya ibn Sabra ibn Husayn of the Banu Suwa'a ibn 'Amir ibn Sa'sa'a. He was blind. 'Abdullah ibn Mas'ud used to bring him near and close. He was one of his companions and related from him.

Isma'il ibn Ibrahim reported from Shu'ba from al-Hakam ibn 'Utayba from Yahya ibn al-Jazzar that Abu al-'Ubaydayn was a man of the Banu Numayr who was blind.

Muhammad ibn Sa'd said, "This is what Isma'il and Numayr ibn 'Amir said. They are brothers of Suwa'a ibn 'Amir ibn Sa'sa'a.'"

Mu'ammil ibn Isma'il reported from Sufyan from Abu Sinan that Abu al-Hudhayl said, "Abu al-'Ubaydayn, one of the companions of 'Abdullah, said, "Abdullah, when they constrict you, eat your loaf and drink the water of the Euphrates and hold fast to your *deen*.'" He had few *hadith*s.

Hurayth ibn Zuhayr

He related from 'Abdullah ibn Mas'ud and 'Ammar ibn Yasar.

Muslim ibn Sa'id

'Ubaydullah ibn Musa reported from Isra'il from Abu al-Ya'fur that Muslim ibn Sa'id said, "I entered with Ibn Mas'ud with Zayd ibn Khulayda and he said, 'A day will come on you when you will wish that you do not own other than a camel and its saddle.'"

Qabisa ibn Burma

Qabisa ibn Burma ibn Mu'awiya ibn Sufyan ibn Munqidh ibn Wahb ibn Numayr ibn Nasr ibn Qu'ayn ibn al-Harith ibn Tha'laba ibn Dudan ibn Asad ibn Khuzayma. Qabisa was a master and noble among his people. He related from 'Abdullah ibn Mas'ud.

Talq ibn Ghannam an-Nakha'i reported that Ja'far ibn Sallam al-Asadi said, "I saw Qabisa ibn Burma al-Asadi using yellow dye."

Sila ibn Zufar al-'Absi

He related from 'Abdullah, Hudhayfa and 'Ammar.

Muhammad ibn 'Abdullah al-Asadi and Musa ibn Mas'ud reported from Sufyan from al-A'mash that Abu Wa'il said, "I met Sila ibn Zufar, and, as far as I knew, he was pious and I said to him, 'Is there any of this disease among your people?' 'No,' he answered, 'because we fear more making them err than making them get it right.'"

Musa ibn Mas'ud said in his *hadith* that his *kunya* was Abu al-'Ala'.

He died in Kufa in the time of Mus'ab ibn az-Zubayr. He was trustworthy and had *hadiths*.

Abu ash-Sha'tha' al-Muharibi

His name was Sulaym ibn al-Aswad. He related from 'Abdullah and died in Kufa in the time of al-Hajjaj ibn Yusuf.

Al-Mustawird ibn al-Ahnaf al-Fihri

He related from 'Abdullah. He was trustworthy and had *hadiths*.

'Amir ibn 'Abada

He related: "The bones of the son of Adam are made ready to prostrate." His *kunya* was Abu Iyas. He was from Bajila and was present at al-Qadisiyya.

Ibn Mu'ayyiz as-Sa'di

He related orally from 'Abdullah. He said, "I went out to mount a horse of mine at dawn." He said, "I passed by the mosque of the Banu Hanifa."

Shaddad ibn al-Azma'

Shaddad ibn al-Azma' ibn Abi Buthayna ibn 'Abdullah ibn Murr ibn Malik ibn Harb ibn al-Harith ibn Sa'd ibn 'Abdullah ibn Wada'a of Hamdan. He and his brother al-Harith ibn al-Azma' were nobles in Kufa. Shaddad died in Kufa while Bishr ibn Marwan was governor. He was trustworthy and had few *hadith*s.

'Abdullah ibn Rabi'a as-Sulami

He was the maternal uncle of 'Amr ibn 'Utba ibn Faraqas as-Sulami. He related from Ibn Mas'ud. He was trustworthy and had few *hadith*s.

'Itris ibn 'Urqub ash-Shaybani

He related from 'Abdullah ibn Mas'ud.

'Amr ibn al-Harith ibn al-Mustaliq

He related from 'Abdullah.

Thabit ibn Qutba al-Muzani

He related from 'Abdullah. He was trustworthy and had a lot of *hadith*s.

Abu 'Aqrab al-Asadi

He related from 'Abdullah. I went to him one day and met him above the house. He did not descend to us until the sun rose. He said, "We went to 'Abdullah and I heard him say that the Prophet ﷺ said, 'The Night of Power is in the last seven nights.'"

'Abdullah ibn Ziyad al-Asadi

His *kunya* was Abu Maryam.

Muhammad ibn 'Ubayd at-Tanafisi reported from Mis'ar from Ash'ath ibn Abi ash-Sha'tha' that Abu Maryam said, "I heard 'Abdullah say when he was in *ruku'*, 'There is no power nor strength except by Allah.'"

Sulayman Abu Dawud at-Tayalisi and Abu 'Amir al-'Aqadi reported from Shu'ba from al-Ash'ath that Abu Dawud said in his *hadith*, "I listened to Abu Maryam 'Abdullah ibn Ziyad al-Asadi."

Abu 'Amir said in his *hadith*, "I heard that Abu Maryam, a man of the Banu Asad, listened to 'Abdullah recite in *Zuhr*. He said that he also related from 'Ammar ibn 'Amir.

233

Kharija ibn as-Salt al-Burjumi

One of the Banu Tamim. He related from 'Abdullah ibn Mas'ud. He had few *hadith*s.

Suhaym ibn Nufayl al-Ashja'i

He related from 'Abdullah ibn Mas'ud. His father was a Companion. He had few *hadith*s.

'Abdullah ibn Mirdas al-Muharibi

He related from 'Abdullah. He had few *hadith*s.

Al-Haytham ibn Shihab as-Sulami

He related from 'Abdullah.

Muhammad ibn al-Fudayl ibn Ghazwan reported from al-Husayn that al-Haytham ibn Shihab said, "I heard Ibn Mas'ud say, 'I prefer to sit on hot coals than to sit cross-legged in the prayer.'" He had few *hadith*s.

Marwan Abu 'Uthman al-'Ijli

He related from 'Abdullah.

Yazid ibn Harun reported from ar-Rabi' ibn Muslim from Marwan Abu 'Uthman al-'Iji who said that he heard 'Abdullah ibn Mas'ud say, "Procrastination is the injustice of the wealthy. If the fault had taken the form of a man, it would have been an evil man."

Abu Hayyan

He related from 'Abdullah.

Yazid ibn Harun reported from Shu'ba from Husayn ibn 'Abd ar-Rahman from Hilal ibn Yasaf that his in-law Abu Hayyan said, "I heard 'Abdullah ibn Mas'ud say, 'When one of you lifts his head from prostration before the imam and prostrates again, he should remain for the amount of time that he raises his head.'"

Abu Yazid

He related from 'Abdullah.

Isma'il ibn Ibrahim reported from Layth from Ash'ath ibn Abi ash-Sha'tha' that Abu Yazid said, "I saw Ibn Mas'ud recite behind the imam." I think that he said that it was in *Zuhr* or in *'Asr*.

'Abida ibn Rabi'a al-'Abdi

He related from 'Uthman, 'Abdullah ibn Mas'ud and Salman.

Al-Fadl ibn Dukayn reported from Abu Ishaq that 'Abida ibn Rabi'a said that he heard 'Abdullah say, "I repeat to those whose sides shun the beds: 'what no eye has seen nor ear heard.'"

Al-Akhnas Abu Bukayr ibn al-Akhnas

He was called Bukayr ad-Dakhm. He related from 'Abdullah.

Yazid ibn Harun reported from Abu Janab from Bukayr ibn al-Akhnas that his father said, "While we were sitting with 'Abdullah a man came to him and asked him about a man who commits fornication with a woman and then marries her. 'Abdullah recited to him, '*It is He who accepts repentance from His slaves and pardons evil acts and knows what you do.*' (42:25)"

Abu Majid al-Hanafi

He related from 'Abdullah.

Abu al-Ja'd

He is Abu Salim ibn Abi al-Ja'd al-Ashja'i, a *mawla* of theirs. He related from 'Abdullah.

'Affan ibn Muslim reported from Hammam from Qatada from Salim ibn Abi al-Ja'd from his father from Ibn Mas'ud about a man who fornicates with a woman and then marries her. He said: "They are both fornicators as long as they are together." He said, "I asked Salim, 'What was your father?' He replied, 'He was a reciter of the Book of Allah.'" He had few *hadith*s.

Sa'd ibn al-Akhram

He related from 'Abdullah.

Dirar al-Asadi

He related from 'Abdullah: "Greediness was divided into ten parts and one part was put in Syria."

Abu Kanf

He related from 'Abdullah.

The uncle of Muhajir ibn Shammas

He related from 'Abdullah and Hudhayfa.

Abu Layla al-Kindi

He related from 'Uthman, 'Abdullah and Salman.

Abu Usama reported from 'Abd al-Malik ibn Abi Sulayman that Abu Layla al-Kindi said, "I was present with 'Uthman when he was under siege when he looked down at them and said, 'Do not murder me.'" It is a long *hadith*.

Al-Khishf ibn Malik at-Ta'i

He related from 'Abdullah ibn Mas'ud. He had few *hadith*s.

Al-Minhal

He is not Ibn 'Amr.

He heard 'Abdullah say, "If there had been anyone with more knowledge of the Qur'an who could be reached by animal, I would go to him."

Nufay'

A *mawla* of 'Abdullah ibn Mas'ud. He related from 'Abdullah.

Waki' ibn al-Jarrah reported from al-Mas'udi from Sulayman ibn Mina that Nufay', a *mawla* of 'Abdullah, said, "'Abdullah was one of the most fragrant of people and had the whitest clothes."

'Adasa at-Ta'i

He related that 'Abdullah said, "'Abdullah was brought a bird which had been caught in a snare and said, "I wish that I could be this bird which was caught."

Sulayman ibn Shihab al-'Absi

He related from 'Abdullah, and Husayn and Hallam ibn Salih related from him.

Muhammad ibn 'Abdullah ibn Numayr reported a long *hadith* about the Dajjal from his father from Hallam ibn Salih from Sulayman ibn Shihab al-'Absi from 'Abdullah ibn Mu'attim al-'Absi.

Muhammad said, "One of his family told me that Ibn Mu'attim was one of those who was at al-Qadisiyya. They relate that he was a Companion."

Mu'thir ibn Ghafawa

He related that 'Abdullah said, "On the Night Journey, the Messenger of Allah ☀ was taken..."

Walan

He related that 'Abdullah was asking about the slaughtering done by a slave of his.

'Amira ibn Ziyad al-Kindi

He related from 'Abdullah: "When you want to go on *hajj*, make a stipulation."

Abu ar-Radrad

He related from 'Abdullah from the Prophet ☀ about the prayer.

Abu Zayd

He heard 'Abdullah say, "I was with the Prophet ☀ on the night of the jinn..."

Wa'il ibn Muhana al-Hadrami

He related from 'Abdullah. He had few *hadith*s.

Ballaz ibn 'Isma

He related from 'Abdullah. He had few *hadith*s.

Wa'il ibn Rabi'a

He related from 'Abdullah: "The thickness of every heaven and earth is five hundred years."

Ishaq ibn Mansur reported from Zuhayr from Abu Ishaq that Shamir ibn 'Atiyya said, "Zirr visited Wa'il ibn Rabi'a when he was very ill and Wa'il said, 'Zirr, say the *takbir*s over me as you did over your brother.' He said the *takbir*s over him seven times."

Al-Fadl ibn Dukayn reported from Qays that Abu Huzayn said, "I saw Wa'il ibn Rabi'a wearing rough silk." He said that al-Musayyab ibn Rafi' related from Wa'il ibn Rabi'a.

Al-Walid ibn 'Abdullah al-Bajali then al-Qasari

One of the Banu Khuzayma. He related from 'Abdullah.

'Abdullah ibn Hallam al-'Absi

He related from 'Abdullah. He had few *hadith*s.

Falfala al-Ju'fi

He related from 'Abdullah. He had few *hadith*s.

Yazid ibn Mu'awiya al-'Amiri

He related from 'Abdullah.

Al-Fadl ibn Dukayn reported from 'Uqba ibn Wahb who heard his father related from Yazid ibn Mu'awiya al-'Amiri who heard Ibn Mas'ud say, "How will you be when you see a people who come to you with flat faces?"

Arqam ibn Ya'qub

He related from 'Abdullah.

'Ubaydullah ibn Musa reported from Isra'il from Abu Ishaq that Arqam ibn Ya'qub said, "'Abdullah said, 'How will you be when you are driven out to the wormwood and southern-wood?' They asked, 'Who will drive us off?' 'The Turks,' he answered."

Hanzala ibn Khuwaylid ash-Shaybani

He related from 'Abdullah: "'Abdullah looked at the dam and said, 'O Allah, I ask you for its good and the good of its people.'"

'Abd ar-Rahman ibn Bishr al-Azraq al-Ansari

He related from 'Abdullah ibn Mas'ud and Abu Mas'ud. He had few *hadith*s.

Al-Bara' ibn Najiya al-Kahili

He related from 'Abdullah: "The millstone of Islam revolves…"

Tamim ibn Hadhlam ad-Dabbi

He related from 'Abdullah.

Hawt al-'Abdi

He related from 'Abdullah and Shurayh.

Al-Fadl ibn Dukayn reported from Mis'ar from 'Abd al-Malik that Hawt al-'Abdi said, "'Abdullah put me in charge of the treasury. When I found a counterfeit coin, I broke it." He had few *hadith*s.

'Amr ibn 'Utba ibn Farqad as-Sulami

His uncle was 'Abdullah ibn Rabi'a as-Sulami. His father 'Utba ibn Farqad was a Companion. He related from 'Abdullah. 'Amr was one of those who strove in worship.

Ahmad ibn 'Abdullah ibn Yunus said, "I heard one of my companions mention that 'Utba ibn Farqad asked one of his family, 'Did 'Amr dye his hair yellow?' He mentioned to him his weakness and made a place for him when he saw him and that 'Amr came and stood in prayer and recited until he reached this *ayat*: *'Warn them of the Day of Immediacy when the hearts rise choking to the throat.'* (40:18) He wept until he stopped. He sat and then stood. He repeated, *'Warn them of the Day of Immediacy when the hearts rise choking to the throat.'* (40:18) He wept until he stopped.' He said, 'He did that until morning.'" 'Utba said, "This is what he did, o sons of work!"

Muhammad ibn Sa'd said in a different account than this that 'Amr ibn 'Utba and Mi'dad ibn Yazid al-'Ijli built a mosque on the back of Kufa. Ibn Mas'ud came to him and he said, "I came to break the mosque of disappointment."

'Ubaydullah ibn Musa reported from Isra'il from Ibrahim ibn al-Munhajir from Ibrahim that 'Amr ibn 'Utba was asked to testify and 'Alqama prayed over him. He was trustworthy and had few *hadith*s.

Qays ibn 'Abd al-Hamdani

He is the uncle of 'Amir ibn Sharahil ash-Sha'bi. He related from 'Abdullah.

Qays ibn Jabtar

He related from 'Abdullah: "How excellent are the two disliked ones!"

Al-'Anbus ibn 'Uqba al-Harami

He related from 'Abdullah.

Al-Fadl ibn Dukayn reported from al-A'mash that Yazid ibn Hayyan said, "'Anbus ibn 'Uqba used to prostrate until the sparrows would land on his back thinking that he was a root of a wall." He had few *hadith*s.

Laqit ibn Qabisa al-Fazari

He related from 'Abdullah.

Husayn ibn Qabisa al-Fazari

He related from 'Abdullah and Salman al-Farisi.

Shubruma ibn at-Tufayl

He related from 'Abdullah.

Ya'la ibn 'Ubayd at-Tanafisi reported from Abu Hayyan at-Taymi from Iyas ibn Nudhayr from Shubruma ibn Tufayl that 'Abdullah ibn Mas'ud said, "A man visits the ruler with his *deen* but leaves without the *deen*. A man said, 'How is that, Abu 'Abd ar-Rahman?' He said, 'He pleases him with what angers Allah.'"

'Abd ar-Rahman ibn Khunays al-Asadi

He related from 'Abdullah: "I saw Ibn Ma'sud with clean clothes and a good scent."

'Umayr Abu 'Imran ibn 'Umayr

A *mawla* of 'Abdullah ibn Mas'ud by emancipation. He related from 'Abdullah.

Abu Mu'awiya ad-Darir reported from Hajjaj from 'Imran ibn 'Umayr that his father said, "I went out with 'Abdullah to Makka and he prayed two *rak'at*s on the bridge of Hira."

Al-Fadl ibn Dukayn reported from Muhammad ibn Qays from 'Imran ibn 'Umayr (and his mother was a concubine of 'Abdullah who was with his father) that his father prayed with 'Abdullah on Friday. He said, "'Abdullah rode and my father went with him to an estate he had outside of al-Qadisiyya. When he reached the river of Hira, he prayed '*Asr* with two *rak'at*s."

Kardus ibn 'Abbas ath-Tha'labi

One of the tribe of Ghatafan. He related from 'Abdullah and had few *hadith*s.

Salama ibn Suhayba

Abu Ishaq ash-Shuba'i related from him his words, i.e. the words of Salama. He was one of the companions of 'Abdullah.

'Abda an-Nahdi

He related from 'Abdullah.

Abu 'Ubayda ibn 'Abdullah ibn Mas'ud al-Hudhali

He related a lot from his father.

Muhammad ibn Sa'd said that they mentioned that he did not listen to anything from him. He listened to Abu Musa and Sa'id ibn Zayd al-Ansari. He was trustworthy and had many *hadith*s.

Abu Dawud Sulayman at-Tayalisi reported from Shu'ba that 'Amr ibn Murra said, "I asked Abu 'Ubayda, 'Do you remember anything from 'Abdullah?' 'No,' he replied."

Shihab ibn 'Abbad reported from Ibrahim ibn Humayd ar-Rawasi that Isma'il ibn Abi Khalid said, "I saw Abu 'Ubayda ibn 'Abdullah ibn Mas'ud as an old man with good eyes." He said, "Sulayman ibn Harb said from Hammad ibn Zayd that Yunus ibn 'Ubayda said, 'I saw Abu 'Ubayda ibn 'Abdullah on a mount as if his face was round as a dinar.'"

Al-Fadl ibn Dukayn reported that al-Walid ibn 'Abdullah ibn Jumay' said, "I saw Abu 'Ubayda ibn 'Abdullah wearing a burnous of rough silk."

Waki' ibn al-Jarrah reported from 'Uthman ibn Abi Hind, "I saw 'Abu 'Ubayda wearing a black turban."

Muhammad ibn Sa'd said: "I reported that Yahya ibn Sa'id al-Qattan said, 'They preferred Abu 'Ubayda ibn 'Abdullah.'"

'Ubayd ibn Nudayla al-Khuza'i

He related from 'Abdullah. It is said, "The Qur'an was recited to him and he recited to 'Alqama."

Yahya ibn Adam said that he heard al-Hasan ibn Salih say, "Yahya ibn Waththab recited to 'Ubayd ibn Nudayla and 'Ubayd ibn Nudayla recited to 'Alqama and 'Alqama recited to Ibn Mas'ud. Which recitation is firmer than this?"

'Ubayd ibn Nudayla died in Kufa while Bishr ibn Marwan was governor. He was trustworthy and had a lot of *hadiths*.

Part of this generation are those who related from 'Uthman, Ubayy ibn Ka'b, Mu'adh ibn Jabal, Talha, az-Zubayr, Hudhayfa, Usama ibn Zayd, Khalid ibn al-Walid, Abu Mas'ud al-Ansari, 'Amr ibn al-'As, 'Abdullah ibn 'Amr and others but none of them related anything from 'Umar, 'Ali and 'Abdullah

Musa ibn Talha

Musa ibn Talha ibn 'Ubaydullah ibn 'Uthman ibn 'Amr ibn Ka'b ibn Sa'd ibn Taym ibn Murra. His mother was Khawla bint al-Qa'qa' ibn Ma'bad ibn Zurara of the Banu Tamim. Musa ibn Talha moved to Kufa and settled there and died there in 103 AH. The prayer was said over him by as-Saqar ibn 'Abdullah al-Muzani. He was an agent for 'Umar ibn Hubayra over Kufa.

Al-Fadl ibn Dukayn reported that Musa ibn Talha died in 104 AH.

Al-Fadl ibn Dukayn reported that Tu'ma ibn 'Anr al-Ja'fari said, "I saw that Musa ibn Talha bound his teeth with gold."

Ma'n ibn 'Isa reported from Abu az-Zubayr al-Asadi that Musa ibn Talha bound his teeth with gold.

'Ubaydullah ibn Musa reported that 'Isa ibn 'Abd ar-Rahman said, "I saw Musa ibn Talha wearing a burnous of rough silk."

Al-Fadl ibn Dukayn reported that 'Amr ibn 'Uthman ibn 'Abdullah ibn Mawhab said, "I saw Musa ibn Talha using black dye."

Muhammad ibn 'Umar said, "I saw those before us and the people of the house of Musa using the *kunya* Abu 'Isa. Musa ibn Talha related from 'Uthman, Talha, az-Zubayr and Abu Dharr. He was trustworthy and had *hadith*s. As for Rawh ibn 'Ubada and Sulayman ibn Harb, they reported from al-Aswad ibn Shayban from Khalid ibn Sumayr in a *hadith* which he related from Musa ibn Talha when he came to them in Basra in the time of al-Mukhtar ibn 'Ubayd. He said in his *hadith* that the *kunya* of Musa was Abu Muhammad."

Salama ibn Sabra

He said, "Mu'adh addressed us." Salama related from Salman al-Farisi and Abu Wa'il related from Salama ibn Sabra.

'Azra ibn Qays al-Bajali

One of Ahmas, one of the Banu Duhn. He related from Khalid ibn al-Walid. He was with him in his Syrian expeditions. Abu Wa'il related from 'Azra ibn Qays.

Aws ibn Dam'aj al-Hadrami

He related from Salman and Abu Mas'ud al-Ansari. Aws was the same age as 'Aliya. He was trustworthy and known, with few *hadith*s. He was alive in the *Jahiliyya*.

Al-Ashtar

His name was Malik ibn al-Harith ibn 'Abd Yaghuth ibn Maslama ibn Rabi'a ibn al-Harith ibn Jadhima ibn Sa'd ibn Malik ibn an-Nakha' of Madhhij.

He related that Khalid ibn al-Walid used to beat people for praying after *'Asr*. Al-Ashtar was one of the companions of 'Ali ibn Abi Talib and was present with him at the Camel, Siffin and all his battles. 'Ali appointed him over Egypt and he went there. When he was at al-'Arish, he drank some honey and died.

Yahya ibn Rafi' ath-Thaqafi

He related from 'Uthman and was known. He had few *hadith*s.

Bilal al-'Absi

He related that 'Ammar led them in the prayer on Friday.

Abu Dawud

He was present at Hudhayfa's *khutba* at Mada'in.

Al-Haytham ibn al-Aswad

Al-Haytham ibn al-Aswad ibn Aqyash ibn Mu'awiya ibn Sufyan ibn Hilal ibn 'Amr ibn Jusham ibn 'Awf ibn an-Nakha'. He was one of the men of Madhhij. He was a *khatib* and poet. He related from 'Abdullah ibn 'Amr ibn al-'As. His father, al-Aswad ibn Aqyash, was present at al-Qadisiyya and was killed on that day. His son al-'Uryan ibn al-Haytham was one of the men and nobles of Madhhij mentioned. He was put in the charge of the police for Khalid ibn 'Abdullah al-Qasari in Kufa.

Abu 'Abdullah al-Fa'ishi of Hamdan

He related from Hudhayfa and Qays ibn Sa'd ibn 'Ubada. He was trustworthy and had few *hadith*s.

Abu Rashid

'Ammar ibn Yasir addressed us in the *khutba* and said, "The Messenger of Allah ﷺ forbade us to make *khutba*s long."

Fa'iq ibn Bukayr al-'Absi

He related from Hudhayfa.

Khalid ibn Rabi' al-'Absi

He related from Hudhayfa.

Sa'd ibn Hudhayfa ibn al-Yaman

He related from his father.

'Abdullah ibn Abi Basir al-'Abdi

He related from Ubayy ibn Ka'b.

Sulaym ibn 'Abd

He related from Hudhayfa.

Abu al-Hajjaj al-Azdi

He related from Salman and Abu Ishaq as-Subay'i related from him.

Mujamma' Abu ar-Rawwa' al-Arhabi

He related from Hudhayfa.

Shabath ibn Ri'bi

His *kunya* was 'Abd al-Quddus ibn Husayn ibn 'Uthaym ibn Rabi' ibn Zayd ibn Rabah ibn Yarbu' ibn Hanzala of the Banu Tamim.

Al-Fadl ibn Dukayn reported from Hafs ibn Ghiyath who heard al-A'mash say, "I attended the funeral of Shabath and they put al-'Ubayd on one side and al-Jawari one side, and the horses on one side, the camels on one side and the she-camels on another side," and he mentioned the classes.

Al-Musayyab ibn Najba

Al-Musayyab ibn Najba ibn Rabi'a ibn Riyah ibn 'Awf ibn Hilal ibn Shamkh ibn Fazra. He was present at al-Qadisiyya and was present with 'Ali ibn Abi Talib in all his battles. He was killed in the Battle of 'Ayn al-Warda with the Penitents who went out and repented for having disappointed al-Husayn. Al-Husayn ibn Numayr sent the head of al-Musayyab ibn Najba with Adham ibn Muhriz al-Bahili to 'Ubaydullah ibn Ziyad and he sent to Marwan ibn al-Hakam and he put it up in Damascus.

Milhan ibn Tharwan

He related from Hudhayfa.

Al-Fudayl ibn Bazwan

Musa ibn Mas'ud related from Sufyan from al-A'mash who said, "It was said to Fudayl ibn Bazwan, 'So-and-so insults you.' He said, 'I am cross with the one who instructed him,' i.e. Shaytan. May Allah forgive him and me.'"

Among this generation those who related from 'Ali ibn Abi Talib

Hujr ibn 'Adi

Hujr ibn 'Adi ibn Jabala ibn 'Adi ibn Rabi' ibn Mu'awiya al-Akramim ibn al-Harith ibn Mu'awiya ibn al-Harith ibn Mu'awiya ibn Thawr ibn Muratta' ibn Kindi. He is Hujr al-Khayr (the Good). His father, 'Adi al-Adbar, was stabbed with his back to the enemy and so was called al-Adbar. Hujr ibn 'Adi lived both in the *Jahiliyya* and Islamic periods. One of the transmitters of knowledge mentioned that he came to the Prophet 嫴 with his brother, Hani' ibn 'Adi.

Hujr was present at al-Qadisiyya and he is the one who conquered Marj 'Adhra. He had a stipend of one thousand five hundred dirhams. He was one of the companions of 'Ali ibn Abi Talib and was present with him at the Battle of the Camel and Siffin.

When Ziyad ibn Abi Sufyan arrived as governor of Kufa, he summoned Hujr ibn 'Adi and said, "Know that I recognise you. You and I have been involved in what you know (i.e. love for 'Ali ibn Abi Talib) but something else has happened. I ask you by Allah to not shed a drop of your blood for me so that I have to finish all of it. Hold your tongue and keep to your home. This is my seat and it is your assembly. I will settle your needs, so spare me your life. I know well your hastiness. I beseech you by Allah, Abu 'Abd ar-Rahman, to take care of yourself. Beware of the riff-raff and those fools who try to make you err in your opinion. If you disdain me or if I seek to lighten your due, I will not single you out for that in myself."

Hujr said, "I have understood." He went to his house and his brothers among the Shi'a came to him and demanded, "What did the governor say to you?" He answered and told them what he had said. They said, "He has not given you good advice." He got up and there was some resistance in him. The Shi'a continued to frequent him and said, "You are our shaykh and the most entitled person to object to this governor." When he went to the mosque, they went with him.

'Amr ibn Hurayth sent for him. At that time he was the deputy of Ziyad in charge of Kufa while Ziyad was in Basra. He said, "Abu 'Abd ar-Rahman, what is happening with this group when you have assured the governor of yourself what you know?" He said to the messenger, "Do you deny what you are in when what you left behind you is better for you?" 'Amr ibn Hurayth wrote to Ziyad about that and said, "You are needed in Kufa, make haste." Ziyad therefore travelled to Kufa and sent for 'Adi ibn Hatim, Jarir ibn 'Abdullah al-Bajali, and Khalid ibn 'Urfuta al-'Udhri, the ally of the Banu Zuhra, and a number of the nobles of Kufa. He then sent them to Hujr ibn 'Adi to plead with him and to forbid him to attend that gathering and to tell him to refrain from speaking about what he was speaking about.

They went to him and he did not agree to anything and did not speak to any of them. He began to say, "Boy, fodder the young camel." The young camel was in the corner of the house. 'Adi ibn Hatim said to him, "Are you mad? I say what I say to you and then you say to the boy, 'Fodder the young camel?'" 'Adi said to his companions, "I only think that this wretch has reached the weakness in all that you see."

The people left him and went to Ziyad and told him some and kept back some and said that his business was good. They asked Ziyad to be kind to him. He said, "Then I would not be for Abu Sufyan." He sent the police and Bukhariya troops to go to him and they fought those who were with them who then scattered, leaving him. They took him to Ziyad and his companions. He said to him, "Bother you! What are you doing?" He answered, "I still have my allegiance to Mu'awiya. I have not cancelled it nor asked it to be cancelled."

Ziyad collected seventy notables of the people of Kufa and said, "Write down your testimony against Hujr and his companions." They did it and then he sent them as a delegation to Mu'awiya and he also sent Hujr and his companions to him. 'A'isha heard about the news and sent 'Abd ar-Rahman ibn al-Harith ibn Hisham al-Makhzumi to Mu'awiya asking him to let him go. 'Abd ar-Rahman ibn 'Uthman ath-Thaqafi said, "Amir al-Mu'minin, scrap it! Scrap it! You will not be bothered an iota after this year!" Mu'awiya said, "I do not want to see them. Read me the letter of Ziyad." It was read to him and the witnesses came and testified.

Mu'awiya ibn Abi Sufyan said, "Take them out to 'Adhra' and kill them there." They were taken to it and Hujr said, "What is this town?" "'Adhra'," they answered. He said, "Praise be to Allah. I am the first Muslim to have their dogs bark in the Cause of Allah and then be brought there today in chains." Every man of them was handed over to be killed by one of the men of Syria. Hujr was handed over to a man of Himyar and he brought him forward to kill him. He said, "Let me pray two *rak'ats*." They left him and he did *wudu'* and prayer two *rak'ats* which were long. It was said to him, "You were long. Are you afraid?" He turned and said, "I only did *wudu'* to pray and I have not prayed a lighter prayer than this. If I am afraid, I have seen a sword unsheathed, a shroud spread out and a grave dug."

Their clans had brought shrouds and dug graves for them. It is said that Mu'awiya was the one who had the graves dug for them and sent the shrouds to them. Hujr said, "O Allah, we ask for Your help against our Community. The people of Iraq have testified against us and the people of Syria have killed us." Hujr was told, "Stretch out your neck." He said, "That is blood which I will not help you with." He was brought forward and his neck struck.

Mu'awiya sent a man from the Banu Salaman ibn Sa'd called Hudba ibn Fayyad who killed them. He was blind in one eye. A man of them from Khath'am looked at him and said, "If the birds spoke the truth, half of us will be killed and half saved." When seven were killed, Mu'awiya sent a messenger to spare all of them. So seven were killed and six saved, or six were killed and seven saved. He said that there were thirteen men.

'Abd ar-Rahman ibn al-Harith ibn Hisham brought 'A'isha's letter to Mu'awiya after they had been killed. He said, "Amir al-Mu'minin! Where is the forbearance of Abu Sufyan in you?" He said, "It vanished when those like you of my people vanished from me."

Hind bint Zayd ibn Mukharriba al-Ansariyya, a Shi'ite, said when Hujr was sent to Mu'awiya:

Rise, O shining moon, rise!
  Do you see Hujr setting out?
He is travelling to Mu'awiya ibn Harb
  who will kill him as the reporter claims.
The tyrants strutted proudly after Hujr
  and al-Khawarnaq and as-Sadir were good for them.
The land is barren for his sake
  as if rain did not give it life.

O Hujr! Hujr of the sons of 'Adi!
    May safety and joy meet you!
I fear for you that which destroyed 'Adi
    while an old man is roaring in Damascus.
If you die, then every leader of a people
    of those in this world will suffer destruction.

Hammad ibn Mas'ada reported from Ibn 'Awn that Muhammad said, "When Hujr was brought, he commanded that he be killed and said, 'Bury him in my garment. I will be raised as a litigant.'"

Yahya ibn 'Abbad reported from Yunus ibn Abi Ishaq from 'Umayr ibn Qumaym that a slave of Hujr ibn 'Adi al-Kindi said, "I said to Hujr, 'I saw your son enter the lavatory and then did not perform *wudu'*.' He said, 'Bring me the page from the small window.' He read, 'In the name of Allah, the All-Merciful, Most Merciful. This is what I heard 'Ali ibn Abi Talib mention: purity is half of faith.'" He was trustworthy and known, and did not relate anything from other than 'Ali.

Sa'sa'a ibn Suhan

Sa'sa'a ibn Suhan ibn Hujr ibn al-Harith ibn al-Hijris ibn Sabira ibn Hidrijan ibn 'Isas ibn Layth ibn Hudad ibn Zalim ibn Dhuhl ibn 'Ijl ibn 'Amr ibn Wadi'a ibn Afsa ibn 'Abd al-Qays of Rabi'a. Sa'sa'a was the brother of Zayd ibn Suhan by his father and mother. Sa'sa'a's *kunya* was Abu Talha. He was one of the people who laid out Kufa. He was a *khatib*. He was one of the companions of 'Ali ibn Abi Talib and he was present with him at the Battle of the Camel with his brothers Zayd and Sayhan, the sons of Suhan. Sayhan was the *khatib* before Sa'sa'a. He held a banner in his hand on the Day of the Camel and he was killed. Zayd took it and was killed. Sa'sa'a took it. Sa'sa'a related from 'Ali ibn Abi Talha. He said, "I said to 'Ali, 'Forbid us what the Messenger of Allah ﷺ forbade us.'" Sa'sa'sa also related from 'Abdullah ibn 'Abbas. He died in Kufa while Mu'awiya ibn Abi Sufyan was caliph. He was trustworthy, and had few *hadith*s.

'Abd Khayr ibn Yazid al-Khaywani of Hamdan

He related from 'Ali ibn Abi Talib and was at Siffin with him. He went forward and was killed. His *kunya* was Abu 'Umara. *Hadith*s are related from him.

Muhammad ibn Sa'd

Muhammad ibn Sa'd ibn Abi Waqqas ibn Uhayb ibn 'Abd Manaf ibn Zuhra. He moved to Kufa and settled there. He went out with 'Abd ar-Rahman ibn Muhammad ibn al-Ash'ath and he was present at Dayr al-Jamajim and then was brought to al-Hajjaj after that and he killed him.

Yazid ibn Harun reported from Ibrahim ibn 'Uthman from Abu Bakr ibn Hafs ibn 'Umar ibn Sa'd that the *kunya* of Muhammad ibn Sa'd was Abu al-Qasim. He was trustworthy and had *hadith*s.

Mus'ab ibn Sa'd ibn Abi Waqqas

He related from 'Ali and settled in Kufa and died there in 103 AH. Isma'il ibn Abi Khalid and others related from him. He was trustworthy and had many *hadith*s.

'Asim ibn Damra as-Saluli

One of Qays 'Aylan. He related from 'Ali and died in Kufa while Bishr ibn Marwan was governor. He was trustworthy and had *hadith*s.

Zayd ibn Yuthayya'

He related from 'Ali and Hudhayfa ibn al-Yaman. He had few *hadith*s.

Shurayh ibn an-Nu'man as-Sa'idi from Hamdan

He related from 'Ali ibn Abi Talib. He had few *hadith*s.

Hani' ibn Hani' al-Hamdani

He related from 'Ali ibn Abi Talib. He was a Shi'ite. His *hadith*s are not acknowledged.

Abu al-Hayyaj al-Asadi

He related from 'Ali ibn Abi Talib.

'Ubayd ibn 'Amr al-Khariji of Hamdan

He related from 'Ali and Abu Ishaq as-Subay'i related from him. He was known and had few *hadith*s.

Maysara Abu Salih, the *mawla* of Kinda

He related from 'Ali ibn Abi Talib. He has *hadith*s. 'Ata' ibn as-Sa'ib related from him.

Maysara ibn 'Aziz al-Kindi

He related from 'Ali.

'Abdullah ibn Numayr reported from al-Ajlah that Maysara ibn 'Aziz al-Kindi said, "A *mawla* of mine died and left a son. We went to 'Ali and he gave me half and gave the son half."

Maysara Abu Jamila at-Tuhuri of the Banu Tamim

He related from 'Ali: "A slave-girl of the family of the Messenger of Allah ﷺ went…"

Maysara ibn Habib an-Nahdi

Abu Usama reported from al-Fudayl ibn Mazruq that Maysara ibn Habib an-Nahdi said, "'Ali passed by some people who were playing chess and said, 'What are these images to which you are inclining?'"

Abu Zabyan al-Janni

His name was Husayn ibn Jundub ibn 'Amr ibn al-Harith ibn Malik ibn Wahshi ibn Rabi'a ibn Munabbih ibn Yazid ibn Harb ibn 'Ulla ibn Jald ibn Malik ibn Udad of Madhhij. It is said that there were six sons of Yazid ibn Harb Janb. One of them was Munabbih ibn Zayd. Abu Zabyan related from 'Ali, Abu Musa al-Ash'ari, Usama ibn Zayd and 'Abdullah ibn 'Abbas. He died in Kufa in 90 AH. He has *hadith*s, and was trustworthy.

Hujayya ibn 'Adi al-Kindi

He related from 'Ali ibn Abi Talib. He was well-known but was not actually as was said.

Hind ibn 'Amr al-Jamali of Murad

He related from 'Ali ibn Abi Talib.

Hanash ibn al-Mu'tamir al-Kinani

His *kunya* was Abu al-Mu'tamir. He related from 'Ali ibn Abi Talib.

Asma' ibn al-Hakam al-Fazari

He related from 'Ali ibn Abi Talib. He had few *hadith*s.

Al-Asbagh ibn Nubata

Al-Asbagh ibn Nubata ibn al-Harith ibn 'Amr ibn Fatik ibn 'Amir ibn Mujashi' ibn Darim of the Banu Tamim. He related from 'Ali ibn Abi Talib and was one of his companions.

Shabbaba ibn Sawwar reported that Muhammad ibn al-Furat said, "I listened to al-Asbagh ibn Nubata ibn al-Harith ibn 'Amr. He was in charge of the police for 'Ali."

Al-Fadl ibn Dukayn reported that Fitr said, "I saw al-Asbagh dyeing his beard yellow." He was a Shi'ite. His transmission was weak.

Qabus ibn al-Mukhariq

He related from 'Ali ibn Abi Talib.

Rabi'a ibn Najidh al-Azdi

He related from 'Ali.

'Ali ibn Rabi'a al-Azdi

From Azd and then one of the Banu Waliba. He related from 'Ali, Zayd ibn Arqam and 'Abdullah ibn 'Umar.

Waki' ibn al-Jarrah reported from Sa'id ibn 'Ubayd at-Ta'i and Muhammad ibn Qays al-Asadi that the *kunya* of 'Ali ibn Rabi'a was Abu al-Mughira.

Al-Fadl ibn Dukayn reported that Fitr said, "I saw 'Ali ibn Rabi'a with a white beard passing by us when we were boys among the wheat-dealers. He greeted us." He was trustworthy and well known.

Abu Salih as-Samman

His name was Dhakwan. He is Abu Suhayl ibn Abi Salih, the *mawla* of Juwayriya, a woman of Qays. He was one of the people of Madina. He went to Kufa a lot and settled among the Banu Kahil and was their imam. He related from 'Ali, and among the people of Kufa who related from Abu Salih were al-Hakam ibn 'Utayba, 'Asim ibn Abi an-Nujud, and al-A'mash, and among the people of Madina were 'Abdullah ibn Dinar, al-Qa'qa' ibn Hakim and Zayd ibn Aslam.

Abu Salih was trustworthy and had a lot of *hadith*s.

Abu Salih az-Zayyat

His name was Sumay'. He had few *hadith*s.

Abu Salih al-Hanafi

His name is 'Abd ar-Rahman ibn Qays, the brother of Tulayq ibn Qays al-Hanafi. He was trustworthy and had few *hadith*s.

'Umara ibn Rabi'a al-Jarmi

He related from 'Ali ibn Abi Talib.

'Umara ibn 'Abd as-Sululi

He related from 'Ali and Hudhayfa.

Abu Salih al-Hanafi

His name is Mahan.

Abu 'Abdullah al-Jadali

His name was 'Abda ibn 'Abdullah ibn Abi Ya'mar ibn Habib ibn 'A'idh ibn Malik ibn Wathila ibn 'Amr ibn Naji ibn Yashkur ibn 'Adwan. His name is al-Harith ibn Amr ibn Qays ibn Amr ibn Qays ibn 'Aylan ibn Mudar. Al-Harith is named 'Adwan because he attacked against his brother, Fahm ibn 'Amr, and killed him. The mother of 'Adwan and Fahm was Jadila bint Murr ibn Tabikha, the sister of Tamim ibn Murr, and they were ascribed to her. Her *hadiths* were thought weak. He was a strong Shi'ite. They claim that he was in charge of the police of al-Mukhtar who sent him against 'Abdullah ibn az-Zubayr with eight hundred men from the people of Kufa to attack them and to protect Muhammad ibn al-Hanafiyya from what Ibn az-Zubayr wanted to do to him.

Muslim ibn Nudhayr as-Sa'di

One of the Banu Sa'd ibn Zayd Manat ibn Tamim. He is the cousin of 'Utayy ibn Damra as-Sa'di who related from Ubayy ibn Ka'b. Muslim ibn Nudhayr related from 'Ali and Hudhayfa. He had few *hadiths* and they mention that he believed in *raj'a*.

Abu Khalid al-Walibi

His name was Hurmuz, a *mawla* of the Banu Waliba of the Banu Asad. He related from 'Ali ibn Abi Talib.

Najiya ibn Ka'b

He related from 'Ali ibn Abi Talib and 'Ammar ibn Yasir.

'Amira ibn Sa'd

He said, "We were with 'Ali on the bank of the Euphrates and a ship passed by with its sails up."

'Abd ar-Rahman ibn Zayd ibn Kharid al-Fa'ishi

One of Hamdan. He had few *hadiths*. He related from 'Ali.

Yahya ibn 'Abbad reported from Shu'ba from Abu Ishaq that 'Abd ar-Rahman ibn Zayd ibn Kharif said, "We went out with 'Ali when he was making for Maskin and he prayed two *rak'at*s between the bridge and the viaduct."

'Ubaydullah ibn Musa reported from Isra'il from Abu Ishaq that 'Abd ar-Rahman ibn Zayd al-Hamdani said, "I saw 'Ali when he was dividing and I asked, 'Will you not give me some of what you are dividing?' He said, 'I have good clothes.' He saw that I had a good appearance and said, 'What? When you have no need of it?' I replied, 'Yes.' He said, 'There is no good for you in it.'"

Al-Fadl ibn Dukayn reported from Zuhayr from Abu Ishaq that he mentioned 'Abd ar-Rahman ibn Zayd al-Fa'ishi and he said, "He was beautiful and had a lot of poetry. I saw him wearing cut cloaks and garments."

Zabyan ibn 'Umara

He related from 'Ali.

Muhammad ibn 'Ubayd reported from Suwayd ibn Najih Abu Qutba from Zabyan ibn 'Umara said, "Some people of 'Ukl brought to 'Ali a man and a woman they found in a sheet and they had with them a drink and basil." 'Ali said, 'Two foul ones made foul.' He said, 'Flog them, but less than the *hadd* punishment.'"

'Abd ar-Rahman ibn 'Awsaha an-Nahmi

One of Hamdan. He related from 'Ali.

Ar-Rayyan ibn Sabira al-Hanafi

He related from 'Ali.

Abu Usama reported from Isma'il ibn Zarabi that ar-Rayyan ibn Sabira al-Hanafi was present at the Battle of an-Nahrawan and was among those who removed Dhu ath-Thudayya (the Kharijite) and he brought 'Ali good news before he reached him. He said, "We reached him while he was in prostration and threw it (the arm) down."

'Abdullah ibn al-Khalil al-Hadrami

He related from 'Ali ibn Abi Talib. He had few *hadith*s.

Yazid ibn Hulayl an-Nakha'i

He related from 'Ali and had few *hadith*s.

Suwayd ibn Jahbal al-Ashja'i

He related from 'Ali ibn Abi Talib. He was not well known and they related from him.

Hajjar ibn Abjur

Hajjar ibn Abjur ibn Jabir ibn Bujayr ibn 'A'idh ibn Sharit ibn 'Amr ibn Malik ibn Rabi'a of 'Ijl. He was a noble and related from 'Ali.

'Adi ibn al-Faras

One of the Banu 'Ubayd ibn Ruwas. His name was al-Harith ibn Kilab ibn Rabi'a ibn 'Amir ibn Sa'sa'a.

Yahya ibn 'Abbad reported from Abu Waki' ibn al-Jarrah ibn Malih from al-Hazhaz that 'Adi ibn Faras gave his wife a choice of a treble divorce in one gathering in which she could choose herself. 'Ali ibn Abi Talib made her finally divorce him.

Qabisa ibn Dubay'a al-'Absi

He related from 'Ali ibn Abi Talib. He had few *hadith*s.

Al-Mughira ibn Hadhf

He related from 'Ali.

Ya'la ibn 'Ubayd reported from al-Ajlah from Zuhayr that al-Mughira ibn Hadhf said, "I was sitting with 'Ali when a man of Hamdan came to him and said, 'Amir al-Mu'minin, I bought a pregnant cow to sacrifice and it has given birth. What do you think about it and its calf?' He said, 'Do not milk it except for what is extra to its calf. On the day of *al-Adha*, slaughter it and its calf for seven of your family.'"

Ar-Rayyash ibn Rabi'a

He related from 'Ali.

Muhammad ibn 'Ubayd related from Isma'il ibn Abi Khalid from 'Amir that Rayyash ibn Rabi'a said, "'Ali was asked about a man who said to his wife, 'You are finally divorced.' He said that he made it a treble divorce."

Ka'b ibn 'Abdullah

He related from 'Ali.

'Ubaydullah ibn Musa reported from Isra'il from az-Zibriqan ibn 'Abdullah al-'Abdi who heard Ka'b ibn 'Abdullah say, "I saw 'Ali stand, urinate and then perform *wudu'* and wipe over his (leather) socks and sandals. Then he stood and led us in *Zuhr*."

Khalid ibn 'Ar'ara

He related from 'Ali ibn Abi Talib.

Habib ibn Himaz al-Asadi

'Ubaydullah ibn Musa related this name from Isra'il from Simak. Abu 'Awana says Habib ibn Hammaz. Habib related from 'Ali.

Ibn an-Nabbah

He was the *mu'adhdhin* of 'Ali. He was a *mukatab*. He related a *hadith* from 'Ali about a *mukataba*.

Qabisa ibn 'Uqba reported from Sufyan from Abu Ja'far al-Farra' from Ja'far ibn Abi Tharwan al-Harithi that Ibn an-Nabbah said, "I made a *kitaba* and I went to 'Ali and I said, 'I made a *kitaba*.' He asked, 'Do you have anything?' 'No,' I answered. He said, 'Collect for your brother.' He said, 'They collected my *kitaba* for me and there was some left over, so I brought it to 'Ali.' He said, 'Use it for the *mukatab*s.'"

Hurayth ibn Mikhash al-Qaysi

He related from 'Ali ibn Abi Talib.

Tariq ibn Ziyad

He related from 'Ali.

'Ubaydullah ibn Musa reported from Isra'il from Ibrahim ibn 'Abd al-A'la that Tariq ibn Ziyad said, "We went out with 'Ali to the Kharijites." Then he mentioned the *hadith* about the Kharijites.

Nujayy al-Hadrami

He related from 'Ali ibn Abi Talib. He had few *hadith*s.

His son, 'Abdullah ibn Nujayy al-Harami

He also related from 'Ali ibn Abi Talib.

'Abdullah ibn Sab'

He related from 'Ali ibn Abi Talib.

Abu al-Khalil

He related from 'Ali ibn Abi Talib.

Yazid ibn 'Abd ar-Rahman al-Awdi

He is the father of Dawud and Idris.

His *hadith* is: "We used to meet with 'Ali and then return and have a midday nap."

'Antara

He is Abu Harun ibn 'Antara. He related from 'Ali ibn Abi Talib. His *kunya* was Abu Waki'.

Al-Walid ibn 'Utba al-Laythi

He related from 'Ali ibn Abi Talib.

Al-Fadl ibn Dukayn reported from Humayd ibn 'Abdullah al-Asamm who heard al-Walid ibn 'Utba al-Laythi say, "We fasted the month of Ramadan in the time of 'Ali as twenty-eight days and 'Ali commanded him to make up a day."

Yazid ibn Madhkur al-Hamdani

He related from 'Ali ibn Abi Talib.

Yazid ibn Qays al-Kharifi or al-Arhabi from Hamdan

He related from 'Ali ibn Abi Talib. He had few *hadith*s.

Abu Mariyya ash-Shaybani

He related from 'Ali ibn Abi Talib.

'Abd al-A'la Abu Ibrahim ibn 'Abd al-A'la

He related from 'Ali ibn Abi Talib.

Hayyan ibn Marthad

He related from 'Ali ibn Abi Talib: "The one who locks a door or lets the curtain down [with his bride] has the bride-price obliged for him." He related from Salman.

Ibn 'Ubayd al-Abras al-Asadi

He related from 'Ali ibn Abi Talib.

Abu Bashir

He related from 'Ali about the Rain Prayer.

Tamim ibn Mushayyij

He related from 'Ali ibn Abi Talib about the foundling.

Sharik ibn Hanbal al-'Absi

He related from 'Ali ibn Abi Talib. He was well-known and had few *hadith*s.

Kathir ibn Namir al-Hadrami

He related from 'Ali ibn Abi Talib.

Abu Hayya al-Wadi'i of Hamdan

He related from 'Ali that he saw him urinate at ar-Rahba and then perform *wudu'*. He related another *hadith* from him: "When you do *wudu'*, inhale."

Tha'laba ibn Yazid al-Himmani of the Banu Tamim

He related from 'Ali ibn Abi Talib. He had few *hadith*s.

'Asim ibn Shurayb az-Zubaydi

He related from 'Ali ibn Abi Talib.

Ar-Rayyash ibn 'Adi al-Kindi

He related from 'Ali ibn Abi Talib.

Qanbar

A *mawla* of 'Ali ibn Abi Talib.

Muslim

A *mawla* of 'Ali ibn Abi Talib. He related from 'Ali.

'Abdullah ibn Numayr and Muhammad ibn 'Ubayd reported from Hashim ibn al-Barid from al-Qasim ibn Muslim, a *mawla* of 'Ali ibn Abi Talib, that his father said, "'Ali called for a drink and he was brought a cup of water and he blew in it and returned it and refused to drink. He said, 'You drink it.'"

Abu Raja'

He related from 'Ali: 'Ali went out with a sword of his to the market and said, "If I had the price of a waist-wrapper, I would not sell it." His name was Yazid ibn Muhjan ad-Dabbi.

Kharasha ibn Habib

He related from 'Ali about a man having sex with his wife and not ejaculating. He said, "He does not do *ghusl* if he shakes it."

Ziyad ibn 'Abdullah

He related from 'Ali.

Abu Usama reported from Ishaq ibn Sulayman ash-Shaybani from his father from al-'Abbas ibn Dhurayh that Ziyad ibn 'Abdullah an-Nakha'i said, "We were sitting with 'Ali ibn Abi Talib when Ibn an-Nabbah came to him to announce the *'Asr* prayer to him. He said, 'The prayer! The prayer!' Then he stood up after that and led us in the *'Asr* prayer. We knelt towards the saddles and could see that the sun had declined."

Abu Nasr

He related from 'Ali.

Muhammad ibn 'Ubayd reported from Muhammad ibn Abi Isma'il from 'Abd ar-Rahman ibn Abi Nasr that his father said, "I went out on *hajj* and met 'Ali at Dhu al-Hulayfa and he said the *talbiya* for both *'umra* and *hajj*." It is a long *hadith*.

Ma'qil al-Ju'fi

He related from 'Ali ibn Abi Talib.

Muhammad ibn 'Ubayd reported from Muhammad ibn Abi Isma'il that Ma'qil al-Ju'fi said, "'Ali urinated in the square and then performed *wudu'* and wiped over his sandals."

Abu Rashid as-Salmani

He related from 'Ali.

Muhammad ibn 'Ubayd reported from 'Abd al-'Aziz ibn Siyah Abu Yazid that Abu Rashid as-Salmani said, "I went to 'Ali in his house and called, 'Amir al-Mu'minin! Amir al-Mu'minin!' He said, 'At your service!' I said, 'Amir al-Mu'minin, I was among the milk camels of my people herding them and a camel of them fell and I feared that it would die so I hurried and stabbed it with an implement either in its side or its hump and mentioned the Name of Allah. I brought its meat separately from all the camels to my family and they refused to eat and said, 'You did not slaughter it.' He said, 'Bother you! Give me its hump! Give me its hump!'"

Abu Ramla

He related from 'Ali.

Muhammad ibn 'Ubayd reported from Yusuf ibn Shuhayb from Habib ibn Yasar from Abu Ramla that 'Ali went out to the square after the sun rose and there was no leader of anyone there. He asked about them, "Where are they?" They answered, "In the mosque, Amir al-Mu'minin." He went for them and called them and asked the man, "What did you find them doing?" He replied, "Some were standing in prayer or sitting talking." When they came to him, 'Ali said, "O people, beware of the prayer of Shaytan! When the sun is the amount of two spears, then pray two *rak'ats*. That is the prayer of the penitent."

Abu Sa'id ath-Thawri

He is 'Aqis. He related from 'Ali.

Muhammad ibn 'Ubayd reported from Abu Sa'id ath-Thawri who said that he heard 'Ali say, "The merchant is impious unless he takes and gives the right."

Abu al-Gharif

His name is 'Ubaydullah ibn Khalifa al-Hamdani. He related from 'Ali. He said, "I was with 'Ali in the square and he urinated and then called for water and washed his hands. Then he recited the beginning of the Qur'an." He had few *hadith*s.

Al-Musaffah al-'Amiri

He related from 'Ali.

Yazid ibn Harun reported from Fudayl ibn Marzuq from Jabala bint al-Musaffah that her father said, "'Ali said to me, 'Brother of the Banu 'Amir, ask me about what Allah and His Messenger said. We the people of the House know best what Allah and His Messenger said.'" He related from 'Ali.

'Abd ar-Rahman ibn Suwayd al-Kahili

He related from 'Ali.

Al-Fadl ibn Dukayn reported from Hamza az-Zayyat from Habib ibn Abi Thabit that 'Abd ar-Rahman ibn Suwayd al-Kahili said, "'Ali did the *qunut* in this mosque while I was listening. He said, 'O Allah, You we worship and to You we pray and prostrate. To You we hasten and hurry to serve. We hope for Your mercy and fear Your punishment. Your punishment will reach the unbelievers. O Allah, we ask for Your help and ask for Your forgiveness and praise You and do not deny You and remove and leave the one who is impious to You."

Husayn ibn Jundub

He related from 'Ali.

Al-Fadl ibn Dukayn reported from Hanash ibn al-Harith from Qabus ibn Husayn ibn Jundub that his father said, "I saw 'Ali urinate in the square and then he wiped over his sandals and prayed."

Malik ibn al-Jawn

He related from 'Ali.

Al-Fadl ibn Dukayn reported from Mas'ud ibn Sa'd ibn Sa'd al-Ju'fi from 'Amr ibn Ways from Khalid ibn Sa'id that Malik ibn al-Jawn said, "I saw 'Ali sit and urinate and then call for water and perform *wudu'* and wipe over his socks and sandals."

Al-Harith ibn Thuwab

He related from 'Ali.

Al-Fadl ibn Dukayn reported from Sharik from Dhurayh that al-Harith ibn Thuwab said, "'Ali led us in the Friday prayer and when he said the *salam*, he said, 'Slaves of Allah, complete the prayer.' Then he stood up and entered his quarters."

Abu Yahya

He related from 'Ali.

'Ubaydullah ibn Musa reported from Isra'il from Jabir that Abu Yahya said, "I saw 'Ali admit Yazid ibn Mukaffaf."

As-Sa'ib Abu 'Ata' ibn as-Sa'ib

He related from 'Ali.

Al-Fadl ibn Dukayn reported from Mindal from 'Ata' ibn as-Sa'ib that his father said, "I visited 'Ali and he said, 'Sa'ib, shall we give you something to drink by which you will remain full for the rest of your day?' I said, 'Yes, Amir al-Mu'minin.' He called for a drink for me and I drank and then he said, 'Do you know what it is?' 'No,' I answered. He said, 'A third milk, a third honey and a third ghee.'"

'Abdullah ibn Abi al-Mujill

He related from 'Ali.

Ishaq ibn Yusuf al-Azraq reported from Sufyan ath-Thawri from 'Abdullah ibn Sharik from 'Abdullah ibn Abi al-Mujill that 'Ali experienced an eclipse at Babel and continued to pray during it until it had passed.

Nahik ibn 'Abdullah as-Saluli

He related from 'Ali that Shaytan went to a monk in a hermitage where he had worshipped Allah for sixty years.

Al-Agharr ibn Sulayk

He is also said that he is al-Agharr ibn Hanzala. He related from 'Ali ibn Abi Talib.

Muhammad ibn Sa'd said, "Perhaps he is ascribed to his grandfather, Sulayk ibn Hanzala."

Abu 'Amir al-'Aqadi reported from Shu'ba that Simak said that he heard al-Agharr ibn Sulayk relate that 'Ali said, "There are three whom Allah hates: an old man who fornicates, an unjust rich man, and a proud pauper."

'Ubaydullah ibn Musa reported from Isra'il from Simak that al-Agharr ibn Hanzala said, "'Ali stood up and said, 'Among His creation Allah hates a fornicating grey-haired man, an unjust rich person and a proud poor man." His *kunya* was Abu Muslim.

'Amr Dhu Marr

He related from 'Ali.

'Ubaydullah ibn Musa reported from Hasan ibn Salih from Abu Ishaq that 'Amr Dhu Marr said, "I saw 'Ali performing *wudu'*. Then he took a handful of water and poured it on his head and then he rubbed it."

'Abdullah ibn Abi al-Khalil al-Hamdani

He related three *hadith*s from 'Ali from the *hadith* of Abu Ishaq.

'Amr ibn Ba'ja

He related from 'Ali.

'Ubaydullah ibn Musa reported from Isra'il from Abu Ishaq that 'Amr ibn Ba'ja said, "I saw 'Ali in Mada'in. He brought a mule of a *dihqan*. When he put his hand on the saddlebow and asked, 'What is this?' They answered, 'Brocade.' He refused to ride it."

Humayd ibn 'Arib

He related from 'Ali and 'Ammar about the man who fell on 'A'isha in the Battle of the Camel.

Sa'id ibn Dhi Huddan

He related from 'Ali.

'Ubaydullah ibn Musa reported from Isra'il from Abu Ishaq from Sa'id ibn Dhi Huddan that 'Ali said, "Allah made war deceit on the tongue of His Prophet." He also related from Ibn 'Abbas.

Rafi' ibn Salama al-Bajali

He listened to 'Ali and related from him.

Aktal ibn Shammakh al-'Ukli

He related from 'Ali.

Muhammad ibn 'Abdullah al-Asadi and al-Fadl ibn Dukayn reported from Sufyan from Jabir from 'Abdullah ibn Nujayy that 'Ali ibn Abi Talib said, "Anyone who is happy to look at the eloquent handsome man should look at Aktal ibn Shammakh."

Aws ibn Mi'laq al-Asadi

He related from 'Ali.

'Affan ibn Muslim reported from Abu 'Awana from Sinan ibn Habib from Nabl bint Badr from her husband Aws ibn Mi'laq al-Asadi heard 'Ali say, "Let this wall be blood which reaches the horse's fetlock."

Tarif

He related from 'Ali.

'Affan ibn Muslim reported from Shu'ba from Sulayman al-A'mash from Musa ibn Tarif that his father, who was in charge of the treasury for 'Ali ibn Abi Talib, that 'Ali drank *nabidh* made in a green vessel.

Second generation of those who related from 'Abdullah ibn 'Umar, Abdullah ibn 'Abbas, 'Abdullah ibn 'Amr, Jabir ibn 'Abdullah, an-Nu'man ibn Bashir, Abu Hurayra and others

'Amir ibn Sharahil ibn 'Abd ash-Sha'bi

He is from Himyar but is counted as part of Hamdan.

'Abdullah ibn Muhammad ibn Murra ash-Sha'bani reported from some shaykhs of Sha'ban, including Muhammad ibn Abi Umayya, who was a scholar, that it rained in Yemen and the flood uprooted a place and exposed a vault which had a stone door. The lock was broken, and he entered and found a large courtyard in which there was a seat of gold on which was a man. We measured him with our hands and his height was twelve spans. He was wearing a gown of silk brocade embroidered with gold. Beside him was a gold staff on the top of which was a red ruby. He was a man with white hair and beard and had two plaits. Also beside him was a tablet on which was written in Himyarite: "In Your Name, O Allah, Lord of Himyar. I am Hassan ibn 'Amr al-Qil (the King). There is no king (*qil*) but Allah. I lived in hope and died at the end of the days of the terrible plague. What was the terrible plague! In it twelve thousand kings died, and I was the last of them to die. I went to the mountain of Dhu ash-Sha'bayn to guard myself from death and it betrayed me." Beside him was a sword on which was written in Himyarite: "I am Qubar and vengeance is achieved by me."

'Abdullah ibn Muhammad ibn Murra ash-Sha'bani said, "This was Hassan ibn 'Amr ibn Qays ibn Mu'awiya ibn Jusham ibn Shamas ibn Wa'il ibn Ghawth ibn Qatan ibn 'Arib ibn Zuhayr ibn Zuhayr ibn Ayman ibn al-Hamaysa' ibn Himyar. Hassan is Dhu ash-Sha'bayn which is a mountain in Yemen. He and his children settled there and he was buried there, and he and his children were named after it. Whoever at Kufa are called Sha'bi, including 'Amir ash-Sha'bi, those in Syria who are called Sha'bani, those in Yemen who are called the family of Dhu Sha'bayn, and those in Egypt and the

Maghrib who are called al-Ash'ub, are all the descendants of Hassan ibn 'Amr Sha'bayn."

The Banu 'Ali ibn Hassan ibn 'Amr were the clan of 'Amir ibn Sharahil ibn 'Abd ash-Sha'bi. They joined Ahmur of Hamdan in the Yemen and are counted as part of them: Ahmur includes Kharif, as-Sa'idiyyun, Al Dhi Bariq, as-Sabi', Al Dhi Huddan, Al Dhi Ridwan, Al Dhi La'wa and Al Dhi Marran, and the bedouin of Hamdan: Ghudar, Yam, Nihm, Shakir and Arhab.

There are many tribes in Hamdan in Himyar, including the family of Dhu Hawal who had been in the vanguard of Tubba', and Ya'fir ibn as-Sabbah who control provinces of San'a today.

They said that ash-Sha'bi's *kunya* was Abu 'Amr. He was thin and lean and he had a twin brother. He was asked, "Abu 'Amr, why are you gaunt?" He answered, "I was crowded in the womb."

'Amir saw 'Ali ibn Abi Talib and described him. He related from Abu Hurayra, Ibn 'Umar, Ibn 'Abbas, 'Adi ibn Hatim, Samura ibn Jundub, 'Amr ibn Hurayth, 'Abdullah ibn Yazid al-Ansari, al-Mughira ibn Shu'ba, al-Bara' ibn 'Azib, Zayd ibn Arqam, Ibn Abi Awfa, Jabir ibn Samura, Abu Juhayfa, Anas ibn Malik, 'Imran ibn Husayn, Burayda al-Aslam, Jarir ibn 'Abdullah, al-Ash'ath ibn Qays, Abu Musa al-Ash'ari, al-Hasan ibn 'Ali, 'Abdullah ibn 'Amr ibn al-'As, an-Nu'man ibn Bashir, Jabir ibn 'Abdullah, Wahb ibn Khanbash at-Ta'i, Hubshi ibn Junada as-Saluli, 'Amir ibn Shahr, Muhammad ibn Sayfi, 'Abdullah ibn Ja'far ibn Abi Talib, 'Urwa al-Bariqi, Fatima bint Qays, 'Abd ar-Rahman ibn Abza, 'Alqama ibn Qays, Farwa ibn Nawfal al-Ashja'i, 'Abd ar-Rahman ibn Abi Layla, al-Harith al-A'war, Zuhayr ibn al-Qayn, 'Awf ibn 'Amir, al-Aswad ibn Yazid, Sa'id ibn Dhi La'wa, Abu Salama ibn 'Abd ar-Rahman and Abu Thabit Ayman who related from Ya'la ibn Murra.

'Abd ar-Rahman ibn Yunus reported from Sufyan ibn 'Uyayna that as-Siri ibn Isma'il said, "I heard ash-Sha'bi say, 'I was born in the year of Jalula'.'"

Hajjaj reported from Shu'ba, "I asked Abu Ishaq, 'Who is older: you or ash-Sha'bi?' He replied, 'He is two years older than me and 'Abd ar-Rahman ibn Abi Sabra Abu Khaythama ibn Malik, al-Harith ibn Barsa' and Abu Jabira ibn ad-Dahhak.'"

'Abdullah ibn Idris reported that he heard, "I heard Layth mention that ash-Sha'bi said, 'I stayed in Madina with 'Abdullah ibn 'Umar for eight or ten months.'"

Muhammad ibn Sa'd said that the reason that he stayed in Madina was that he feared al-Mukhtar and fled from him to Madina and stayed there.

Al-Fadl ibn Dukayn reported from 'Abd as-Salam ibn Abi al-Musli that ash-Sha'bi said, "I learned reckoning from al-Harith al-A'war."

'Ubaydullah ibn Musa reported from Isra'il that 'Isa ibn Abi 'Azza said, "I remained with 'Amir in Khurasan for ten months in which he did not perform more than two *rak'ats*."

Muhammad ibn Sa'd said, "He had a diwan. He used to attack in it. He had been a Shi'ite, but saw things they did and heard their words and their excess and then he abandoned their opinion and criticised them."

Abu Mu'awiya ad-Darir reported from Malik ibn Mighwal that ash-Sha'bi said, 'If the Shi'ites had been birds, they would have been vultures. If they had been animals, they would have been donkeys."

'Abd al-Hamid ibn 'Abd ar-Rahman al-Himmani reported from al-Wassafi that 'Amir ash-Sha'bi said, "I love the righteous Muslims and the righteous people of the Banu Hashim. Do not be a Shi'ite. Hope for what you do not know. Do not be a Murji'ite. Know that good is from Allah and evil is from yourself. Do not be a Qadarite like from the one whom you see doing good while he has his nose split like an Indian."

Muhammad ibn Sa'd said, "Our companions said, 'Ash-Sha'bi was one of those who rebelled with the *qurra'* against al-Hajjaj and was present at the Battle Dayr al-Jamajim. He was among those who slipped away and he hid for a time. He wrote to Yazid ibn Abi Muslim to speak about him to al-Hajjaj. He conveyed to him, 'By Allah, I am not bold enough to do that, but pick a time when he sits for the common people and then go to him and present yourself before him and you can give your excuse and admit your wrong action. Ask me to testify to what you want and I will testify.' Ash-Sha'bi did that and al-Hajjaj was not aware of him until he was standing before him. He said to him, 'Ash-Sha'bi?' 'Yes,' he replied, 'may Allah make the governor thrive.' He said, 'Did I not come to the town when your stipend was such-and-such and then I increased your stipend when someone the like of you does not get an increase?' He replied, 'Yes, may Allah make the governor thrive.' He said, 'Did I not acknowledge you over your people and not acknowledge your like?' He replied, 'Yes, may Allah make the governor thrive.' He continued, 'Did I not let you lead your people in the prayer when someone like you does not do so?' He answered, 'Yes, may Allah make the governor thrive.' He said, 'Did I not bring you to the Amir al-Mu'minin and someone like you is not brought there?' He answered, 'Yes, may Allah make the governor thrive.' He asked, 'What made you go out with enemy of the All-Merciful?' He answered, 'May Allah make you thrive. The sedition confused us and we were neither righteous and godfearing nor impious and strong in it. I wrote to Yazid ibn Abi Muslim to inform him of my regret for my excess and my recognition of the truth which I had abandoned and I asked him to inform the governor of that and to obtain a safe-conduct for me. He did not do it.' Al-Hajjaj turned to Yazid and asked, 'Is that the case, Yazid?' He replied, 'Yes, may Allah make the governor thrive.' He said, 'What kept you from informing me of his letter?' He replied, 'Business, governor.' Al-Hajjaj said, 'First go.' Ash-Sha'bi went to his house secure.'"

Muhammad ibn al-Fudayl ibn Ghazwan reported from Shubruma that ash-Sha'bi said, "I did not write black on white at all and no one related to me a *hadith* but that I wanted 'Ali to repeat it."

Qabisa ibn 'Uqba reported from Sufyan that someone heard ash-Sha'bi say, "I wish that I had only of my knowledge what is neither for me or against me."

'Abdullah ibn 'Amr al-Munqari reported from 'Abd al-Warith ibn Sa'id from Muhammad ibn Juhada that 'Amir ash-Sha'bi was asked about something and he did not have anything to report about it. It was said to him, "Speak your opinion." He said, "What will you do with my opinion? Rather on my opinion."

Muhammad ibn 'Abdullah al-Ansari reported that Ibn 'Awn said, "Ash-Sha'bi used to relate a *hadith* in meaning [rather than exact words]."

'Abd al-'Aziz ibn al-Khattab ad-Dabbi reported from Mindal from al-Hasan ibn 'Uqba Abi Kibran al-Muradi that ash-Sha'bi said, "Write what you heard from me, even on a wall."

Qabisa ibn 'Uqba reported from Sufyan from 'Abdullah ibn Abi as-Safar that ash-Sha'bi said, "I am not a scholar and I do not leave a scholar. Abu Husayn is a righteous man."

Ahmad ibn 'Abdullah ibn Yunus reported from Abu Shihab from Adam that a man asked Ibrahim about a question and he said, "I do not know." 'Amir ash-Sha'bi passed by him and said to a man, "Ask that shaykh and then come back and tell me." He returned to him and said, "I do not know." Ibrahim said, "This, by Allah, is true *fiqh*."

Ahmad ibn 'Abdullah reported from Abu Shihab that as-Salt ibn Bihram said, "I did not see a man who conveyed what ash-Sha'bi conveyed who more often said, 'I do not know.'"

Muhammad ibn 'Abdullah al-Ansari reported from Salih ibn Muslim, "I was with ash-Sha'bi whose hand was in mine or my hand in his. We went to the mosque and found Hammad in the mosque with his companions around him. There was a hubbub and voices. He said, 'By Allah, I hate those of this mosque so much that they made it more hated to me than the rubbish of my house. Companies of rabble.' He left and returned and we also returned."

Qabisa ibn 'Uqba reported from Sufyan from 'Abdullah ibn Abi as-Safar from ash-Sha'bi who said, "A time was when there was no assembly which I loved more to sit in than this mosque, and now I prefer to sit in the rubbish heaps today than to sit in this mosque." He used to say as he passed by them, "What are those wretches saying?" Or he said "Sons of its backside." (Qabisa was unsure which he said.) "If they speak their opinion, urinate on it. If they relate from the Companions of Muhammad 🏵, take it."

'Abd al-Hamid ibn 'Abd ar-Rahman al-Himmani reported from Abu Hanifa who said, "I saw ash-Sha'bi wearing rough silk and sitting with poets. I asked him about a question and said, 'What do the sons of the backside say about it (meaning the *mawali*).'"

Al-Fadl ibn Dukayn reported from Sufyan from Abu Hasin that ash-Sha'bi said, "I wished that my stipend had been in the urine of a donkey. How many have had their stipends lead them to the Fire!'"

'Arim ibn Fadl reported from Hammad ibn Zayd from Ayyub that 'Atiyya as-Sarraj said, "I passed with ash-Sha'bi by one of the mosques of Juhayna. He said, 'I testify that such-and-such of the people of this mosque, three hundred of the Companions of the Prophet 🏵, drank the *nabidh* made in gourds in weddings.'"

Al-Fadl ibn Dukayn reported from Abu Isra'il said, "I saw ash-Sha'bi judging in a corner at the Bab al-Fil."

Al-Fadl ibn Dukayn reported from Abu Usama who said, "I brought a creditor who owed me some dirhams to ash-Sha'bi. He said, "If you give it or it comes to you another time, I will imprison you, even if you are the son of 'Abd al-Hamid.'"

Muhammad ibn Sa'd said that 'Abd al-Hamid ibn 'Abd ar-Rahman ibn Zayd ibn al-Khattab was the governor of 'Umar ibn 'Abd al-'Aziz over Iraq. He appointed 'Amir ash-Sha'bi as qadi of Kufa.

Waki' ibn al-Jarrah reported from al-Hasan ibn Salih that his father said, "I saw ash-Sha'bi wearing a white turban whose ends hung down and he did not object to it."

'Umar ibn Shabib al-Mussali reported, "My father said to me, 'I saw ash-Sha'bi wearing a red blanket which was very red.'"

'Abdullah ibn Idris reported that he heard Layth said, "I saw ash-Sha'bi and did not know whether his blanket or his beard was a stronger red."

Hajjaj ibn Nusayr reported that al-Aswad ibn Shayban said, "I saw ash-Sha'bi in Kufa wearing a red robe without a cloak and a red turban made from Yemeni cloth: both the robe and turban." He said, "I saw it when he was the qadi in Kufa on that day and he was giving judgement in the mosque."

Al-Fadl ibn Dukayn reported that Fitr said, "I saw ash-Sha'bi using henna dye."

'Amr ibn al-Haytham reported, "I asked Mu'arrif ibn Wasil, 'Did ash-Sha'bi use dye?' He answered, 'Henna.'"

Al-Fadl ibn Dukayn reported that Abu Umayya az-Zayyat said, "I saw ash-Sha'bi wearing a robe of yellow rough silk."

Yazid ibn Harun reported that 'Urwa al-Bazzaz Abu 'Abullah said, "I saw 'Amir wearing a robe of green rough silk."

Rawh ibn 'Ubada reported that Ibn 'Awn said, "I saw ash-Sha'bi wearing a tall hat of green rough silk."

'Abdullah ibn Ja'far ar-Raqqi reported from 'Ubaydullah ibn 'Amr from Isma'il that ash-Sha'bi had a robe of rough silk which he wore with different colours.

'Affan ibn Muslim reported from Hammad ibn Salama from Dawud ibn Abi Hind that ash-Sha'bi used to wear saffron dye.

Ishaq ibn Yusuf al-Azraq and 'Abdullah ibn Numayr reported that Malik ibn Mighwal said, "I saw ash-Sha'bi wearing a red mantle."

Ibn Numayr said in his *hadith*: "a yellow waist-wrapper."

Ishaq said in his *hadith*, "I said, 'Shi'ite?' He said, 'Yes.'"

'Ubaydullah ibn Musa reported that 'Isa ibn 'Abd ar-Rahman said, "I saw ash-Sha'bi wearing a red mantle and a yellow waist-wrapper."

Al-Fadl ibn Dukayn reported that 'Ubayd ibn 'Abd al-Malik said, "I saw ash-Sha'bi sitting on a lion-skin."

Al-Fadl ibn Dukayn reported from Salih ibn Abi Shu'ayb al-'Ukli, "I asked 'Amir about wearing fur when he had on a fur coat. I said, 'What do you think about wearing it?' He said, 'Good. There is nothing wrong with it. They used to think that tanning was its purification.'"

Al-Fadl ibn Dukayn reported that Qays ibn Mujalid said, "I saw ash-Sha'bi wearing a robe of sable."

Muhammad ibn 'Abdullah al-Asadi reported that Yunus ibn Abi Ishaq said, "I saw ash-Sha'bi praying in a fur coat."

Al-Fadl ibn Dukayn reported that 'Uthman ibn Abi Hind al-'Absi said, "I met ash-Sha'bi on the day of the *'Id al-Fitr* or *Adha* wearing an 'Adani mantle."

Al-Fadl ibn Dukayn reported from Hibban that Mujalid said, "Ash-Sha'bi came to us wearing a sable robe in which he used to pray. He used to pray in fox skins."

Al-Hajjaj ibn Muhammad reported that he heard Shu'ba say, "I asked Abu Ishaq who said, 'Who is older: you or ash-Sha'bi?' He answered, 'Ash-Sh'abi is one or two years older.'"

Shu'ba said, "Abu Ishaq saw 'Ali and he described him to us as having a large belly and bald.

'Abd ar-Rahman ibn Mahdi reported from Ibn al-Mubarak from 'Abd ar-Rahman ibn Yazid that Makhul said, "I did not see anyone who had more knowledge of a past *sunna* than ash-Sha'bi."

Sufyan said from Ibn Shubruma that ash-Sha'bi said, "When the circle was big, it was a call or salvation."

Al-Fadl ibn Dukayn reported from Abu Kibran that ash-Sha'bi said, "Al-Hajjaj sent me to Rutbil who admitted me and asked me, 'What is this dye? Hair is white and black.' I replied, 'It is the *sunna*.'"

Ahmad ibn 'Abdullah ibn Yunus reported from Abu al-Ahwas that Tariq ibn 'Abd ar-Rahman said, "I visited ash-Sha'bi when he was ill and he stood to pray in a shirt and waist-wrapper without any cloak."

Khalf ibn Tamim ibn Malik reported from his father that ash-Sha'bi used to not leave his gathering until he had said, "I testify that there is no god but Allah alone with no partner and I testify that Muhammad is His slave and Messenger. I testify that the *deen* is as He prescribed and I testify that Islam is as He described. I testify that the Book is as it was revealed and that the word is as it was spoken. I testify that Allah is the Clear Truth." When he went to get up, he said, "Allah mentioned Muhammad with the *salam* from us."

Muhammad ibn 'Abdullah al-Ansari reported that Ibn 'Awn said that a man said in the presence of ash-Sha'bi, "Allah said." Ash-Sha'bi said, "Why do you not say what Allah said?"

'Amr ibn 'Asim al-Kilabi reported from Abu Bakr ibn Shu'ayb ibn al-Habhab who heard 'Amir ash-Sha'bi when my father said to him, "Why is your waist-wrapper hanging, Abu 'Amr?" He said that he was wearing a rose waist-wrapper. Ash-Sha'bi said, "There is nothing here to hold it up," and he struck his hand on his buttocks. My father asked him, "How much do you think that you have been given, Abu 'Amr? Ash-Sha'bi answered:

My soul complains to me, "Death is creeping.
    I carried you for seventy and seven."
If you speak of hope, lying soul,
    three will make a full eighty.

Abu Bakr ibn Shu'ayb said that he was seventy-seven when he composed it.

Muhammad ibn 'Umar reported that Ishaq ibn Yahya ibn Talha said, "Ash-Sha'bi died in Kufa in 105 AH when he was seventy-seven."

Abu Nu'aym al-Fadl ibn Dukayn reported that ash-Sha'bi died in 104 AH.

That is how Sa'id ibn Jamil related that Aban ibn 'Umar ibn 'Uthman said, "Ash-Sha'bi died in 104 AH."

Muhammad ibn Sa'd that others, including Abu Burda ibn Abi Musa, said that he died in 103 AH on *Jumu'a*.

Muhammad ibn al-Fudayl ibn Ghazwan reported that 'Asim reported the death of ash-Sha'bi to al-Hasan and he said, "May Allah have mercy on him. He had a position in Islam." He said that ash-Sha'bi died suddenly.

Sa'id ibn Jubayr

His *kunya* was Abu 'Abdullah, a *mawla* of the Banu Waliba ibn al-Harith of the Banu Asad ibn Khuzayma.

Sulayman Abu Dawud at-Tayalisi, 'Affan ibn Muslim and Abu al-Walid at-Tayalisi reported from Shu'ba from al-Fadl ibn Dukayn from Abu ar-Rabi' as-Samman, all from Abu Bishr Ja'far ibn Iyas, that Sa'id ibn Jubayr said, "Ibn 'Abbas asked me, 'Who are you from?' I replied, 'From the Banu Asad.' 'From their Arabs or their *mawali*?' he asked. I answered, 'From their *mawali*.' He said, 'Say: 'I am one of those whom Allah has blessed of the Banu Asad.'"

Yazid ibn Harun reported from Hammam ibn Yahya from Muhammad ibn Juhada from Abu Ma'shar that Sa'id ibn Jubayr said, "Abu Mas'ud al-Badri saw me on the Day of the *'Id*. I had a lock of hair and he said, 'Boy, there is no prayer on a day like this before the prayer of the imam. Pray two *rak'at*s after them and recite long.'"

Muhammad ibn Sa'd said. Sa'id ibn Jubayr also related from Ibn 'Umar, Ibn 'Abbas and others.

Rawh ibn 'Ubada reported from Shu'ba from Sulayman that Mujahid said, "Ibn 'Abbas said to Sa'id ibn Jubayr, 'Relate.' He said, 'Are you here?' He said, 'Is it not a blessing of Allah to you that you relate while I am present? If you are correct, it is that. If you err, I will inform you.'"

Muhammad ibn 'Abdullah al-Ansari reported from 'Abdullah ibn Ma'dan from al-Hasan ibn Muslim from Sa'id ibn Jubayr that he asked Ibn 'Abbas before he went blind and he was not able to write with him. When Ibn 'Abbas went blind, he wrote. He heard about that and was angry.

Yahya ibn 'Abbad reported from Ya'qub ibn 'Abdullah from Ja'far ibn Abi al-Mughira that Sa'id ibn Jubayr said, "Sometimes I went to Ibn 'Abbas and wrote in my page until he dictated until it was full and I wrote on my sandal until it was full and I wrote on my sleeve. Sometimes I went to him and did not write down a single *hadith* until I went back. No one asked him about anything."

'Abd al-Wahhab ibn 'Ata' reported from 'Amr ibn Abi al-Miqdam that the *mu'adhdhin* of the Banu Wada'a said, "I visited 'Abdullah ibn 'Abbas while he was reclining on a silk pillow. Sa'id ibn Jubayr was at his feet and he was saying. 'Look at how you relate from me! You have preserved a lot of *hadith*s from me.'"

Ahmad ibn 'Abdullah ibn Yunus reported from Abu Bakr ibn 'Ayyash that Abu Hasin said, "I asked Sa'id ibn Jubayr, 'Did you ask Ibn 'Abbas about all that I heard you relate?' He answered, 'No. I was sitting and did not speak until I got up. They related and I memorised.'"

'Abd al-'Aziz ibn 'Abd al-Khattab ad-Dabbi reported from Ya'qub from Ja'far that Sa'id said, "I used to go to Ibn 'Abbas and write from him."

Abu 'Asim an-Nabil reported that 'Abdullah ibn Muslim ibn Hurmuz said, "Sa'id ibn Jubayr disliked writing down *hadith*s."

'Affan reported from Shu'ba from Ayyub that Sa'id ibn Jubayr said, "I used to ask Ibn 'Umar about the page and if he knew what was in it, it was the arbiter between me and him." He said, "I asked him about *ila'* and he said, 'Do you want to say that Ibn 'Umar said that and Ibn 'Umar said?' I said, 'Yes, we are satisfied with your statement.' He said that the rulers spoke about that."

'Affan ibn Muslim reported from Wuhayb from Ayyub that Sa'id ibn Jubayr said, "When we used to disagree about something in Kufa, I would write it and keep it with me until I met Ibn 'Umar and asked him about it."

Muhammad ibn 'Abdullah al-Asadi and Qabisa ibn 'Uqba reported from Aslam al-Munqari that Sa'id ibn Jubayr said, "A man came to Ibn 'Umar and asked him about the shares of inheritance. He said, "Go to Sa'id ibn Jubayr. He knows reckoning better than I do and he will prescribe of it what I prescribe.'"

Al-Fadl ibn Dukayn reported from Isra'il from Thawr that Sa'id ibn Jubayr said, "Engraved on my ring was 'My Lord is mighty and decrees.' He said, 'Ibn 'Umar read it and forbade it. So I erased it and wrote, 'Sa'id ibn Jubayr.'"

Abu Mu'awiya ad-Darir reported from al-A'mash that Mas'ud ibn Malik said, "'Ali ibn Husayn asked me, 'What did Sa'id ibn Jubayr do?' I said, 'He was righteous.' He said, 'That is a man who used to pass by us and he would ask him about the obligatory shares and things by which Allah benefited us. In our view, he was not one of those who made a target of us,' and he pointed with his hand at Iraq."

Malik ibn Isma'il reported from Kamil that Habib said, "The companions of Sa'id ibn Jubayr reproached him for relating and he said, 'I prefer to relate to you and your companions than to take it with me to my grave.'"

Qabisa ibn 'Uqba reported from Sufyan that 'Ata' ibn as-Sa'ib said that Sa'id ibn Jubayr said, "No one comes to me to ask me."

Musa ibn Isma'il reported from Hammad ibn Zayd from Ayyub that Sa'id ibn Jubayr related a *hadith*. He said, "I followed him to ask him to repeat it. He said, 'It is not every time I give milk, so drink.'"

Musa ibn Isma'il reported from Hammad ibn Zayd that 'Ata' ibn as-Sa'ib said, "I went to Sa'id ibn Jubayr and he asked me, 'Who is the most ascetic of people?' He used to come to me at such-and-such an hour to question me."

'Affan ibn Muslim and Musa ibn Isma'il reported from 'Abd al-Wahid ibn Ziyad that Abu Shihab said, "Sa'id ibn Jubayr reported to us twice every day after the *Fajr* prayer and after *'Asr*."

Yazid ibn Harun reported from 'Abd al-Malik ibn Abi Sulayman that Sa'id ibn Jubayr used to recite the entire Qur'an every two nights."

Yazid ibn Harun reported from Sufyan that Hammad said that Sa'id ibn Jubayr said, "I recited the Qur'an in one *rak'at* in the Ka'ba."

Al-Fadl ibn Dukayn reported from al-Hasan ibn Salih that Qada' said, "Sa'id ibn Jubayr used to come between *Maghrib* and *'Isha'* and recite the Qur'an in Ramadan."

Al-Fadl ibn Dukayn reported from Qays ibn ar-Rabi' from as-Sa'b ibn 'Uthman that Sa'id ibn Jubayr said, "Two nights has not passed for me since al-Husayn was killed but that I recited the Qur'an in it, except when I was on a journey or ill."

'Arim ibn al-Fadl reported from Hammad ibn Zayd from Abu Hasim that Sa'id ibn Jubayr said, "I recite my part of the Qur'an, even if the imam is speaking on Friday."

Musa ibn Isma'il reported from 'Abd al-Wahid ibn Ziyad that Abu Shihab said, "Sa'id ibn Jubayr used to lead us in the prayer in Ramadan, and he would make his voice quaver and sometimes he repeated an *ayat* twice."

Qabisa ibn 'Uqba reported from Sufyan from 'Ata' ibn as-Sa'ib that Sa'id ibn Jubayr asked a man, "What did you relate after me?" He said, "We did not relate anything after you." He said, "Yes. Al-A'ma and Ibn as-Sawqal will chant the Qur'an to you."

Qabisa ibn 'Uqba reported from Sufyan that Sa'id ibn 'Ubayd said, "I saw Sa'id ibn Jubayr leading them in the prayer. I heard him repeating this *ayat, 'They have shackles and chains around their necks and are dragged along the ground.'* (40:71)"

Musa ibn Isma'il reported from 'Abd al-Wahid ibn Ziyad that Abu Shihab said, "Sa'id ibn Jubayr used to lead us in the *'Isha'* prayer in Ramadan and then go back and remain for a short time. Then returned and led us in six *tarawih* and did the *witr* with three. He did the *qunut* for the amount of about fifty *ayat*s."

Yusuf ibn al-Ghariq reported from Juwayriya ibn Bashir from Sa'id ibn Hammad that when Sa'id ibn Jubayr finished a *sura* in his voluntary prayer, he said, "The Truthful God spoke the truth."

Ahmad ibn 'Abdullah ibn Yunus reported from Isra'il from 'Abd al-Karim that Sa'id ibn Jubayr said, "I prefer to be hit with whips on my head than to speak while the imam is speaking on the Day of *Jumu'a*."

Sa'id ibn Mansur reported from Jarir that Habib ibn Abi 'Amra said, "I spoke to Sa'id ibn Jubayr after dawn but he did not speak to me."

Qabisa ibn 'Uqba reported that Sufyan said, "I was told by someone who saw Sa'id ibn Jubayr kiss his son when he was a man."

Al-Hasan ibn Musa reported from Hammad ibn Salama from 'Ata' ibn as-Sa'ib that when Sa'id ibn Jubayr finished his food, he said, "O Allah, You made us full and quenched us and so make us strong. You provided and gave a lot and were good, so give us more."

Kathir ibn Hisham reported from Ja'far ibn Burqan that Abu Hamza, a *mawla* of Yazid ibn al-Muhallab, said, "I was praying beside Sa'id ibn Jubayr and when the imam said, *'Not those with anger on them nor the misguided'* (1:7), Sa'id said, 'O Allah, forgive me. Ameen.' When the imam said, *'Allah hears whoever praises Him,'* Sa'id said, 'O Allah, our Lord, praise is Yours the extent of the heavens and the extent of the seven earths and the extent of what is between them and the extent of whatever You wish of anything more.'" He said, "Perhaps he continued to say that until he went into prostration and said, 'Allah is greater.'"

Al-Walid ibn al-Agharr al-Makki reported from 'Attab ibn Bashir from Salim (i.e. al-Aftas) that Sa'id ibn Jubayr performed an *'aqiqa* for himself after he was a man.

Muhammad ibn Mus'ab al-Qarqashani reported that Jabala ibn Sulayman al-Walibi al-Kufi said, "I saw Sa'id ibn Jubayr doing *i'tikaf* in the mosque of his people."

Malik ibn Isma'il reported from Isra'il from Abu al-Jahhaf from Muslim al-Batin that Sa'id ibn Jubayr did not hear anyone who back-bit someone in his presence without saying, "If you mean that, then say it to his face."

Sa'id ibn 'Amir reported from Hammam from Layth that Sa'id ibn Jubayr saw a pearl and did not take it.

Al-Fadl ibn Dukayn reported from Humayd ibn 'Abdullah al-Asamm who heard 'Abd al-Malik ibn Sa'id ibn Jubayr say, "My father said, 'Show despair for what is in the hands of people. It is a burden. Beware of what is excused. Good is not excused.'"

Al-Fadl ibn Dukayn reported from Mindal that Ja'far ibn Abi al-Mughira said, "I saw Sa'id ibn Jubayr using kohl while he was fasting." He said, "I saw Sa'id ibn Jubayr praying wth a sword and he had no cloak on other than it."

Al-Fadl ibn Dukayn reported from Isma'il ibn 'Abd al-Malik said, "I saw Sa'id ibn Jubayr praying in the arch and he did not perform the *qunut* in *Subh*." He said that he used to wear a turban and had it hanging down a span behind him.

Al-Fudayl ibn Dukayn reported from Sufyan that Hilal ibn Khabbab said, "I saw Sa'id ibn Jubayr assume *ihram* from Kufa."

Qabisa ibn 'Uqba reported from Hamza az-Zayyat from Abu Ishaq: "I saw Sa'id ibn Jubayr doing *tawaf* walking slowly."

Qabisa ibn 'Uqba reported from Sufyan from Habib ibn Abi Thabit that Muslim al-Batin said, "Sa'id ibn Jubayr was asked, 'Which is better: thankfulness or patience?' He answered, 'I prefer patience and well-being.'"

Muslim ibn Ibrahim reported from Hazm that Hilal ibn Khabbab said, "I met Sa'id ibn Jubayr in Makka and I asked, 'Where will the destruction of people come from?' He replied, 'From their scholars.'"

Muhammad ibn 'Abdullah al-Asadi reported from Sufyan from al-A'mash from Sa'id ibn Jubayr about His words, *'My earth is wide'* (29:56): "When acts of rebellion are committed in it, then go out."

Ad-Dahhak ibn Makhlad reported from Abu Yunus al-Qazzi who said, "I asked Sa'id ibn Jubayr about the words of Allah: *'Except for the men, women and children who really are oppressed.* (4:98)' He answered, 'Some people in Makka were wronged' (or 'subjugated.') I said, 'I have come to you from some people like that (i.e., the time of al-Hajjaj).' He said, 'Nephew, we desired and strove but Allah refused anything other than what He willed.'"

Hisham Abu al-Walid at-Tayalisi reported from Abu 'Awana from Isma'il ibn Salim from Habib ibn Abi Thabit that Sa'id ibn Jubayr was appointed by Matar ibn Najiya during the civil insurrection of al-Ash'ath over the two river barriers of Kufa and collecting *sadaqa* and land taxes.

Habib said, "He travelled and I travelled with him until we reached the barrier on the river and a man came to us who was building ships before that for the one before him. He entered the ship carrying a currycomb and Sa'id ibn Jubayr said to him, 'To you! To you!' He removed him and then Sa'id ibn Jubayr looked and he was the first to ride to him. Among those who came to him on that day was a merchant of the people of the *dhimma* and he did not take anything from him and he did not think that they owed land tax. He examined the people of Islam and took *zakat* from them on what they had with them."

Muhammad ibn Sa'd said that they said, "Sa'id ibn Jubayr was among the *qurra'* who rose against al-Hajjaj and he was present at Dayr al-Jamajim."

Sa'id ibn Muhammad ath-Thaqafi reported from az-Zibriqan al-Asadi: "I asked Sa'id ibn Jubayr about al-Jamajim and said, 'I am a slave and my master is with al-Hajjaj. Do you fear for me if I am killed that it will be a sin against me?' He answered, 'No. Fight, even if your master fights with himself and with you.'"

Musa ibn Isma'il reported from 'Umara ibn Zadhan that Abu as-Sahba' said, "Sa'id ibn Jubayr said when he was told that al-Hasan said that there is *taqiyya* in Islam, 'There is no *taqiyya* in Islam.' He said, 'I thought that he was tested and taken from the front.'"

Muhammad ibn Sa'd said, "When the people of Ibn al-Ash'ath were defeated at Dayr al-Jamajim, Sa'id fled and went to Makka."

'Arim ibn al-Fadl and Sulayman ibn Harb reported from Hammad ibn Zayd from Yahya ibn 'Atiq that Muhammad ibn Sirin said, "Sa'id ibn Jubayr was unsuccessful and did what he did and then went to Makka to give *fatwa*s to people."

Muhammad ibn Sa'd said, "The one who seized Sa'id ibn Jubayr was Khalid ibn 'Abdullah al-Qasari. He was the governor of 'Abd al-Malik over Makka. He sent him to al-Hajjaj.

Musa ibn Isma'il reported from 'Abdullah ibn Marwan that Sharik Hisham ad-Dastuwa'i said, "I saw Sa'id ibn Jubayr doing *tawaf* of the House in chains, and I saw him enter the Ka'ba as one of ten chained men."

Yazid ibn Harun reported from 'Abd al-Malik ibn Abi Sulayman who said, "Khalid ibn 'Abdullah heard the sound of chains and he asked, 'What is this?' He was told, 'Sa'id ibn Jubayr, Talq ibn Habib and their people are doing *tawaf* of the House.' He said, 'Stop their *tawaf*.'"

'Ubaydullah ibn Musa reported that ar-Rabi' ibn Abi Salih said, "I visited Sa'id ibn Jubayr when he was brought to al-Hajjaj. A man of the people wept and Sa'id asked, 'Why are you weeping?' He replied, 'Because of your affliction.' He said, 'Do not weep. It was in the knowledge of Allah that it would be.' Then he recited, *'Nothing occurs, either in the earth or in yourselves, without it being in a Book. We make it happen.'* (57:22)"

Muhammad ibn 'Ubayd reported that he heard a shaykh mention that he was sitting with al-Hajjaj when Sa'id ibn Jubayr was brought with two girths. He spoke to him for a time and said, "Guards, take him and strike off his head." He was taken and said, "Let me pray two *rak'at*s." He turned towards the *qibla* and al-Hajjaj said, "What did he say to you?" He said, "Let me pray two *rak'at*s." He said, "No, only to the east." Sa'id said, *"'Wherever you turn, the face of Allah is there.'* (2:115)" Then he stretched out his neck and it was struck.

Wahb ibn Jarir ibn Hazim reported from his father who heard al-Fadl ibn Suwayd, who was in the care of al-Hajjaj, relate and his father had instructed al-Hajjaj: "Al-Hajjaj sent me for a need and it was said that Sa'id ibn Jubayr had been brought. I returned to see what he would do with him. I stood at the head of al-Hajjaj and al-Hajjaj said to him, 'Sa'id, did I not appoint you? Did I not share with you in my trust?' 'Yes,' he replied. He said so that we thought that he would let him go. He said, 'What moved you to rebel against me?' He said, 'I was asked to.' Al-Hajjaj flew into a fury and said, 'Ha! Did you think that the request of the enemy of the All-Merciful to you was a right? Do you think that Allah and the Amir al-Mu'minin are not due any right from you? Strike off his head!' and his head was struck off. His head fell in a white hat with no wrap which was on his head."

'Ali ibn Muhammad reported that Abu al-Yaqathan said, "Sa'id ibn Jubayr said on the day of Dayr al-Jamajim when they were fighting, 'Fight them for their injustice in rule, their abandoning the *deen*, their subjugating the servants of Allah, their making the prayer unperformed, and abasing the Muslims.' When the people of Dayr al-Jamajim were defeated, Sa'id ibn Jubayr went to Makka and Khalid ibn 'Abdullah seized him and sent him to al-Hajjaj with Isma'il ibn Awsat al-Bajali. Their driver was Zayd ibn Masruq, one of the Banu Dabari ibn 'Ubayd ibn Tha'laba ibn Yarbu'. He was brought to al-Hajjaj by Isma'il ibn Awsat. He said to him, 'Did I not come to Iraq and honour you?' He mentioned the things which he had done and he answered, 'Yes.' He said, 'What brought you out against me?' He replied, 'Ibn al-Ash'ath had my allegiance and asked me.' Al-Hajjaj became angry and said, 'Do you think that the enemy of Allah is owed what you did not show to Allah, the Amir al-Mu'minin or me? I will not lift my foot until I kill you and send you immediately to the Fire. Bring me a heavy sword!' Muslim al-A'war stood with a heavy Hanafi sword and struck his neck. Al-Hasan said, 'How extraordinary Sa'id ibn Jubayr is! He fought al-Hajjaj in a place and he ordered his killing. Then he fled to Makka and did not control himself.'"

Muhammad ibn 'Umar said that Sa'id ibn Jubayr was killed in 94 AH. At that time he was forty-nine.

Zuhayr Abu Khaythama reported from Jarir from Wasil ibn Sulaym that 'Abdullah ibn Sa'id ibn Jubayr said, "Sa'id ibn Jubayr was killed when he was forty-nine."

Ahmad ibn 'Abdullah ibn Yunus reported from Abu Bakr ibn 'Ayyash from al-A'mash or Mughira from Ibrahim that Sa'id was mentioned to him and he said, "That was a man who made himself famous."

One of them said, "It was said to Ibrahim that Sa'id ibn Jubayr was killed and he said, 'May Allah have mercy on him. He did not leave his like behind.'"

Muhammad ibn 'Abdullah al-Asadi reported from Sufyan from 'Amr ibn Maymun ibn Mihran that Maymun ibn Mihran said, "Sa'id ibn Jubayr died and there was no man on the surface of the earth but that he needed Sa'id."

'Abd ar-Rahman ibn Mahdi reported from 'Abd al-Wahid that Wiqa' ibn Iyas said, "I saw 'Azra frequent Sa'id ibn Jubayr who had a *tafsir* in a book and with it was an ink-well."

Ad-Dahhak ibn Makhlad reported from 'Abdullah ibn Muslim ibn Hurmuz that Sa'id ibn Jubayr disliked for a man to lean on something in his prayer. He said, "I did not see him pray at all except that it was as if he was taut."

Sufyan ibn 'Uyayna reported that Salim ibn Abi Hafsa said, "When al-Hajjaj commanded that Sa'id ibn Jubayr be killed, he said, 'Let me pray two *rak'ats*.'"

Al-Fadl ibn Dukayn reported from Mu'awiya ibn 'Ammar adh-Dhahani from 'Abd al-Malik that Sa'id ibn Jubayr said, "I saw him crowding me in the presence of Ibn 'Abbas (meaning al-Hajjaj)."

Waki' ibn al-Jarrah reported from Fitr: "I saw Sa'id ibn Jubayr with a white beard."

'Arim ibn al-Fadl reported from Hammad ibn Zayd that Ayyub said, "Sa'id ibn Jubayr had a very white beard."

'Arim ibn al-Fadl and Malik ibn Isma'il reported from Hammad ibn Zayd that Ayyub said, "Sa'id ibn Jubayr was asked about dyeing the hair black and he disliked it. He said, 'Allah clothes His slave with light in his face and then he extinguishes it with black!'"

Waki' ibn al-Jarrah related that Isma'il ibn 'Abd al-Malik said, "I saw Sa'id ibn Jubayr wearing a white turban."

Waki' ibn Jubayr and al-Fadl ibn Dukayn reported that Abu Shihab Musa ibn Nafi'said, "I saw Sa'id ibn Jubayr praying in his burnous without putting his hands out of it."

Waki' reported that Abu Shihab Musa ibn Nafi' said, "I saw Sa'id ibn Jubayr praying *sadl* in the voluntary prayer wearing a mantle with two sides wrapped up."

Waki' reported that Isma'il ibn 'Abd al-Malik said, "I saw Sa'id ibn Jubayr wearing a white turban."

Al-Fadl ibn Dukayn reported that 'Umar ibn Dharr said, "I heard my father say, 'Sa'id ibn Jubayr used to assume *ihram* in a variegated mantle."

'Umar said, "My father went into *ihram* in a variegated mantle."

Abu Burda ibn Abi Musa al-Ash'ari

His name was 'Amir ibn 'Abdullah ibn Qays.

Muhammad ibn Humayd al-'Abdi reported from Ma'mar from Sa'id ibn Abi Burda that Abu Burda said, "My father sent me to 'Abdullah ibn Salam to learn from him. I went to him and he asked me, 'Who are you?' I told him. He greeted me and I said, 'My father sent me to you to ask you and learn from you.' He said, 'Nephew, you are in a land of merchants. If someone owes you some money and gives you a load of straw, do not accept it. It is usury.'"

'Arim ibn al-Fadl reported from Hammad ibn Zayd from Layth that Abu Burda said, "I went to Madina and met 'Abdullah ibn Salam and said, 'Will you not enter a house which the Messenger of Allah 🌸 entered and pray in a house in which the Messenger of Allah 🌸 prayed and we will feed you dates and *sawiq*?' 'Abdullah ibn Salam said, 'Nephew, you are in a land where usury is widespread and hidden. Is there not among you those who when they have made a loan, allow the one with a debt to bring a load of food or a load of fodder? That is usury.'"

Ya'qub ibn Isma'il al-Hadrami reported from Abu 'Awana that Muhajir Abu al-Hasan said, "Abu Wa'il and Abu Burda were in charge of the treasury."

Abu Nu'aym said, "Abu Burda was appointed qadi in Kufa after Shurayh."

Al-Fadl ibn Dukayn reported that Yazid ibn Mardawayh said, "I saw Abu Burda riding on a mount and the copy of the Qur'an was hanging from the front of the saddle."

Talq ibn Ghannam an-Nakha'i reported from Abu Ghannam ibn Talq ibn Mu'awiya an-Nakha'i said, "I saw Abu Burda ibn Abi Musa attend the funeral of a *mawla* who had died among us. He put the imam of the quarter forward to lead the prayer."

Muhammad ibn Sa'd said that Muhammad ibn 'Umar said, "Abu Burda related from his father. He was appointed qadi of Kufa."

Muhammad ibn 'Umar and others said that Abu Burda died in Kufa in 103 AH.

Al-Fadl ibn Dukayn and Sa'id ibn Jamil reported from Aban ibn 'Umar ibn 'Uthman ibn Abi Khalid that Abu Burda died in 104 AH.

His brother, **Musa ibn Abi Musa** al-Ash'ari

His mother was Umm Kulthum bint al-Fadl ibn 'Abbas ibn 'Abd al-Muttalib. He related from his father.

Their brother, **Abu Bakr ibn Abi Musa** al-Ash'ari

Abu Bakr was his actual name. He related from his father and others. He had few *hadith*s and is thought weak. He died while Khalid ibn 'Abdullah was governor. He was older than Abu Burda.

'Urwa ibn al-Mughira ibn Shu'ba ath-Thaqafi

His *kunya* was Abu Ya'fur. He related from his father.

Muslim ibn Ibrahim reported from Sallam ibn Miskin from Abu an-Nadr al-Mazini from ash-Sha'bi that 'Urwa ibn al-Mughira ibn Shu'ba was governor over Kufa, and he was one of the best people of that house.

Al-'Aqqar ibn al-Mughira ibn Shu'ba ath-Thaqafi

He also related from his father.

Ya'fur ibn al-Mughira ibn Shu'ba ath-Thaqafi

He also related from his father.

Hamza ibn al-Mughira ibn Shu'ba ath-Thaqafi

He also related from his father.

Ibrahim an-Nakha'i

He is Ibrahim ibn Yazid ibn al-Aswad ibn 'Amr ibn Rabi'a ibn Haritha ibn Sa'd ibn Malik ibn an-Nakh'i of Madhhij. His *kunya* was Abu 'Imran. He was one-eyed.

Hammad ibn Mas'ada reported from Ibn 'Awn that Muhammad ibn Sirin said one day: "I reckon that the Ibrahim who was mentioned was a young man who sat with us, as far as I know, with Masruq as if he was not with us when he was with us."

'Affan ibn Muslim reported from Sulaym ibn Akhdar that Ibn 'Awn said, "I described Ibrahim to Muhammad ibn Sirin and he said, 'Perhaps he is that one-eyed young man who used to sit with us with 'Alqama among the people as if he was not in them."

Hajjaj ibn Muhammad al-A'war and 'Amr ibn al-Haytham Abu Qatan reported from Shu'ba from Mansur that Ibrahim said, "I did not write anything."

Abu Qatan said and Shu'ba said that Mansur said, "I would prefer not to write than this and that."

Muhammad ibn al-Fudayl ibn Ghawan reported from 'Abd al-Malik ibn Abi Sulayman who said, "I saw Sa'id ibn Jubayr being asked for a *fatwa*. He stated, 'Do you ask me for a *fatwa* when Ibrahim is among you?'"

Al-Fadl ibn Dukayn reported from Sufyan that his father said, "I often heard Ibrahim exclaim in astonishment, 'I am made needed! I am made needed!'"

'Ubaydullah ibn Musa reported that he heard al-A'mash say, "We used to go to Shaqiq and we would go to that and go to this and we do not think that Ibrahim had anything."

Muhammad ibn 'Abdullah al-Asadi and Qabisa ibn 'Uqba reported from Sufyan that al-A'mash said, "I did not mention a *hadith* to Ibrahim at all but that he added to it."

Qabisa ibn 'Uqba reported from Sufyan ibn Abjar that Zubayd said, "I did not ask Ibrahim about anything at all but that I recognised dislike in him."

Al-Fadl ibn Dukayn and Qabisa ibn 'Uqba reported from Sufyan that Mughira said, "We used to be in awe of Ibrahim as we would be in awe of a ruler."

Al-Fadl ibn Dukayn reported that Malik ibn Mighwal said, "I heard Talha say, 'There was no one in Kufa I liked more than Ibrahim and Khaythama."

Ahmad ibn 'Abdullah ibn Yunus reported from Abu Shihab from al-Hasan ibn 'Amr that Fudayl said, "I said to Ibrahim, 'I have come to you having compiled questions. It was as if Allah has snatched them from me and I see that you dislike writing.' He said, 'Rarely does a human being write a book but that he relies on it. Rarely does a man seek knowledge but that Allah brings him what will be enough for him.'"

'Abd al-Wahhab ibn 'Ata' reported from Sa'id ibn Abi 'Aruba from Abu Mash'ar from Ibrahim that he used to visit one of the wives of the Prophet ﷺ, namely 'A'isha, and saw them wearing red garments. Ayyub asked Abu Mash'ar, "How did he go in where they were?" He said, "He used to perform *hajj* with his paternal uncle, his maternal uncle 'Alqama and al-Aswad before he reached puberty. There was brotherhood and love between them and 'A'isha."

Waki' reported from Malik ibn Mighwal that Zubayd said, "I asked Ibrahim about a question and he said, 'I did not find in what was between me and you anyone to ask except me.'"

Qabisa ibn 'Uqba reported from Sufyan that Abu Hasin said, "I went to Ibrahim to ask him about a question and he said, 'I did not find in what was between me and you anyone to ask except me?'"

Muhammad ibn 'Abdullah al-Ansari reported that Ibn 'Awn said, "Ibrahim used to relate *hadith*s by meanings [rather than exact wording]."

Qabisa ibn 'Uqba reported from Sufyan that al-Hasan ibn 'Ubaydullah said, "I asked Ibrahim, 'Will you not relate to me?' He replied, 'Do you mean that I will be like so-and-so? Go to the mosque of the quarter. If someone comes who is asked about anything, listen to him.'"

'Amr ibn al-Haytham Abu Qatan reported from Shu'ba that al-A'mash said, "I said to Ibrahim, 'When you relate to me from 'Abdullah, give the *isnad*.' He said, 'When you say, "'Abdullah said,' I heard it from more than one of his companions. When I say, 'So-and-so related to me,' then so-and-so related from me.'"

'Arim ibn al-Fadl reported from Hammad ibn Zayd that Abu Hashim said, "I said to Ibrahim, 'Abu 'Imran, has a *hadith* reached you from the Prophet ﷺ which you relate to us?' 'Yes,' he said, 'but I say, "'Umar said. 'Alqama said. Al-Aswad said." I find that easier for me.'"

Ahmad ibn 'Abdullah ibn Yunus reported from Abu Bakr ibn 'Ayyash that 'Asim said, "When someone went to Abu Wa'il to ask him for a *fatwa*, he said to him, 'Go and ask Abu Razin. Then come to me and tell me what reply he gives you.' Abu Razin was with him in the house. Also when he was asked, he said, 'Go to Ibrahim and ask him and then come and tell me what he said to you.'"

'Affan ibn Muslim reported from Abu 'Awana from Mughira that Ibrahim disliked to lean against a pillar.

Muhammad ibn 'Abdullah al-Asadi reported from Sufyan that Abu Qays says, "I saw Ibrahim as a shaved boy holding to 'Alqama by the stirrup on Friday."

Al-Fadl ibn Dukayn reported that Abu Bakr ibn 'Ayyash said, "I asked al-A'mash, 'How many gathered with Ibrahim?' He answered, 'Four or five.'"

Abu Bakr said, "I did not see ten with Habib and I did not see two asking him."

Muhammad ibn 'Abdullah al-Ansari reported from Mindal that al-A'mash said, "Khaythama said to me, 'You and Ibrahim should go and sit in the Great Mosque and the *'arif*s and police will sit for you.' I mentioned that to Ibrahim and he said, 'I prefer that we will sit in the mosque with the *'arif*s and police sitting with us than to withdraw and people accuse us of an opinion which is overthrown.'"

Al-Fadl ibn Dukayn, Muhammad ibn 'Abdullah and Qabisa ibn 'Uqba reported from Sufyan that al-Hasan ibn 'Amr said, "Ibrahim said, 'I have never disputed with any man at all.'"

'Amr ibn 'Asim reported from Hammad ibn Zayd that Ibn 'Awn said, "I sat with Ibrahim an-Nakha'i and he mentioned the Murji'ites and made a statement about them which he later changed for a better one."

Malik ibn Isma'il reported from al-Hasan ibn Salih from his father from al-Harith al-'Ukli that Ibrahim said, "Beware of the people of this innovated opinion," meaning the Murji'ites.

Muhammad ibn 'Abdullah al-Ansari reported that he said, "I heard Muhill relating that Ibrahim said, "*Irja'* is innovation.'"

Muhammad ibn 'Abdullah reported that Muhill said, "A man called Muhammad was sitting with Ibrahim. Ibrahim heard that he espoused *irja'* and Ibrahim said to him, 'Do not sit with me.'"

Muhammad ibn 'Abdullah al-Ansari reported from Abu Salama as-Sa'igh from Muslim al-A'war that Ibrahim said, "They left this *deen* finer than the finest cloth."

Muhammad ibn 'Abdullah reported that Muhill said, "I said to Ibrahim, 'What should we do if they ask us if we are believers?' He replied, 'When they ask you, say, *"We believe in Allah and what has been sent down to us and what has been sent down to Ibrahim..."* (2:136)'"

Muhammad ibn 'Abdullah reported that Muhill said, "Ibrahim said to us, 'Do not let them sit with us,' meaning the Murji'ites."

Muhammad ibn 'Abdullah reported from Sa'id ibn Salih from Hakim ibn Jubayr that Ibrahim said, "We fear for this community from the Murji'ites more than we fear more for them that same number of Azraqites."

'Ubaydullah ibn Musa reported from Isra'il from Ghalib Abi al-Hudhayl that he was with Ibrahim when some of the Murji'ites came to him. They spoke to him and he became angry. He said, "This is what they say, so do not visit me."

Malik ibn Isma'il reported from Ja'far ibn Ziyad from Abu Hamza that Ibrahim said, "If the Companions of Muhammad ﷺ had not wiped over nails, I would not have washed them to do extra. We have enough of a burden against people who ask us about their understanding when we disagree with their business."

Muhammad ibn as-Salt reported from Mansur ibn Abi al-Aswad that al-A'mash said, "The Murji'ites were mentioned in the presence of Ibrahim and he said, 'By Allah, they are more hated to me than the People of the Book.'"

Ahmad ibn 'Abdullah ibn Yunus reported from Fudayl ibn 'Iyad from Mughira that Ibrahim said, "Whoever turns away from wiping turns away from the *Sunna*. I only think that that is from Shaytan."

Fudayl said that he meant abandoning wiping.

Ahmad ibn 'Abdullah ibn Yunus reported from Ja'far al-Ahmar from Mughira that Ibrahim said, "Whoever turns away from wiping has turned away the *Sunna* of the Prophet ﷺ."

Qabisa ibn 'Uqba reported from Sufyan that al-A'mash said, "I asked Ibrahim, 'Can I come to you and present to you?' He said, 'I disliked to say of something it is like this when it is like this.'"

Ahmad ibn 'Abdullah ibn Yunus reported that he heard Abu Bakr ibn 'Ayyash say, "Ibrahim and 'Ata' did not speak until they were asked."

Kathir ibn Hisham reported from Ja'far ibn Burqan from Rabi' ibn Abi Zaynab al-Kufi from Abu al-Minjab al-Basri that a man used to go to Ibrahim an-Nakha'i and learn from him. He would listen to some people mention 'Ali and 'Uthman. He asked Ibrahim an-Nakha'i about that and he said, "I am not a Sabali [Jabrite] nor a Murji'ite."

Ahmad ibn Yunus reported from Abu al-Ahwas from Mufaddal ibn Muhalhil from Mughira that Ibrahim said, "A man said to Ibrahim, 'I prefer 'Ali to Abu Bakr and 'Umar.' Ibrahim said, 'As for 'Ali, if he had heard your words, he would have pained your back. If you sit with us with this, then do not sit with us.'"

Jarir ibn 'Abd al-Hamid ad-Dabbi reported that ash-Shaybani said that Ibrahim said, "I prefer 'Ali to 'Uthman and I would prefer to fall from the sky than to bring evil to 'Uthman."

Ahmad ibn 'Abdullah ibn Yunus reported from Mindal from Yahya ibn Hammad from Abu 'Awana, all from al-A'mash that Ibrahim said, "When he stood, he said the *salam*. When we asked him about something, he repeated the *salam* and sealed with it."

Mu'ammil ibn Isma'il and 'Arim ibn al-Fadl reported from Hammad ibn Zayd that Shu'ayb ibn al-Habhab said that Hunayda, the wife of Ibrahim, related that Ibrahim used to fast every other day.

Musa ibn Isma'il reported from Abu 'Awana that Abu Miskin said, "Ibrahim used to like for there to be dates in his house. When someone entered and he did not have anything, he said, 'Bring us dates.' If a beggar came, he would give him a date."

Al-Fadl ibn Dukayn and Muhammad ibn 'Abdullah reported from Sufyan from al-Hasan ibn 'Amr that Ibrahim used to not go to the *'Ids* and *Jumu'a* when he was afraid.

Al-Fadl ibn Dukayn reported from Abu Isma'il that Fudayl said, "I asked permission for Hammad to visit Ibrahim when he was hiding in the house of Abu Mash'ar."

Muhammad ibn 'Abdullah al-Asadi reported from Sa'id ibn Salih al-Ashajj from Hajim ibn Jubayr that Ibrahim said, "There is no *'arif* [overseer] there who is not an unbeliever."

Muhammad ibn 'Abdullah al-Ansari reported that Ibn 'Awn said, "We were with Ibrahim when a man came and said, 'Abu 'Imran, pray to Allah to heal me!' I saw that he disliked it intensely so that I saw the dislike in his face, or until I recognised the dislike of that in his face. Then he said, 'A man came to Hudhayfa and said, 'Pray to Allah to forgive me.' He said, 'May Allah not forgive you.' The man went to a corner and sat down. After that he said, 'May Allah admit you as Hudhayfa was admitted. Are you pleased now?' He added, 'One of you comes to a man as if he calculated his business, and as if...' Ibrahim mentioned the *Sunna* and he desired it and he mentioned what people have innovated and he disliked it and spoke about it."

'Affan ibn Muslim reported from Ya'qub ibn Ishaq that Ibn 'Awn said, "Ibrahim used to go to the rulers and ask them for stipends."

Qabisa ibn 'Uqba reported from Sufyan from Mansur and Ibrahim ibn Muhajir (or from one of them) that Ibrahim went out to Ibn al-Ashtar and he gave him a stipend and he accepted.

Muhammad ibn Rabi'a al-Kilani reported that al-'Ala' ibn Zuhayr al-Azdi said, "Ibrahim came to my father when he was in charge of Hulwan and gave him a mule to ride, clothed him in garments and gave him a thousand dirhams which he accepted."

'Abd al-Hamid ibn 'Abd ar-Rahman reported that al-A'mash said, "Nu'aym ibn Abi Hind gave Ibrahim a jar of thickened grape juice and he accepted it and found it very sweet. So he cooked it and made it *nabidh*."

Muhammad ibn Rabi'a al-Kilabi reported that al-A'mash said, "I saw that Ibrahim had a good voice and did not quaver."

Ahmad ibn 'Abdullah ibn Yunus reported from Abu Shihab from al-Hasan ibn 'Amr from Fudayl ibn 'Amr that when Ibrahim wanted to strike his servant, he said, "I praise Allah that I strike you." He called for a whip and then said, "Stretch!" and hit him like that.

Ahmad ibn 'Abdullah ibn Yunus reported from Abu Shihab from al-Hasan ibn 'Amr from Fudayl ibn 'Amr from Ibrahim who said, "They used to say that when a man reaches forty years with a certain character, he will not change from it until he dies. It used to be said to someone who was forty, 'Guard yourself.'"

Ahmad ibn 'Abdullah ibn Yunus reported from Abu Shihab from al-Hasan ibn 'Amr that Farqad as-Sabakhi saw a man with Ibrahim who had loosened his waist-wrapper and whose hair was long and in locks. Farqad said, "Abu 'Imran, will you not stop this one from loosening his waist-wrapper and having these locks in his hair?" Ibrahim said, "I do not know whether the coarseness of the Banu Asad has dominated you or the error of the Banu Tamim. As for this

291

man, he finds that it is hot and loosens his waist-wrapper and this one lets his hair down when he wants to pray, Allah willing."

Ahmad ibn 'Abdullah ibn Yunus reported from Abu Shihab from al-Hasan ibn 'Amr that Farqad said, "Abu 'Imran, this morning I was concerned about my tax which was six dirhams. The new moon came and I did not have it, so I made a supplication. While I was walking on the edge of the Euphrates I found six dirhams. I took them and weighed them and they were only six: no more, no less." He answered him, "Give it away as *sadaqa*. It is not yours."

Ahmad ibn 'Abdullah ibn Yunus reported from Abu Shihab from al-Hasan ibn 'Amr that Fudayl ibn 'Amr said that Ibrahim said, "It used to be disliked for a man when he was given with something to turn away from it."

Qabisa ibn Uqba reported from Sufyan that al-A'mash said, "Sometimes I saw Ibrahim carrying something while he was saying, 'I hope that there is a reward for it (meaning for carrying it).'"

Qabisa ibn 'Uqba reported from Sufyan from Mansur from Ibrahim and Mujahid that they disliked al-Jamajim.

Malik ibn Isma'il reported from Sharik that Mughira said, "I heard the sound of jangles in the house of Ibrahim."

Malik ibn Isma'il reported from Isra'il from Mughira that Ibrahim said was asked, "How are you this morning?" He answered, "In blessing from Allah."

Malik ibn Isma'il reported from 'Abd as-Salam ibn Harb from Khalaf from someone who mentioned that Ibrahim said, "I did not recite this *ayat* at all but that I remembered cold water: *'A barrier will be set up between them and the thing that they desire.'* (34:54)"

Qabisa ibn 'Uqba reported from Sufyan that al-A'mash said, "Sometimes I saw Ibrahim pray and then come to us and he remained for a time of the day as if he was ill."

Qabisa ibn "Uqba reported from Sufyan from Fudayl ibn Ghazwan from Abu Mash'ar that Ibrahim said, "If I had thought it lawful to fight anyone of the people of the *qibla*, I would allow fighting those Khashabiyya."

Al-Mu'alla ibn Asad reported from 'Abd al-'Aziz ibn al-Mukhtar from Khalid al-Hadhdha' that Abu Mash'ar said, "I saw Ibrahim on Friday turning from the imam. 'When he did not hear the *khutba*, he glorified Allah."

Al-Mu'alla ibn Asad reported from Bayhas Abu Habib from Nahshal from Hammad ibn Abi Sulayman that an-Nakha'i passed by some people and he did not greet them, and people objected to that. He refuted them and some of them said, "Abu 'Imran passed by us and did not greet us." He said, "I saw you busy and I disliked to make you sin."

Muhammad ibn 'Abdullah al-Asadi reported from Sufyan that Mansur said, "I mentioned to Ibrahim cursing al-Hajjaj or one of the tyrants and he said, 'Did not Allah say, "The curse of Allah is on the unjust"?'"

Al-Fadl ibn Dukayn reported from Sufyan from Zayd, a shaykh on Muharib, who said, "I heard Ibrahim cursing al-Hajjaj."

Muhammad ibn 'Abdullah al-Asadi reported from Sufyan from Mansur that Ibrahim said, "It is enough for me, my uncle, that a man is blind to the business of al-Hajjaj."

Al-Fadl ibn Dukayn and Muhammad ibn 'Abdullah al-Asadi reported from Suyfan that ash-Shaybani said, "It was mentioned that Ibrahim at-Taymi sent to the Kharijites to summon them and Ibrahim an-Nakha'i said to him, 'To whom are you calling them? To al-Hajjaj?'"

'Abd al-Hamid ibn 'Abd ar-Rahman al-Himmani reported from Abu Hanifa that Hammad said, "I gave Ibrahim the good news of the death of al-Hajjaj and he prostrated."

Hammad said, "I did not see anyone weep from joy until I saw Ibrahim weep from joy."

Abu 'Ubayd reported that al-'Awwam ibn Hawshab said, "The office of Ibrahim was at Radhan. Abu Hawshab ibn Yazid ash-Shaybani was in charge of this area. The army asked his permission to visit their dependants and he gave permission to them and set a term for them. He said, 'If anyone is absent for longer than the term, I will give him a lash for each day.' I said to Ibrahim, 'You stay for as long as you wish. It is not disliked for you.' So he stayed for twenty days beyond the term. My father made the people present themselves and when he came on the name of every man of them who was absent, he began to hit them until he called Ibrahim. He had been absent for twenty days beyond the term and he had commanded it. We, who were ten brothers, went to him. He said to us, 'Whoever has a free mother is divorced, and whoever has a slave mother is free if you do not sit and speak until my command is carried out as I carried it out on others.' We sat until he hit him twenty lashes."

Yahya ibn Adam reported from Sufyan that Yazid ibn Abi Ziyad said, "I saw Ibrahim wearing a hat of fox-fur."

'Ubaydullah ibn Musa reported from al-Hasan ibn Salih that Abu al-Haytham al-Qassab said, "I saw Ibrahim wearing a Persian hat in the front of which was a fox skin."

Al-Fadl ibn Dukayn reported from Sufyan that Yazid ibn Abi Ziyad said, "I saw Ibrahim wearing a hat of fox-fur or lined with fox."

Al-Fadl ibn Dukayn reported that Muhill said, "I saw Ibrahim wearing a fur coat. I asked about fur and he said, 'Tanning is its purification.'"

Yazid ibn Harun reported that al-'Awwam ibn Hawshab said, "I saw Ibrahim an-Nakha'i wearing a red mantle. I visited him in his house and saw him wearing red garments."

Ishaq ibn Yusuf al-Azraq reported from Malik that Salama ibn Kuhayl said, "I did not see Ibrahim in the summer wearing anything except a red mantle and yellow waist-wrapper."

Muhammad ibn 'Ubayd at-Tanafisi reported that Sulayman ibn Yusayr said, "I saw Ibrahim wearing two yellow mantles in which he went out to the General Mosque and red ones in which he prayed here."

Al-Fadl ibn Dukayn reported that Hanash ibn al-Harith said, "I saw Ibrahim wearing a shirt and two garments dyed with saffron."

Al-Fadl ibn Dukayn reported that Muhill said, "I saw Ibrahim wearing a mantle which was sometimes red that had been washed."

Muhammad ibn 'Abdullah al-Asadi reported that al-Walid ibn Jumay' said, "I saw Ibrahim wearing a red mantle."

Yahya ibn 'Abbad reported from Malik ibn Mighwal that Ujayl said, "I did not see Ibrahim at all in the summer wearing anything but a red mantle and yellow waist-wrapper."

Al-Fadl ibn Dukayn reported that Muhill said, "I saw Ibrahim wrapped in a mantle and on it with an additional mantle, and he prayed, being the imam."

Al-Fadl ibn Dukayn reported from Isra'il that Mansur saw Ibrahim wearing an embellished shawl.

Waki' reported from Sufyan that a shaykh of an-Nakha' said, "I saw Ibrahim beginning the prayer in the winter in his robe."

'Amr ibn al-Haytham Abu Qatan reported that Shu'ba said, "Al-Hakam led us in the prayer in a robe. We said, 'Has pride moved you to this?' He said, 'When it is substantial, there is no harm in it.' Ibrahim used to lead them in the prayer wearing a long shirt and mantle."

Al-Fadl ibn Dukayn reported that Bukayr ibn 'Amir said, "I saw Ibrahim wearing a turban with its end hanging down behind him."

Al-Fadl ibn Dukayn reported that Muhill said, "I saw Ibrahim wearing an iron ring on his left hand."

'Abd ar-Rahman ibn Mahdi reported from Hammad ibn Zayd from Abu al-Hakam that Maymun ibn Mihran said, "I met Ibrahim and said, 'What is this doubt which reached me about you?'"

It is reported from Yahya ibn Sa'id who said, "Ibrahim was not with Ibn al-Ash'ath."

Muhammad ibn 'Abdullah al-Ansari reported from Sufyan from Mughira that Ibrahim wore his turban with a tail behind him.

Mu'ammil ibn Isma'il reported from Sufyan that al-A'mash said, "I saw an iron ring on the hand of Ibrahim."

'Ubaydullah ibn Musa reported from Isra'il that al-A'mash said, "Ibrahim's iron ring was on his left hand."

Ahmad ibn 'Abdullah ibn Yunus reported from Za'ida that al-A'mash said, "Ibrahim's ring was on his left hand."

Al-Fadl ibn Dukayn reported from Sufyan that Mansur said, "Engraved on Ibrahim's ring was 'The end is to Allah and we are His.'"

Al-Fadl ibn Dukayn reported from Isra'il that Abu al-Haytham said, "I visited Ibrahim while he was ill and he wept. I said, 'What is making you weep, Abu 'Imran?' He replied, 'I am not weeping out of anxiety for this world, but for these two daughters of mine.' I came the following day and he had died. His wife had taken him out of the house to the Suffa and was weeping for him."

Waki' ibn al-Jarrah, Yazid ibn Harun, Abu Usama and Muhammad ibn "Abdullah al-Ansari reported that Ibn 'Awn said, "When Ibrahim died, we went to his house and asked, 'What were his instructions?' They said, 'He instructed that no 'arzami bricks be put in his grave, a *lahd* be made and he not be followed with fire.'"

Waki' reported from Umayy as-Sayrafi from Abu al-Haytham that Ibrahim instructed: "When there are four of you, do not announce my death to anyone."

Isma'il ibn Ibrahim reported that Ibn 'Awn said, "We buried Ibrahim at night in fear."

Isma'il ibn Ibrahim ibn 'Ulayya and Muhammad ibn 'Abdullah al-Ansari reported that Ibn 'Awn said, "I went to ash-Sha'bi after Ibrahim's death and he asked me, 'Were you among those who attended the burial of Ibrahim?' I turned to him and he said, 'By Allah, his like is not left after them.' I said, 'In Kufa?' He answered, 'Not in Kufa or Basra or Syria or there or there.'"

Muhammad ibn 'Abdullah added, "nor in the Hijaz."

Muhammad ibn al-Fudayl ibn Ghazwan ad-Dabbi reported that Ibn Abjur said, "I told ash-Sha'bi about the death of Ibrahim and he said, 'I praise Allah. He did not leave his equal to replace him.' He added, 'Dead, he has more *fiqh* than alive.'"

Jarir ibn 'Abd al-Hamid ad-Dabbi reported from Mughira that ash-Sha'bi said, "Ibrahim has more *fiqh* dead than alive."

Ahmad ibn 'Abdullah ibn Yunus reported that he heard Abu Bakr ibn 'Ayyash say, "Ibrahim an-Nakha'i reached the age of about fifty."

Muhammad ibn Sa'd and others said: they agree that he died in 96 AH in Kufa while al-Walid ibn 'Abd al-Malik was caliph, when he was forty-nine and had not reached fifty. It reached him that Yahya ibn Sa'id al-Qattan used to say, "Ibrahim died when he was about fifty."

Abu Nu'aym said, "I asked the son of Ibrahim's daughter about his death and he said, 'Four or five months after al-Hajjaj.'"

Abu Nu'aym said that it was as if he died at the beginning of 96 AH.

Ibrahim at-Taymi

He was Yazid ibn Sharik from Taym ar-Rabbab. His *kunya* was Abu Asma'.

Yazid ibn Harun reported that al-'Awwam ibn Hawshab said, "I saw Ibrahim at-Taymi wearing a red mantle and I visited him in this house and I saw red garments."

Ishaq ibn Yusuf al-Azraq reported that al-'Awwam ibn Hawshab said, "I saw Ibrahim at-Taymi wearing a red mantle."

'Ali ibn Muhammad reported: the reason for the imprisonment of Ibrahim at-Taymi was that al-Hajjaj sought for Ibrahim an-Nakha'i and the one who sought him came and said, 'I want Ibrahim.' Ibrahim at-Taymi said, 'I am Ibrahim.' So he took him while he knew that he meant Ibrahim an-Nakha'i and it was not lawful for him to point him out. He was brought to al-Hajjaj and he commanded that he be imprisoned in Dimas prison. He had no shade from the sun nor shelter from the cold. Every two men were chained together. Ibrahim changed and his mother came to him in prison and did not recognise him until he spoke to her. He died in prison. Al-Hajjaj dreamt that someone said, 'A man from the people of the Garden has died in this town tonight.' In the morning, he asked, 'Has anyone died in Wasit in the night?' They answered, 'Yes. Ibrahim at-Taymi died in prison.' He said, 'A dream which is one of the pricks of Shaytan,' and commanded that he be thrown on the rubbish heap."

Al-Fudayl ibn Dukayn, Muhammad ibn 'Abdullah al-Asadi and Qabisa ibn 'Uqba reported from Sufyan ath-Thawri from Abu Hayyan that Ibrahim at-Taymi said, "I did not compare my words to my actions but that I feared that I would be a liar."

Muhammad ibn 'Abdullah al-Asadi reported from Sufyan that his father said, "Ibrahim at-Taymi knew stories and he dreamt that he was distributing basil. Ibrahim an-Nakha'i heard about that and said, 'Basil has a sweet scent and bitter taste.'"

'Ubaydullah ibn Musa reported from Isra'il from Ibrahim ibn Muhajir from Ibrahim that he mentioned Ibrahim at-Taymi and said, "I reckon that he sought the Face of Allah by his stories. I wish that he had been satisfied with sufficiency so that it was neither for him nor against him."

Muhammad ibn 'Abdullah al-Asadi reported from Sufyan that Hammam said, "When Ibrahim at-Taymi related a story, his father Yazid ibn Sharik expelled him."

'Abdullah ibn 'Amr Abu Ma'mar al-Minqari reported from 'Abd al-Warith ibn Sa'id from Muhammad ibn Juhada from Sulayman that Ibrahim at-Taymi said, "My father was wearing a shirt of cotton whose sleeves reached his palms. I told him, 'Father, you should put something on.' He said, 'I went to Basra and got thousands. I did not have greater joy in it nor tell myself to go again. I wished that every wholesome morsel I ate had been in the mouth of the person I most hated. I heard Abu ad-Darda' say, 'The one with two dirhams on the Day of Rising will suffer a stronger reckoning that the one with one dirham.'"

Khaythama ibn 'Abd ar-Rahman ibn Abi Sabra

Abu Sabra's name was Yazid ibn Malik ibn 'Abdullah ibn ad-Dhu'ayb ibn Salama ibn 'Amr ibn Dhuhl ibn Nurran ibn Ju'fi ibn Sa'd al-'Ashira of Madhhij.

'Ubaydullah ibn Musa and 'Abd al-Wahhab reported from Isra'il from Hisham Abu al-Walid at-Tayalisi, Yahya ibn 'Abbad and Wahb ibn Jarir from Shu'ba all from Abu Ishaq that Khaythama said, "When my father was born, my grandfather named him 'Aziz. Then he mentioned that to the Prophet ﷺ and he said, 'His name is 'Abd ar-Rahman.'"

'Ubaydullah said in his *hadith* that he was born in Madina.

Al-Fadl ibn Dukayn reported from Yunus ibn Abi Ishaq from Abu Ishaq that Khaythama said, "My grandfather had a son born to him and named him 'Aziz. He went to the Prophet ﷺ and said, 'I have had a son.' He asked, 'What did you name him?' He replied, "Aziz.' He said, 'Rather he is 'Abd ar-Rahman.'"

Khaythama said that he was his father.

'Abd al-Wahhab ibn 'Ata' reported from 'Abdullah al-'Umari from Nafi' that Ibn 'Umar said, "The names which the Messenger of Allah ﷺ most loved were 'Abdullah and 'Abd ar-Rahman."

Al-Fadl ibn Dukayn reported from Hafs ibn Ghiyath that al-A'mash said, "Al-Musayyab had a son and Khaythama bought a gazelle and sent it to him."

Yahya ibn 'Abbad reported from Malik ibn Mighwal that Talha said, "I visited Khaythama. He was one of the people of Kufa who most admired Ibrahim and Khaythama. They stood and I stood. He said, 'And you as well.' He took my hand and kissed it and I kissed his hand. Malik said, 'Talha did it to me and I did it to him.'"

'Abdullah ibn Idris reported from Shu'ba that Nu'aym ibn Abi Hind said, "I saw Abu Wa'il at the funeral of Khaythama on a donkey saying, 'Sorrow!' or words to that effect." Khaythama related orally from Ibn 'Umar. He said that he related from Isra'il from Hakim ibn Jubayr that Khaythama ibn 'Abd ar-Rahman met thirteen of the Companions of the Prophet ﷺ, and none of them changed anything."

Tamim ibn Salama al-Khuza'i

He died in 100 AH while 'Umar ibn 'Abd al-'Aziz was caliph. Al-A'mash related from him. He was trustworthy and had *hadith*s.

'Umara ibn 'Umayr at-Taymi

One of Taymullah ibn Tha'laba. Al-A'mash related from him. He died while Sulayman ibn 'Abd al-Malik was caliph.

Al-Fadl ibn Dukayn reported from Hafs that al-A'mash said, "'Umara met a man in an expedition and said, 'I recognise you. Are you not the one who sat with us with Ibrahim?' He said, 'Yes.' He had sixty dinars with him. He opened his bag and gave him thirty dinars of it."

Abu ad-Duha Muslim ibn Subayh al-Hamdani

He died while 'Umar ibn 'Abd al-'Aziz was caliph. He related from Masruq and the companions of 'Abdullah. He was trustworthy and had many *hadith*s.

Tamim ibn Tarafa at-Ta'ifi

He died in the time of al-Hajjaj in 94 AH. He was trustworthy and had few *hadith*s.

Hakim ibn Jabir ibn Abi Tariq al-Ahmasi of Bajila

He died at the end of the rule of al-Hajjaj in the caliphate of al-Walid ibn 'Abd al-Malik. He was trustworthy and had few *hadith*s.

'Abd ar-Rahman ibn al-Aswad

'Abd ar-Rahman ibn al-Aswad ibn Yazid ibn Qays ibn 'Abdullah ibn Malik ibn 'Alqama ibn Salaman ibn Kahl ibn Bakr ibn 'Awf ibn an-Nakha'i of Madhhij.

Al-Fadl ibn Dukayn reported from al-'Ala' ibn Zuhayr al-Azdi that 'Abd ar-Rahman ibn al-Aswad said, "I used to go to visit 'A'isha without permission until the year I reached puberty. I greeted and asked permission and she recognised my voice and said, 'Enemy of his self, did you do it?' I said, 'Yes, mother.' She said, 'Enter, son.' She received me and asked me about my father and his companions and I informed her. Then I asked her about what I had been sent to ask."

'Arim ibn al-Fadl reported from Hammad ibn Zayd from as-Saq'ab ibn Zuhayr that 'Abd ar-Rahman ibn al-Aswad said, "My father sent me to 'A'isha to ask her about something in the year I reached puberty. I went to her and called to her from behind the screen. She said, 'Did you do it, boy?' I said, 'My father asks what obliges *ghusl*?' She answered, 'When the shaved parts meet.'"

Talq ibn Ghannam reported that he heard Abu Isra'il say, "When I saw 'Abd ar-Rahman ibn al-Aswad, I said, 'He is one of the *dihqan*s of the Arabs in their garments, perfume, and mounts.' He said, 'I saw him riding on a mule.'"

Al-Fadl ibn Dukayn reported that Fitr said, "'Abd ar-Rahman ibn al-Aswad came on a mule."

Al-Fadl ibn Dukayn reported that Fitr said, "I saw 'Abd ar-Rahman ibn al-Aswad wearing coarse silk."

Al-Fadl ibn Dukayn reported that Fitr said, "I saw 'Abd ar-Rahman ibn al-Aswad using henna dye."

Talq ibn Ghannam an-Nakha'i reported that Abu Ghannam ibn Talq said, "There were ties of birth between us and al-Aswad ibn Yazid in the *Jahiliyya*. 'Abd ar-Rahman ibn al-Aswad rarely went on a journey or came from a journey without coming to us to greet us to maintain that birth."

Muhammad ibn 'Abdullah al-Asadi reported from Isra'il that Sinan ibn Habib as-Sulami said, "I went out with 'Abd ar-Rahman ibn al-Aswad to the bridge and no Jew or Christian crossed over it but that he greeted him. I said to him, 'You greet these when they are the people of idolatry?' He answered, 'Peace is the mark of the Muslim. I wanted them to know that I am a Muslim.'"

Shihab ibn 'Abbad reported from Hafs that al-Hasan ibn 'Ubaydullah said, "'Abd ar-Rahman ibn al-Aswad used to lead us in the prayer on the night of *Fitr* and he soaked his feet in water when he was fasting."

Ahmad ibn 'Abdullah ibn Yunus reported from Muhammad ibn Talha from Zubayd that Abd ar-Rahman ibn al-Aswad was leading his people in twelve *tarawih* prayers in Ramadan and he prayed for himself twelve *ra'kat*s between each two *tarawih*. He recited for them a third of the Qur'an every night. He used to pray with them on the night of the *Fitr* and said, "It is a night of *'Id*."

Talq ibn Ghannam an-Nakha'i reported that he heard Malik ibn Mighwal say, "When 'Abd ar-Rahman ibn al-Aswad ibn Yazid stopped at the well of Maymun, he said, 'I am a hajji son of a hajji.'"

'Abdullah ibn Murra al-Hamdani

He died while 'Umar ibn 'Abd al-'Aziz was caliph. He was trustworthy and had sound *hadith*s.

Salim ibn Abi al-Ja'd al-Ghatafani

A *mawla* of Ghatafan.

'Ubaydullah ibn Musa and Muhammad ibn 'Abdullah al-Asadi reported that Sufyan that Mansur said, "When Salim related, he related a lot. When Ibrahim related, he was succinct. I spoke to Ibrahim, and he said that Salim used to write."

Al-Fadl ibn Dukayn reported from Qays from 'Ata' ibn as-Sa'ib that 'Alqama, al-Aswad, Ibn Nudayla and Ibn Ma'qil made an allowance for Salim ibn Abi al-Ja'd to buy the *wala'* of a *mawla* of his from 'Amr ibn Hurayth for ten thousand dirhams to help him with his worship. They said that he died in the caliphate of 'Umar ibn 'Abd al-'Aziz in 100 or 101 AH.

Abu Nu'aym said that he died before that in the caliphate of Sulayman ibn 'Abd al-Malik. He was trustworthy and had a lot of *hadith*s.

His brother, 'Ubayd ibn Abi al-Ja'd

He is also related from. He had few *hadith*s.

Their brother, 'Imran ibn Abi al-Ja'd

He is also related from.

Their brother, Ziyad ibn Abi al-Ja'd

He is also related from.

Their brother, **Muslim ibn Abi al-Ja'd**

He is also related from. They said that there were six sons of Abu al-Ja'd. Two were Shi'ites, two were Murji'ites and two held the opinion of the Kharijites. Their father used to say to them, "My sons, Allah has caused disagreement among you."

Abu al-Bakhtari at-Ta'i

His name, as mentioned by 'Ali ibn Ja'far, was Sa'id ibn Abi 'Imran. Another said that it was Sa'id ibn Jubayr. He was a *mawla* of the Banu Nabhan of Tayy'.

Sulayman Abu Dawud at-Tayalisi reported from Shu'ba that 'Amr ibn Murra said, "On the day of Jamajim, the *qurra'* wanted to put Abu al-Bakhtari in charge of them. Abu al-Bakhtari said, 'Do not do it. I am a man of the *mawali*. Put one of the Arabs in command over you.'" They said that Abu al-Bakhtari was present with 'Abd ar-Rahman ibn al-Ash'ath on the Day of Dujayl and was killed on that day in 83 AH.

'Affan ibn Muslim reported from Hammad ibn Salama from 'Ata' ibn as-Sa'ib from Abu al-Bakhtari and his companions that when one of them heard any praise of him which might bring pride in his heart, he bent his shoulders and said, "I am humble to Allah." Perhaps Hammad said, "He bent his back."

Zuhayr ibn Harb reported from 'Ali ibn Thabit from Sharik that 'Ata' ibn as-Sa'ib said, "Abu al-Bakhtari heard wailing and wept."

Muhammad ibn 'Ubayd reported that ar-Rabi' ibn Hassan said, "I saw Abu al-Bakhtari praying in a robe."

Muhammad ibn Sa'd said that Hajjaj said that Shu'ba said, "Abu al-Bakhtari did not meet 'Ali nor did he see him."

'Abdullah ibn Idris reported that Shu'ba said, "I asked al-Hakam ibn 'Utayba about Zadhan and he said, 'More.' I asked Salama ibn Kuhayl and he said, 'I prefer Abu al-Bakhtari to him.' Abu al-Bakhtari has a lot of *hadith*s and his *hadith* are *mursal* and he related from the Companions of the Messenger of Allah ﷺ but did not listen to a great Companion. Those of his *hadith*s which he heard are good. Those which say 'from' are weak."

Dharr ibn 'Abdullah

Dharr ibn 'Abdullah ibn Zurara ibn Mu'awiya ibn 'Amira ibn Munabbih ibn Ghalib ibn Waqsh ibn Qasim ibn Murhaba of Hamdan. Dharr was one of the most eloquent of people in recounting stories. He was a Murji'ite. He is Abu 'Umar ibn Dharr. He was one of those *qurra'* who went out with 'Abd ar-Rahman ibn Muhammad ibn al-Ash'ath against al-Hajjaj ibn Yusuf.

Al-Fadl ibn Dukayn reported from Abu Isra'il al-Mala'i that al-Hakam said that he heard Dharr say at Dayr al-Jamajim, "Is it only cold steel in the hand of a deluded unbeliever?"

Al-Musayyab ibn Rafi' al-Asadi

Ma'n ibn 'Isa reported from Ishaq ibn Yahya ibn Talha from al-Musayyab ibn Rafi that 'Umar ibn Hubayra called him to appoint him qadi. He said, "It would not delight me to be appointed qadi and have pillars of this mosque of yours in gold."

They said that al-Musayyab ibn Rafi' died in 105 AH.

Thabit ibn 'Ubayd al-Ansari

He met Zayd ibn Thabit and said, "I prayed behind al-Mughira ibn Shu'ba for two *rak'at*s." He was trustworthy with a lot of *hadith*s. He related from al-A'mash and others.

Abu Hazim al-Ashja'i

His name was Salman, a *mawla* of 'Azza al-Ashja'iyya. He related from Abu Hurayra and died in the caliphate of 'Umar ibn 'Abd al-'Aziz. He was trustworthy and had sound *hadith*s.

Murayy ibn Qatari

He related from 'Adi ibn Hatim.

Malik ibn al-Harith as-Salami

He was trustworthy and sound *hadith*s. Al-A'mash related from him.

Yahya ibn al-Jazzar

He was a *mawla* of Bajila.

Yahya ibn Sa'id al-Qattan reported from Shu'ba that al-Hakam said, "Yahya ibn al-Jazzar was a Shi'ite. He was excessive in his position." They said that he was trustworthy and had *hadith*s.

Al-Hasan al-'Urani of Bajila

They said that he was trustworthy and had *hadith*s.

Qabisa ibn Hulb

Qabisa ibn Hulb ibn Yazid ibn 'Adi ibn Qunafa ibn 'Adi ibn 'Abd Shams ibn 'Adi ibn Akhzam. He related from his father. His father came to the Prophet 鷺 and listened to him.

Abu Malik al-Ghifari

He was the author of the *tafsir*. He had few *hadith*s.

Abu Sadiq al-Azdi

His name is 'Abdullah ibn Najidh. It is said that his name was Muslim ibn Yazid of Azd Shanu'a.

Al-Fadl ibn Dukayn reported that Abu Salama as-Sa'igh said, "I saw that Abu Sadiq had a white beard."

Muslim ibn Ibrahim reported that Abu Bakr ibn Shu'ayb ibn al-Habhab said, "I saw Abu Sadiq with a white beard and hair."

Muslim ibn Ibrahim reported that Abu Bakr ibn Shu'ayb said, "I saw Abu Sadiq praying in breaches and a thick soft garment."

Abu Mu'awiya ad-Darir reported that al-A'mash said, "I saw Abu Sadiq going out and I saw him wearing breaches."

Muslim ibn Ibrahim reported from Mahdi ibn Maymun that Shu'ayb ibn al-Habhab said, "Abu Sadiq did not do voluntary fasting for a single day nor did he pray any *rak'at* except the obligatory either before it or after it. He was a marvel in scrupulousness." He had few *hadith*s and they used to say things about him.

Abu Salih

His name is Badham, the *mawla* of Umm Hani bint Abi Talib. He is the one with a *tafsir* which he related from Ibn 'Abbas which was then related from Abu Salih by Abu Salih al-Kalbi, Muhammad ibn as-Sa'ib. Simak ibn Harb and Isma'il ibn Abi Khalid also related from Abu Salih.

Al-Fadl ibn Dukayn reported from Abu Bakr ibn 'Ayyash that 'Asim said, "Abu Salih had a large beard and used his fingers to penetrate it."

Yazid ibn al-Bara'

Yazid ibn al-Bara' ibn 'Azib ibn al-Harith al-Ansari of the Banu Haritha of Aws. He related from his father and Adi ibn Thabit related from him.

Suwayd ibn al-Bara' ibn 'Azib

He related from his father and he was governor of 'Uman. He was like one of the best of governors.

Musa ibn 'Abdullah

Musa ibn 'Abdullah ibn Yazid ibn Zayd al-Khatmi of the Ansar from Aws. His mother was the daughter of Hudhayfa ibn al-Yaman.

Ibrahim ibn Jarir ibn 'Abdullah al-Bajali

'Abd al-Malik ibn 'Umayr related from him.

Ahmad ibn Muhammad ibn al-Walid al-Azraqi reported that 'Amr ibn Yahya ibn Sa'id ibn 'Amr ibn Sa'id ibn al-'As said, "I saw Ibrahim and Aban, the sons of Jarir ibn 'Abdullah, and my grandfather dyeing using henna and *katm*." He lived long and was born after the death of Jarir and remained until Sharik and Asad ibn 'Amr met him.

Abu Zur'a ibn 'Amr

Abu Zur'a ibn 'Amr ibn Jarir ibn 'Abdullah al-Bajali. He related from his grandfather and from Abu Hurayra.

Hilal ibn Yasaf al-Ashja'i

Yahya ibn 'Isa ar-Ramli reported from Sufyan that 'Amr ibn Murra said, "The *kunya* of Hilal ibn Yasaf was Abu al-Hasan. He was trustworthy and had a lot of *hadith*s.

Sa'd ibn 'Ubayda as-Sulami

Al-A'mash and Husayn related from him. He died while 'Umar ibn Hubayra was governor of Kufa. He was trustworthy and had a lot of *hadith*s.

Muhammad ibn 'Abd ar-Rahman ibn Yazid an-Nakha'i

He was the nephew of al-Aswad ibn Yazid an-Nakha'i.

He said: "I heard Husayn ibn 'Ali al-Ju'fi say that Muhammad ibn 'Abd ar-Rahman ibn Yazid had the *kunya* Abu Ja'far. He was called 'the astute' because of his fineness in worship."

Muhammad ibn al-Fudayl reported from Ghazwan that his father said, "That was mentioned to Muhammad ibn 'Abd ar-Rahman ibn Yazid al-Mardi, who was called al-Kayyis (the astute) and was also called ar-Rafiq (fine)."

'Ali ibn 'Abdullah ibn Ja'far reported from Sufyan that Malik said, "Muhammad ibn 'Abd ar-Rahman ibn Yazid has a righteous wife and she only saw him making supplication for her."

Sufyan said that he was called ar-Rafiq. He had few *hadith*s.

'Abd ar-Rahman ibn Abi Nu'm al-Bajali

His *kunya* was Abu al-Hakam. He was the one who assumed *ihram* from one year to the next. He was trustworthy and had *hadith*s.

Abu as-Safar Sa'id ibn Yuhmid ath-Thawri of Hamdan

He died while Khalid ibn 'Abdullah al-Qasri was governor of Kufa. He was trustworthy and had few *hadith*s.

'Abdullah al-Bahi

Waki' reported from Sufyan from as-Suddi from al-Bahi, a *mawla* of az-Zubayr, who said that he was trustworthy and was known and had few *hadith*s.

Abu al-Waddak

His name was Jabr ibn Nawf ibn Rabi'a al-Hamdani. He had few *hadith*s.

Yahya ibn Waththab

A *mawla* of the Banu Kahl of the Banu Asad ibn Khuzayma.

Yahya ibn Adam reported from Abu Bakr ibn 'Ayyash that 'Asim said, "Yahya ibn Adam learned from Waththab from 'Ubayd ibn Nudayla *ayat* by *ayat*, and, by Allah, he was a reciter."

Waki' said that al-A'mash said, "When Yahya ibn Waththab was in the prayer it was as if he was speaking directly to a man."

'Ubaydullah ibn Musa reported that al-A'mash said, "I saw Yahya ibn Waththab praying in a fur coat." He said that Yahya ibn Waththab died in Kufa in 103 AH in the caliphate of Yazid ibn 'Abd al-Malik. He was trustworthy and had few *hadith*s, and knew the Qur'an.

Abu Hilal 'Umayr ibn Qumaym ibn Yaram at-Taghlibi

He was known with few *hadith*s.

At-Tamimi

Abu Ishaq as-Subay'i related from him.

Muhammad ibn 'Abdullah al-Asadi said, "I asked Isra'il about the name of at-Tamimi and he said, 'Arbad.'"

Jirwa ibn Humayl ibn Malik at-Ta'i

He had few *hadith*s.

Ad-Dahhak ibn Muzahim al-Hilali

His *kunya* was Abu al-Qasim.

Qabisa ibn 'Uqba reported from Juwaybir that ad-Dahhak said, "My mother bore me in two years, (i.e. the pregnancy was two years.)" Yazid said that Juwaybir reported that ad-Dahhak said that a woman can be pregnant for two years.

'Abd al-Malik ibn 'Amr Abu 'Amm al-'Aqadi and al-Fadl ibn Dukayn reported from Qurra ibn Khalid who said, "The ring of ad-

Dahhak was silver in which was the like of crystal. Engraved on it was the form of a bird."

Al-Fadl ibn Dukayn reported that Bashir ibn Salman said, "I was in the squadron of ad-Dahhak ibn Muzahim."

Al-Fadl ibn Dukayn reported that Sufyan said, "Ad-Dahhak taught and did not take anything for it."

Al-Qasim ibn Malik al-Muzani reported that a man said, "I saw ad-Dahhak wearing a hat of fox-fur."

Abu Dawud reported from Shu'ba that Mushash said, "I asked ad-Dahhak if he had met Ibn 'Abbas and he answered, 'No.'"

Abu Dawud al-Hafri reported from Shu'ba that 'Abd al-Malik ibn Maysara said, "Ad-Dahhak did not meet Ibn 'Abbas. He met Sa'id ibn Jubayr in Rayy and took the *tafsir* from him."

Qabida ibn 'Uqba reported from Sufyan from a man that ad-Dahhak said, "I met my companions and they only learned scrupulousness."

Muslim ibn Ibrahim al-Azdi reported from Salama ibn 'Abdullah ibn Fadala Abu 'Amira az-Zahrawi from Muhammad ibn Bakr ar-Rahabi from a man of Kufa that the brother of ad-Dahhak ibn Muzahim said, "When ad-Dahhak was dying, he sent for me and said, 'I only think that death will come to me before morning. When I die, I should not find you announcing, 'Ad-Dahhak has died. Ad-Dahhak has died.' Whoever hears the call has come. Use your hand to wash me. Put a lot of perfume on the points of prostration and shroud me in white shrouds of medium quality. Beware of what people have innovated in graves. Bury me in a *lahd*. When the men carry me on their shoulders. Do not walk with me as in a bridal procession, but walk with a medium gait, less than a trot and more than a walk. If you find bricks, then use them. Otherwise use the wood from the earth. When you place me in my *lahd*, level the bricks over me and raise a brick at the head of your brother. Then look at where he lies and then end your business. When you have buried me, and the hands of the men are free of me, stand at the head of my grave and face the *qibla*. Then call with three voices which your companions can hear: 'O Allah, You have set ad-Dahhak in his grave to ask him about his Lord, his *deen* and his Prophet ﷺ. Make him firm in the firm speech in this life and in the Next World.' Then depart.'"

Ahmad ibn 'Abdullah ibn Yunus reported that he heard Abu Bakr ibn 'Ayyash relate that al-Ajlah said, "Ad-Dahhak ibn Muzahim said to me, 'Act before you are unable to act.'"

Al-Ajlah said, "Is it this?" He answered, "I want to act today and cannot."

Al-Fadl ibn Dukayn reported from 'Ubayd ibn Tufayl that ad-Dahhak said when he was dying to his brother, "No one but you should pray over me. Do not allow the governor to pray over me. Mention what you know of me."

They said, "Ad-Dahhak went to Khurasan and stayed there and they listened to him." He died in 105 AH.

Al-Qasim ibn Mukhaymira al-Hamdani

Shihab ibn 'Abbad reported from Ibrahim ibn Humayd ar-Rawwasi that al-Qasim ibn Mukhaymira was a *mu'adhdhin* or a teacher.

Hajjaj ibn Muhammad reported from Muhammad ibn 'Abdullah ash-Shu'aythi from al-Qasim ibn Mukhaymira that he used to pray for death. When he was dying, he said to his *umm walad*, "I used to pray for death but when it comes to me, I dislike it!" They said that al-Qasim ibn Mukhaymira died while 'Umar ibn 'Abd al-'Aziz was caliph. He was trustworthy and had *hadith*s.

Al-Qasim ibn 'Abd ar-Rahman

Al-Qasim ibn 'Abd ar-Rahman ibn 'Abdullah ibn Mas'ud al-Hudhali. He was appointed qadi in Kufa.

Al-Fadl ibn Dukayn reported that Abu Isra'il said, "I saw al-Qasim ibn 'Abd ar-Rahman giving judgement at his door."

'Abdullah ibn Numayr reported that al-A'mash said, "I used to sit with al-Qasim ibn 'Abd ar-Rahman when he was the qadi."

Hajjaj ibn Muhammad reported from al-Mas'udi that al-Qasim used to dislike taking something for four things: for reciting the Qur'an, giving *adhan*, acting as qadi, and distributing.

Sa'id ibn Mansur reported from Sufyan from Mis'ar that Muharib ibn Dithar said, "We accompanied al-Qasim ibn 'Abd ar-Rahman on a journey and he dominated us in three things: long silence, many prayers and generosity."

Al-Fadl ibn Dukayn reported that Fitr said, "I saw al-Qasim ibn 'Abd ar-Rahman dyeing his hair with henna." He said that al-Qasim died in Kufa while Khalid ibn 'Abdullah al-Qasri was governor.

Ma'n ibn 'Abd ar-Rahman

He was younger than al-Qasim. He related *hadith*s from him. He was trustworthy and had few *hadith*s.

'Atiyya ibn Sa'd ibn Junada al-'Awfi

One of Jadila Qays. His *kunya* was Abu al-Hasan.

Yazid ibn Harun reported from Fudayl that 'Atiyya said, "When I was born, my father brought me to 'Ali and informed him, he allotted for me in the hundred. Then my father was given my stipend he brought ghee and honey with it."

Sa'd ibn Muhammad ibn al-Hasan ibn 'Atiyya said, "Sa'd ibn Junada came to 'Ali ibn Abi Talib when he was in Kufa and said, 'Amir al-Mu'minin, I have had a son, so name him.' 'Ali said, 'This is a gift (*'atiyya*) of Allah.' So he was named 'Atiyya. His mother was a Greek *umm walad*. 'Atiyya rebelled against al-Hajjaj with Ibn al-Ash'ath. When the army of Ibn al-Ash'ath was defeated, 'Atiyya fled to Persia. Al-Hajjaj wrote to Muhammad ibn al-Qasim ath-Thaqafi to summon 'Atiyya to curse 'Ali ibn Abi Talib. If he did not, then he was to inflict forty lashes on him and shave his head and beard. He summoned him and read the letter of al-Hajjaj to him. 'Atiyya refused to do it. He dealt him forty lashes and shaved his head and beard. When Qutayba was appointed over Khurasan, 'Atiyya went to him. He did not stay in Khurasan until 'Umar ibn Hubayra was appointed over Iraq. 'Atiyya wrote to him to ask him for permission to come and he gave him permission. He went to Kufa and stayed there until he died in 111." He was trustworthy, Allah willing, and had sound *hadith*s. Some people did not think that he was authoritative.

Yazid ibn Suhayb al-Faqir

His *kunya* was Abu 'Uthman. He was one of the people of Kufa and then he moved to Makka and settled there. He listened to Jabir ibn 'Abdullah. Mis'ar, and al-Mas'udi, and the Kufans related from him.

Ziyad ibn Abi Maryam

He is related from.

'Abdullah ibn al-Harith ash-Shaybani

Al-Minhal ibn 'Amr related from him.

Al-Fadl ibn Dukayn reported that Sufyan said that 'Abdullah ibn al-Harith was a teacher and did not take any wage.

Abu Bakr ibn 'Amr ibn 'Uqba

Al-Mas'udi related from him.

Muhammad ibn al-Muntashar ibn al-Ajda'

He is 'Abd ar-Rahman ibn Malik ibn Umayya ibn 'Abdullah ibn Sulayman ibn Ma'mar ibn al-Harith ibn Sa'd ibn 'Abdullah ibn Wada'a of Hamdan. He was the nephew of Masruq ibn al-Ajda'. He related from his uncle.

Muhammad ibn 'Abdullah al-Ansari reported from al-Muthanna ibn Sa'id that Muhammad ibn al-Muntashar was the deputy of 'Abd al-Hamid ibn 'Abd ar-Rahman ibn Zayd ibn al-Khattab over Wasit. He was trustworthy and had few *hadith*s.

His brother, al-Mughira ibn al-Muntashir ibn al-Ajda'

He is related from.

Sulayman ibn Maysara al-Ahmasi

Al-A'mash related from him.

Sulayman ibn Mushar

Al-A'mash related from him.

Nu'aym ibn Abi Hind al-Ashja'i

He died while Khalid ibn 'Abdullah al-Qasri was governor of Kufa. He was trustworthy and had *hadith*s.

Third Generation

Muharib ibn Daththar

One of the Banu Sadus ibn Shayban ibn Dhuhl ibn Tha'laba ibn 'Ukaba ibn Sa'b ibn 'Ali ibn Bakr ibn Wa'il. His *kunya* was Abu Mutarrif. He was appointed qadi of Kufa. It is related that he said, "I wept and my dependants wept. When I was dismissed as qadi, I wept and my dependants wept."

Sufyan ibn 'Uyayna said, "I saw him." Sufyan was asked, "Where did you see him?" He replied, "In a corner giving judgement. When those (the Banu Hashim) came, Muhammad ibn 'Abd ar-Rahman ibn Abi Layla sat with the companions of Muharib and spoke. Muharib died while Khalid ibn 'Abdullah al-Qasri was governor of Kufa in the caliphate of Hisham ibn 'Abd al-Malik. He had *hadiths* but they did not consider him to be authoritative. He was one of the first Murji'ites who expressed hope for both 'Ali and 'Uthman and did not testify to faith or disbelief."

Al-'Ayzar ibn Hurayth al-'Abdi

Al-Fadl ibn Dukayn reported that 'Uqba ibn Abi Hafsa said, "Al-'Ayzar ibn Hurayth was an *'arif*."

Muslim ibn Abi 'Imran al-Batin

Al-Fadl ibn Dukayn reported from Qays that Hajjaj said, "I saw Muslim al-Batin had a Samangan rug made of foxes and he prayed while on it."

Talha ibn Musarrif

Talha ibn Musarrif ibn 'Amr ibn Ka'b ibn Juhdub ibn Mu'awiya ibn Sa'd ibn al-Harith ibn Dhuhl ibn Salama ibn Dadawl ibn Jusham ibn Yam of Hamdan. His *kunya* was Abu 'Abdullah. He was the reciter of the people of Kufa. They recited the Qur'an to him. When he saw that they were too much for him and it seemed as if he disliked that for himself, he went to al-A'mash and recited to him. So people inclined to al-A'mash and left Talha.

'Ali ibn 'Abdullah ibn Ja'far reported that Sufyan said, "I asked Ibn Abjur, 'Who is the best of those you have seen?' He was silent for a time and then said, 'May Allah have mercy on Talha.'"

Talq ibn Ghannam an-Nakha'i reported from Malik ibn Mighwal that Talha said, "He and I went to an alley and he went before me in it. Then he turned to me and said, 'If I knew that you were older than me by a hour (or a day), I would not have gone in front of you.'"

'Ali ibn 'Abdullah ibn Ja'far reported that he asked Sufyan, "Who is older: Talha or Zubayd?" He answered, "How close they are!" Then he said, "Talha offered his daughter to Zubayd and Zubayd said, 'What will stop me from seeking that from you except that I do not know whether that will agree with me or not?'"

Al-Fadl ibn Dukayn reported from Malik that Talha said, "I went to Khaythama to visit him with a group (or 'with some people') when he was ill. When they got up, I went to stand and he said, 'And you?' He took my hand and kissed it and I kissed his hand."

Malik said, "I visited Talha and he did it to me and I did it to him."

Al-Fadl ibn Dukayn reported that Musa ibn Qays said, "The Yamis wake their children on the night of the 27th." He meant Talha and Zubayd, during the month of Ramadan.

Ahmad ibn 'Abdullah ibn Yunus reported from Abu Shihab that al-Hasan ibn 'Amr said, "Talha ibn Musarrif said, 'If it were not that I am in *wudu'*, I would tell you what the Shi'ites say.'" They said, "Talha went out with the *qurra'* from the people of Kufa who left for al-Jamajim in the time of al-Hajjaj." He died after that in 112 AH.

Yahya ibn Abu Bukayr reported that he heard Shu'ba say, "I was at the funeral of Talha and Abu Mash'ar Ziyad ibn Kulayb praised him: 'There is no one like him left." He was trustworthy and had sound *hadith*s.

Zubayd ibn al-Harith

Zubayd ibn al-Harith ibn 'Abd al-Karim ibn Juhdub ibn Dhuhl ibn Malik ibn al-Harith ibn Dhuhl ibn Salama ibn Dadwal ibn Jushum ibn Yam of Hamdan. His *kunya* was Abu 'Abdullah.

Muhammad ibn 'Abdullah al-Asadi reported from Sufyan that Husayn said, "Zubayd went to Ibrahim wearing a burnous. He said, 'This is not the time of burnouses.'"

Yahya ibn Bukayr reported from Nu'aym ibn Maysara that Sa'id ibn Jubayr said, "If I had been given a choice to be in someone's skin, I would have chosen Zubayd al-Yami."

Abu Nuh Qurad reported that he heard Shu'ba say, "I did not see a shaykh in Kufa who was better than Zubayd."

Shu'ba said, "I was with him one day sitting in a mosque and a woman passed by who had a ball of cotton with her. The ball dropped and she was not aware of it but Zubayd was. He stood up and left me sitting and hurried after her until he caught up to her and gave her the ball and then returned to me."

Al-Fadl ibn Dukayn and Muhammad ibn 'Umar reported that Zubayd died in 122 AH in the time of Zayd ibn 'Ali. He was trustworthy and had *hadith*s.

Shamir ibn 'Atiyya ibn 'Abd ar-Rahman al-Asadi

One of the Banu Murra ibn al-Harith ibn Sa'd ibn Tha'laba. He was trustworthy and had sound *hadith*s.

Bakr ibn Ma'iz ath-Thawri

He had few *hadith*s.

Abu Ya'la Mundhir ath-Thawri

He was trustworthy and had few *hadith*s.

'Abd ar-Rahman ibn Sa'id ibn Wahb al-Hamdani

He had few *hadith*s.

Abu Hubayra

His name was Yahya ibn 'Abbad al-Ansari. He died while Yusuf ibn 'Umar was governor. He had few *hadith*s.

Bukayr ibn al-Akhnas

He had few *hadith*s.

'Ali ibn Mudrik an-Nakha'i

Talq ibn Ghannam reported that Bakkar ibn 'Abdullah al-Qurashi said, "'Ali ibn Mudrik an-Nakha'i died when Yusuf ibn 'Umar came to Iraq in 120 at the end of the caliphate of Hisham ibn 'Abd al-Malik."

Khalid ibn 'Abdullah and Yusuf ibn 'Umar both minted dirhams in that year. He had few *hadith*s and Shu'ba related from him.

'Ali ibn al-Aqmar

'Ali ibn al-Aqmar ibn 'Amr ibn al-Harith ibn Mu'awiya ibn 'Amr ibn al-Harith ibn Rabi'a ibn 'Abdullah ibn Wada'a of Hamdan. There is also his brother, Kulthum ibn al-Aqmar al-Wada'i of Hamdan.

Jabala ibn Suhaym ash-Shaybani

He died in the civil war of al-Walid ibn Yazid.

Wabara ibn 'Abd ar-Rahman al-Musli of Madhhij

He died while Khalid ibn 'Abdullah was governor of Kufa for Hisham ibn 'Abd al-Malik.

Abu az-Zanba'

His name was Sadaqa ibn Salih.

Abu 'Awn ath-Thaqafi

His name was Muhammad ibn 'Ubaydullah. He died while Khalid ibn 'Abdullah al-Qasri was governor. He was trustworthy and had *hadith*s. Sufyan and Shu'ba related from him.

'Abd al-Jabbar ibn Wa'il ibn Hujr al-Hadrami

He was trustworthy, Allah willing, with few *hadith*s. They spoke about his transmission from his father and they said that he did not meet him.

His brother, 'Alqama ibn Wa'il

He was trustworthy and had few *hadith*s.

Yahya ibn 'Ubayd al-Bahrani

His *kunya* was Abu 'Umar.

'Awn ibn 'Abdullah ibn 'Utba ibn Mas'ud al-Hudhali

When 'Umar ibn 'Abd al-'Aziz became caliph, 'Awn ibn 'Abdullah, Abu as-Sabbah Musa ibn Abi Kathir and 'Umar ibn Hamza travelled to him and spoke to him about *irja'* and debated with him and claimed that he agreed with them and did not disagree with them about any of it. He was trustworthy and had a lot of *mursal* transmissions.

'Abdullah ibn Abi al-Mujalid

A *mawla* of Azd. He is the son-in-law of Mujahid.

Abu Ishaq as-Subay'i

His name was 'Amr ibn 'Abdullah ibn 'Ali ibn Ahmad ibn Dhi Yahmad ibn as-Subay' ibn Sabu' ibn Sa'b ibn Mu'awiya ibn Kathir ibn Malik ibn Jusham ibn Hashid ibn Jusham ibn Khayran ibn Nawf of Hamdan.

Al-Hasan ibn Musa reported from Zuhayr that Abu Ishaq said, "My grandfather al-Khiyar went to 'Uthman who asked, 'How many of your dependants are with you, shaykh?' He said, 'I have with me,' and he mentioned them. He said, 'As for you, shaykh, we have allotted you fifteen (i.e. fifteen hundred dirhams) and one hundred thousand dirhams for your dependants."

Al-Aswad ibn 'Amir said that Sharik said, "Abu Ishaq as-Subay'i was born in 'Uthman's rule. I reckon that Sharik said that it was three years before the end."

Sufyan said, "Our shaykhs said, 'Ash-Sha'bi and Abu Ishaq met and ash-Sha'bi said to him, "You are better than me, Abu Ishaq." He said, "No, by Allah, I am not better than you. You are better than me and older than me.""'

Ahmad ibn 'Abdullah ibn Yunus reported from Zuhayr that Abu Ishaq related that he prayed *Jumu'a* behind 'Ali. He said, "He prayed it at midday after the sun had declined and he saw him standing with a white beard and bald."

Al-Fadl ibn Dukayn reported from Yunus ibn Abi Ishaq that Abu Ishaq said, "I saw 'Ali. My father said to me, 'Get up, 'Amr, and look at the Amir al-Mu'minin.' I looked at him and saw that he dyed his beard and it was a thick beard."

Rawh ibn 'Ubada reported that Shu'ba said, "I heard Abu Ishaq said, 'We were in Khurasan in the time of Mu'awiya and did not gather.'"

Hajjaj said that Shu'ba said, "Abu Ishaq was older than Abu al-Bakhtari at-Ta'i."

Al-Hasan ibn Musa reported that Zuhayr said, "I saw Abu Ishaq when he was leading us in the prayer taking his cap from the ground or taking it from his head and putting it on the ground."

Ahmad ibn 'Abdullah ibn Yunus reported that he heard Abu Bakr ibn 'Ayyash saying, "Abu Ishaq died when he was a hundred or a year short of that."

Abu Nu'aym reported: "Abu Ishaq reached ninety-eight or ninety-nine and died in 128."

Yahya ibn Sa'id al-Qattan said: Abu Ishaq died on the day that ad-Dahhak entered Kufa in 129."

Musa ibn Dawud said that he heard Sufyan ath-Thawri say in 158 AH, "I am sixty-one and Abu Ishaq as-Subay'i died thirty years ago. Perhaps I heard Abu Ishaq say, 'Sila related to us for sixty years.'"

'Amr ibn Murra al-Jamali of Murad

Murad is part of Madhhij.

Abu Nuh Qurad reported from Shu'ba: "I did not see 'Amr ibn Murra in a prayer but that I thought that he did not leave until he was answered."

Muhammad ibn 'Umar said that he heard Sufyan ath-Thawri say, "'Amr ibn Murra died in 118."

Al-Fadl ibn Dukayn reported: "'Amr ibn Murra died in 110."

Muhammad ibn 'Abdullah ibn Numayr reported from Ahmad ibn Bashir that Mis'ar said: "I heard 'Abd al-Malik ibn Maysara in the funeral of 'Amr ibn Murra say, 'I reckon that he is the best of men.'"

'Abd al-Malik ibn 'Umayr al-Lakhmi

His *kunya* was Abu 'Umar. He was an ally of the Banu 'Adi ibn Ka'b of Quraysh.

Khalaf ibn Tamim reported: "I asked Isma'il ibn Ibrahim ibn Muhajir about the birth of 'Abd al-Malik ibn 'Umayr and he said, 'You asked me about it and he told me that he was born when there were three years left of 'Uthman's rule.'"

Sufyan ibn 'Uyayna said, "They are the great of the people of Kufa at that time. This one was a hundred and that one was a hundred (i.e. 'Abd al-Malik ibn 'Umayr and Ziyad ibn 'Ilaqa.)"

Sufyan said that he heard 'Abd al-Malik ibn 'Umayr say, "By Allah, I relate a *hadith* and I do not omit a letter of it."

Ahmad ibn 'Abdullah ibn Yunus reported from Abu Bakr ibn 'Ayyash: "Abu Ishaq said to us, 'Ask 'Abd al-Malik ibn 'Umayr and Simak ibn Harb. Simak did not have all of that. He had *hadith*s.'" They said that 'Abd al-Malik ibn 'Umayr was appointed qadi in Kufa before ash-Sha'bi. His title was al-Qitbi. He died in Kufa in Dhu al-Hijja 136 AH.

Al-Haytham ibn 'Adi said, "I went behind in his funeral."

It was related to me that Hafs ibn Ghiyath said, "I saw 'Abd al-Malik ibn 'Umayr as an old man sitting on a chair and oiled from his crown to his foot."

Ziyad ibn 'Ilaqa ath-Tha'labi of Ghatafan

His *kunya* was Abu Malik.

Salama ibn Kuhayl al-Hadrami

He died in 122 AH when Zayd ibn 'Ali was killed in Kufa.

Abu Nu'aym said that Zayd was killed on 'Ashura' of this year. Salama had a lot of *hadith*s.

Maysara ibn Habib an-Nahdi

Sufyan ath-Thawri related from him.

Qays ibn Muslim al-Jadali of Jadila Qays

Waki' reported from Sufyan that Qays ibn Muslim Abi 'Amr al-Jadhali said, "I heard Abu Nu'aym al-Fadl ibn Dukayn say, 'Qays ibn Muslim died in 120 in Kufa.'" He was trustworthy and was firm and had righteous *hadith*s.

Nusayr ibn Dhu'luq

His *kunya* was Abu Tu'ma ath-Thawri.

Jawwab ibn 'Ubaydullah at-Taymi, Taym ar-Ribab

Sufyan said that Khalaf said, "Jawwab used to tremble in remembrance. Ibrahim an-Nakha'i said to him, 'If you own it I do not care if it prepares me. If you do not own it, you differ from the one who is better than you.'"

Isma'il ibn Raja' az-Zubaydi

Al-A'mash related from him.

Muhammad ibn al-Fadl said from al-A'mash that Isma'il ibn Raja' gathered children and related to them so that they would not forget his *hadith*s.

Jami' ibn Shaddad al-Muharibi

His *kunya* was Abu Sakhra.

Talq ibn Ghannam an-Nakha'i reported: I heard Qays ibn ar-Rabi' say, "Jami' ibn Shaddad died on the last Friday night of Ramadan 118."

Ma'bad ibn Khalid al-Jadali

Talq ibn Ghannam an-Nakha'i reported that Muhammad ibn 'Umar al-Asadi said that Ma'bad died in 118 AH while Khalid ibn 'Abdullah al-Qasri was governor.

Wasil ibn Hayyan al-Ahdab al-Asadi

One of the Banu Sa'd ibn al-Harith ibn Tha'laba ibn Dudan. His mother was one of the children of Abu Sammal the poet.

Al-Fadl ibn Dukayn reported that Wasil died in Kufa in 120 AH.

'Abd al-Malik ibn Maysara az-Zarrad

He was a *mawla* of the Banu Hilal ibn 'Amir.

He said that he heard Waki' ibn Jarrah mention 'Abd al-Malik ibn Maysara and said, "That is az-Zarrad." He was trustworthy and had a lot of *hadith*s.

He died while Khalid ibn 'Abdullah al-Qasri was governor of Kufa.

Ash'ath ibn Abi ash-Sha'tha' al-Muharibi

The name of ash-Sha'tha' was Sulaym ibn al-Aswad. He died while Yusuf ibn 'Umar was governor of Kufa.

Khalifa ibn al-Husayn ibn Qays ibn 'Asim al-Minqari

He related from his father that his grandfather became Muslim in the time of the Prophet 襟. The Messenger of Allah 襟 commanded him to have a *ghusl* with water and lote-leaves.

Habib ibn Abi Thabit al-Asadi

He was a *mawla* of the Banu Kahil. His *kunya* was Abi Yahya. The name of Abu Thabit was Qays ibn Dinar.

Abu Hudhayfa Musa ibn Mas'ud reported from Sufyan that Habib ibn Abi Thabit said, "I sought knowledge and I did not have an intention. Then Allah provided the intention."

Ahmad ibn 'Abdullah ibn Yunus reported from Abu Shihab from al-Hasan ibn 'Amr that Habib ibn Abi Thabit said, "I have no letter on the earth except one *hadith* in my box."

Ahmad ibn 'Abdullah ibn Yunus reported that Abu Bakr ibn 'Ayyash said, "I heard Habib ibn Abi Thabit say, 'I am seventy-three.'"

Abu Bakr ibn 'Ayyash said, "There were only three and no more in Kufa: Habib ibn Abi Thabit, al-Hakam ibn 'Utayba and Hammad ibn Abi Sulayman. Those three are the people of *fatwa* and they are famous. There was no one in Kufa who did not humble himself to Habib."

Al-Fadl ibn Dukayn and Muhammad ibn 'Umar reported that Habib ibn Abi Thabit died in 119 AH.

He said, "It was related to me that Hafs ibn Ghiyath said, 'I saw Habib ibn Abi Thabit: a tall one-eyed man.'"

'Asim ibn Abi an-Najud al-Asadi

He is 'Asim ibn Bahdala, a *mawla* of the Banu Jadhima ibn Malik ibn Nasr ibn Qu'ayn ibn Asad.

Al-Fadl ibn Dukayn reported from Abu al-Ahwas that 'Asim ibn Abi an-Najud had the *kunya* Abu Bakr.

'Affan ibn Muslim reported from Hammad ibn Salama that 'Asim said, "I never came to Abu Wa'il from a journey at all but that he kissed my hand."

Musa ibn Isma'il reported from Aban ibn Yazid al-'Attar from 'Asim that Abu Wa'il used to withdraw to the countryside. When he came, he met 'Asim, took his hand and he kissed it. They said that 'Asim was trustworthy but that there were a lot of errors in his *hadith*s.

Abu Hasin

His name was 'Uthman ibn 'Asim ibn Hasin. He was from the Banu Jusham ibn al-Harith ibn Sa'd ibn Tha'laba ibn Dudan ibn Asad ibn Khuzayma and their number in the Banu Kabir ibn Zad ibn Murra ibn al-Harith ibn Sa'd.

Sufyan ibn 'Uyayna said that ash-Shaybani said, "I entered the mosque with ash-Sha'bi and he said, 'Look and see who among our companions we sit with. Do you see Abu Hasin?'"

Sufyan said from a man of the people of Kufa, "''Amir was asked when he was dying, 'Who do you command us?' He said, 'I do not know and I have not left a scholar. Abu Hasin is a righteous man.'"

Sufyan said that Mis'ar said that Abu Hasin said, "''Abdullah ibn Ma'qil met me and said, 'Commerce distracted you.' I answered, 'Power distracted you.'"

Sufyan said, "Someone appointed him and sent to him two thousand dirhams which he refused."

Sufyan said, "I said, 'Abu Hasin, why did you refuse them?' He replied, 'Out of modesty and nobility.'"

Sufyan said, "Abu Ishaq said to me, 'He died with us (meaning Abu Hasin).' A man got up and said, 'Who is this? This is a gooddoer. By Allah, no one is capable of his prayer!'"

Muhammad ibn 'Umar said that Abu Hasin died in 128 AH.

Abu Juwayriya al-Jarmi

His name was Hittan ibn Khufaf.

Abu Qays al-Awdi

His name was 'Abd ar-Rahman ibn Tharwan.
Al-Fadl ibn Dukayn reported that Abu Qays died in 120 AH.

Isma'il ibn 'Abd ar-Rahman as-Suddi

He is the author of the *tafsir*. He died in 127 AH.

Abu al-Muhajjal

His name was Rudayni ibn Murra.

Husayn ibn 'Abd ar-Rahman an-Nakha'i

Talq ibn Ghannam an-Nakha'i reported that he heard Hafs ibn Ghiyath say, "Malik ibn Mighwal mentioned the excellence of Talha ibn Musarrif. A man asked him, 'Have you seen Husayn ibn 'Abd ar-Rahman an-Nakha'i?' 'No,' he replied. He said, 'If you had seen him, you would not have mentioned Talha,' i.e. due to his excellence."

Talq ibn Ghannam reported that he said that he heard Hafs ibn Ghiyath say, "In the daytime in the winter Husayn ibn 'Abd ar-Rahman an-Nakha'i wore a robe, edged with eighty veils, and a blanket at night."

Abu Sakhra

His name was Jami' ibn Shaddad al-Muharibi. He died in 127 AH. Abu Nu'aym said it was in 118 AH.

Abu as-Sawda' an-Nahdi

His name is 'Amr ibn 'Imran.

'Uthman ibn al-Mughira ath-Thaqafi

His *kunya* was Abu al-Mughira. He is also called 'Uthman al-A'sha and 'Uthman ibn Abi Zur'a.

Ar-Rukayn ibn ar-Rabi' ibn 'Umayla al-Fazari

He saw Asma' bint Abi Bakr as-Siddiq. He died in the civil war of al-Walid ibn Yazid ibn 'Abd al-Malik.

Abu az-Za'ra'

His name was 'Amr ibn 'Amr ibn 'Awf al-Jushami. He was the nephew of Abu al-Ahwas from whom 'Abdullah ibn Mas'ud related.

Hilal al-Wazzan al-Juhani

His *kunya* was Abu Umayya. He is Hilal as-Sarraf. He was the nephew of Abu Humayd who is Ibn Miqlas.

Al-Mu'alla ibn Asad and Abu Hisham al-Makhzumi reported from Abu 'Awana that Hilal ibn Abi Humayd said, "''Urwa ibn az-Zubayr gave me a *kunya* before I had a child."

Thuwayr ibn Abi Fakhita

His *kunya* was Abu al-Jahm. He was a *mawla* of Umm Hani' bint Abi Talib and he had descendants. He was old and lived long.

Malik ibn Isma'il reported to Isra'il from Thuwayr that he accompanied his father to Makka with 'Alqama, al-Aswad and 'Amr ibn Maymun. Not one of them had a whip and did not bridle their animals.

Musa ibn Abi 'A'isha al-Hamdani

Sufyan ibn Uyayna said that 'Amr ibn Qays said, "I did not raise my head but that I saw him praying on his roof," meaning Musa ibn Abi 'A'isha.

Sa'id ibn Masruq ath-Thawri

He is the father of Sufyan ath-Thawri. He died in 128 AH while 'Abdullah ibn 'Umar ibn 'Abd al-'Aziz was governor of Iraq.

Sa'id ibn 'Amr

Sa'id ibn 'Amr ibn Sa'id ibn al-'As ibn Sa'id ibn al-'As ibn Umayya. Al-Aswad ibn Qays related from him.

Sa'id ibn Ashwa' al-Hamdani

He was appointed qadi of Kufa and died while Khalid ibn 'Abdullah al-Qasri was governor.

His brother, **Rabi' ibn Abi Rashid**

Khallad ibn Yahya reported that he heard Sufyan ibn 'Uyayna say, "When ar-Rabi' ibn Abi Rashid appeared to Habib ibn Abi Thabit and his companions, he said to them, "Refrain. Ar-Rabi' has come.'"

Abu al-Jahhaf

His name is Dawud ibn Abi 'Awf. Sufyan ath-Thawri and Sufyan ibn 'Uyayna related from him.

Thabit ibn Hurmuz

His *kunya* is Abu al-Miqdam al-'Ijli. He is Abu 'Amr ibn Abi al-Miqdam.

'Abda ibn Abi Lubaba, a *mawla* of Quraysh

'Amr ibn Sa'id reported from Sa'id ibn 'Abd al-'Aziz that 'Abda ibn Abi Lubana whose *kunya* was Abu al-Qasim. Makhul gave him his *kunya* when he met him.

Sinan ibn Habib as-Sulami

His *kunya* was Abu Habib.

Abu Nahik

His name was al-Qasim ibn Muhammad al-Asadi.

Abu Farwa al-Hamdani

His name was 'Urwa ibn al-Harith.

Abu Farwa al-Juhani

His name was Muslim ibn Salim.

Abu Na'ama al-Kufi

His name was Shayba ibn Nu'ama. Sufyan ath-Thawri, Hushaym and Jarir related from him.

Abu Ja'far al-Farra'

He has *hadith*s.

Abu Ma'shar Ziyad ibn Kulayb at-Taymi

He died while Yusuf ibn 'Umar was governor of Iraq. He had few *hadith*s.

Shibak ad-Dabbi

He was a companion of Ibrahim an-Nakha'i. Mughira related from him. He was trustworthy, Allah willing, and had few *hadith*s.

Bayan ibn Bishr

His *kunya* was Abu Bishr. He was a *mawla* of Ahmas ibn Bajila.

Ibrahim ibn al-Muhajir ibn Jabir al-Bajali

He was one of Bajila. His father was one of the scribes of al-Hajjaj ibn Yusuf. Ibrahim was trustworthy.

Al-Hakam ibn 'Utayba

Al-Fadl ibn Dukayn reported from Abu Isra'il that al-Hakam ibn 'Utayba had the *kunya* Abu 'Abdullah.

Muhammad ibn Sa'd said, "I walked with 'Abdullah ibn Idris for a need of his. When we reached the crossroads of Kinda, he stopped at the door of a house on the street and asked me, 'Do you know to whom this house belongs? This is the house of al-Hakam ibn 'Utayba.'" He was a *mawla* of Kinda. Al-Hakim and Ibrahim an-Nakha'i were the same age and were born in the same year.

Muhammad ibn Sa'd said that 'Abd ar-Razzaq that Ma'mar said, "Az-Zuhri was among his companions like al-Hakam ibn 'Utayba was among his companions."

Al-Fadl ibn Dukayn reported that Fitr said, "I saw al-Hakam with a white beard."

Al-Fadl ibn Dukayn reported from Abu Isra'il that al-Hakam wore a fine turban. He said, "He led us in the prayer wearing a jubbah and I said, 'Abu 'Abdullah!' He said, 'One of the Companions of the Prophet ﷺ would pray or lead in one jubbah when he did not have any other.'"

Al-Hajjaj ibn Muhammad said that he heard Abu Isra'il say, "The first day on which I recognised al-Hakam ibn 'Utayba was the day that ash-Sha'bi died. He said, 'A man asked about a question and they said, 'You must have al-Hakam ibn 'Utayba.'"

Muhammad ibn 'Abdullah ibn Numayr ibn Idris reported that Shu'ba said, "Al-Hakam died in Kufa in 115 while Hisham ibn 'Abd al-Malik was caliph."

Ibn Idris said, "I was born in it."

Al-Hakam ibn 'Utayba was trustworthy, a lofty elevated *faqih* scholar with a lot of *hadith*s.

Hammad ibn Abi Sulayman

His kunya was Abu Isma'il, the *mawla* of Ibrahim ibn Abi Musa al-Ash'ari.

Al-Fadl ibn Dukayn reported from Abu Isra'il that the name of Abu Sulayman, the father of Hammad, was Muslim. He was one of those whom Mu'awiya ibn Abi Sufyan sent to Musa al-Ash'ari when he was at Dumat al-Jandal.

Yahya ibn 'Abbad reported from Sharik that Jami' ibn Shaddad said, "I saw Hammad writing with Ibrahim on tablets, saying, 'By Allah, I do not intend this world by it.'"

Ahmad ibn 'Abdullah ibn Yunus reported from Abu Bakr ibn 'Ayyash that Mughira said, "When Ibrahim died, we saw that the one who appointed him was al-A'mash. We came to him and asked him about the lawful and unlawful. When he had nothing, we asked him about shares of inheritance. He had that.' He said, 'We went to Hammad and asked him about shares of inheritance and he had nothing. We asked him about the lawful and unlawful and he had it.' He said, 'We took shares of inheritance from al-A'mash and we took the lawful and unlawful from Hammad from Ibrahim.'"

'Abdullah ibn Numayr reported that Malik ibn Mighwal said, "I saw Hammad praying wearing a yellow waist-wrapper and a red mantle."

Malik ibn Isma'il reported that he heard his mother, the daughter of Isma'il ibn Hammad ibn Abi Sulayman, say, "Sometimes I saw the copy of the Qur'an in the room of my grandfather Hammad ibn Abi Sulayman and his tears were on the paper."

They all agree that Hammad ibn Abi Sulayman died in 120 AH while Hisham ibn 'Abd al-Malik was caliph.

Hammad ibn Abi Sulayman went to Basra to Bilal ibn Abi Burda while he was its governor and Hisham ad-Dastuwa'i, Hammad ibn Salama and others listened to him in that visit.

Hammad ibn Zayd said, "Ayyub did not go to anyone we did not go to. When Ayyub did not go to someone, we did not go to him. When Hammad returned to Kufa, we asked, 'How did you find the people of Basra?' He said, 'A piece of the people of Syria who alighted among us,' i.e. not like us in command over us." They said, "Hammad was weak in *hadith*s and muddled things at the end of his life." He was a Murji'ite. He had a lot of *hadith*s.

Muhammad ibn 'Abdullah ibn Numayr reported from Abu Bakr ibn 'Ayyash that Mughira said, "I asked Ibrahim, 'Who should we ask after you?' He answered, 'Hammad.'"

'Affan ibn Muslim reported from Sallam ibn Abi al-Mundhir that 'Uthman al-Batti said, "When Hammad spoke his opinion, he was correct. When he spoke from other than Ibrahim, he erred."

Al-Fudayl ibn 'Amr al-Fuqaymi

He died while Khalid ibn 'Abdullah al-Qasri was governor. He was trustworthy and had *hadith*s.

Al-Harith al-'Ukli

Hushaym reported from Mughira that al-Harith al-'Ukli and Ibn Shubruma were discussing judgement after *'Isha'* and Abu al-Mughira passed by them and said, "At this hour! Is it not enough for you what you have in the day so that you also discuss it at this time?" He was trustworthy and had few *hadith*s.

Al-Harith ibn Hasira of Azd

One of Azd themselves. Sufyan ath-Thawri related from him.

'Abdullah ibn as-Sa'ib

He related from Zadhan and Sufyan ibn Sa'id ath-Thawri related from him.

'Abd al-A'la ibn 'Amir at-Taghlabi

Sufyan ath-Thawri and Isra'il related from him.

'Abd ar-Rahman ibn Mahdi said that Sufyan related the *hadith* of 'Abd al-A'la. He said, "We used to think that it was from a book. 'Abd al-A'la used to relate from Ibn al-Hanafiyya from 'Ali and did that a lot. Sufyan said, 'We used to think that it was from a book.'" He was weak in *hadith*.

Adam ibn Sulayman

He was a *mawla* of Khalid ibn Khalid ibn 'Umara ibn al-Walid ibn 'Uqba ibn Abi Mu'ayt. He said, "That is how Sufyan ath-Thawri mentioned it when he related it in what Mu'ammil ibn Isma'il reported. He is Abu Yahya ibn Adam the *muhaddith* who was in Kufa. Khalid ibn Khalid was a generous noble man.

Muhammad ibn Juhada

He was a *mawla* of the Banu Awd.

Sulayman ibn Harb reported from Hammad ibn Zayd that Muhammad ibn Juhada said, "My father died on the road to Makka and Talha ibn Musarrif came to console us. He said, 'It is said that those who die in finishing one of three will go to the Garden: *hajj*, *'umra* or an expedition.'"

'Abd al-Malik ibn Abi Bashir

'Arim ibn al-Fadl reported from Hammad ibn Zayd that Ghalib al-Qattan said, "I went to al-Hasan with the letter of 'Abd al-Malik ibn Abi Bashir and he said, 'Read it.' I read it and it contained a supplication. Al-Hasan said, 'Many of your brothers have not yet been born.'"

Salim ibn Abi Hafsa

His *kunya* was Abu Yunus.

328

They said that Salim was a strong Shi'ite. In the reign of the Banu Hashim, Dawud ibn 'Ali went on *hajj* with the people that year: 132 AH. Salim ibn Abi Hafsa performed *hajj* that year and entered Makka saying the *talbiya*, saying, 'At Your service. At Your service, destroyers of the Banu Umayya. At Your service.' He was a loud man and Dawud ibn 'Ali heard him and asked, 'Who is this?' They replied, 'Salim ibn Abi Hafsa.' They reported his business and his opinion.

Aban ibn Salih ibn 'Ubayd

They say that Abu 'Ubayd was one of the captives of Khuza'a whom the Prophet ﷺ attacked in the expedition to the Banu al-Mustalaq. He was taken by Usayd ibn Abi al-'Is ibn Umayya and went afterwards to 'Abdullah ibn Khalid ibn Usayd ibn Abi al-'Is who set him free. Salih ibn 'Umayr was killed at Rayy. The Azraqites attacked them at night. They were killed in their army in the time of al-Hajjaj.

'Abdullah ibn 'Umar ibn Muhammad ibn Aban ibn Salih reported from his uncle, Aban ibn Muhammad, who heard his father say, "My father (meaning Aban ibn Salih ibn 'Umayr) visited 'Umar ibn 'Abd al-'Aziz and he asked him, 'Are you in the register?' He said, 'I used to dislike that with other than you. As with you, I do not mind.'" It was allotted to him. Aban ibn Salih was born in 60 AH and died in 'Asqallan in about 110 AH when he was fifty-five. His *kunya* was Abu Bakr.

❋❋❋❋❋

Also from this generation are: **'Abdullah ibn Hanash** al-Awdi, **'A'idh ibn Nusayb** al-Kahili of Banu Asad, **Mujammi' at-Taymi,** **'Abdullah ibn 'Usaym** al-Hanafi, **Simak ibn Harb** adh-Dhuhli, **Shabib ibn Gharqada** al-Bariqi, **Kulayb ibn Wa'il** al-Bakri, **Muhammad ibn Qays** al-Hamdani, **Tariq ibn 'Abd ar-Rahman** al-Ahmasi, **Muhariq ibn 'Abdullah** al-Ahmasi, **'Abd al-'Aziz ibn Rufay',** **'Abd al-'Aziz ibn Hakim** al-Hadrami, **'Abdullah ibn Sharik** al-'Amiri, **Sa'id ibn Abi Burda** ibn Abi Musa al-Ash'ari, **'Abd ar-Rahman ibn 'A'ish** an-Nakha'i, **'Ayyash ibn 'Amr** al-

'Amiri, **al-Aswad ibn Qays** al-'Abdi, **Ziyad ibn Fayyad** al-Khuza'i, **Hakim ibn Jubayr** al-Asadi, **Hakim ibn Daylam, Jami' ibn Abi Rashid, Qays ibn Wahb** al-Hamdani, **Al-Miqdam ibn Shurayh** ibn Hani' al-Harithi, **Muhill ibn Khalifa** at-Ta'i, **Zuhayr ibn Abi Thabit** al-'Absi, **'Amir ibn Shaqiq** ibn Hamza al-Asadi, **al-Mughira ibn an-Nu'man** an-Nakha'i, **Zayd ibn Jubayr** al-Jushami, **Badr ibn Dithar** ibn Rabi'a, **Az-Zubayr ibn 'Adi** al-Yami of Hamdan, **Al-Hurr ibn as-Sabbah** an-Nakha'i, and **'Alqama ibn Marthad** al-Hadrami.

Fourth Generation

Mansur ibn al-Mu'tamir as-Sulami

His *kunya* was Abu 'Attab.

Ahmad ibn 'Abdullah ibn Yunus reported from Mindal that Mansur ibn al-Mu'tamir said, "We sought knowledge and without having that intention in it but then Allah provided us with it afterwards." Mindal said, "Allah provided insight after it." He said, "We were young."

'Ali ibn 'Abdullah ibn Ja'far reported that he heard Sufyan ibn 'Uyayna and he mentioned Mansur ibn al-Mu'tamir. He said, "He went blind from weeping. He had a rag with which he wiped the tears from his eyes." Sufyan said that they claimed that he fasted and prayed for sixty years.

Yahya ibn Sa'id al-Qattan said that Sufyan ath-Thawri said, "When I was young, al-A'mash was one of the companions of Ibrahim. When I mentioned Mansur, he was silent."

Abu Nu'aym said that he heard Hammad ibn Zayd say, "I saw Mansur in Makka." He said, "I think that he was part of this Khashabiyya." He said, "I do not think that he used to lie." They said that Mansur died at the end of 123 AH. He was trustworthy and secure with a lot of *hadith*s, and was high, elevated.

Al-Mughira ibn Miqsam ad-Dabbi

He was a *mawla* of Dabba whose *kunya* was Abu Hisham. He was blind. He died in 136 AH. He was trustworthy and had a lot of *hadith*s.

'Ata' ibn as-Sa'ib ath-Thaqafi

His *kunya* was Abu Zayd. He died in 136 AH. He was trustworthy. The early ones related from him. His memory became weak at the end of his life and he muddled at the end of his life.

Ibn 'Ulayya said: "He is weaker than Layth in my opinion, and al-Layth was weak."

Ibn 'Ulayya said, "I only wrote one tablet from 'Ata' and I erased one of the sides." He said, "I asked Shu'ba about him and he said,

'When he relates from one man, he is trustworthy. When he combines and says 'Zadhan and Maysara and Abu al-Bakthari,' then be careful about him. The shaykh's memory became faulty."

Husayn ibn 'Abd ar-Rahman as-Sulami

He was one of the tribe themselves.

'Abdullah ibn Abi as-Safar al-Hamdani

He died in the caliphate of Marwan ibn Muhammad. He was trustworthy and did not have a lot of *hadith*s.

Abu Sinan Dirar ibn Murra ash-Shaybani

Shihab ibn 'Abbad al-'Abdi reported: "Our companions said, 'The weepers in Kufa were four: Dirar ibn Murra, 'Abd al-Malik ibn Abjur, Muhammad ibn Suqa and Mutarrif ibn Tarif.' Dirar ibn Murra dug his grave fifteen years before his death. He used to go to him and do the entire Qur'an with him." He was trustworthy and safe.

Abu Yahya al-Qattat

He was a *mawla* of Yahya ibn Ja'da ibn Hubayra. He is weak.

Abu al-Haytham al-'Attar al-Asadi

He was trustworthy.

'Amr ibn Qays al-Masir

He was a *mawla* of Kinda. He spoke about *irja'* and other things.

Musa ibn Abi Kathir al-Ansari

His *kunya* was Abu as-Sabbah. The name of Abu Kathir was as-Sabbah. Musa was one of the *mutakallimun* who delved into *irja'* and other things. He was one of those who went to 'Umar ibn 'Abd al-'Aziz and spoke to him about *ijra'*. He was trustworthy in *hadith*.

Mu'awiya ibn Ishaq ibn Talha ibn 'Ubaydullah at-Taymi

He was trustworthy.

Qabus ibn Abi Zibyan al-Janni

He has some weakness and is not authoritative.

'Ubayd al-Mukattab ibn Mihran

He was a *mawla* of the Banu Dabba. He was trustworthy with few *hadith*s.

Muhammad ibn Suqa

He was a *mawla* of Bajila. He was a merchant who sold rough silk. He was scrupulous.

'Abdullah ibn az-Zubayr al-Humaydi reported that Sufyan ibn 'Uyayna said, "Raqba ibn Masqala came to me in my house. When he wanted to go to Muhammad ibn Suqa, his route passed by us. He said, 'Take me to Muhammad ibn Suqa.' I heard Talha say at Kufa, 'Two men wanting Muhammad ibn Suqa and 'Abd al-Jabbar ibn Wa'il.'"

Habib ibn Abi 'Amra al-Qassab al-Azdi

He related from Sa'id ibn Jubayr. He was trustworthy and had few *hadith*s. Ath-Thawri related from him.

Yazid ibn Abi Ziyad

His *kunya* was Abu 'Abdullah. He was a *mawla* of 'Abdullah ibn al-Harith ibn Nawfal al-Hashimi. He died in 130 AH. He was trustworthy in himself but muddled things at the end of his life and did extraordinary things.

'Ammar ibn Abi Mu'awiya ad-Duhni

He was a *mawla* of Ahmas. His *kunya* was Abu 'Abdullah. He had *hadith*s.

Al-Hasan ibn 'Amr al-Fuqaymi

Muhammad ibn 'Abdullah al-Asadi reported from Sufyan that al-Hasan ibn 'Amr said, "My father took me to Sa'id ibn Jubayr when I was young. He said, 'Learn the Qur'an from someone like this.'"

Muhammad ibn 'Abdullah al-Asadi reported from Sufyan that al-Hasan ibn 'Amr said, "Ibrahim left me his clothes in his will."

They said that he died at the beginning of the caliphate of Abu Ja'far al-Mansur.

'Asim ibn Kulayb ibn Shihab al-Jarmi

He died at the beginning of the caliphate of Abu Ja'far al-Mansur. He was trustworthy and is used as authoritative. He did not have a lot of *hadith*s.

Abu Miskin

He was a companion of Ibrahim. His name was al-Hurr, a *mawla* of the Banu Awd. He had few *hadith*s.

Abu Ishaq Ibrahim ibn Muslim al-Hajari

He was a man of the Arabs who came to Kufa from Hajar. He was weak in *hadith*s.

Al-A'mash

His name was Sulayman ibn Mihran. His *kunya* was Abu Muhammad al-Asadi. He was a *mawla* of the Banu Kahil. He stayed with the Banu 'Awf of the Banu Sa'd. He used to pray in the mosque of the Banu Haram of the Banu Sa'd.

Waki' reported that al-A'mash said, "My father was carried and his brother died and Masruq inherited from him."

Muhammad ibn Sa'd said that he heard someone mention that his father was present at the killing of al-Husayn ibn 'Ali. Al-A'mash had knowledge of the Qur'an, shares of inheritance, as well as knowledge of *hadith*. Talha ibn Musarrif recited the Qur'an to him. He used to recite to people and did not stop doing that at the end of his life. He used to recite a known amount of the Qur'an to people every day in every Sha'ban until he was old and weak. They would bring their copies of the Qur'an and compare them and correct what was in them. Abu Hayyan at-Taymi used to bring a copy of the Qur'an which was the soundest of those Qur'ans and they would also correct theirs by what was in it. Al-A'mash used to recite the reading of 'Abdullah ibn Mas'ud. Al-A'mash used to recite to Yahya ibn Waththab and Yahya ibn Waththab recited to 'Ubayd ibn Nudayla al-Khuza'i, and 'Ubayd ibn Nudayla recited to 'Alqama, and 'Alqama recited to 'Abdullah.

Ahmad ibn 'Abdullah ibn Yunus reported that Abu Bakr ibn 'Ayyash said that he heard al-A'mash say, "By Allah, you do not go to anyone but that you compel him to lie. By Allah, I do not know of anyone who is worse than them."

Abu Bakr said, "I did not acknowledge this because they did not give full *isnad*s." He said that Abu Bakr then mentioned their *tadlis*.

'Abdullah ibn Ja'far ar-Raqqi reported from 'Ubaydullah ibn 'Amr that Abu Ishaq ibn Rashid said, "When az-Zuhri indicated the people of Iraq, he considered their knowledge weak. I said, 'In Kufa there is a *mawla* of the Banu Asad who relates four thousand *hadith*s.' He said, 'Four thousand *hadith*s!' I said, 'Yes. If you wish, I will bring you some of his knowledge.' I presented it to him. He began to read and recognised alterations in it. He said, 'By Allah, this is knowledge. I did not think that anyone knew this.'"

'Affan ibn Muslim reported that Abu 'Awana said, "Al-A'mash, in my view, had goods and I used to say to him, 'I have profited by this and that from you.' He said, 'I will not move any goods afterwards.'"

'Affan ibn Muslim reported that 'Umar ibn 'Ali al-Muqaddami said, "Al-Hajjaj ibn Atra'a came and asked permission to visit al-A'mash and he said, 'Tell him that Abu Arta'a is at the door.' He said, 'Do you use your *kunya* with me? Do you use your *kunya* with me? Do not give him permission to enter!'"

Waki' said that al-A'mash said, "When I and Abu Ishaq met, we brought a *hadith* of 'Abdullah which he had without permission."

Sufyan said, "I went to al-A'mash and said, 'I say that I did not ask Abu Muhammad about something but that he answered me.' He said, 'Hasan ibn 'Ayyash informed me that he related a matter after him.' Al-A'mash said, 'A man said to me, "I sat with az-Zuhri and I mentioned you to him and he said, 'Do you have any of his *hadith* with you?'"'"

Sufyan said: "Al-A'mash used to ask me about the *hadith* of Ibn 'Iyad and Ibn 'Ajlan. Sufyan ath-Thawri was the person with the most knowledge of the *hadith* of al-A'mash. Sometimes al-A'mash erred and Sufyan rejected it."

Al-Fadl ibn Dukayn and Waki' reported that al-A'mash was born on the day that al-Husayn ibn 'Ali ibn Abi Talib was killed. That was 'Ashura' in Muharram 60 AH. He died in 148 AH when he was eighty-eight. As for Yahya ibn 'Isa ar-Ramli, he said that al-A'mash was born in 58 AH.

Al-Haytham ibn 'Adi said that he died in 147 AH.

Muhammad ibn 'Umar al-Waqidi and al-Fadl ibn Dukayn said that he died in 148 AH.

Isma'il ibn Abi Khalid

He was a *mawla* of the Banu Ahmas of Bajila. His *kunya* was Abu 'Abdullah. He was two years younger than Ibrahim an-Nakha'i.

Al-Hasan ibn Musa al-Ashyab reported from Zuhayr from Abu Ishaq that 'Amir said, "Isma'il ibn Abi Khalid drank knowledge greatly."

Shihab ibn 'Abbad al-'Abdi reported: "Isma'il ibn Abi Khalid saw six of those who saw the Prophet 靆: Anas ibn Malik, 'Abdullah ibn Abi Awfa, Abu Kahil, Abu Juhayfa, 'Amr ibn Hurayth and Tariq ibn Shihab."

Al-Fadl ibn Dukayn and others reported that Isma'il ibn Abi Khalid died in Kufa in 146 AH.

Someone heard 'Ali ibn Mushir say that he heard Sufyan ath-Thawri say, "We consider the *huffaz* to be four: 'Abd al-Malik ibn Abi Sufyan, Isma'il ibn Abi Khalid, 'Asim al-Ahwal and Yahya ibn Sa'id al-Ansari."

Firas ibn Yahya al-Hamdani

He was a companion of ash-Sha'bi. He was trustworthy, Allah willing.

Jabir ibn Yazid al-Ju'fi

Al-Fadl ibn Dukayn reported that he heard Sufyan say (and he mentioned that Jabir ibn Yazid al-Ju'fi said), "When he tells him, 'He related to me' or 'I heard,' it is that. When he says, 'He said,' it is like *tadlis*."

Al-Fadl ibn Dukayn reported that Jabir died in 128 AH.
Muhammad ibn 'Umar reported the like of that from Qays ibn ar-Rabi'. He said that he was very weak in opinion and *hadith*.

Abu Ishaq ash-Shaybani

His name was Sulayman ibn Abi Sulayman, their *mawla*.
Muhammad ibn 'Umar said that he died in 129 AH.
Another said that he died when there were two years left of the caliphate of Abu Ja'far.

Mutarrif ibn Tarif al-Harithi

Sufyan ibn 'Uyayna said, "Mutarrif met me and said, 'Why do you not come to me?' He was on a mule. I said, 'Would that there was some *sadaqa*.' He wept and said, 'Do you ignore me?' It was as if he praised him."

Sufyan said that Mutarrif used to say, "By Allah, you are dearer to me than my family."

Mutarrif died while Abu Ja'far al-Mansur was caliph.

Isma'il ibn Sami' al-Hanafi

He was trustworthy, Allah willing.

Al-'Ala' ibn 'Abd al-Karim al-Yami of Hamdan

He was the nephew of Zubayd Lahha. He died while Abu Ja'far al-Mansur was caliph.

'Isa ibn al-Musayyab al-Bajali

He was qadi for Khalid ibn 'Abdullah al-Qasri over Kufa, but he had a long life and Jabir ibn Yazid al-Ju'fi used to sit with him since he sat for judgement. He died while Abu Ja'far al-Mansur was caliph.

Muhammad ibn Abi Isma'il as-Sulami

Abu Isma'il's name was Rashid. They were three brothers from whom people related. Isma'il ibn Rashid was the oldest of them and the first to die. Husayn and his brother Muhammad ibn Abi Isma'il also related from him. Muhammad died in 142 AH while Abu Ja'far al-Mansur was caliph. Ath-Thawri also related from Muhammad ibn

337

Abi Isma'il and others. 'Umar ibn Rashid related from Hafs ibn Ghiyath, 'Abdullah ibn Numayr and Yahya al-Qattan and ath-Thawri.

Khalid ibn Salama ibn al-'As ibn Hisham al-Makhzumi

He fled from Kufa when the mission of the 'Abbasids appeared to Wasit and was killed with Ibn Hubayra. They say that Abu Ja'far al-Mansur cut out his tongue and then killed him. He has descendants in Kufa.

Bukayr ibn 'Utayq

He said that he heard Muhammad ibn al-Fudayl ibn Ghazwan ad-Dabbi say, "Bukayr ibn 'Utayq performed sixty *hajj*s." He was trustworthy.

Al-Ja'd ibn Dhakwan

He was a *mawla* of Qadi Shurayh. His house was at the crossroads of Kinda. He had few *hadith*s.

Hallam ibn Salih al-'Absi

He related from the companions of 'Umar ibn al-Khattab and 'Abdullah ibn Mas'ud.

Abu al-Haytham

He was a seller of cane. He had few *hadith*s.

Az-Zibriqan ibn 'Abdullah al-'Abdi

He had few *hadith*s.

Abu Ya'fur al-'Abdi

Sufyan ibn 'Uyayna said, "Abu Ya'fur said to me, 'There is no man left in Kufa who is older than me.'"

Muhammad ibn Bishr al-'Abdi said, "I saw Abu Ya'fur when his prayer place was here. His name was Waqid ibn Waqdan." He was trustworthy, Allah willing.

'Isa ibn Abi 'Azza

A *mawla* of al-Hamdan. He was trustworthy and had *hadith*s.

Al-'Ala' ibn al-Musayyab ibn Rafi' al-Asadi

He was trustworthy.

Harun ibn 'Antara

He was trustworthy.

Al-Hasan ibn 'Ubaydullah an-Nakha'i

He was trustworthy. He died while Abu Ja'far al-Mansur was caliph.

Mujalid ibn Sa'id al-Hamdani

His *kunya* was Abu 'Umayr. He died in 144 AH while Abu Ja'far al-Mansur was caliph. He was weak in *hadith*.

Yahya ibn Sa'id al-Qattan said, "I did not wish that Mujalid would tell me in a *hadith* of the opinion of ash-Sha'bi from Masruq but that he did so." Yahya ibn Sa'id al-Qattan related from him with this. Sufyan ath-Thawri, Shu'ba and others related from him.

Layth ibn Abi Sulaym

His *kunya* was Abu Bakr, and he was a *mawla* of 'Anbasa ibn Abi Sufyan ibn Harb ibn Umayya.

'Abd ar-Razzaq related that Ma'mar said, "I heard Ayyub say to al-Layth, 'Pay attention to what you hear from these two men and hold to it (meaning Tawus and Mujahid).'"

They said that Layth died at the beginning of the caliphate of Abu Ja'far. He lived in the Jabbana of 'Arzam. His father Abu Sulaym was one of the worshipping striving men in the General Mosque of Kufa. When Shabib the Kharijite entered Kufa, he went to the mosque and spent the night in it and killed them. Abu Sulaym was among those he killed. The people abandoned *tahajjud* that night in the mosque. Layth was a righteous man of worship. He was weak in *hadith*s. It was said that he used to ask 'Ata', Tawus and Mujahid about something and they disagreed about it and he related that they agreed without being deliberate in that.

Al-Ajlah ibn 'Abdullah al-Kindi

His *kunya* was Abu Hujayya. He died while Abu Ja'far was caliph after Muhammad and Ibrahim, the sons of 'Abdullah ibn al-Hasan ibn Hasan had revolted. They revolted in 145 AH. He was very weak.

'Abd al-Malik ibn Abi Sulayman al-'Arzami al-Fazari

He was their *mawla*. His *kunya* was Abu 'Abdullah. Abu Sulayman's name was Maysara. They agree that he died on 10 Dhu al-Hijja 145 AH while Abu Ja'far al-Mansur was caliph. He was firm, secure, trustworthy.

Al-Qasim ibn al-Walid al-Hamdani

He was trustworthy.

'Abdullah ibn Shubruma ad-Dabbi

He was trustworthy and a *faqih* with few *hadith*s.

Yazid ibn Harun reported: "I saw 'Abdullah ibn Shubruma. His *kunya* was Abu Shubruma, an Arab man of good character. Sometimes he dressed until he spent the night in his clothes. 'Isa ibn Musa appointed him qadi over the *kharaj* land."

'Abd ar-Razzaq said that Ma'mar said, "Ibn Shubruma here was governor with us in Yemen. When he was dismissed, I saw him off. When the people left and I was alone with him and no one was with us, he looked at me and said, 'Abu 'Urwa, I praise Allah. I have not replaced this shirt of mine since I entered.' Then he was silent for a time and said, 'I say to you: lawful. As for the unlawful, there is no way to it.'"

They said that 'Abdullah ibn Shurbuma died in 144 AH. He was a poet. He and Muhammad ibn 'Abd ar-Rahman ibn Abi Layla attended 'Isa ibn Musa every night and they remained with him. When they came they remained on their animals until they were given permission. Sometimes 'Iyad, the chamberlain of 'Isa ibn Musa, came out to them and said, "Go."

'Abdullah ibn Shubruma used to refer to those who asked him to be witnesses as hoopoes. A man came to him and he was asked about and dropped. He spoke to him about that and 'Abdullah ibn Shubruma composed:

We asked and he did not care about what we asked.
How many a noble man has been broken by hoopoes!

'Umara ibn al-Qa'qa' ibn Shubruma ad-Dabbi

Sufyan ibn 'Uyayna said: "'Umara ibn al-Qa'qa', the nephew of 'Abdullah ibn Shubruma, and 'Abdullah ibn 'Isa, the nephew of Muhammad ibn 'Abd ar-Rahman ibn Abi Layla. They used to say, 'They are better than their uncle.' Ibn Shubruma said to 'Umara, 'Apply yourself to something in Hira. It was a truce which 'Umar made.'" 'Umara was trustworthy.

Yazid ibn al-Qa'qa' ibn Shubruma ad-Dabbi

He was also related from.

Husayn ibn Hasan al-Kindi

He was appointed qadi of Kufa. He was trustworthy.

Ghaylan ibn Jami' al-Muharibi

He was appointed qadi of Kufa. He died while Yazid ibn 'Umar ibn Hubayra was governor of Iraq. The *Musawwida* killed him when they first came out between Wasit and Kufa. He was trustworthy, Allah willing.

Ibrahim ibn Muhammad ibn al-Muntashir al-Hamdani

He was trustworthy.

Mukhawwal ibn Rashid

Mukhawwal ibn Rashid ibn Abi Rashid ibn Abi Rashid an-Nahdi, a *mawla* of Nahd. He died at the beginning of the caliphate of Abu Ja'far al-Mansur. He was trustworthy, Allah willing.

'Umayr ibn Yazid ibn Abu al-Gharif al-Hamdani

He died at the beginning of the caliphate of Abu Ja'far al-Mansur.

Al-Hajjaj ibn 'Asim al-Muharibi

He was appointed qadi in Kufa.

Al-Fadl ibn Dukayn reported that Sufyan ath-Thawri said, "I saw him on Friday and I saw him another Friday on a bed. He died in the reign of the Umayyads."

Abu Hayyan at-Taymi

His name is Yahya ibn Sa'id. He was trustworthy and had sound *hadith*s.

Musa al-Juhani

His *kunya* was Abu 'Abdullah. He was trustworthy, with few *hadith*s.

Al-Hasan ibn al-Hurr

His *kunya* was Abu Muhammad, and he was a *mawla* of the Banu as-Sayda' of the Banu Asad in Khuzayma. He died in Makka in 133 AH. He was trustworthy, with few *hadith*s.

Al-Walid ibn 'Abdullah ibn Jumay' al-Khuza'i

He was one of Khuza'a. He was trustworthy, and had *hadith*s.

As-Salt ibn Bahram

He was one of the Banu Taymullah ibn Tha'laba. He was trustworthy, Allah willing.

Hanash ibn al-Harith ibn Laqit an-Nakha'i

He was trustworthy, with few *hadith*s.

Wiqa' ibn Iyas al-Asadi

His *kunya* was Abu Yazid. He was trustworthy, Allah willing.

Badr ibn 'Uthman

He was a *mawla* of the family of 'Uthman ibn 'Affan. His home was close to the mosque at the Bab al-Fil. He had *hadith*s.

Sa'id ibn al-Marzuban

His *kunya* was Abu Sa'id al-Baqqal, and he was a *mawla* of Hudhayfa ibn al-Yaman. He had few *hadith*s.

Sulayman ibn Busayr

His *kunya* was Abu as-Sabbah, and he was a *mawla* of al-Hajjaj ibn Arta'a an-Nakha'i.

'Ubayda ibn Mu'attib ad-Dabbi

His *kunya* was Abu 'Abd al-Karim. He was blind. He was very weak. Sufyan ath-Thawri related from him.

Zakariyya' ibn Abi Za'ida

He was a *mawla* of Muhammad ibn al-Muntashir al-Hamdani.

Al-Fadl ibn Dukayn reported that he died in 148 AH in the caliphate of Abu Ja'far al-Mansur. He was trustworthy with a lot of *hadith*s.

Aban ibn 'Abdullah ibn Sakhr ibn al-'Ayla al-Bajali

Sakhr's *kunya* was Abu Hazim. Sakhr was one of the Companions of the Prophet ﷺ. Aban died in Kufa while Abu Ja'far al-Mansur was caliph.

As-Sabbah ibn Thabit al-Bajali

He was from Bajila. He was the imam of the mosque of Jarir ibn 'Abdullah. He was noble and intelligent. He died while Abu Ja'far al-Mansur was caliph.

'Abd ar-Rahman ibn Zubayd al-Yami

His *kunya* was Abu al-Ash'ath. He died a year after the *Mubayyida*, 146 or 147 AH, while Abu Ja'far al-Mansur was caliph.

Sa'id ibn 'Ubayd at-Ta'i

His *kunya* was Abu al-Hudhayl. His maternal uncles were the Banu Asab ibn Khuzayma and he had a house among them and he used to lead them in the prayer. He died while Abu Ja'far al-Mansur was caliph.

Musa as-Saghir ibn Muslim at-Tahhan

Ahmad ibn 'Abdullah ibn Yunus reported, "I heard them mention that Musa as-Saghir at-Tahhan died in prostration at the Maqam."

Mu'arrif ibn Wasil

One of the Banu 'Amr ibn Sa'd ibn Zayd Manat ibn Tamim.

Ahmad ibn 'Abdullah ibn Yunus reported, "Mu'arrif was the imam of the mosque of the Banu 'Amr ibn Sa'd. He had a hernia. He used to recite the Qur'an in full on a journey and when at home in three days. He led his people in the prayer for sixty years and he did not forget in the prayer at all because it was his concern."

'Isa ibn al-Mughira

His *kunya* was Abu Shihab. Muhammad ibn 'Ubayd said, "I met him."

Abu Bahr

Al-Hasan ibn Salih related from him.

Waki' said: "He was our nephew who was with us. I saw him. His name was Burayd ibn Shaddad."

Abu al-'Adabbas

His name was Mani'.

Abu al-'Anbas

Mis'ar related from him. His name was al-Harith.

This generation includes **ar-Rabi' ibn Suhaym** al-Asadi of the Banu Kahil and **Shawdhab Abu Mu'adh.**

Fifth Generation

Muhammad ibn 'Abd ar-Rahman

Muhammad ibn 'Abd ar-Rahman ibn Abi Layla ibn Bilal ibn Bulayl ibn Uhayha ibn al-Jullah al-Ansari, then one of the Banu Jahjaba ibn Kulfa of the Banu 'Amr ibn 'Awf of Aws. They agreed that he died in Kufa in 148 AH and he was appointed qadi for the Umayyads and then for the 'Abbasids while 'Isa ibn Musa was in charge of Kufa and its districts.

Al-Fadl ibn Dukayn reported: "Muhammad ibn 'Abd ar-Rahman ibn Abi Layla was seventy-two on the day that he died."

Ahmad ibn 'Abdullah ibn Yunus reported from Abu Shihab that Ibn Abi Layla said, "I do not know anything of the business of my father other than I know that he had two wives and he had two green jars which he made into *nabidh* on alternate days."

Ash'ath ibn Sawwar ath-Thaqafi

A *mawla* of Thaqif. He used to work with wood. His home was in an-Nakha' and his house was opposite the mosque of Hafs ibn Ghiyath. He died at the beginning of the caliphate of Abu Ja'far al-Mansur. He was weak in *hadith*.

Muhammad ibn as-Sa'ib

Muhammad ibn as-Sa'ib al-Kalbi ibn Bishr ibn 'Amr ibn al-Harith ibn 'Abd al-Harith ibn 'Abd al-'Uzza ibn Imru' al-Qays ibn 'Amir ibn an-Nu'man ibn 'Amir ibn 'Abd Wudd ibn Kinana ibn 'Awf ibn 'Udhra ibn Zayd al-Lat ibn Rufayda ibn Thawr ibn Kalb. His *kunya* was Abu an-Nadr. His grandfather was Bishr ibn 'Amr and his sons, as-Sa'ib, 'Ubayd and 'Abd ar-Rahman were present at the Battle of the Camel with 'Ali ibn Abi Talib. As-Sa'ib ibn Bishr was killed with Mus'ab ibn az-Zubayr. He has what Ibn Warq' an-Nakha'i said:

Who will convey from me to 'Ubayd
    that I, his brother, raised aloft the brandished sword?

If you seek knowledge from him,
   he resides at ad-Dayrayn without a pillow.
I deliberately raised my head from him with the sword,
   and I entrusted him to Sufyan after Muhammad.

Sufyan and Muhammad were the sons of as-Sa'ib. Muhammad ibn as-Sa'ib was present at al-Jamajim with 'Abd ar-Rahman ibn Muhammad ibn al-Ash'ath. Muhammad ibn as-Sa'ib had knowledge of *tafsir* and the lineage and accounts of the Arabs. He died in Kufa in 146 AH while Abu Ja'far al-Mansur was caliph.

Muhammad ibn Sa'd said that he was told all of that by his son, Hisham ibn Muhammad ibn as-Sa'ib. He knew lineage and the accounts and battles of the Arabs.

They said that that is not the case. He was very weak in his transmission.

Al-Hajjaj ibn Atra'a

Al-Hajjaj ibn Atra'a ibn Thawr ibn Hubayra ibn Sharahil ibn Ka'b ibn Salaman ibn 'Amir ibn Haritha ibn Sa'd ibn Malik ibn an-Nakha' of Madhhij. His *kunya* was Abu Arta'a. He was noble. He was one of the companions of Abu Ja'far al-Mansur and he attached himself to al-Mahdi and he remained with him until he died in Rayy while al-Mahdi was there at that time in the caliphate of Abu Ja'far al-Mansur. He was weak in *hadith*.

Abu Janab al-Kalbi

His name was Yahya ibn Abi Hayya. He was weak in *hadith* and died in 147 AH in Kufa while Abu Ja'far was caliph.

Aban ibn Taghlab ar-Rib'i

He died in Kufa while Abu Ja'far was caliph. 'Isa ibn Musa was governor of Kufa. He was trustworthy and Shu'ba related from him.

Muhammad ibn Salim

He was the father of Sahl al-'Absi, who knew the shares of inheritance. He was weak and had a lot of *hadith*s.

Abu Kubran al-Muradi

His name was al-Hasan ibn 'Uqba.

Bashir ibn Salman an-Nahdi

He was a *mawla* of Nahd. His *kunya* was Abu Isma'il. His home was in Hamdan. He was a shaykh and had few *hadith*s.

Bashir ibn al-Muhajir

He was a *mawla*. His home was in Ghanna but he was not their *mawla*.

Bukayr ibn 'Amir al-Bajali

His *kunya* was Abu Isma'il. He was trustworthy, Allah willing.

Muhill ibn Muhriz ad-Dabbi

His *kunya* was Abu Yahya. He was blind. He was weak in *hadith*.

Muhammad ibn Qays al-Asadi of the Banu Walib

His *kunya* was Abu Nasr. He was trustworthy, Allah willing.

Talha ibn Yahya

Talha ibn Yahya ibn Talha ibn 'Ubaydullah ibn 'Uthman ibn 'Amr ibn Ka'b ibn Sa'd ibn Taym ibn Murra. He was trustworthy and had sound *hadith*s.

'Abd ar-Rahman ibn Ishaq

His *kunya* was Abu Shayba. He was weak in *hadith*s. He related from Shu'ba. He is the one from which Abu Mu'awiya ad-Darir and the Kufans related. 'Abd ar-Rahman ibn Ishaq al-Madini was firmer than him in *hadith*. He is the one from whom Isma'il ibn 'Ulayya and the Basrans related.

Ishaq ibn Sa'id

Ishaq ibn Sa'id ibn 'Amr ibn Sa'id ibn al-'As ibn Sa'id ibn al-'As ibn Umayya. He had *hadith*s and was related from.

'Umar ibn Dharr ibn 'Abdullah al-Hamdani

He was one of the Banu Murhiba. His *kunya* was Abu Dharr. He was a qadi.

Muhammad ibn Sa'd said that Muhammad ibn 'Abdullah al-Asadi said that 'Umar ibn Dharr died in 153 AH in the caliphate of Abu Ja'far al-Mansur. He was a Murji'ite. He died and Sufyan ath-Thawri and al-Hasan ibn Salih did not see him. He was trustworthy, Allah willing, and had many *hadiths*.

'Uqba ibn Abi Salih

He is related from.

'Uqba ibn Abi al-'Ayzar

He was a *mawla* of Banu Awd of Madhhij. He had few *hadiths*.

'Abd al-'Aziz ibn Siyah al-Asadi

He was a *mawla*. He was one of the best people and had *hadiths*. His house was with Habib ibn Abi Thabit. He died while Abu Ja'far al-Mansur was caliph.

Yusuf ibn Suhayb

Abu Nu'aym said that he was from the Banu Badda' of Kinda and I think that he was their *mawla*.

Yunus ibn Abi Ishaq as-Subay'i

His *kunya* was Abu Isra'il. He reached a great age. He related from most of the men of his father. He died in Kufa in 159 AH. He was trustworthy and had many *hadiths*.

Dawud ibn Yazid ibn 'Abd ar-Rahman al-Awdi

He was from Awd of Madhhij. He was weak and had sound *hadiths*.

Idris ibn Yazid ibn 'Abd ar-Rahman al-Awdi

The brother of Dawud ibn Yazid. He is Abu 'Abdullah ibn Idris. He has *hadiths*.

'Abdullah ibn Habib ibn Abi Thabit

He was a shaykh. Abu Nu'aym and Qabisa ibn 'Uqba related from him.

Fitr ibn Khalifa al-Hannat

His *kunya* was Abu Bakr. He died in Kufa shortly after 'Ali ibn Hayy and so it seems that he died in 155 AH while Abu Ja'far al-Mansur was caliph. He was trustworthy, Allah willing. Some people thought him weak. Waki', Abu Nu'aym and others related from him. He did not let anyone write with him and he lived a very long time and met many people. He related from Abu Wa'il and others.

Abu Hamza ath-Thumali

His name was Thabit ibn Abi Safiyya. He died while Abu Ja'far al-Mansur was caliph. He was weak.

Mis'ar ibn Kidam

Mis'ar ibn Kidam ibn Zuhayr ibn 'Ubaydullah ibn al-Harith ibn 'Abdullah ibn 'Amr ibn 'Abd Manaf ibn Hilal ibn 'Amir ibn Sa'sa'a. His *kunya* was Abu Salama.

Muhammad ibn 'Abdullah al-Asadi said that Mis'ar died in Kufa in 152 AH.

Abu Nu'aym said that it was in 155 AH while al-Mansur was caliph.

Someone reported that he heard Sufyan ibn 'Uyayna say, "Sometimes I saw Mis'ar when a man came to him and he related something to him when he knew it better than him but he listened to him and was silent."

Al-Haytham said, "Mis'ar did not hear a *hadith* at all except in the General Mosque. He had a worshipping mother and used to carry her felt and walk with her until they entered the mosque and he spread out the felt for her and she rose and prayed. He went to the front of the mosque and prayed. Then he sat and those who wanted to meet with him and he related to them. Then he went to his mother and carried her felt and went with her. He had no refuge except for his house and the mosque. He was a Murji'ite. He died and Sufyan ath-Thawri and al-Hasan ibn Salih ibn Hayy did not attend his funeral.

Malik ibn Mighwal

Malik ibn Mighwal ibn 'Asim ibn Malik ibn Ghaziyya ibn Haritha ibn Khadij ibn Jabir ibn 'Awdh ibn al-Harith ibn Suhayba ibn Anmar, which is Bajila. His *kunya* was Abu 'Abdullah. He died in Kufa at the end of Dhu al-Hijja 158 AH in the same month that Abu Ja'far al-Mansur, the Amir al-Mu'minin, died.

As-Saqr ibn 'Abd ar-Rahman ibn Malik ibn Mighwal reported all of that to me. He was trustworthy, safe, with a lot of *hadith*s, excellent, good.

Abu Shihab al-Akbar

His name was Musa ibn Nafi', a *mawla* of the Banu Asad. He related from Sa'id ibn Jubayr, 'Ata' and Mujahid. Ath-Thawri, Sharik, Hafs, Waki' and Ibn Numayr relate from him. He was trustworthy, with few *hadith*s.

Abu 'Umays

His name was 'Utba ibn 'Abdullah ibn 'Utba ibn 'Abdullah ibn Mas'ud al-Hudhali, the ally of the Banu Zuhra. He was trustworthy.

Al-Mas'udi

His name was 'Abd ar-Rahman ibn 'Abdullah ibn 'Utba ibn 'Abdullah ibn Mas'ud. He died in Baghdad. He was trustworthy with a lot of *hadith*s although he muddled things at the end of his life. Older people related from him.

'Abd al-Jabbar ibn 'Abbas ash-Shabbami of Hamdan

There was some weakness in him. He is related from.

Umayy ibn Rabi'a as-Sayrafi

Abu Usama said that his *kunya* was Abu 'Abd ar-Rahman. He was trustworthy and had few *hadith*s.

Bassam as-Sayrafi

He related from Abu Ja'far Muhammad ibn 'Ali.

Abu Nu'aym said, "I reckon that he was a slave and I do not know that he had a father. He lived at the baths of 'Antara. He related from Abu Ja'far Muhammad ibn 'Ali. His *kunya* was Abu 'Abdullah.

Musa ibn Qays al-Hadrami

His *kunya* was Abu Muhammad. He died while Abu Ja'far al-Mansur was caliph. He had few *hadith*s.

Dawud ibn Nusayr at-Ta'i

One of Tayy'. His *kunya* was Abu Sulayman. He listened to *hadith* and *fiqh* and knew grammar and knew the battles and battles of people, and then worshipped. He did not say anything about that.

Al-Fadl ibn Dukayn reported from Abu Dawud al-Hafari that the companion of Dawud at-Ta'i said, "I went to him for twenty nights and discussed *hadith* with him. That day he told me, 'Do not ever again discuss any with me of what you have just been discussing with me.'"

Al-Fadl ibn Dukayn said, "I heard Zufar say, 'I and Dawud at-Ta'i went to al-A'mash and Dawud said, 'A voice which is not usual after a time.' Al-A'mash said, 'By Allah, I am not concerned if you do not think me usual.' Dawud said, 'I did not see anyone drawing near to me with long separation and benefit from than other than you.'"

Al-Fadl ibn Dukayn reported: "I used to see that Dawud at-Ta'i did not resemble the reciters. He wore a black hat which the merchants wore. He sat in his house for twenty years or less until he died. His funeral came. I could not see him due to the large number of people. He died in 165 AH while al-Mahdi was caliph."

Suwayd ibn Najih

His kunya was Abu Qutba. He used to live among the Banu Haram, and was the neighbour of al-A'mash. He died while Abu Ja'far al-Mansur, the Amir al-Mu'minin, was caliph.

Muhammad ibn 'Ubaydullah al-'Arzami al-Fazari

He listened a lot and wrote and then buried his books. After that he related again. His books were gone and people found his *hadith*s weak because of that. He died while Abu Ja'far was caliph.

Al-Hasan ibn 'Umara al-Bajali

He was a *mawla* of Bajila. His *kunya* was Abu Muhammad. He died in 153 AH while Abu Ja'far al-Mansur was caliph. He was weak in *hadith*. Some of them did not write down his *hadith*s.

Harun ibn Abi Ibrahim ath-Thaqafi

Abu Ibrahim is Harun al-Barbari. 'Abdullah ibn Idris and others related from him. He had sound *hadith*s.

Mujammi' ibn Yahya al-Ansari

He was one of the family of Jariya ibn al-'Attaf, but he settled in Kufa. His origins were Madinan. The Kufans related from him. He had *hadith*s.

Abu Hanifa

His name was an-Nu'man ibn Thabit. Thabit was a *mawla* of the Banu Taymullah ibn Tha'laba ibn Bakr ibn Wa'il. He has opinion (*ra'y*). They agree that he died in Baghdad in Rajab or Sha'ban 150 AH while Abu Ja'far al-Mansur was caliph.

Muhammad ibn 'Umar reported that Hammad ibn Abi Hanifa said, "Abu Hanifa died when he was seventy."

Muhammad ibn 'Umar said, "On the day he died in Kufa I was expecting his arrival and then news of his death came." He was weak in *hadith*.

Abu Rawq

His name was 'Atiyya ibn al-Harith al-Hamdani from a sub-tribe of them called the Banu Wathn. He had *tafsir*. He related from ad-Dahhak ibn Muzahim and others.

Abu Ya'fur as-Saghir

'Abdullah ibn Numayr, Hafs ibn Ghiyath, Muhammad ibn al-Fudayl ibn Ghazwan and Yahya ibn Zakariyya' ibn Abi Za'ida related from him. His name was 'Abd ar-Rahman ibn 'Ubayd ibn Nistas al-Baka'i. Mansur ibn al-Mu'tamir related from his father, 'Ubayd ibn Nistas.

As-Sari ibn Isma'il al-Hamdani

One of the Sa'idis. He was a scribe for ash-Sha'bi. He related shares of inheritance and other things from him. As-Sari was appointed qadi of Kufa. He had few *hadith*s.

Isma'il ibn 'Abd al-Malik ibn Rufay'

He was the nephew of 'Abd al-'Aziz ibn Rufay', a *mawla* of the Banu Waliba from the Banu Asad ibn Khuzayma. He died while Abu Ja'far al-Mansur was caliph.

Dalham ibn Salih al-Kindi

One of Kinda. He died while Abu Ja'far al-Mansur was caliph.

Muhammad ibn 'Ali as-Sulami

They related from him.

'Isa ibn 'Abd ar-Rahman as-Sulami

He died early while Abu Ja'far al-Mansur was caliph.

Sixth Generation

Sufyan ibn Sa'id

Sufyan ibn Sa'id ibn Masruq ibn Habib ibn Rafi' ibn 'Abdullah ibn Mayhaba ibn Ubayy ibn 'Abdullah ibn Munqidh ibn Nasr ibn al-Harith ibn Tha'laba ibn 'Amir ibn Milkan ibn Thawr ibn 'Abd Manat ibn Udd ibn Tabikha ibn Ilyas ibn Mudar ibn Nizar. His *kunya* was Abu 'Abdullah.

Muhammad ibn Sa'd said that Muhammad ibn 'Umar said, "Sufyan was born in 97 while Sulayman ibn 'Abd al-Malik was caliph." He was trustworthy, safe, secure, with a lot of *hadith*s, and authoritative. They agreed that he died in Basra while he was in hiding in Sha'ban 161 AH while al-Mahdi was governor.

'Affan ibn Muslim reported from Khalid ibn al-Harith from Sufyan that Hammad ibn Abi Sulayman said, "This lad is a proper follower," i.e. Sufyan himself.

Qabisa ibn 'Uqba reported that he heard Sufyan say, "My father was a Darani and I did not take any *hadith* about it which he did not like."

Khalaf ibn Tamim reported that he heard Sufyan ath-Thawri say, "I found my heart put right in Makka and Madina with exiled people, the people of houses and cloaks."

Qabisa ibn 'Uqba reported from a man that Sufyan said, "Learn this knowledge. When you learn it, then preserve it. When you preserve it, act by it. When you act by it, promulgate it."

Bakkar reported that Sufyan ath-Thawri often said, "O Allah, make safe! Make safe!"

Yahya ibn Abi Bakr reported that he heard Shu'ba say, "Sufyan did not relate a *hadith* from as-Suddi which I asked him about but that it was as he related to me."

They used to relate that Sufyan once accepted wealth and connection from one of the governors but then he abandoned that and did not accept anything from anyone. He used to go to Yemen and trade. He divided what he had to some of his brothers to invest for him and would settle on the *'Id* festival every year. He would meet them, carry out the reckoning and take their profit. He had about two hundred dinars. He had an only son and Sufyan used to say, "There is nothing in this world which I love more than him and I want for him to precede me." His son died and he left everything after the death of his son to the son of his sister and her children. 'Ammar ibn Muhammad was the son of his sister. His brother al-Mubarak ibn Sa'id did not inherit anything from him.

He said that Sufyan was sought and left for Makka. Al-Mahdi, the Amir al-Mu'minin, wrote to Muhammad ibn Ibrahim, who was in charge of Makka, to look for him. Muhammad sent for Sufyan and informed him of that. He said, "If you want for people to come, then show yourself so that I can send you to them. If you do not want that, then hide." Sufyan hid. Muhammad ibn Ibrahim sought him and commanded that a caller call out in Makka, "Whoever brings Sufyan will have such-and-such." He remained in hiding in Makka and only appeared to the people of knowledge and those he did not fear.

'Abd ar-Rahman ibn Ishaq reported from Sa'id ibn Sulayman that Abu Shihab al-Hannat said, "The sister of Sufyan ath-Thawri sent with me a bag to Sufyan while he was in Makka which contained cake and brown bread. I came to Makka and asked after him and was told, 'Perhaps he is sitting behind the Ka'ba next to the Bab al-Hannatin.' I went there. He was a friend of mine and I found him lying down. I greeted him and he did not ask me that question nor greet me as I used to know from him. I said to him, 'Your sister has sent you a bag of cake and brown bread which is with me.' He said, 'Give it to me quickly.' He sat up. I said, 'Abu 'Abdullah, I come to you and I am your friend. I greeted you and you did not return the greeting to me. When I told you that I had brought you a bag of cake not worth anything, you sat up and spoke to me.' He said, 'Abu Shihab, do not blame me. I have not tasted anything for three days.' I excused him."

When Sufyan was afraid in Makka of being sought out, he went out to Basra and came to it and stayed near the house of Yahya ibn Sa'id al-Qattan. He said to one of the people of the house, "Are you near one of the people of *hadith*?" They said, "Yes, Yahya ibn Sa'id." He said, "Bring him to me." He brought him and he said, "Here I have been for six or seven days." Yahya moved to his side and opened a door between them. He used to come to him with the *hadith* transmitters of the people of Basra to greet him and listen to him. Among those who came to him were Jarir ibn Hasim, al-Mubarak ibn Fudala, Hammad ibn Salama, Marhum al-'Attar, Hammad ibn Zayd and others. 'Abd ar-Rahman ibn Mahdi went to him and attached himself to him. Yahya and 'Abd ar-Rahman used to write those days from him. Whenever Abu 'Awana came to him, he refused and said, "A man who does not know me – how can I go to him?" That was because Abu 'Awana had greeted him in Makka and Sufyan did not return the greeting to him. He was spoken to about that and he said, "I do not recognise him."

When Sufyan was afraid that it would be known that he was staying in Basra, he approached Yahya ibn Sa'id and said to him, "Move me from this place." He moved him to the house of al-Haytham ibn Mansur al-A'raji of the Banu Sa'd ibn Zayd Manat ibn Tamim. He remained among them and Hammad ibn Zayd asked him about his withdrawal from the sultan. He said, "This is the action of the people of innovations. What do you fear from them?" So Sufyan and Hammad agreed to go to Baghdad. Sufyan wrote to al-Mahdi or to Ya'qub ibn Dawud. He began with himself and it was said to them that they would be angry if he did that, so he began with them and the answer to his letter brought him what was necessary of being brought near, honour, listening to him and obedience.

He was about to go out to him and came down with a fever and was very ill and was dying. He was anxious and Marhum ibn 'Abd al-'Aziz said to him, "Abu 'Abdullah, what is this anxiety? You are going to the Lord whom you worshipped." He was silent and calm and said, "Look and see who is here of our Kufan companions." They sent to 'Abadan and 'Abd ar-Rahman ibn 'Abd al-Malik ibn Abjur and al-Hasan ibn 'Ayyash, the brother of Abu Bakr ibn 'Ayyash came to him and he instructed 'Abd ar-Rahman ibn 'Abd al-Malik to pray over him. They stayed with him until he died and his bier was brought out to the people of Basra suddenly and they heard about his death. The people attended and 'Abd ar-Rahman ibn 'Abd al-Malik prayed over him. He was a righteous man with whom Sufyan was pleased for himself. He went down into his grave and Khalid ibn al-Harith and others went down with him and they buried him. Then 'Abd ar-Rahman ibn 'Abd al-Malik and al-Hasan ibn 'Ayyash left for Kufa and informed its people of Sufyan's death. May Allah have mercy on him.

Isra'il ibn Yunus ibn Abi Ishaq as-Subay'i

His *kunya* was Abu Yusuf. He died in Kufa in 162 AH. Abu Nu'aym said it was 160 AH. He was trustworthy and people related many *hadith*s from him. Some of them thought that he was weak.

Yusuf ibn Ishaq ibn Abi Ishaq as-Subay'i

He is related from. He died while Abu Ja'far al-Mansur was the Amir al-Mu'minin. He had few *hadith*s.

'Ali ibn Salih

The name of Salih was Hayy ibn Salih ibn Muslim ibn Hayyan ibn Shufayy ibn Hunayy ibn Rafi' ibn Qumli ibn 'Amr ibn Mati' ibn Sahlan ibn Zayd ibn Thawr ibn Malik ibn Mu'awiya ibn Duman ibn Bakil ibn Jusham of Hamdan. His *kunya* was Abu Muhammad.

Al-Fadl ibn Dukayn reported: "''Ali and Hasan, the sons of Salih Taw'am were born in Batin. 'Ali was a bit earlier. I did not hear Hasan ever called by his name. He used to be called: "Abu Muhammad."

Muhammad ibn Sa'd said that 'Ali had the Qur'an.

'Ubaydullah ibn Musa said, "I read the Qur'an to him. 'Ali died in 154 while Abu Ja'far was caliph. He was trustworthy."

Hisham ibn Muhammad said: "The mother of 'Ali and Salih, the sons of Salih ibn Hayy, was Umm al-Aysar the daughter of al-Miqdam ibn Muslim ibn Hayyan ibn Shufayy ibn Hunayy ibn Rafi' ibn Qumli." He was trustworthy, Allah willing, with few *hadith*s.

His brother, Hasan ibn Hayy

He is Hasan ibn Salih. His *kunya* was Abu 'Abdullah. He was a devoted worshipping *faqih*.

Al-Fadl ibn Dukayn reported: "I did not see al-Hasan ibn Hayy sit cross-legged at all."

A beggar came to him one day and asked him and he removed his socks and gave them to him. He said, "I saw him on *Jumu'a* and he hid on Sunday night and remained in hiding for seven years until he died in 167 while hiding in Kufa. At that time Rawh ibn Hatim ibn Qabisa ibn al-Muhallab was governor over it for al-Mahdi. Hasan ibn

Hayy was a Shi'ite. 'Isa ibn Zayd ibn 'Ali married his daughter and went into concealment with him in the same place in Kufa until 'Isa ibn Zayd died in hiding. Al-Mahdi had sought them and made strenuous efforts in seeking them but was not able to get them until they died. Hasan ibn Hayy died six months after 'Isa ibn Zayd."

I heard Abu Nu'aym al-Fadl ibn Dukayn say, "I saw Hasan ibn Salih on *Jumu'a* with people and then he concealed himself on the Sunday that his son died. At that time he was sixty-two or sixty-three. He was trustworthy and had many sound *hadith*s. He was a Shi'ite."

Asbat ibn Nasr al-Hamdani

One of Hamdan. He was the transmitter of as-Suddi. He also related *tafsir*. He related from Mansur and others.

Muhammad ibn Talha ibn Musarrif al-Yami

One of Hamdan. His *kunya* was Abu 'Abdullah. He died in 167 AH while al-Mahdi was caliph. He had *hadith*s which are not acknowledged.

'Affan said: "Muhammad ibn Talha related from his father and his father died early. People seemed to call him a liar but no one was so bold as to say to Muhammad ibn Talha, 'You are lying.'" It was part of his excellence.

Zuhayr ibn Mu'awiya

Zuhayr ibn Mu'awiya ibn Hudayj ibn ar-Ruhayl ibn Zuhayr ibn Khaythama ibn Abi Humran. His name was al-Harith ibn Mu'awiya ibn al-Harith ibn Malik ibn 'Awf ibn Sa'd ibn Harim ibn Ju'fi ibn Sa'd al-'Ashira of Madhhij. His *kunya* was Abu Khaythama. He moved to Jazira and settled there until he died there.

'Amr ibn Khalid al-Misri reported that he heard Sa'id ibn Mansur praised well and commanded that he be written from.

Zuhayr ibn Mu'awiya went to Jazira in 164 AH or the beginning of 173 AH while Harun was caliph. He was trustworthy, firm, trusted and had a lot of *hadith*s.

ar-Ruhayl ibn Mu'awiya ibn Hudayj ibn ar-Ruhayl

The brother of Zuhayr. He is also related from.

Hudayj ibn Mu'awiya ibn Hudayj ibn ar-Ruhayl

Their brother. He is also related from. He was weak in *hadith*.

Shayban ibn 'Abd ar-Rahman

His *kunya* was Abu Mu'awiya an-Nahawi, a *mawla* of the Banu Tamim and his origins were from Basra. He was the teacher of the children of Dawud ibn 'Ali ibn 'Abdullah ibn 'Abbas. He died in Baghdad in 164 AH while al-Mahdi was caliph. He was buried in the cemetery of al-Khayzaran in Baghdad. He was trustworthy, with a lot of *hadith*s.

Qays ibn ar-Rabi' al-Asadi

One of the children of al-Harith ibn Qays who became Muslim while he had nine wives. The Prophet ﷺ commanded him to keep four of them and divorce the rest. His *kunya* was Abu Muhammad.

Qays was called al-Hawwal because of the great amount of his listening and knowledge. Qays died in Kufa in 168 AH while al-Mahdi was caliph.

Qabisa ibn Jabir al-Asadi

He had a lot of *hadith*s and was weak in them.

Za'ida ibn Qudama ath-Thaqafi

His *kunya* was Abu as-Salt.

Mu'awiya ibn 'Amr al-Azdi reported that Za'ida died in Byzantine territory in the year in which al-Hasan ibn Qahtaba raided in the summer of 161 or 160 AH. He was trustworthy, secure and held to the *Sunna* and the Community.

Abu Bakr an-Nahshali

One of the Banu Tamim. He was the son of 'Abdullah ibn Qattaf. He was a Murji'ite. He was a devout worshipper. He had *hadith*s and some people thought that he was weak.

Sharik ibn 'Abdullah ibn Abi Sharik

Abu Sharik is al-Harith ibn Aws ibn al-Harith ibn Wahbik ibn Sa'd ibn Malik ibn an-Nakha' of Madhhij. His *kunya* was Abu 'Abdullah. He was born in Bukhara in the land of Khurasan. His grandfather had been present at al-Qadisiyya.

Al-Fadl ibn Dukayn reported *hadith*s from Sharik from Abu Mash'ar before he became qadi. He said, "I am Sharik ibn 'Abdullah ibn Abi Sharik. Abu Sharik, my grandfather, was present at al-Qadisiyya. See me in Kufa and I will sit with you." Sharik was one of the men of Kufa. Abu Ja'far al-Mansur summoned him and said, "I want to appoint you qadi of Kufa." He said, "Spare me, Amir al-Mu'minin!" He stated, "I will not spare you." He said, "Let me go today and return." The Amir al-Mu'minin saw what he thought. He said, "You want to leave and hide from me. By Allah, you will do it or I will give fifty of your people what you dislike!" When Sharik heard his oath, he returned to him and did not hide. He appointed him qadi of Kufa and he remained qadi until Abu Ja'far died and al-Mahdi came to power. He confirmed his appointment as qadi and then later dismissed him. Sharik died in Kufa on Saturday the beginning of Dhu al-Qa'da 177 AH. Harun, the Amir al-Mu'minin, was in Hira and his governor at that time was Musa ibn 'Isa ibn Musa ibn Muhammad ibn 'Ali. He attended Sharik's funeral and prayed over him. Harun, the Amir al-Mu'minin, came from Hira to pray over him and found that the prayer had been performed over him. He left the bridge. Sharik was trustworthy, secure, with a lot of *hadith*s. He often erred.

'Isa ibn al-Mukhtar

'Isa ibn al-Mukhtar ibn 'Abdullah ibn Abi Layla al-Ansari.

He listened to the *Musannaf* of Muhammad ibn 'Abd ar-Rahman ibn Abi Layla and he listened to it from 'Isa Bakr ibn 'Abd ar-Rahman, the Qadi of Kufa.

Abu al-Ahwas

His name is Sallam ibn Sulaym, a *mawla* of the Banu Hanifa. He died in Kufa in 179 AH while Harun was caliph. He had a lot of *hadith*s and was sound in it.

Kamil ibn al-'Ala' at-Tamimi

His *kunya* was Abu al-'Ala'. He had few *hadith*s, and was not known for that.

'Amr ibn Shamir al-Ju'fi

He was the imam of the Ju'fi mosque for sixty years. He was a qadi and he had *hadith*s. He was very weak and his *hadith*s were abandoned. He died while Abu Ja'far was caliph.

Muhammad ibn Salama ibn Kuhayl al-Hadrami

Sufyan ibn 'Uyayna related from him. Muhammad ibn Salama related from his father. He was weak.

His brother, Yahya ibn Salama ibn Kuhayl al-Hadrami

He died while Musa al-Hadi was the Amir al-Mu'minin. He was very weak.

Abu Isra'il al-Mula'i al-'Absi

His name was Isma'il ibn Abi Ishaq. They used to say that he was truthful. Bahz ibn Asad related that he heard Abu Isra'il accepting 'Uthman and things about this which he related from him.

Al-Jarrah ibn Malih

Al-Jarrah ibn Malih ibn 'Adi ibn al-Faris ibn Sufyan ibn al-Harith ibn 'Amr ibn 'Ubayd ibn Ru'as ibn Kilab ibn 'Amir ibn Rabi'a ibn 'Amir ibn Sa'sa'a. He is Abu Waki' ibn al-Jarrah. He was appointed over the treasury in Madinat as-Salam while Harun ar-Rashid was caliph. He was difficult in *hadith*.

Mufaddil ibn Yunus

He died in 172 AH while Harun ar-Rashid was Amir al-Mu'minin. He was trustworthy.

Mufaddil ibn Muhalhil

He was trustworthy and Abu Usama Hammad ibn Usama and others related from him.

Hibban ibn 'Ali al-'Anazi

His *kunya* was Abu 'Ali. He was older than his brother Mindal; al-Mahdi liked to see the two of them. He wrote to Kufa about their personalities. When they entered where he was, they greeted him and he asked, "Which of you is Mindal?" Mindal said, "This is Hibban, Amir al-Mu'minin." Hibban died in Kufa in 171 AH while Harun was caliph. Hibban was weak in *hadith*, weaker than Mindal.

His brother, Mindal ibn 'Ali al-'Anazi

His *kunya* was Abu 'Abdullah. He was more intelligent and retained more than Hibban. He was younger than him. Mindal died in Kufa in 167 or 168 AH while al-Mahdi was present before his brother Hibban. He had some weakness. Some people desired his *hadith*s and thought him trustworthy. He was good, excellent, one of the people of the *Sunna*.

Abu Zubayd

His name was 'Abthar ibn al-Qasim of the Banu Zubayd of Madhhij. He died in Kufa in 178 AH while Harun ar-Rashid was caliph. He was trustworthy and had a lot of *hadith*s.

Abu Kudayna

His name was Yahya ibn al-Muhallab al-Bajali of the Banu ar-Rib'a. He was trustworthy, Allah willing.

Huraym ibn Sufyan al-Bajali

He was trustworthy, Allah willing.

Hani' ibn Ayyub al-Ju'fi

He had *hadith*s and there was weakness in him.

Mansur ibn Abi al-Aswad

He was a *mawla* of the Banu Layth. He was a merchant and he had a lot of *hadith*s.

His brother, **Salih ibn Abi Aswad**

He also used to relate *hadith*s.

'Abd ar-Rahman ibn Humayd ar-Ru'asi

He was the father of Hamid ibn 'Abd ar-Rahman. He was trustworthy and had *hadith*s.

His brother, **Ibrahim ibn Humayd** ar-Ru'asi

The companion of Isma'il ibn Abi Khalid. He had a lot of transmission from Isma'il.

Ja'far ibn Ziyad al-Ahmar

A *mawla* of Muzaham ibn Zufar from Taym ar-Ribab.

I heard Abu Nu'aym say that Ja'far died in Kufa in 177 AH while Harun was caliph.

'Amr ibn Abi al-Miqdam al-'Ijli

He died while Harun was caliph. The name of Abu al-Miqdam was Thabit. 'Amr did not have anything in *hadith* in their view. Some of them did not write down his *hadith*s because of his weakness and opinion. He was an extreme Shi'ite.

Salama ibn Salih al-Ahmar al-Ju'fi

His *kunya* was Abu Ishaq. He sought *hadith* and then his memory became confused and so people thought him weak. He was appointed qadi of Wasit and then dismissed. He died in Baghdad in 188 AH while Harun ar-Rashid was caliph.

Hashraj ibn Nabata

His *kunya* was Abu Mukarram. He related from Sa'id ibn Jamhan.

Al-Qasim ibn Ma'n

Al-Qasim ibn Ma'n ibn 'Abd ar-Rahman ibn 'Abdullah ibn Mas'ud al-Hudhali, the ally of the Banu Zuhra of Quraysh. His *kunya* was Abu 'Abdullah. He was appointed qadi of Kufa and he did not seek to be paid anything until he died. He was trustworthy, a scholar of *hadith*, *fiqh*, poetry and the battles of people. He was called the ash-Sha'bi of his time. He was generous.

Abu Shayba

His name was Ibrahim ibn 'Uthman al-'Absi of the children of Abu Sa'da. He related *hadith*s from Abu Sa'd and Abu Sa'd related from Ibn 'Abbas. Abu Shayba was appointed qadi of Wasit and died while Harun ar-Rashid was caliph. He was weak in *hadith*. Yazid ibn Harun related from him.

Abu al-Muhayya

His name was Yahya ibn Ya'la ibn Harmala ibn al-Jalid ibn 'Ammar ibn Arta'a ibn Zuhayr ibn Umayya ibn Jusham ibn 'Adi ibn al-Harith ibn Taym Allah ibn Tha'laba. He died in Kufa in 1-8 [sic] AH while Harun was caliph when he was seventy-six.

Al-Mubarak ibn Sa'id ibn Masruq

The brother of Sufyan ath-Thawri. He died in Kufa at the beginning of 189 AH. He had *hadith*s.

Hamza az-Zayyat ibn 'Umara

His *kunya* was Abu 'Umara, a *mawla* of the family of 'Ikrima ibn Rib'i at-Taymi. He used to bring oil from Kufa to Hulwan and brought cheese and almonds from Hulwan to Kufa. He was the companion of the reciters of the Qur'an and knew shares of inheritance.

Muhammad ibn Sa'd said that he was told that Sufyan ibn Sa'id ath-Thawri said to him, "Ibn 'Umara, as for recitation and shares of inheritance, we do not read to you regarding them." Hamza died in Hulwan in 156 AH while Abu Ja'far was caliph. Hamza was a righteous man, and he had *hadith*s. He was truthful and followed the *Sunna*.

Muhammad ibn Aban

Muhammad ibn Aban ibn Salih ibn 'Umayr ibn 'Ubayd, a *mawla* of 'Abdullah ibn Khalid ibn Usayd ibn Abi al-'Is ibn Umayya ibn

'Abd Shams. His *kunya* was Abu 'Amr. He had transmission of *hadith*. He died on the Day of Ru'us in Sunday 11 Dhu al-Hijja in 175 AH while Harun ar-Rashid was caliph when he was eighty-one. He was married to 'Usayma the sister of Husayn ibn 'Ali al-Ju'fi. His sons were 'Umar, Aban and Ibrahim. He had descendants and progeny in Kufa among Ju'fi.

Ya'la ibn al-Harith al-Muharibi, **Maslama ibn Ja'far, Isma'il ibn Ibrahim** ibn al-Muhajir al-Bajali were also in this generation.

Seventh Generation

Abu Bakr ibn 'Ayyash

He was a *mawla* of Wasil ibn Hayyan al-Ahdab al-Asadi. It is from the generation before this, but he lived long so that he was written among the new. He was one of the worshippers.

Waki' said that he saw him praying on Friday until the imam said the *taslim* for 'Asr. He said, "I have known this shaykh with this prayer for forty years." Abu Bakr died in Kufa in Jumada al-Ula in 193 AH in the same month in which Harun, the Amir al-Mu'minin, died in Tus. Abu Bakr was trustworthy and knew *hadith* and knowledge although he had a lot of errors.

Su'ayr ibn al-Khims

One of the Banu 'Amr ibn Sa'd ibn Zayd Manat ibn Tamim. He was a noble man to whom his companions gathered. He was familiar. He followed the *Sunna* and the Community and he had *hadith*s.

'Abd as-Salam ibn Harb al-Mula'i

His *kunya* was Abu Bakr. He died in Kufa in 187 AH while Harun ar-Rashid was caliph. He had some weakness in hadith. He was difficult.

Al-Muttalib ibn Ziyad ibn Abi Zuhayr al-Qurashi

His *kunya* was Abu Muhammad. He lived among Thaqif and was the mawla of Jabir ibn Samura as-Suwa'i. Jabir was the ally of the Banu Zuhra from Quraysh. That is why he is called al-Muttalib ibn Zayd al-Qurashi. He was very weak in *hadith*. He died in Kufa in 185 AH while Harun was caliph.

Sayf ibn Harun al-Burjumi

One of the Banu Tamim. He is related from.

His brother, Sinan ibn Harun

He is related from.

'Umar ibn 'Ubayd at-Tanafisi

His *kunya* was Abu Hafs, and he was a *mawla* of Iyad ibn Nizar ibn Ma'add. He died in Kufa in 185 AH while Harun was caliph. He was an old shaykh. He was trustworthy, Allah willing.

Zufar ibn al-Hudhayl al-'Anbari

He listened to *hadith* and looked at opinion. It dominated him and was attributed to him. He died in Basra and left his instructions with Khalid ibn al-Harith and 'Abd al-Wahid ibn Ziyad. His father al-Hudhayl was in charge of Isbahan. His brother was Sabbah ibn al-Hudhayl who was in charge of the *zakat* of Banu Tamim. Zufar did not have anything in *hadith*.

'Ammar ibn Muhammad

The nephew of Sufyan ath-Thawri. He died in Muharram 182 AH while Harun was caliph. He was trustworthy and was related from.

'Ali ibn Mushir

His *kunya* was Abu al-Hasan from 'A'idha Quraysh themselves. He was appointed qadi in Mosul. He was trustworthy and had a lot of *hadith*s.

Ma'sud ibn Sa'd al-Ju'fi

He is related from.

'Umar ibn Shabib al-Musli of Madhhij

He was also related from.

'Ammar ibn Sayf ad-Dabbi

He was the executor of the will of Sufyan ath-Thawri. He left his books with him and said, "Bury them when I die."

Muhammad ibn al-Fudayl ibn Ghazwan ad-Dabbi.

He was a *mawla* of Dabba. His *kunya* was Abu 'Abd ar-Rahman.

Muhammad ibn Sulaym al-'Abdi reported that he heard Muhammad ibn al-Fudayl say, "My grandfather Ghazwan was present at al-Qadisiyya with his *mawla*, a man of the Banu Dabba. I asked, 'What was Ghazwan?' He replied, 'Greek.'"

Muhammad ibn al-Fudayl died in Kufa in 195 AH and his funeral was attended by Waki' ibn al-Jarrah. He was trustworthy, truthful, with a lot of *hadith*, and a Shi'ite. Some did not use him as authoritative.

'Abdullah ibn Idris

'Abdullah ibn Idris ibn Yazid ibn 'Abd ar-Rahman al-Awdi of Madhhij. His *kunya* was Abu Muhammad.

Talq ibn Ghannam reported that 'Abdullah ibn Idris ibn Yazid was born in 115 AH while Hisham ibn 'Abd al-Malik was caliph and died in Kufa on 10 Dhu al-Hijja 192 AH at the end of the caliphate of Harun ar-Rashid. He was trustworthy, secure, with a lot of *hadith*s, authoritative, the possessor of *Sunna* and the Community.

Musa ibn Muhammad al-Ansari

He is related from.

Hafs ibn Ghiyath

Hafs ibn Ghiyath ibn Talq ibn Mu'awiya ibn Malik ibn al-Harith ibn Tha'laba ibn 'Amir ibn Rabi'a ibn Jusham ibn Wahbil ibn Sa'd ibn Malik ibn an-Nakha' of Madhhij.

Talq ibn Ghannam reported that Hafs ibn Ghiyath was born in 117 AH while Hisham ibn 'Abd al-Malik ibn Hisham was caliph. His *kunya* was Abu 'Umar. Harun, the Amir al-Mu'minin, appointed him qadi at Baghdad at ash-Sharqiyya and then he was appointed qadi of Kufa and continued to be qadi there until he became very ill and died on 10 Dhu al-Hijja 194 AH while Muhammad ibn Harun was caliph. He was trustworthy, secure, and firm, although he employed *tadlis*.

Ibrahim ibn Humayd ibn 'Abd ar-Rahman ar-Ru'asi

His *kunya* was Abu Ishaq. He died in 178 AH while Harun ar-Rashid was caliph.

Al-Qasim ibn Malik al-Muzani

His *kunya* was Abu Ja'far al-Mansur. He was trustworthy, with sound *hadith*s.

'Abd ar-Rahman ibn 'Abd al-Malik ibn Abjar al-Kinani

He died in 181 AH while Harun ar-Rashid was caliph. He prayed over Sufyan ath-Thawri in Basra. He was good, excellent, someone holding to the *Sunna*.

'Abda ibn Sulayman

'Abda ibn Sulayman ibn Hajib ibn Zurara ibn 'Abd ar-Rahman ibn Surad ibn Sumayr ibn Mulayl ibn 'Abdullah ibn Abi Bakr ibn Kilab. The one who reached Islam and became Muslim was Surad. 'Abda's *kunya* was Abu Muhammad. His name was 'Abd ar-Rahman and then he got the title 'Abda and it was usually used for him. He died in Kufa on 27 Rajab 188 AH while Harun ar-Rashid was caliph and Muhammad ibn Rabi'a al-Kilabi prayed over him. He was trustworthy.

Abu Khalid al-Ahmar Sulayman ibn Hayyan

He was a *mawla* of the Banu Ja'far ibn Kilab. He died in Kufa in Shawwal 187 AH while Harun was caliph. He was trustworthy, with a lot of *hadith*s.

Yahya ibn al-Yaman al-'Ijli

His *kunya* was Abu Zakariyya'. He died in Kufa in Rajab 189 AH while Harun was caliph. He had a lot of *hadith*s with a lot of errors and was not used as authoritative when he changed.

Abu Shihab al-Hannat

His name was 'Abd Rabbihi ibn Nafi'. He was trustworthy and had a lot of *hadith*s.

'Ubaydullah ibn 'Abd ar-Rahman al-Ashja'i

He was trustworthy.

'Ali ibn Ghurab

He was a *mawla* of al-Walid ibn Sakhr al-Fazari from whom Isma'il ibn Raja' related the *hadith* of al-A'mash about 'Uthman. His *kunya* was Abu al-Hasan. He died in Kufa at the beginning of 184 AH while Harun was caliph. 'Ali was truthful and had some weakness. He accompanied Ya'qub ibn Dawud and so people left him.

Abu Malik al-Jubni

His name was 'Amr ibn Hashim. He was truthful, but he used to err a lot.

'Ali ibn Hashim ibn al-Barid

He died in Kufa in Rajab or Sha'ban 181 AH while Harun ar-Rashid was caliph. He was correct in *hadith* and truthful.

'Abd ar-Rahman ibn Muhammad al-Muharibi

His *kunya* was Abu Muhammad. He died in Kufa in 195 AH while Muhammad ibn Harun was caliph. He was a trustworthy shaykh, but with many errors.

'Aththam ibn 'Ali

He was one of the Banu al-Wahid. His *kunya* was Abu 'Ali. He died in Kufa in 195 AH while Muhammad ibn Harun was caliph. He was trustworthy.

Abu Mu'awiya ad-Darir

His name was Muhammad ibn Khazin, a *mawla* of the Banu 'Amr ibn Sa'd ibn Zayd Manat ibn Tamim, the group of Su'ayr ibn al-Khims. He was trustworthy, with a lot of *hadith*, and used *tadlis*. He was a Murji'ite. He died in Kufa in 195 AH. Waki' did not see him.

'Abd ar-Rahman ibn Sulayman ad-Darani

His root was from Rayy, but he grew up in Kufa and listened to *hadith*. His *kunya* was Abu 'Ali. He died in Kufa in 184 AH. He was a *mawla* of the Banu Kinana. He was known as al-Khulqani. He was related from.

Yahya ibn 'Abd al-Malik ibn Abi Ghaniyya

His *kunya* was Abu Zakariyya'. He lived in the Banu Sa'd ibn Hammam. He died in Kufa in 186 or 187 AH while Harun was caliph. He was trustworthy and had sound *hadith*s.

Yahya ibn Zakariyya ibn Abi Za'ida

His *kunya* was Abu Sa'id. He died in Mada'in while he was its qadi in 183 AH while Harun was caliph. He was trustworthy, Allah willing, and Harun the Amir al-Mu'minin, asked to appoint him qadi.

Asbat ibn Muhammad al-Qurashi

His *kunya* was Abu Muhammad. He died in Kufa in Muharram 200 AH while al-Ma'mun was caliph. He was trustworthy, truthful although there is some weakness in him. They related from him.

Muhammad ibn Bishr ibn al-Furafisa al-'Abdi

His *kunya* was Abu 'Abdullah. He died in Kufa in Jumada al-Ula 203 AH while al-Ma'mun was caliph. He was trustworthy, with a lot of *hadith*s.

'Abdullah ibn Numayr

'Abdullah ibn Numayr ibn 'Abdullah ibn Abi Hayya ibn Sarh ibn Salama ibn Sa'd ibn al-Hakam ibn Salman ibn Malik. He is Kharif ibn 'Abdullah ibn Kathir ibn Malik ibn Jusham ibn Hashid of Hamdan al-Hamdani then al-Kharifi. His *kunya* was Abu Hisham. He died in Kufa in Rabi' al-Awwal 199 AH. Muhammad ibn Bishr al-'Abdi prayed over him. He was his friend. He died while 'Abdullah al-Ma'mun was caliph. He was trustworthy, with a lot of *hadith*s, truthful.

Waki' ibn al-Jarrah

Waki' ibn al-Jarrah ibn Malih ibn 'Adi ibn al-Faras ibn Sufyan ibn al-Harith ibn 'Amr ibn 'Ubayd ibn Ru'as ibn Kilab ibn Rabi'a ibn

'Amir ibn Sa'sa'a. His kunya was Abu Sufyan. He performed *hajj* in 196 AH and then having finished *hajj* died at Fayd in Muharram 197 AH while Muhammad ibn Harun was caliph. He was trustworthy, secure, an elevated scholar with many *hadiths*, an authority.

Abu Usama

His name was Hammad ibn Usama ibn Zayd ibn Sulayman ibn Ziyad. He was a freed man, a *mawla* of al-Hasan ibn Sa'd, a *mawla* of al-Hasan ibn 'Ali ibn Abi Talib.

He said, "I heard someone mention that Ziyad, the freed man was the *mawla* of al-Hasan ibn 'Ali ibn Abi Talib. They used to live with the family of al-Hasan ibn Sa'd on the same road." Bad feelings arose between them and Zayd ibn Sulayman said, "We and you are the same." They moved away from them and the child of al-Hasan ibn Sa'd claimed that they were their *mawla*s and people ascribed them to them. As for Abu Usama, his son and others who reported their business reported that they did not hear any mention of this at all.

Abu Usama died in Kufa on Sunday 19 Shawwal 201 AH while al-Ma'mun was caliph when he was eighty. Muhammad ibn Isma'il ibn 'Ali ibn 'Abdullah ibn 'Abbas al-Hashimi prayed over him. He attended his funeral and they had him lead the prayer because of his age and position. He was not governor at that time. He was trustworthy and secure with a lot of *hadiths*. He used *tadlis* and his *tadlis* is evident. He held to the *Sunna* and the Community.

Al-Hasan ibn Thabit of the Banu Taghlib

He was known as Ibn ar-Ruzkar. His *kunya* was Abu 'Ali. He was one of the companions of 'Abdullah ibn Idris and his peers. He related from al-A'mash and others. Then he refused to transmit *hadith* and did not relate until he died. He was known for *hadith*.

'Uqba ibn Khalid as-Sakuni

He related from al-A'mash and Isma'il ibn Abi Khalid, 'Abd al-Malik ibn Abi Sulayman, Hisham ibn 'Urwa, 'Ubaydullah ibn 'Umar, and Musa ibn Muhammad ibn Ibrahim. He died in Kufa in 188 AH while Harun was caliph.

Ziyad ibn 'Abdullah ibn at-Tafil al-Bakka'i

One of the Banu 'Amr ibn Sa'sa'a. His *kunya* was Abu Muhammad. He listened to Mansur ibn al-Mu'tamir, Mughira, Isma'il ibn Abi Khalid and the men of the people of Kufa. He listened to shares of inheritance from Muhammad ibn Salim and listened to expeditions from Muhammad ibn Ishaq. He went to Baghdad and related to them expeditions, shares of inheritance and other things. Then he returned to Kufa where he died in 183 AH while Harun was caliph. He was weak with them and they related from him.

Ahmad ibn Bashir

His *kunya* was Abu Bakr, and he was a *mawla* of the Banu Shayban. He related from al-A'mash, Hisham ibn 'Urwa, Isma'il ibn Abi Khalid, 'Abd al-Malik ibn Abi Sulayman and others.

Ja'far ibn 'Awn

Ja'far ibn 'Awn ibn Ja'far ibn 'Amr ibn Hurayth al-Makhzumi. His *kunya* was Abu 'Awn. He died in Kufa on Monday 11 Sha'ban 209 AH while al-Ma'mun was caliph. He was trustworthy, with a lot of *hadith*s.

Husayn ibn 'Ali al-Ju'fi

His *kunya* was Abu 'Abdullah. He and a brother of his called Muhammad were twins. Muhammad married and had children while Husayn never married. He did not have ease and gave the *adhan* in the Ju'fi mosque for sixty years. He was a devout worshipper who had excellence, reciting the Qur'an to people. He related from Layth ibn Abi Sulaym, Musa al-Juhani, al-A'mash, Hisham ibn 'Urwa and others. Sufyan ibn 'Uyayna respected him.

Someone who saw him reported that Husayn came to Makka on *hajj* and Sufyan ibn 'Uyayna met him and greeted him and took his hand and kissed it. 'Abdullah ibn Idris, Abu Usama and the shaykhs of Kufa respected him and went to him and related to him. He was familiar with the people of the Qur'an and the people of good. He died in Kufa in Dhu al-Qa'da 203 AH while al-Ma'mun was caliph.

'A'idh ibn Habib

The vendor of al-Harawi. His *kunya* was Abu Ahmad. He was a *mawla* of the Banu 'Abs. He was the neighbour of 'Ubaydullah ibn Musa, an intimate companion of his house. He was trustworthy, Allah willing.

Ya'la ibn 'Ubayd ibn Abi Umayya at-Tanafisi

His *kunya* was Abu Yusuf, a *mawla* of Iyad.

Talq ibn Ghannam an-Nakha'i reported that Ya'la was born in 117 AH while Hisham ibn 'Abd al-Malik was caliph. He died in Kufa on Sunday 25 Shawwal 209 AH while al-Ma'mun was caliph. He was trustworthy, with a lot of *hadith*s.

Muhammad ibn 'Ubayd ibn Abi Umayya at-Tanafisi

The brother of Ya'la. His *kunya* was Abu 'Abdullah. He descended in Baghdad for a time and then returned to Kufa. He died there before Ya'la in 204 AH while al-Ma'mun was caliph. He was trustworthy and had a lot of *hadith*s. He held to the *Sunna* and the Community.

'Imran ibn 'Uyayna

The brother of Sufyan ibn 'Uyayna. His *kunya* was Abu Ishaq. He died in 199 AH while al-Ma'mun was caliph. He related from Abu Hayyan at-Taymi and others.

Yahya ibn Sa'id

Yahya ibn Sa'id ibn Aban ibn Sa'id ibn al-'As ibn Sa'id ibn al-'As ibn Umayya ibn 'Abd Shams. His *kunya* was Abu Ayyub. He related from al-A'mash, Hisham ibn 'Urwa, Yahya ibn Sa'id. Isma'il ibn Abi Khalid and others. He related expeditions from Muhammad ibn Ishaq. He moved and settled in Baghdad where he died.

His brother, 'Abd al-Malik ibn Sa'id

He was a man of letters, with knowledge of the stars and the battles of people.

Muhadir ibn al-Muwarri' al-Hamdani, then al-Yami

His *kunya* was Abu al-Muwarri'. He used to live at Jabbana of Kinda. He related from al-A'mash, Hisham ibn 'Urwa and others. He was trustworthy, truthful, refusing to relate *hadith* but then he related them after that. He died in Kufa in Shawwal 206 AH while al-Ma'mun was caliph.

Humayd ibn 'Abd ar-Rahman ibn Humayd ar-Ra'asi

His *kunya* was Abu 'Awf. He was imam of the mosque of Waki' ibn al-Jarrah. He related from al-A'mash and he related from al-Hasan ibn Salih a lot. He died in Kufa in 170 AH while Harun was caliph. He was trustworthy, with a lot of *hadith*s and people did not write all that he had.

Muhammad ibn Rabi'a

His *kunya* was Abu 'Abdullah. He died in Baghdad and is related from.

Sa'id ibn Muhammad ath-Thaqafi al-Warraq

His *kunya* was Abu al-Hasan. He died in Baghdad. He was weak and they wrote from him.

Qurran ibn Tammam al-Asadi

His *kunya* was Abu Tammam. He came to Baghdad and died there. He had *hadith*s. Some of them thought him weak.

Yunus ibn Bukayr

A *mawla* of the Banu Shayban. His *kunya* was Abu Bakr. He was the companion of Muhammad ibn Ishaq, the one with expeditions. He died in Kufa in 197 AH while al-Ma'mun was caliph.

'Abd al-Hamid ibn 'Abd ar-Rahman al-Himmani

His *kunya* was Abu Yahya. He was weak.

'Ubaydullah ibn Musa ibn al-Mukhtar al-'Absi

His *kunya* was Abu Muhammad. He read to 'Isa ibn 'Umar and 'Ali ibn Salih ibn Hayy. He used to recite the Qur'an in his mosque. He related from al-A'mash, Hisham ibn 'Urwa, Isma'il ibn Abi Khalid, Zakariyya' ibn Abi Za'ida, 'Uthman ibn al-Aswad, Muhammad ibn 'Abd ar-Rahman ibn Abi Layla and others. He was the person who related the most in his time from Isra'il ibn Yunus ibn Abi Ishaq. He died in Kufa at the end of Shawwal 213 AH while al-Ma'mun was caliph. He was trustworthy, truthful, Allah willing, with many *hadiths* and a good appearance. He was a Shi'ite and related *hadiths* about Shi'ism which are *munkar*. He was thought weak because of that by most people. He knew the Qur'an.

Abu Nu'aym al-Fadl

Abu Nu'aym al-Fadl ibn Dukayn ibn Hammad ibn Zuhayr, a *mawla* of the family of Talha ibn 'Ubaydullah at-Taymi. He related from al-A'mash, Zakariyya' ibn Abi Za'ida, Mis'ar ibn Kidam, Ja'far ibn Burqan and others. He died in Kufa on Tuesday night and was buried Tuesday, at the end of Sha'ban 219 AH.

'Abdus ibn Kamil reported: "We were with Abu Nu'aym ibn Dukayn one day in the month of Rabi'a al-Awwal 217 in Kufa when Ibn Muhadir ibn al-Muwarri' came to him and Abu Nu'aym said to him, 'I saw your father yesterday in a dream and it seemed that he gave me two and a half dirhams. What do you say about this?' We said, 'You have had a good dream.' He said, 'I interpreted it as meaning that I will live for two and a half days, or two and a half months, or two and a half years and then join the group.'" He died in Kufa on Tuesday night and was buried on Tuesday at the end of Sha'ban 219 AH. That was thirty full months after his dream. I was told by those who were present that he fell ill a day and a night before he died and did not speak until *Zuhr*. Then he spoke and instructed his son 'Abd ar-Rahman to care for a young son of a son of his called Maytham who had died before him. On Monday evening, he was stabbed in his neck and he appeared with a weapon in his hand. He died on Tuesday and he was prepared at night and brought out early and many people did not know about it. He was taken to the cemetery and a man of the family of Ja'far ibn Abi Talib called Muhammad ibn Dawud came and his son, 'Abd ar-Rahman ibn Abi Nu'aym, put him forward and he led the prayer over him. Then the governor, who was Muhamamd ibn 'Abd ar-Rahman ibn 'Isa ibn Musa al-Hashimi came and blamed them for not telling him about his death. Then he went to a side of the grave and he and his companions and those people who joined him prayed over him. He died while al-Mu'tasim Abu Ishaq was caliph. He was trustworthy, secure, with a lot of *hadith*s, an authority.

Muhammad ibn al-Qasim al-Asdi

His *kunya* was Abu Ibrahim. He used to sell red camels and other camels at Kunasa. He related from al-Awza'i and others. He died in Kufa. He had *hadith*s.

Muhammad ibn 'Abd al-A'la ibn Kunasa al-Asad

He is the nephew of Ibrahim ibn Adham az-Zahid. He related from al-A'mash, Hisham ibn 'Urwa and others. He was a scholar in Arabic, the battles of people and poetry. He died in Kufa on 27 Shawwal 209 AH while al-Ma'mun was caliph.

'Ali ibn Zabyan al-'Absi

His *kunya* was Abu al-Hasan. He was appointed qadi of ash-Sharqiyya in Baghdad. Then Harun, the Amir al-Mu'minin, appointed him qadi with him in his army wherever he was. He used to sit in the mosque which was ascribed to al-Khuld for judgement. He went out with Harun when he went to Khurasan and he died in Qarmasin in 192 AH. 'Ali ibn 'Ubaydullah ibn 'Amr, Ibn Abi Layla and others related from him.

Eighth Generation

Yahya ibn Adam ibn Sulayman

His *kunya* was Abu Zakariyya', a *mawla* of Khalid ibn Khalid ibn 'Umara ibn 'Uqba ibn Abi Mu'ayt. He died at Fam as-Sukh in the month of Rabi' al-Awwal 203 AH while al-Ma'mun was caliph. He related from Sufyan ath-Thawri and others. He was trustworthy.

Zayd ibn al-Hubbab al-'Ukli

He was a *mawla* of Ukl. His *kunya* was Abu al-Husayn. He died in Kufa in Dhu al-Hijja 203 AH while al-Ma'mun was caliph.

Abu Ahmad az-Zubayri

His name was Muhammad ibn 'Abdullah ibn az-Zubayr, a *mawla* of the Banu Asad. He was the nephew of Fudayl ar-Rammani. He died in Ahwaz in Jumada al-Ula 203 AH while al-Ma'mun was caliph. He was truthful, with a lot of *hadith*s.

Abu Dawud al-Hafari

His name was 'Amr ibn Sa'd. He was a teacher. Abu Dawud 'Amr ibn Sa'd was a devout, humble ascetic. He was one of the companions of Sufyan ath-Thawri. He died in Kufa in Jumada al-Akhira 203 AH while al-Ma'mun was caliph.

Qabisa ibn 'Uqba

His *kunya* was Abu 'Amir of the Banu Suwa'a ibn 'Amir ibn Sa'sa'a. He died in Kufa in Safar 215 AH while al-Ma'mun was caliph. He was trustworthy, truthful, with a lot of *hadith*s from Sufyan ath-Thawri.

'Amr ibn Muhammad al-'Anqazi

He used to sell goods called 'anqaz. He was a *mawla* of the family of Ziyad ibn Abi Sufyan. He had the *hadith*s of the Prophet and others. He was a neighbour of Abu Dawud al-Hafari in Kufa. They prayed in the mosque and their house was in Hafar as-Subay'.

Mu'awiya ibn Hisham al-Qassar

A *mawla* of the Banu Asad. His *kunya* was Abu al-Hasan. He died in Kufa and was truthful, with a lot of *hadith*s.

'Abd al-'Aziz ibn Aban al-Qurashi

One of the children of Sa'id ibn al-'As. His *kunya* was Abu Khalid. He was appointed qadi of Wasit. Then he was dismissed and came to Baghdad and settled there. He died there on Wednesday 14 Rajab 207 AH while al-Ma'mun was caliph. He had a lot of transmission from Sufyan and then he muddled things after that and they withheld from his *hadith*s.

'Ali ibn Qadim

His *kunya* is Abu al-Hasan. He died in Kufa in 213 AH while al-Ma'mun was caliph. He was denied and his *hadith*s are *munkar*. He was an extreme Shi'ite.

Thabit ibn Muhammad al-Kinani

His *kunya* is Abu Isma'il. He was a devout worshipper who related from Mis'ar ibn Kidam and others. He died in Kufa in Dhu al-Hijja 215 AH while al-Ma'mun was caliph.

Abu Ghassan

His name was Malik ibn Isma'il ibn Ziyad ibn Dirham, the *mawla* of Kulayb ibn 'Amir an-Nahdi, one of the Banu Khuzayma. The mother of Abu Ghassan was the daughter of Isma'il ibn Hammad ibn Abi Sulayman and Hammad ibn Abi Sulayman, the maternal uncle of Isma'il ibn Abi Ghassan. Abu Ghassan died in Kufa at the beginning of Rabi' al-Akhir 219 AH while Abu Ishaq al-Mu'tasim was caliph. Abu Ghassan was trustworthy, truthful, a very strong Shi'ite.

Ahmad ibn 'Abdullah ibn Yunus

His *kunya* was Abu 'Abdullah, and he was a *mawla* of the Banu Yarbu' from the Banu Tamim. He died in Kufa on Friday on 25 Rabi' al-Akhir 227 AH. He was trustworthy, truthful, and held to the *Sunna* and Community.

Talq ibn Ghannam

Talq ibn Ghannam ibn Talq ibn Mu'awiya ibn Malik ibn al-Harith ibn Tha'laba ibn 'Amir ibn Rabi'a ibn 'Amir ibn Jusham ibn Wahbil ibn Sa'd ibn Malik ibn an-Nakha' of Madhhij. His *kunya* was Abu Muhammad. He was the cousin of Hafs ibn Ghiyath, the Qadi Lahha. He acted as his scribe while he was qadi.

Talq ibn Ghannam reported: "My grandfather Malik ibn al-Harith was at al-Qadisiya. My grandfather, Talq ibn Mu'awiya, was born in 140 at the end of the caliphate of Abu al-'Abbas as-Saffah. Talq ibn Ghannam died in 211 while al-Ma'mun was caliph. He was trustworthy and truthful. He had *hadith*s."

Ishaq ibn Mansur as-Saluli

He was one of their *mawla*s. He died in Kufa in 205 AH while al-Ma'mun was caliph.

Bakr ibn 'Abd ar-Rahman

Bakr ibn 'Abd ar-Rahman ibn 'Abdullah ibn 'Isa ibn 'Abd ar-Rahman ibn Abi Layla al-Ansari. He listened to the *Musannaf* of Muhammad 'Abd ar-Rahman ibn Abi Layla from 'Isa ibn al-Mukhtar ibn 'Abdullah ibn Abi Layla. He related it from him. Bakr was appointed qadi of Kufa for about ten years and then dismissed. He died after that in Kufa.

Khalid ibn Makhlad al-Qatawani

He is attributed to Bajila. His *kunya* was Abu al-Haytham. He had *hadith*s from the men of Madina. He was a Shi'ite. He died in Kufa in the middle of Muharram 213 AH while al-Ma'mun was caliph. His *hadith*s about Shi'ism were *munkar* and extreme. They wrote from him only out of necessity.

Ishaq ibn Mansur

Ishaq ibn Mansur ibn Hayyan ibn al-Husayn ibn Malik ibn Akhi Abi al-Hayyaj al-Asadi. He was good, excellent. He related from Abu Kudayna, Sharik and Abu al-Ahwas.

'Ubayd ibn Sa'id

'Ubayd ibn Sa'id ibn Aban ibn Sa'id ibn al-'As ibn Umayya. He related from Sufyan and others.

'Anbasa ibn Sa'id

His brother, 'Anbasa ibn Sa'id ibn Aban ibn Sa'id ibn al-'As. His *kunya* was Abu Khalid. He was trustworthy, with a lot of transmission from 'Abdullah ibn al-Mubarak and others.

Rabah ibn Khalid

His *kunya* was Abu 'Ali. He related from Zuhayr, Hasan ibn Salih, Qays and Sharik. He had a lot of *hadith*s. He died in Kufa before he was written from.

Nawfal

His *kunya* was Abu Mas'ud ad-Dabbi from the tribe of Dabba. Nawfal related from Zuhayr, Abu al-Ahwas, Sharik, Ibn al-Mubarak and others. He had a lot of *hadith*s. He died in Kufa before he was written from.

'Abd ar-Rahim ibn 'Abd ar-Rahman

'Abd ar-Rahim ibn 'Abd ar-Rahman ibn Muhammad al-Muharibi. His *kunya* was Abu Ziyad. He related from Za'ida ibn Qudama and others. He died in Kufa in Sha'ban 211 AH while al-Ma'mun was caliph. He was trustworthy and truthful.

Zakariyya' ibn 'Adi

His *kunya* was Abu Yahya, a *mawla* of the Banu Taymullah. He died in Baghdad in Jumada al-Ula 212 AH while al-Ma'mun was caliph. Zakariyya' was a righteous man, truthful.

'Abd ar-Rahman ibn Mus'ab al-Ma'ni

His *kunya* is Abu Yazid. He was a devout worshipper. He had *hadith*s.

'Ali ibn 'Abd al-Hamid al-Ma'ni

One of Azd. He was also good, excellent. He was the cousin of 'Abd ar-Rahman ibn Mus'ab. He had *hadith*s.

'Awn ibn Sallam

A *mawla* of Quraysh. His *kunya* was Abu Muhammad. He related from Isra'il, Zuhayr, Asbat ibn Nasr, Mansur ibn Abi al-Aswad, 'Isa ibn 'Abd ar-Rahman as-Sulami and others.

Yahya ibn Ya'la ibn al-Harith al-Muharibi

He died in Kufa in 216 AH while al-Ma'mun was caliph.

'Amr ibn Hammad ibn Talha al-Qannad

His *kunya* was Abu Muhammad, the one with the *tafsir* of Asbat ibn Nasr from as-Suddi. He died in Kufa in Rabi' al-Awwal 222 AH. He said that he originated from Isbahan and his grandfather went to Kufa and the governor of Hamdan and settled with them at the crossroads of Hamdan. He died while Abu Ishaq al-Mu'tasim was caliph. He was trustworthy, Allah willing.

Muhammad ibn as-Salt

His *kunya* was Abu Ja'far, and he was a *mawla* of the Banu Asad ibn Khuzayma.

Isma'il ibn Aban al-Warraq

His *kunya* was Abu Ishaq, and he was a *mawla* of Kinda.

Al-Hasan ibn ar-Rabi'

His *kunya* was Abu 'Ali. He was the brother of Mutayr, the companion of al-Bawari. Al-Hasan was one of the companions of 'Abdullah ibn al-Mubarak. He was present with him when he died in

Hit and he closed his eyes. Al-Hasan died in Kufa on Saturday at the beginning of Ramadan 221 AH while Abu Ishaq was caliph.

'Abd al-Hamid ibn Salih

His *kunya* was Abu Muhammad. He used to stay among the Banu Shaytan in Kufa. He related from Zuhayr and Huraym.

Ahmad ibn al-Mufaddal

He was a *mawla* of Quraysh, the cousin of 'Amr al-'Anqari. He died in Dhu al-Qa'da 215 AH. He transmitted from Asbat ibn Nasr.

'Uthman ibn Hakim al-Awdi

He related from Sharik and others. He was trustworthy.

Shihab ibn 'Abbad al-'Abdi

He died in Kufa on Saturday 28 Jumada al-Ula 224 AH while Abu Ishaq ibn Harun was caliph.

Al-Haytham ibn 'Ubaydullah

A *mufti* of Quraysh. His *kunya* was Abu Muhammad.

Yahya ibn 'Abd ar-Rahman al-Himmani

His *kunya* was Abu Zakariyya'. He died in Samarra in Ramadan 230 AH.

Yusuf ibn al-Buhlul

His *kunya* was Abu Ya'qub of the Banu Aban ibn Darim of the Banu Tamim from themselves. He is the author of the expeditions which he heard from 'Abdullah ibn Idris from Muhammad ibn Ishaq. He died in Kufa in Rabi' al-Akhir or Jumada al-Ula 218 AH while al-Ma'mun was caliph.

Sa'id ibn Shurahbil al-Kindi

His *kunya* is Abu 'Uthman. Sa'id went to Egypt and wrote from Ibn Lahi'a and others.

'Uthman ibn Zufar ibn al-Hudhayl

He died in Kufa in Rabi' al-Akhir or Jumada al-Ula 218 AH while al-Ma'mun was caliph.

Yahya ibn Bishr ibn Kathir

His *kunya* was Abu Zakriyya al-Asadi al-Hariri. His house was close to the mosque of Simak. He was a merchant who came to Damascus, and he listened to Sa'id ibn 'Abd al-'Aziz, Sa'id ibn Bashir and Mu'awiya ibn Sallam, the companion of Yahya ibn Abi Kathir. He died in Kufa in Jumada al-Ula 229 AH while Harun al-Wathiq was caliph.

Hisham ibn al-Miqdam and **Suwayd ibn 'Amr** al-Kalbi are part of this generation.

Ninth Generation

Isma'il ibn Musa

Isma'il ibn Musa ibn bint Isma'il ibn 'Abd ar-Rahman as-Suddi. His *kunya* was Abu Muhammad. He related from Sharik ibn 'Abdullah and others.

Hamdan ibn Muhammad ibn Sulayman al-Isbahani

He related from Sharik and others. He died in Kufa.

Al-Munjab ibn al-Harith at-Tamimi

His *kunya* was Abu Muhammad. He related from Sharik and 'Ali ibn Mushir and others.

'Uthman ibn Muhammad

'Uthman ibn Muhammad ibn Ibrahim ibn 'Uthman al-'Absi. His *kunya* was Abu al-Hasan. He was one of the children of Abu Sa'da. He related *hadith* from Abu Sa'da, and Abu Sa'da related from Ibn 'Abbas and Ibn az-Zubayr. 'Uthman ibn Abi Shayba mentioned that he related from the Prophet ﷺ. 'Uthman related from Sharik, Abu al-Ahwas and 'Ali ibn Mushir. He wrote the books of Jarir. He travelled to him in Rayy and listened to his books.

His brother, 'Abdullah ibn Muhammad

'Abdullah ibn Muhammad ibn Abi Shayba. His *kunya* was Abu Bakr. He related from Sharik, 'Ali ibn Mushir and the Kufans. He travelled to Basra and wrote from those of his shaykhs he met.

Ahmad ibn Asad ibn 'Asim ibn Mighwal al-Bajali

He was the son of the daughter of Malik ibn Mighwal. His *kunya* was Abu 'Asim. He died in Kufa in Safar 229 AH while Harun al-Wathiq billah was caliph.

'Umar ibn Hafs ibn Ghiyath an-Nakha'i

He died in Kufa in Rabi' al-Awwal 222 AH while Abu Ishaq al-Mu'tasim billah was caliph.

Thabit ibn Musa

His *kunya* was Abu Yazid. He died in Kufa in 229 AH while Harun al-Wathiq billah was caliph.

Muhammad ibn 'Abdullah

Muhammad ibn 'Abdullah ibn Numayr al-Hamdani, then al-Kharifi. His *kunya* was Abu 'Abd ar-Rahman. He died in Kufa in 234 AH.

Harun ibn Ishaq al-Hamdani

His *kunya* was Abu al-Qasim.

Muhammad ibn al-'Ala'

His *kunya* was Abu Kurayb. He settled in Matmura in Kufa close to the house of Abu Usama in Hafar.

'Ubaydullah ibn Ya'ish

His *kunya* was Abu Muhammad. He died in Kufa in Ramadan 229 AH while Harun ibn Abi Ishaq was caliph. He was trustworthy.

Yusuf ibn Ya'qub as-Saffar

His *kunya* was Abu Ya'qub.

Layth ibn Harun al-'Ukli

His *kunya* was Abu 'Utba. Zayd ibn al-Hubbab was their *mawla*. He died in Kufa at the end of 228 AH while Harun ibn Abi Ishaq was caliph.

Abu Hisham ar-Rifaʻi

His name was Muhammad ibn Yazid ibn Kathir ibn Rifaʻa of the Banu ʻIjl.

Abu Saʻid al-Ashajj

His name was ʻAbdullah ibn Saʻid al-Kindi.

Saʻid ibn ʻAmr

One of the children of al-Ashʻath ibn Qays al-Kindi. His *kunya* was Abu ʻUthman. He listened to Abu ʻAwana, ʻAbthar and others. He was trustworthy, truthful, secure. He died in Kufa in Safar 230 AH while Harun ibn Abi Ishaq was caliph.

Jubara ibn al-Mughallas al-Maliki

He was the imam of the mosque of the Banu Himman. He is thought weak.

Dirar ibn Surad at-Tahhan

His *kunya* was Abu Nuʻaym. He died in Kufa in the middle of Dhu al-Hijja 229 AH while Harun ibn Abi Ishaq was caliph.

Ismaʻil ibn Muhammad ibn Abi al-Hakam ath-Thaqafi

One of the children of al-Mukhtar ibn Abi ʻUbayd ath-Thaqafi. His grandfather was Abu al-Hakam. He related from al-Aʻmash.

Ismaʻil ibn Bahram

He related from al-Ashjaʻi.

ʻAbdullah ibn Barrad al-Ashʻari

One of the children of Abu Musa. His *kunya* was Abu ʻAmir. He died in Kufa in 234 AH.

Husayn ibn ʻAbd al-Awwal al-Ahwal

His *kunya* was Abu ʻAbdullah.

Yazid ibn Mihran

His *kunya* was Abu Khalid al-Khabbaz. He related from Abu Bakr ibn 'Ayyash and he died in Kufa in Shawwal 228 AH while Harun ibn Abi Ishaq was caliph.

Marwan ibn Ja'far

Marwan ibn Ja'far ibn Sa'd ibn Samura ibn Jundub al-Fazari. He related from Abu Bakr ibn 'Ayyash. He was responsible for the will of Samura to his sons.

Masruq ibn al-Marzuban al-Kindi

His *kunya* was Abu Sa'id. He related from Yahya ibn Zakariyya' ibn Abi Za'ida and others.

Farwa ibn Abi al-Maghra' and **Al-'Ala' ibn 'Umar al-Hanafi** were also from this generation.

Glossary

'Abd al-Qays, Banu: a branch of Rabi'a located in Bahrayn. It was the first Arab tribe outside of Madina to accept Islam.

Abiward: also Baward, a town on the northern slopes of the mountains of Khurasan.

abna': the descendants of the Persian troops sent by Khosraw I to the Yemen in 575 to assist Sayf ibn Abi Yazan, the Himyari chief, in the fight against Abyssinian occupation.

Abu Qubays: a mountain in Makka.

'Ad: an ancient people in southern Arabia to whom the Prophet Hud was sent.

adhan: the call to prayer.

Ajnadayn: site of the first major battle between the Byzantines and Muslims under Khalid ibn al-Walid in 13/634 in which the Muslims decisively defeated the Byzantine forces who numbered about 100,000.

akhmas: slaves from the fifth of the state (*khums*).

Amir al-Mu'minin: "the Commander of the Believers", the title of the Caliph.

'Amwas plague: a major plague which broke out in Syria in 18/639 which killed many of the Companions.

Anmar: one of the Yemeni tribes from Saba' which was a branch of Kahlan which had moved to Yathrib in pre-Islamic times.

Ansar: the "Helpers", the people of Madina who welcomed and aided the Prophet ﷺ.

'Aqaba: lit. the steep slope, a mountain pass to the north of Makka just off the caravan route to Madina, where the Prophet ﷺ met with the first Muslims from Yathrib (Madina) in two successive years. On the first occasion, they pledged to follow the Messenger, and on the second or Great Pledge of 'Aqaba, to defend him and his Companions as they would their own wives and children.

'Aqiq: a valley about seven kilometres west of Madina.

'aqiqa: a sacrifice in celebration of the birth of a child.

'Arafa: a plain fifteen miles to the east of Makka on which stands the Jabal ar-Rahma, the Mount of Mercy. One of the essential rites of *hajj* is to stand on 'Arafa on the 9th of Dhu al-Hijja.

'arif (plural *'urafa'*): literally "one who knows", an overseer, an official in charge of a military division (*'irafa*) in early Basra and Kufa.

Asad, Banu: a major Arab tribe who were a sub-branch of Rabi'a. They rebelled after the death of the Prophet ﷺ and supported the false prophet Tulayha.

'Ashura': the 10th day of Muharram, the first month of the Muslim lunar calendar. As al-Husayn ibn 'Ali was killed on 'Ashura', the day became a major Shi'ite festival commemorating the event.

Aslam, Banu: a sub-tribe of Khuza'a who were located to the north of Madina. They were enthusiastic supporters of the Prophet ﷺ and he gave them the status of Muhajirun whether or not they emigrated.

'Asr: the obligatory afternoon prayer.

al-Aswad ibn Ka'b al-'Ansi: "The black man of 'Ans", better known as 'Abhala ibn Ka'b. He claimed prophethood in Yemen towards the end of the Prophet Muhammad's ﷺ lifetime, around 10/630. He went on to invade Najran and most of the Yemen. He was eventually assassinated in 11/632.

Aws: along with Khazraj, one of the two major tribes in Madina.

ayat: a verse of the Qur'an.

'Ayn al-Warda: a place near the Syrian border where in 65/684, the Penitents or *Tawwabun* faced the Umayyad army and were defeated.

Azd: major sub-tribe of Qahtan in Yemen. When the Ma'rib dam collapsed for the third time in the third century CE, a large number of the Azd tribe left Yemen and emigrated in many directions.

Azraqites: or Azariqa, a group of Kharijites who take their name from their leader, Nafi' ibn al-Azraq who took their ideas to an extreme position, holding that anyone who did not leave and join them was an unbeliever.

Bab al-Fil: one of the gates of the mosque in Kufa.

Bab al-Hannatin: "Gate of the Embalmers", one of the gates of the Masjid al-Haram in Makka.

Badr: a place near the coast, about ninety-five miles to the south of Madina where, in 2 AH, in the first battle fought by the newly established Muslim community, three hundred Muslims led by the Messenger of Allah overwhelmingly defeated more than one thousand Makkan idolaters.

Bajila: an Arab tribe who are considered to be a sub-division of Anmar. There was some uncertainty about their ancestry: they were either Yemeni or Nizari, but they are generally considered to be Yemeni.

Bajumayra: a place near Takrit in the region of Mosul.

Balanjar: a Khazar city located in the North Caucasus region, between the cities of Derbent and Samandar. 'Abd ar-Rahman ibn Rabi'a and his army met a Khazar force outside Balanjar and were annihilated.

Banu: lit. sons, a tribe or clan.

Baqi': the cemetery in Madina.

Baraz ar-Ruz: a town located between an-Nahrawan and ad-Daskara.

al-Butah: the site of a battle in the Ridda War in which the Muslim forces, led by Khalid ibn al-Walid defeated the Banu Yarbu', a branch of Banu Tamim, under their chief, Malik ibn Nuwayra.

Buwana: a place in Arabia where there may or may not have been an idol in pre-Islamic times, according to different reports.

al-Buzakha: site of a battle in 11/632 in the Ridda War where the Muslims under Khalid ibn al-Walid defeated Tulayha, a false prophet of the tribe of Asad.

cafiz: or **qafiz** (plural *aqfiza*), a measure of grain consisting of twelve *sa'*s.

Camel, Battle of the: one of the major incidents of the first Civil War (*Fitna*) in which the forces of 'Ali defeated the forces of 'A'isha, Talha, and az-Zubayr in a battle fought outside Basra in 36/656.

Chosroes: or Khosraw, the title of the Persian Sasanid emperor. It comes from Khosraw Anushakruwan, most illustrious of the Sasanian king of kings whose name became the common designation of the ruler.

Daba: *see Dibba.*

Dabba: a tribe which originated from Yamama and lived in close proximity with Banu Tamim. They did not join Tamim in the Ridda War. They took part in the Muslim campaign against the Sasanids and supported 'A'isha in the Battle of the Camel. They settled in Basra.

Dajjal: the false Messiah whose appearance marks the imminent end of the world.

Daylam: a province of Persia. The Daylamites inhabited the mountainous regions of northern Iran on the southern shore of the Caspian Sea. They were employed as soldiers from the time of the Sasanid Empire. There was a group of four thousand who participated in the Battle of Qadisiyya under Rustam. After the battle, they became Muslim and settled in Kufa.

Dayr al-Jamajim: *see Jamajim.*

Deen: the life-transaction, literally the debt between two parties, in this usage between the Creator and created.

Dhat as-Salasil: a place about ten days' walk north of Madina, a military expedition led by 'Amr ibn al-'As which took place a month after the Battle of Mu'ta in 8/629.

dhikr: remembrance of Allah.

dhimma: obligation or contract, in particular a treaty of protection for non-Muslims living in Muslim territory.

Dhu al-Hijja: the twelfth month of the Muslim lunar calendar in which the *hajj* takes place.

Dhu al-Khalasa: an idol belonging to Khath'am, Daws and Bajila in the pre-Islamic period located in Tabala in Yemen. It was known as the Yamani Ka'ba.

Dhu al-Majaz: a market in the Hijaz which was held in the first eight days of Dhu al-Hijja.

Dhu al-Qa'da: the eleventh month of the Muslim calendar.

Dhu ath-Thudayya: al-Mukhdaj, or the one with the deformed arm, one leader of the Kharijites who was killed in the Battle of Nahrawan in 38/658. 'Ali sent people to look for him among the slain because of the *hadith* about "a people who would pass through Islam like an arrow through game" would have with them a man with a deformed arm.

Dibba: a place in Oman, one of the major ports of Arabia and the capital of the Banu Azd. One of the major battles of the Ridda War took place there between Azd under Laqit ibn Malik and the Muslim forces under 'Ikrima in which Laqit was killed and the Muslims were victorious.

dihqan: landlord, one of the class of Persian landlords who administered sub-districts.

Dimas: a large prison in Wasit built by al-Hajjaj.

Ditch, Battle of the: or Battle of the Trench. In 5/627, the Makkans, assisted by the Jewish tribe of Banu Nadr and the Arab tribes of Banu Ghatafan and Banu Asad, marched on Madina with an army of ten thousand soldiers. The Prophet ﷺ ordered a ditch to be dug on the unprotected side of Madina and manned constantly. The Makkans were forced to undertake a siege which failed.

diwan: Originally the register of soldiers and pensions under 'Umar. Subsequently it became a governmental department for the finance and records of the government.

Duha: forenoon, in particular the voluntary morning prayer.

Duhn, Banu: also called Wa'ila, a branch of the Banu Bakr.

Dujayl: site of a battle in 77/767 against the Kharijites in which Shabib, their leader was drowned.

Dumat al-Jandal: an important caravan town and agricultural oasis, now in north-western Saudi Arabia which was conquered by Khalid ibn al-Walid in 11/633.

Fajr: the obligatory dawn prayer.

Fakhkh: site of a battle in 169/786, located about five miles outside of Makka, where al-Husayn ibn al-Husayn ibn 'Ali ibn Abi Talib rebelled against the 'Abbasids and was killed and defeated.

Fam as-Sukh: a village slightly to the north of Madina.

faqih: (plural *fuqaha'*), a man learned in knowledge of *fiqh* who by virtue of his knowledge can give a legal judgement.

Fatiha: "the Opener", the first *sura* of the Qur'an.

fatwa: an authoritative statement on a point of law.

fidya: a ransom, compensation paid for rites or acts of worship missed or wrongly performed.

al-Fihl: site of a battle in the Jordan valley fought between the Byzantines and the Muslim forces led by Khalid ibn al-Walid in 13/635 which resulted in a Muslim victory.

fiqh: the science of the application of the *Shari'a*. A practitioner or expert in *fiqh* is called a *faqih*.

fuqaha': plural of *faqih*.

Ghamid, Banu: a tribe in western Arabia which originated from Yemen.

Ghanm, Banu: a branch of Tamim found in Madina.

Ghiyara, Banu: allies of the Banu Zuhra.

ghusl: major ablution of the whole body with water required to regain purity after menstruation, lochia and sexual intercourse.

hadd: (plural *hudud*), Allah's boundary limits for the lawful and unlawful. The *hadd* punishments are specific fixed penalties laid down by Allah for specified crimes.

hadith: reported speech of the Prophet ﷺ.

hafiz: a *hadith* master who has memorised at least 100,000 *hadith*s – texts, chains of transmissions and meanings. It is also used for someone who has memorised the entire Qur'an.

Hajar: a mountain chain in northern 'Uman.

Hajj: the annual pilgrimage to Makka which is one of the five pillars of Islam.

al-Hajjaj: al-Hajjaj ibn Yusuf al-Thaqafi, the governor first of the Hijaz, Yamama and Yemen and then of Iraq for the Umayyads. His name, which is a title, means "the Bone Crusher". He played a critical role in consolidating the administrative structure of the Umayyad dynasty during its early years. He was an extremely harsh ruler.

al-Hajun: a cemetery on a hill near Makka, now known as Janna al-Mu'alla.

Hamdan: a large sub-tribe of Qahtan in Yemen, renowned for bravery. All fourteen thousand members of the powerful Hamdan tribe are said to have embraced Islam in a single day.

Hanifa, Banu: an ancient Arab tribe inhabiting the area of al-Yamama in central Arabia. The tribe belonged to the great Rabi'a branch of North Arabian tribes.

hanut: an aromatic compound of camphor, reed perfume and red and white sandalwood used for perfuming shrouds.

Haram: Sacred precinct, the area around the Ka'ba in Makka.

al-Harith, Banu: the dominant tribe in Najran in the early period of Islam. It was one of the southern Arabs. It is also known as Balharith.

al-Harra: a stony tract of black volcanic rock east of Madina where a terrible battle took place in 63 AH (26 August 683) between the forces of Yazid I and 'Abdullah ibn az-Zubayr which ended in Madina being sacked and plundered.

Haruriyya: the first Kharijites or schismatics who separated themselves from 'Ali and based themselves at Harura', a town two miles from Kufa.

Hashim, Banu: descendants of the family of Hashim, the great grandfather of the Prophet ﷺ.

Hawazin: one of the large Arab tribes, a sub-tribe of Qays 'Aylan. It was concentrated around Ta'if. The Battle of Hunayn was fought against them.

Hijaz: the region along the western seaboard of Arabia in which Makka, Madina, Jeddah and Ta'if are situated.

Hijra: emigration in the way of Allah. Islamic dating begins with the *Hijra* of the Prophet Muhammad ﷺ from Makka to Madina in 622 CE.

Himman, Banu: a branch of the Arab tribe of Tamim.

Himyar: one of the two main groupings of the southern or Qahtani Arabs. The Himyarite kingdom in Yemen was the dominant state in Arabia until 525 CE.

Hira: an ancient city in Iraq which was the capital of the Lakhmids, the vassals of the Sasanids. It was captured by Khalid ibn al-Walid in 633 CE. It is south of Kufa, which replaced it.

hizb: a set portion of the Qur'an for recitation.

Homage of ar-Ridwan: also referred to as the Tree of ar-Ridwan, a pledge which the Muslims took to avenge 'Uthman ibn 'Affan when they thought that Quraysh had murdered him at al-Hudaybiya in 6/628.

Hudaybiya: a well-known place ten miles from Makka on the way to Jidda where the Homage of ar-Ridwan took place.

hudud: plural of *hadd*.

huffaz: plural of *hafiz*.

Hulwan: an ancient city in the Zagros mountain range in present-day western Persia.

Hunayn: a valley between Makka and Ta'if where a battle took place between the Prophet ﷺ and the tribe of Hawazin in 8/630.

'Id: a festival, either the festival at the end of Ramadan or at the time of the *hajj*.

'Id al-Adha: the festival at the end of the *hajj*.

'Id al-Fitr: the festival at the end of the fast of Ramadan on the 1st of the month of Shawwal.

'idda: a period after divorce or the death of her husband during which a woman must wait before re-marrying.

ihram: the conditions of clothing and behaviour adopted by someone on *hajj* or *'umra*.

'Ijl, Banu: an ancient Arab tribe considered to be part of Bakr ibn Wa'il of Rabi'a. They originally lived in Yamama and in the region around the routes between Makka and southern Iraq. They had ties with the Persians whom they supported against the Muslims in the early days.

ila': a vow by a husband to abstain from sexual relations with his wife. If four months pass, it is considered a divorce.

imam: Muslim religious or political leader, also the leader of the group prayer.

irja': A term with some ambiguity which means suspending or postponing judgement on whether or not someone is a believer. This became the position of the Murji'ites which was to postpone judgement on people's actions. The term was also used politically for suspending judgement between 'Ali and 'Uthman.

'Isha': the obligatory evening prayer.

isnad: a tradition's chain of transmission from individual to individual.

i'tikaf: seclusion, while fasting, in a mosque, particularly in the last ten days of Ramadan.

Jabbana: cemetery, an open area which was later used as a place for holding gatherings.

Jabbana of 'Arzam: a cemetery area in Kufa named after 'Arzam, who used to churn butter there in a cloth.

al-Jabiya: the capital of the Ghassanids, south of Damascus, and 'Umar's headquarters when he visited Syria and where he instituted the diwan and the capital of Syria for twenty years while Mu'awiya was governor.

Jadila, Banu: one of the large branches of the Banu Tayy'.

al-Jahhaf: *see Torrent, Year of the.*

Jahiliyya: the Time of Ignorance before the coming of Islam.

al-Jalula': a battle between the Muslims and Sasanids in 16/637 in which the Persians were defeated.

Jam': al-Muzdalifa, a well-known place between 'Arafa and Mina.

Jamajim: Dayr al-Jamajim: a battle in Iraq in 82/701 which ended the rebellion of Ibn al-Ash'ath.

Jamal, Banu: a sub-tribe of Murad.

jamra: one of the stone pillars at Mina. Stoning them is part of the rites of *hajj*.

al-Janad: a city in southern Yemen close to Ta'izz. It was located on a caravan route.

Jazira: Mesopotamia or north-eastern Syria.

al-Ji'irana: A place, few miles from Makka. The Prophet ﷺ oversaw the distribution of the war booty of the Battle of Hunayn there, and from there he assumed the state of *ihram* to perform *'umra*.

jihad: struggle, particularly fighting for the Cause of Allah to establish or defend Islam.

jinn: inhabitants of the heavens and the earth made of smokeless fire who are usually invisible.

jizya: a protection tax payable by non-Muslims as a tribute to a Muslim ruler.

jubbah: a long loose outer garment with wide sleeves.

Ju'fi: a Yemeni tribe related to Hamdan or Madhhij.

Juhayna: a large nomadic tribe from the Hijaz whose territory covered the routes between Syria and Makka.

Jumada al-Akhira: the sixth month of the Muslim lunar calendar.

Jumada al-Ula: the fifth month of the Muslim lunar calendar.

Jumah, Banu: a clan of Quraysh.

Jumu'a: the day of gathering, Friday, and particularly the *Jumu'a* prayer which is performed instead of the *Zuhr* prayer by those who attend it.

Jurash: a fortified Yemeni city in the 'Asir mountain range of Arabia.

Ka'ba: the cube-shaped building at the centre of the Haram in Makka, originally built by the Prophet Ibrahim. Also known as the House of Allah. It is towards the Ka'ba that Muslims face when praying.

Kahil, Banu: a branch of the Banu Asad.

Kahlan: a sub-group of the Qahtan tribe which consists of Tayy', Azd, 'Amila-Judham and Hamdan-Madhhij.

Kaskar: a town on the Tigris between Kufa and Basra.

katm: a plant used for dyeing hair.

Kazima: a place on the northern coast of Kuwait Bay.

kharaj: taxes imposed on revenue from land or the work of slaves.

Kharijites: the earliest sect in Islamic history, a group who separated themselves from the body of the Muslims and declared war on all those who disagreed with them, stating that a wrong action turns a Muslim into an unbeliever.

Khashabiyya: a disparaging term for the followers of al-Mukhtar because some of the *mawali* used pieces of wood (*khasab*) as weapons.

khatib: a speaker or orator; the one who delivers the *khutba*.

Khwarazm: an ancient state of central Asia, situated in and around the basin of the lower Amu Darya River. It was conquered without fighting in 93/712 by Qutayba ibn Muslim.

Khaybar: Jewish colony to the north of Madina which was besieged and captured by the Muslims in the seventh year after the Hijra.

Khazraj: along with Aws, one of the two major tribes in Madina.

khul': a form of divorce initiated by the wife.

Khurasan: a Persian province southeast of the Caspian Sea; a centre of many dissident movements in early Islamic history.

khutba: a speech, and in particular a standing speech given by the *imam* before the *Jumu'a* prayer and after the two *'Id* prayers.

Khuza'a: a branch of the Azd Qahtani tribes. They were allies of Quraysh and were located on the road between Makka and Madina.

Kinana: a large tribe who lived in the area around Makka. Quraysh was one of its branches.

Kinda: a tribe of south Arabs from a Kahlani branch that was part of the Sabaean Kingdom of Ma'rib (central Yemen) in the early third century CE. They were the kings of Hadramawt from 325 to 425 CE and were part of the Himyar tribal federation and later were kings in Najd.

kitaba: a contract by which a slave acquires his freedom against a future payment, or payment by instalments, to his master.

Kunasa: the dump in Kufa which later became a market.

kunya: a respectful but affectionate way of addressing people as "the father of so-and-so" or "the mother of so-and-so".

lahd: a grave, about five feet deep in which a niche is dug for the body into the side facing *qibla* so that the body is protected by the overhang. The other form of graves is called *shaqq*.

Mada'in: the name given to an ancient metropolis formed by Ctesiphon and Seleucia (also referred to as Seleucia-Ctesiphon) on opposite sides of the Tigris River in Iraq.

Madhhij: an important large Yemeni Arab sub-tribe of Kahlan.

Madinat as-Salam: "the City of Peace", meaning Baghdad.

Maghrib: the obligatory sunset prayer.

Mahdi: "Divinely Guided", the descendant of the Prophet ﷺ who will come at the end of time to bring justice.

Makhzum, Banu: one of the wealthy clans of Quraysh.

Manbaj: a city on the Euphrates, east of Aleppo.

Maqam: Maqam Ibrahim, the place of the stone on which the Prophet Ibrahim stood while he and Isma'il were building the Ka'ba.

Ma'rab: a place in Yemen.

Marj 'Adhra: a village fifteen miles from Damascus which was conquered by Khalid ibn al-Walid.

Marj Rahit: a place east of Damascus in Syria where a battle took place in 64/684 between the forces of ad-Dahhak ibn Qays who supported Ibn az-Zubayr and the Ummayad Marwan which resulted in a Marwanid victory. It is said that the battle re-kindled the feuds between the northern Arab tribes and the southern tribes. It was also the site of an earlier battle in 11/634 in which Khalid ibn al-Walid defeated the Ghassanids.

Marwa: a small hill near the Ka'ba. (*see Safa and Marwa*)

marzban: a military governor of a frontier district under the Sasanids.

Masabadhan: a district in Luristan in Persia which was conquered in 16/637 by Dirar ibn al-Khattab.

Masjid al-Haram: the great mosque in Makka. The Ka'ba is situated in it.

Maskin: a district in Iraq located on the Dujayl river just west of the Tigris and below the border with the territory of Mosul.

Mathani: "the often recited", the *Fatiha*.

mawali: the plural of *mawla*, a person with whom a tie of clientage has been established, usually by having been a slave and then set free. It was also used for a type of political patronage.

mawla: *see mawali*.

Mina: a valley five miles on the road to 'Arafa where the three *jamra*s stand.

mithqal: the weight of one dinar.

mu'adhdhin: someone who calls the *adhan* or call to prayer.

Mubayyida: "the white-clad", a heretical sect who were followers of al-Muqanna' (the veiled one) who claimed to be the Mahdi. Al-Muqanna', or Hisham ibn Hakim al-Marwazi, was a follower of Abu Muslim, the 'Abbasid agent, and then later led his own movement against the 'Abbasids. He died in 166/783.

Mudar: The northern Arab tribes fell into two groups: Mudar, under the leadership of the tribe of Tamim, and Rabi'a. Opposing them were the southern, Yemeni tribes under Azd. The tribes of Rabi'a came to side with the Azdites.

Mufassal: the *sura*s of the Qur'an from *Surat Qaf* (50) to the end of the Qur'an.

mufti: someone qualified to give a legal opinion or *fatwa*.

muhaddith: a scholar who transmits and/or studies *hadith*.

Muhajirun: the Companions of the Messenger of Allah ﷺ who accepted Islam in Makka and emigrated to Madina. The singular is *muhajir*.

Muharib, Banu: a branch of Banu Qays located in Najd.

Muharram: the first month of the Muslim lunar year.

mukatab: a slave who has been given a *kitaba*, a contract to buy his freedom.

al-Mukhtar: al-Mukhtar ibn Abi 'Ubayd ath-Thaqafi, the Shi'ite Muslim leader who in 66/685 championed the Muhammad ibn al-Hanafiyya, a son of 'Ali by a wife other than Fatima, as leader of the Islamic community in opposition to the Umayyad dynasty. He also rallied the *mawali* of Kufa to his cause by preaching the imminent coming of a mahdi, or saviour, who would wipe out ethnic and class distinctions and implant the egalitarian society.

munkar: "denounced", a narration reported by a weak reporter which goes against another authentic *hadith*.

murabit: one who holds fast together in the Cause of Allah with the aim of establishing the *deen* of Allah, derived from the word *'ribat'*.

Murad: a southern Arab tribe.

al-Muraysi': a battle between the Prophet ﷺ and the Banu al-Mustaliq in Sha'ban 6 AH.

Murhiba, Banu: a southern Arab tribe.

Murji'ites: the opponents of the Kharijites. They held that it is faith and not actions which are ultimately important. They also have a political position which suspends judgement on a person guilty of major sins.

mursal: a *hadith* in which a man in the generation after the Companions quotes directly from the Prophet ﷺ without mentioning the Companion from whom he got it.

Musannaf: a *hadith* collection arranged by topical chapters.

al-Musawwida: "the black ones", meaning the 'Abbasids because of their black flags. Eventually al-Ma'mun adopted the colour green to put an end to the partisanship of the white and black flags.

Musaylima: a false prophet of the Banu Hanifa in Yamama who was one of the leaders of the Ridda.

Mustaliq, Banu: a sub-tribe of Khuza'a. The Muslim forces met the Banu Mustaliq in battle at a watering place called al-Muraysi' and defeated them soundly in 5/627.

mutakallimun: those who study the science of *kalam*, the science of investigating theological doctrine.

Mu'tazilite: someone who adheres to the school of the Mu'tazila which is rationalist in its approach to existence. Originally they held that anyone who commits a sin is neither a believer nor an unbeliever. They also held the Qur'an to be created.

muwallad: people of mixed origins.

Muzayna: a tribe which was located south of Madina, most of whom were nomads.

nabidh: a drink made by soaking grapes, raisins, etc., in water without allowing them to ferment to the point of becoming intoxicating.

Nahrawan: site of a decisive battle fought in 38/658 following the Battle of Siffin (37/657) in which 'Ali, the fourth caliph, and his army annihilated most of the Kharijites. Nahrawan is a town on the bridge of the canal of Nahrawan.

Najran: a region in the south of the Arabia peninsula, bordering with Yemen.

Nakha': a southern Arab tribe from Yemen.

nashsh: a weight measure equal to half an *uqiya*.

Negus: a generic term for the King of Abyssinia.

Nihawand: the decisive battle fought near Hamadan in 22/642 which marked the final defeat of the Persians by the Muslims.

an-Nujayr: an old fort in Yemen. During the Ridda War fighters from Kinda took refuge there and were defeated by the Muslims.

an-Nukhayla: a town in Iraq near Kufa, site of a battle which 'Ali fought against the Kharijites in 39 AH. It was also the camp of the Penitents and the site where Mu'awiya stopped when negotiating with al-Hasan ibn 'Ali.

Numayr, Banu: a mostly Bedouin tribe that lived on the western borders of Yamama.

Penitents: the *Tawwabun*, a Shi'ite group. Blaming their own inaction for having caused the death of al-Husayn, they vowed to expiate their guilt by seeking vengeance. It ended in their utter defeat by the Umayyad at the Battle of 'Ayn al-Warda in 65/685.

Qahtan: the ancestor of the southern Arabs via his twenty-four sons. Qahtan divides into the sub-groups of Himyar and Kahlan.

al-Qara: a tribe of Quraysh which was allied with the Banu Zuhra.

qadar: "power". The Qadariyya were a sect who said that people have power (*qadar*) over their actions and hence free will.

Qadariyya: a sect who believed that people have complete power (*qadar*) over their actions and hence free will.

qadi: a judge, qualified to judge all matters in accordance with the *Shari'a* and to dispense and enforce legal punishments

Qadisiyya: site of a decisive four-day battle fought against the Persians in Iraq in 15/636.

Qaran: a sub-tribe of Murad.

Qarmasin: now called Kirmanshah, a town southwest of Hamadhan.

Qarn: Qarn al-Manazil a place between Ta'if and Makka on the Najd road which is the *miqat* of the people of Najd. It is a mountain about 94 km east of Makka, overlooking 'Arafat.

Qarun: the Biblical Korah, mentioned in the Qur'an (28:76-84). He was famed for his incredible wealth and became arrogant on account of it and Allah caused the earth to swallow him up.

qasama: an oath taken by fifty men of the tribe of a person who is being accused of killing somebody.

Qayl: the title of a pre-Islamic king who ruled a district in Yemen.

Qays 'Aylan: a large tribal confederation of Mudar. Ghatafan and Hawazin are two important sub-groups.

qiran: combining *hajj* and *'umra* simultaneously.

Quda'a: a Himyarite tribe that was exiled from Yemen following the trials of the Lakhmids and they settled in the southern part of the Lakhmid Kingdom.

Qudayd: a place located on the Red Sea between Yanbu' and Rabigh on the pilgrim route from Medina to Mecca. Al-Manat's main temple was there in the *Jahiliyya*.

qunut: a supplication said in the prayer.

Qurayza: One of the Jewish tribes of Madina.

qurra': the plural of *qari'*, Qur'an reciter. It is also used historically for those who had not taken part against the Muslims in the Ridda War, so there is often confusion as to who is meant.

Rabadha: a luxuriant oasis about 200 km northeast of Madina, located on a pilgrimage route.

Rabi'a, Banu: one of the two largest tribes in northern Arabia.

Rabi' al-Akhir: the fourth month of the Muslim lunar calendar.

Rabi' al-Awwal: the third month of the Muslim lunar calendar.

ar-Rahba: a town in Syria.

ar-Ra'ish, Banu: a sub-tribe of Kinda.

raj'a: the Shi'ite doctrine that the Imam is hidden and will return.

rajaz: "trembling", a type of poetry with a particular metre which is easy on the ear and easily provokes emotions.

rak'at: unit of the prayer consisting of a series of standing, bowing, prostration and sitting.

Ramadan: the month of fasting, the ninth month in the Muslim lunar calendar.

Raqqa: is a city in north central Syria located on the north bank of the Euphrates River, about 160 km east of Aleppo, one of the main cities of the historical Diyar Mudar, the western part of the Jazira.

ar-Rass: "the men of ar-Rass", a people mentioned in the Qur'an who were destroyed. Ar-Rass may be the name of a well.

ra'y: opinion, personal discretion.

Rayy: one of the four main cities in the Persian district of Jibal.

Razm, Day of: a battle at ar-Razm in southern Najran in Murad territory between Banu Harith and Murad over the possession of the idol Yaghuth. It took place the same day as the Battle of Badr.

ribat: the stronghold traditionally used by the Muslims to prepare for their *jihad* against the enemies of Islam, situated on exposed points of the frontier.

Ridda: the defection of various Arab tribes after the death of the Prophet ﷺ which brought about the Ridda War.

Ridwan: Homage of ar-Ridwan: a pledge which the Muslims took to avenge 'Uthman when they thought that Quraysh had murdered him at al-Hudaybiya in 6/628.

Rukba: a valley near Ta'if.

ruku': bowing, particularly the bowing position in the prayer.

Rustaq: a town in northern 'Uman.

Rutbil: or Zunbil, the king of Kabulistan. Al-Hajjaj sent the Army of Peacocks against him.

sa': measure of volume equal to four *mudd*s, a *mudd* being a double-handed scoop.

Saba': Sheba, a Yemeni tribe. It also is used for the region in which Ma'rab is located where Saba' lived.

sadaqa: charitable giving in the Cause of Allah.

sadl: praying with one's hands at one's sides.

Safa and Marwa: two hills close to the Ka'ba. Running between them is one of the rites of Hajj.

as-Safra': a village between two mountains through which the Prophet ﷺ passed on his way to Badr.

sahur or *suhur*: the early morning meal taken before first light when fasting.

Sakasik: part of the Yemeni tribe of Kinda.

salam: saying *"as-salamu 'alaykum"*, which ends the prayer.

Sawad: lit. "the Black", fertile agricultural region of south-central Iraq which is 'black' or lush with date-palms.

sawiq: a mush made of wheat or barley (also with sugar and dates).

Sha'ban: the eighth month of the Muslim lunar calendar.

Sha'ban, Banu: a sub-tribe of Himyar.

Shabib: Shabib ibn Yazid ash-Shaybani: a famous Kharijite ruler who rebelled against the Umayyads at Mosul. He drowned in 77/697 while trying to escape from al-Hajjaj.

shahada: bearing witness, particularly bearing witness that there is no god but Allah and that Muhammad is the Messenger of Allah. It is one of the pillars of Islam. It is also used to describe legal testimony in a court of law.

Shari'a: The legal modality of a people based on the revelation of their Prophet. The final *Shari'a* is that of Islam.

ash-Sharqiyya: the eastern section of western Baghdad, located to the east of the original city.

Shawwal: the tenth month of the Muslim lunar calendar.

shaytan: a devil, particularly Iblis.

Shayban: an important sub-tribe of Bakr ibn Wa'il of Rabi'a.

Shurta al-Khamis: the police force which developed from the military to maintain order in Kufa under 'Ali.

Siffin: a place in Syria near Raqqa where in 38/657 a battle between 'Ali ibn Abi Talib and Mu'awiya took place.

Sijistan: a province in Persia.

as-Silsila: the chain or barrier which stopped boats on the Euphrates so that they could be taxed.

Sirar: a place three miles from Madina on the road to Iraq.

Subh: the dawn prayer.

Suffa: a verandah attached to the Prophet's Mosque where the poor Muslims used to sleep. In Kufa and Basra, it was the covered hall of the mosque.

Suhrak or **Shahrak:** a site of a major battle against the Persians under the marzban of Fars, Shahrak in the time of 'Umar.

Sunna: the customary practice of a person or group of people. It has come to refer almost exclusively to the practice of the Messenger of Allah ﷺ.

Sunna **and the Community, People of the:** *Ahl as-Sunna wa al-Jama'a,* the technical term designating Sunnis, those who adhere to the doctrine and practice of the majority of the Muslims, free of the sectarianship and strife which arose later, especially adherence to Shi'ite groups. The term developed as a response to sectarianism.

sura: chapter of the Qur'an.

Suwa'a, Banu: a branch of the northern 'Amir ibn Sa'sa'a.

Tabi'un: the second generation of the early Muslims who did not meet the Prophet Muhammad ﷺ, but learned the *Deen* of Islam from his Companions.

Tabuk: a town in northern Arabia close to Jordan. In the ninth year after the Hijra, the Messenger of Allah ﷺ, hearing that the Byzantines were gathering a large army to march against the Muslims, led a large expedition, in his last campaign, to Tabuk.

tadlis: an *isnad* in which the reporter has concealed the identity of his shaykh.

tafsir: Qur'anic commentary.

Taghlib: a large and powerful Arabian tribe of Mesopotamia and northern Arabia located along the middle Euphrates. They were Christian at the time of the Prophet ﷺ.

tahajjud: voluntary prayers performed at night between *'Isha'* and *Fajr.*

Ta'if: an important town in the mountains, fifty miles to the east of Makka.

takbir: saying *"Allahu Akbar"*, "Allah is greater".

talbiya: saying *"Labbayk"* (At Your service) during the *hajj.*

Tamim, Banu: a major tribe located in northeastern Arabia above Bahrayn.

taqiyya: concealment of one's views to escape persecution.

taqwa: awe or fear of Allah, which inspires a person to be on guard against wrong action and eager for actions which please Him.

tarawih: prayers at night in Ramadan.

Tarwiyya: "drawing water", the 8th of Dhu'l-Hijja, the day before 'Arafa when the pilgrims gather water and stay overnight at Mina.

taslim: saying "*as-salamu 'alaykum*" to end the prayer.

tawaf: circumambulation of the Ka'ba, done in sets of seven circuits.

Taym: a sub-tribe of Quraysh.

Tayy': a large tribe belonging to the southern or Qahtanite branch of Arab tribes.

Thamud: a people to whom the Prophet Salih was sent, possibly a group of Nabateans.

Thaniyya al-'Ulya: the upper mountain pass which is an entry into Makka.

Thaqif: one of the tribes of Arabia during Muhammad's era. Thaqif was the main tribe of the town of Ta'if.

Torrent, Year of the: *al-Jahhaf,* 80 AH, a year when there was a great flood in Makka which carried away the pilgrims and their camels along with their loads.

Tree, the: *see Homage of Ridwan.*

Tubba': the title of the king of a south Arabian people. Probably the Himyarites.

Tustar: or Shushtar in Persian, an ancient fortress town in southwestern Iran in Khuzistan on the river Karun.

'Udhra, Banu: a nomadic tribe which is part of Quda'a.

Uhud: a mountain just outside of Madina where five years after the Hijra, the Muslims lost a battle against the Makkan idolaters. Many great Companions, and in particular Hamza, the uncle of the Prophet ﷺ, were killed in this battle.

Umm al-Mu'minin: "Mother of the Believers", an honorific used for the wives of the Prophet ﷺ.

umm walad: a slavegirl who has borne her master's child: she cannot be sold and becomes free upon her master's death.

'umra: the lesser pilgrimage to the Ka'ba in Makka performed at any time of the year.

uqiya: a measure of silver, equal to forty dirhams or 123 gms of silver.

'ushr: land tax.

Wadi'a, Banu: a sub-tribe of Banu Kalb.

wala': the tie of clientage, established between a freed slave and the person who frees him, and by someone becoming the protegé of a tribe.

Waliba (Banu): a clan of the Banu Asad.

wars: a kind of yellow dye and perfume.

Wasit: a military and commercial garrison city in Iraq, established in 83/702 on what was then the right bank of the Tigris River, between Basra and Kufa, by al-Hajjaj. It became a great ship-building and commercial centre as well as the administrative centre. It has since disappeared due to a shift in the course of the Tigris.

witr: lit. "odd", a single *rak'at* prayed immediately after the *shaf'* which makes the number of sunna prayers uneven.

wudu': ritual washing to be pure for the prayer.

Yamama: a major battle between the Muslims and the armies of the East Roman-Byzantine Empire. The battle consisted of a series of engagements that lasted for six days in August 636 near the Yarmuk river. The result of the battle was a complete Muslim victory.

Appendix I

Governors and Qadis of Kufa

'Umar ibn al-Khattab

Sa'd ibn Abi Waqqas 16-21
'Abdullah ibn 'Abdullah ibn 'Itban 21
Ziyad ibn Hanzala 21
'Ammar ibn Yasir 21-22
Abu Musa al-Ash'ari 22
al-Mughira ibn Shu'ba 22-25

Abu Qurra al-Kindi 16-18
Qadi Shurayh 19 -

'Uthman

Sa'd ibn Abi Waqqas 25-26
al-Walid ibn 'Uqba 26-30
Sa'id ibn al-'As 30-34
Abu Musa al-Ash'ari 34
Sa'id ibn al-'As 35

Qadi Shurayh

'Ali

'Umara ibn Shihab 36
Abu Musa al-Ash'ari 36
Qaraza ibn Ka'b 36
Abu Mas'ud al-Ansari (deputy) 36-40

Umayyads

al-Mughira ibn Shu'ba 40-49
Ziyad ibn Abi Sufyan 49-53
'Abdullah ibn Khalid ibn Asid 53
ad-Dahhak ibn Qays 55-58
'Abd ar-Rahman ibn Umm al-Hakam 58
an-Nu'man ibn Bashir 59-60
'Ubaydullah ibn Ziyad 60-64

Qadi Shurayh

Second Civil War

'Amir ibn Mas'ud 64
'Abdullah ibn Yazid al-Khatmi 64-65

Shurayh refused to act in *fitna*
Sa'd ibn Nimran 64

'Abdullah ibn Muti' 65-66
al-Mukhtar 66-67

'Abdullah ibn 'Utba b. Mas'ud 66
'Abdullah ibn Malik 66
Mus'ab ibn Zubayr 67-70

'Abdullah ibn 'Utba ibn
  Mas'ud 67-68
Shurayh 69-78

Umayyads

Qatan ibn 'Abdullah 71
Bishr ibn Marwan 71-75
al-Hajjaj 75-95

Abu Burda ibn Abi Musa 79-81?
Abu Bakr ibn Abi Musa 87?-96

Yazid ibn Abi Kabsha 95
Yazid ibn al-Muhallab 96-98
'Abd al-Hamid ibn
  'Abd ar-Rahman 99-101
Muhammad ibn 'Amr 102

ash-Sha'bi 99-101
al-Qasim ibn 'Abd
  ar-Rahman 102-103

'Umar ibn Hubayra 103-105
Khalid b. 'Abdullah al-Qasri 105-119
Yusuf ibn 'Umar 120-126

Husayn ibn al-Hasan 104-105
Bilal ibn Abi Burda 109-118
Ibn Shubruma 120-121
Ibn Abi Layla 122-128?

Mansur ibn Jumhur 126
'Abdullah ibn 'Umar ibn 'Abd al-Aziz 126-127
an-Nadr ibn al-Harshi 128 - (unrest)
Yazid ibn 'Umar 129-132

al-Hajjaj ibn 'Asim 129-131

'Abbasids

Dawud ibn 'Ali 132
'Isa ibn Musa 133-147
Muhammad ibn Sulayman 147-155
'Amr ibn Zuhayr 155-158
Isma'il ibn Abi Isma'il 158
Ishaq ibn as-Sabbah 159-163
Hashim ibn Sa'id 164-166
Rawh ibn Hatim 167-?

Ibn Abi Layla 132-148

'Abd ar-Rahman b. 'Abdullah 148
'Ubayd ibn bint Abi Layla ? -153
Sharik ibn 'Abdullah 153-164

Appendix II

Charts

CHRONOLOGICAL TABLE OF 'ALIDS

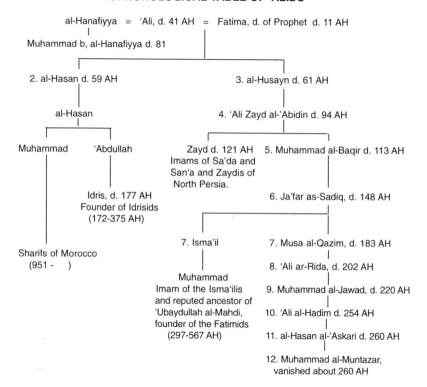

al-Hanafiyya = 'Ali, d. 41 AH = Fatima, d. of Prophet d. 11 AH

Muhammad b, al-Hanafiyya d. 81

2. al-Hasan d. 59 AH

3. al-Husayn d. 61 AH

al-Hasan

4. 'Ali Zayd al-'Abidin d. 94 AH

Muhammad   'Abdullah

Zayd d. 121 AH
Imams of Sa'da and
San'a and Zaydis of
North Persia.

5. Muhammad al-Baqir d. 113 AH

Idris, d. 177 AH
Founder of Idrisids
(172-375 AH)

6. Ja'far as-Sadiq, d. 148 AH

7. Isma'il

7. Musa al-Qazim, d. 183 AH

Sharifs of Morocco
(951 -   )

Muhammad
Imam of the Isma'ilis
and reputed ancestor of
'Ubaydullah al-Mahdi,
founder of the Fatimids
(297-567 AH)

8. 'Ali ar-Rida, d. 202 AH

9. Muhammad al-Jawad, d. 220 AH

10. 'Ali al-Hadim d. 254 AH

11. al-Hasan al-'Askari d. 260 AH

12. Muhammad al-Muntazar,
vanished about 260 AH

Rabi‘a and Mudar Chart

I.
The Descendants of Rabi‘a

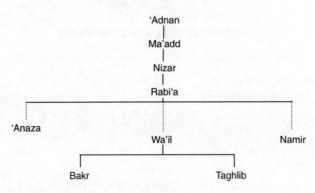

'Adnan
|
Ma'add
|
Nizar
|
Rabi‘a

'Anaza — Wa'il — Namir

Wa'il: Bakr — Taghlib

II.
The Descendants of Mudar

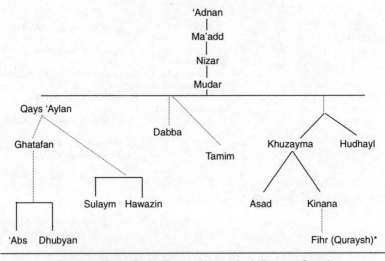

'Adnan
|
Ma'add
|
Nizar
|
Mudar

Qays 'Aylan · Dabba · Tamim · Khuzayma · Hudhayl

Ghatafan

Sulaym · Hawazin

Khuzayma: Asad · Kinana

'Abs · Dhubyan

Kinana: Fihr (Quraysh)*

*The tribes of Dabba, Tamim, Khuzayma, Hudayl, Asad, Kinana and Quraysh
together formed a group which is known as Khindif, and is often distinguished
from Qays 'Aylan.

Index